HOLLYWOOD
RHAPSODY

HOLLYWOOD RHAPSODY

Movie Music and Its Makers
1900 to 1975

GARY MARMORSTEIN

Schirmer Books
An Imprint of Simon & Schuster Macmillan
New York

Prentice Hall International

London Mexico City New Delhi Singapore Sydney Toronto

For Mary and for Rebecca

Schirmer Books
An Imprint of Simon & Schuster Macmillan
1633 Broadway
New York, NY 10019

Library of Congress Catalog Card Number: 97-19891

Printed in the United States of America

Printing number
10 9 8 7 6 5 4 3 2 1

Library of Congress Cataloging-in-Publication Data

Marmorstein, Gary.
   Hollywood rhapsody : movie music and its makers, 1900 to 1975 / Gary
Marmorstein.
      p. cm.
   Includes bibliographical references (p.   ) and index.
   ISBN 0-02-864595-2
   1. Motion picture music—United States—History and criticism.
2. Musicians—California—Los Angeles. I. Title.
ML2075.M246 1997
781.5'42'0973—dc21   97-19891
                                                                            CIP
                                                                            MN

The paper used in this publication meets the minimum requirements of
American National Standard for Information Sciences—Permanence of Paper for
Printed Library Materials. ANSI Z39.48-1992 (Permanence of Paper).

C O N T E N T S

ACKNOWLEDGMENTS

When researching a cultural book project—whether about music, or the movies, or both—a writer tends to be dependent on individuals who provide him with literary, audio, and visual materials. I'm grateful to the following for various contributions: David Benesty; Louise Blackton; David Buechner; Irwin Chusid; George Duning; Tomas Firle; Melodie Hollander; Yvonne Jurmann; Donald Kahn; Miles Kreuger; Arthur Morton; Lisa Phelps; Terry Polesie; David Raksin; Doug Schwalbe; John Strauss; Susanna Moross Tarjan; and John Waxman.

Thanks to Timothy Edwards at the UCLA Archive of Popular Music; Ned Comstock at the USC Doheny Memorial Cinema-Television Library; the staff at the Margaret Herrick Library of the Academy of Motion Picture Arts & Sciences, especially Warren Sherk, Barbara Hall, and Robert Cushman; librarians at the Theatre and Music Collections of the Lincoln Center Library for the Performing Arts; and, from ASCAP's offices in New York City, Maggie Aponte, Jim Steinblatt, and Michael Kerker.

At Schirmer Books, Richard Carlin, Dan Mausner, and Debi Elfenbein endured my tantrums, then quietly went about the business of improving the book. Alicia Williamson was there to help out.

Warmest thanks to Knox Burger and Kitty Sprague, who picked me up and dusted me off before, during, and after each draft of *Hollywood Rhapsody*.

WHERE YOU'RE TERRIFIC IF YOU'RE EVEN GOOD

Movie music: junk; trash; schmalz. One more shallow product of an art form that routinely aims at the lowest common denominator.

These equations have been made since a soundtrack was first spliced onto celluloid. Like all time-worn clichés, they contain degrees of truth. "Go to the movies," instructed Vernon Duke, who spent a fair amount of time composing for the Hollywood studios; "the feature will be accompanied by impressive sounds, scary and treacly by turn, borrowed from the Masters in public domain and subtly disguised as the film composer's own." Duke's is a common assessment among serious composers, even those who, like Duke, earned a comfortable living from the movies.

Most music written for the movies has a singular purpose: to enhance the film. It suggests that film composers and songwriters have never been really free to write what they please; they must address their compositions to the story ideas given to them, in and around the settings and stars of the film, and they must do it under the frequently extreme hardship of the deadline. Since the beginning of the 1930s a ten-week deadline to create an entire film score has been common; three weeks isn't unheard of. The miracle is that out of such time and style restrictions has come some of the most memorable music of our century.

1

And it comes despite the crassness of moviemakers—studio heads, executives, producers—who hire the composers and songwriters. Hugh Fordin describes Oscar Hammerstein's experience writing lyrics, including the gorgeous "The Folks Who Live on the Hill," for *High, Wide and Handsome* (1937):

> The night the film was first sneak-previewed Adolph Zukor walked across the polished floor of the Riviera Country Club in Hollywood to wring Oscar's hand and say, "That's the greatest picture we ever made!" A few months later, with the picture's road-show exhibition backfiring and producing less revenue than expected, Zukor walked past Oscar in a restaurant and stared through him as though he had never seen him before in his life.

Three years earlier, after his first collaborator Larry Hart completed new lyrics for Ernst Lubitsch's version of *The Merry Widow*, Richard Rodgers went to MGM's Culver City studio to say goodbye to Irving Thalberg, his employer of the past few months. "I walked over," Rodgers remembered in his autobiography, "and said, 'Larry and I are leaving today and I just wanted to say goodbye.' Thalberg looked up with an uncomprehending, glassy stare on his boyish face, and I suddenly realized that he hadn't the faintest idea who I was."

Nearly thirty years later, New York–based composer David Amram describes an incident that occurred after he had worked on the music for *Splendor in the Grass* (1961), written by William Inge and directed by Elia Kazan:

> After I had completed the score, Jack Warner came to New York to see a preview. Apparently he fancied himself a kind of stand-up comic. After he had completed a few jokes that I remembered my grandfather telling me and I failed to laugh, he suddenly looked at me and said, "Who are you, the undertaker?"
>
> His retinue automatically roared with laughter.
>
> "No, I'm David Amram," I said. "I wrote the music."
>
> "Well, here's another bright boy," he said. "Listen, there's a lot of young people nobody knows about, they got a big break working with this guy, Kazan. Leonard Bernstein did his first film score, *On the*

Waterfront, for him. Who knows?" he said, looking around at his retinue and throwing up his hands, "this boy may be another Leonard Bernstein." Then, looking at me again, he said, "Who's greater than Leonard Bernstein?"

"Beethoven," I answered. Mr. Warner turned back to his retinue and didn't bother me anymore.

It's a tradition for studio heads and producers to consider a well-known contemporary composer—the more involved with movies or musical theater, the better—far more important than any longhair who didn't earn millions in his lifetime; and Leonard Bernstein, whom Jack Warner could identify as great because he'd worked in the industry and received acclaim for his music, was the last word in composition to him. Amram, wary of the Hollywood juggernaut even before his first visit there, would have none of it, refusing to butt heads with men whose minds were crosshatched with dollar signs. ("That's a nice little quartet, Ludwig, but give us something we can hum.")

Zukor and Thalberg exhibited the obliviousness of studio chiefs toward songwriters—musicians, after all, are not movie stars—while Warner is the jokey lunkhead whose personal, cigar-chomping crassness stands for the crassness of all Hollywood. Yet Warner also stands for one of the great paradoxes of Hollywood: that some men who appear to be devoid of imagination could sponsor, if not actually supervise, the creation of such memorable music. Among the composers and songwriters in Warner's employ, over the course of forty years, were Max Steiner, Dimitri Tiomkin, Erich Korngold, Franz Waxman, Alex North, Harry Warren, Al Dubin, Richard Whiting, Johnny Mercer, Harold Arlen, Jule Styne, Sammy Cahn, and Ira Gershwin. And what was true for Warner was true for the other studio giants, most of them Warner's equal in taste(lessness).

This book is about the men—and a handful of women in a male-dominated industry—whose music accompanied the romances, comings of age, murders, suicides, battles, wars, marriages, miscarriages of justice, and births that movies are about. It covers how these musicians did their work, and the development of that work over the course of seventy-five years, from approximately 1900 to 1975, when the studios' music departments had all but disappeared due to a combination of union squabbles, television, and the new predominance of the rock music soundtrack.

Most of my subjects are composers and songwriters—lyricists as well as melodists. In some cases—particularly regarding Bing Crosby, Fred Astaire, and Frank Sinatra—there was no way to avoid discussing movie stars at length. But orchestrators, conductors, and soundmen have also been important since the advent of the soundtrack. "With the development of recorded music and broadcasting," Robert Russell Bennett wrote in the late 1940s, "orchestration assumes greater and greater importance." This applies as well to the movie soundtrack. Consequently, I discuss the orchestrators who have been at least as responsible as the composers for the film scores. In the movie industry, for the most part, the terms *orchestrator* and *arranger* are used interchangeably, except on vocal numbers, in which their responsibilities are distinct from one another. In discussing movie credits, I tend to assign the possessive to the individual who exerted the most clout during a production. Sometimes this is the producer (e.g., David Selznick's *Gone with the Wind*), sometimes the director (e.g., Alfred Hitchcock's *North by Northwest*), occasionally the star and almost never, sadly, the writer. This isn't arbitrary—there's always a reason for the attribution—but when writing about the collaborative world of moviemaking I'm bound to be wrong here and there. To those who may take offense at arguable attributions, please forgive me.

Although I refer to some foreign film composers, particularly in the material on the silents, they appear here primarily in relation to the American movie industry. I wish I'd had more space to discuss, say, Georges Delerue and Maurice Jarre. Is there any reader who doesn't know a Lara born shortly after 1965, when *Doctor Zhivago* appeared on the screen accompanied by Jarre's music?

John Barry, who composed the James Bond theme for *Dr. No* (although British composer Monty Norman is credited), is a much more important figure than the following text would suggest, as are other British composers such as William Walton, William Alwyn, Richard Addinsell (composer of "The Warsaw Concerto"), John Addison, and Malcolm Arnold. In *The Bridge on the River Kwai*, Arnold's use of the "Colonel Bogey" march, by British military composer Kenneth Alford, was so effective that it influenced almost every war movie to be released in the following decade. From Italy, no film composer has been more prominent than Nino Rota, but most of Rota's work was for Federico Fellini, and there was little room to talk about his blockbusting themes for Zeffirelli's *Romeo and Juliet* and *The Godfather.*

Instead, the focus is on Hollywood, and on its music makers who worked under the familiar tension between art and commerce. Given the strictures of time and style these musicians faced, it's a wonder that so many of them completed their assignments; given the extraordinary music—songs as well as scores—that has come from the movies, their achievement at times is positively heroic.

GM

ONE

SMILE THROUGH YOUR FEAR AND SORROW
FILM MUSIC BEFORE THE SOUNDTRACK

In 1958, when I was five, my mother took me to the Queen Anne Theater in Bogota, New Jersey, to see a revival of Charlie Chaplin's *Modern Times*. The movie was speechless but not silent. Its soundtrack contained recorded music, including the song "Smile," credited to Chaplin. Although *Modern Times* is no longer my favorite Chaplin movie, as a child I hadn't seen anything like it. Only much later I learned that it had been made in 1935, at least seven years after most movies had gone to sound. Chaplin was the last prominent holdout for the feature film that included no recorded speech. But he never worked without music—even in the so-called Silent Era, when he took inspiration for his stories from popular song.

Silent movies had no soundtracks, so there was no speech and no recorded sound effects. But there was almost always music. Music was part of the moviegoing experience long before ads proclaimed JOLSON SINGS!

•   •   •

Before music was routinely recorded right onto celluloid to enhance moving pictures, it was used, understandably, to muffle the noise of projectors. A single upright piano helped to keep customers from being distracted by the metallic ratcheting. Constant keyboard improvisation also enhanced the movie itself. Near the turn of the century, movies took on the kind of amusement status that vaudeville had; the next step was to use vaudeville's music. A pit band or a honky-tonk piano could produce wondrous sounds for an audience watching images. The bump-and-grind rhythms of the burlesque house became a comic movie staple.

After pictures outgrew storefront cinemas and moved into little theaters, an increasing number of these theaters were equipped with keyboard instruments. This coincided with the years of American piano manufacturers' greatest productivity: in 1909 alone, more than 364,000 pianos, new and used, were put on the market. Many of these found their way into cinemas.

A few years earlier, impresario Mitchell Mark opened the Comique Theater in Boston. The Comique boasted an orchestra pit so deep that the musicians couldn't be seen by the audience. Suddenly a picture's musical accompaniment seemed to be coming from nowhere and everywhere at once. Mark took the presentation of movie music a step further in 1907 when he installed the first church organ to be used for the movies at Cleveland's Alhambra Theater.

Movie accompanists, usually keyboard players with a knack for improvisation and hundreds of riffs at their disposal, tended to be attached to the cinemas they worked for, like the projectionist or the concessionaire. The teenage Fats Waller played piano in Washington and New York, presiding for years at Harlem's Lincoln Theater until 1923, when the cinema closed and he moved on to play the huge organ at the Lafayette. By 1915, thirteen-year-old Louis Alter, who would go on to compose the exquisite "Manhattan Serenade" and "Do You Know What It Means to Miss New Orleans?," was working as a cinema pianist in Boston. In Kansas City, Carl Stalling, who would produce the music for Walt Disney's *Steamboat Willie* (1928) and lead the Warners music department in scoring hundreds of cartoons, improvised on organ in various cinemas. Harry Warren began his astonishing professional career by playing piano in an East New York cinema and providing silent star Corinne Griffith with mood music while she acted. In Los Angeles the young Gaylord Carter, who would work into his nineties, played the great downtown picture palaces, with their Mayan or Oriental motifs. These mammoth theaters, the most opulent all over the country, featured Wurlitzers that rose from the floor by hydraulic elevator. (It was from the early cinema organs that we get the phrase "Pull out the stops," referring to the stops on an organ.)

For those musicians who couldn't improvise imaginatively, cue sheets and music books helped immensely. Preeminent among these was *Moving Picture Music* by J. S. Zamecnik. Born in Ohio in 1872, Zamecnik traveled to his parents' native Czechoslovakia to study with Dvořák at the Prague Conservatory. He was an accomplished violinist when he returned to America. After a stint with the Pittsburgh Symphony Orchestra, he went back to his hometown of Cleveland to serve as music director for the Hippodrome Theater, a lavish movie house. Already a facile composer-arranger, Zamecnik's responsibilities led him to catalogue his movie accompaniment riffs. The first volumes of *Moving Picture Music* were published in 1913 by Sam Fox Publishing (no apparent relation to early movie mogul William Fox), and included themes for "Defense of Honor," "Remorse," and "Evil Plotter." The success of the volumes kept Zamecnik working for decades.

Zamecnik's European counterpart was Giuseppe Becce, an Italian whose Kinothek ("film library") music series served Berlin-based filmmakers from 1919. But the Kinothek series only exploited and synthesized Europe's more established history of opera and incidental music. In fact, the first original film score we know of preceded Kinothek by a decade. Camille Saint-Saëns's music for *L'Assassinat du Duc de Guise* (1908); the French movie is lost to us (its subject matter appears to have been close cousin to that of the 1994 French film *Queen Margot*), but the eighteen-minute score survives as the composer's Opus 128 for Strings, Piano, and Harmonium.

o   o   o

America's most innovative filmmaker, David Wark (D. W.) Griffith, was an early champion of film scores. For his 1913 spectacle *Judith of*

Bethulia (the title character exacts revenge from her city's Assyrian attackers), Griffith prepared music cues to be used by the film's exhibitors. These included familiar light classics from Suppé, Rossini, and Grieg, a particular favorite of the director.

But with a running time of 45 minutes, *Judith* was no more than a warmup for Griffith's next, major work. By 1914, when he began to adapt the Thomas Dixon novels *The Clansman* and *The Leopard's Spots* for the screen, movies had become longer—sometimes filling as many as ten reels at a playing time of 160 minutes—to better fit their presentation in the grand picture palaces. To assemble a score for his film, then known as *The Clansman,* Griffith hired twenty-four-year-old Carli Densmore Elinor, a music "fitter" with a knack for compiling odds and ends from the classics. A Bulgarian who "couldn't write his name, frankly," according to composer-orchestrator Hugo Friedhofer, Elinor was a firm believer in the importance of a good music library. Together, Griffith and Elinor patched together a score that was effective enough to excite the film's first two audiences, at the Loring Opera House in Riverside, California, on New Year's Day, 1915, and then at Klune's Auditorium in downtown Los Angeles on February 8. This was where *The Clansman* became *Birth of a Nation,* rechristened by novelist Dixon himself.

But Griffith wanted more changes. One of these was a more streamlined score, to be played by a full orchestra. For this he brought in Joseph Carl Breil.

Until his association with Griffith, Breil's career wasn't at all unusual for American composers of the time. As a child in Pittsburgh, Breil fell in love with opera. He was sent to Milan to study voice, continued his music studies in Leipzig, and sang in various opera companies. Basing himself in New York, he tried his hand at comic operas. He was forty when he had his first production, *Love Laughs at Locksmiths,* produced in Portland, Maine. For money, Breil took over the musical direction of several New York theaters. These jobs spurred his interest in films, which routinely shared the bill with stage productions.

Meanwhile Adolph Zukor, a former furrier who had become treasurer of the Marcus Loew theater chain (and who would eventually run Paramount Pictures), had bought the rights to the French-produced

Queen Elizabeth. Running an hour, the 1912 film starred Sarah Bernhardt. Zukor booked *Queen Elizabeth* into the Lyceum Theater. Because Breil was contracted to conduct anyway, he took a crack at composing his own music for the film. These New York showings, with Breil's score, were a hit.

Breil continued to compose operas. His 1913 operas, *Professor Tattle* and *The Seventh Chord,* brought him to the attention of Griffith, who was also impressed by Breil's work on *Queen Elizabeth.* Together, Griffith and Breil cobbled together a new score for *Birth of a Nation*— about two thirds adapted from the classics, one-third original music by

Sarah Bernhardt in *Queen Elizabeth* (1912). Music composed in 1914 by Joseph Carl Breil
Courtesy of Universal Studios

Breil—meant to be played by a sixty-piece orchestra. In an unpublished autobiography, Dixon described the first Breil showing: ". . . the throb through the darkness of that orchestra rais[ed] the emotional power to undreamed heights."

Birth of a Nation has earned a notorious reputation for its racist elements, which are underscored, in fact, by its music. Within minutes of its opening, the score establishes mood with Stephen Foster's "Swanee River" (composed in 1851). Slaves dance to "Turkey in the Straw," which was first published in 1834 as "Zip Coon," credited to blackface entertainers George Washington Dixon and Bob Farrell. ("Oh, ole Zip Coon he is a larned skolar/Sings posum up a gum tree an' coon-y in a holler.") The wistful "Comin' Thru the Rye" is played at a Southern dance after the battle of Bull Run. As soldiers gather for assembly, we can hear strains of "O Tannenbaum," and, as they march away, "Dixie," with "No Place Like Home" cut in when they're at the front.

Generally, Breil and Griffith exploited America's most popular songs to evoke feelings of home, patriotism, and a union divided. There's much more oom-pah-pahing in the battle scenes than would be acceptable on today's soundtracks; otherwise the music serves the same heart-tugging functions. Some of the earliest movie chase music is used over a sequence when black Union soldiers raid a South Carolina town, looting and shooting indiscriminately. The music is cartoonish and hateful, but so masterfully timed that you can't tear your eyes away. The burning of Atlanta is a scene familiar to many moviegoers from *Gone with the Wind*; for Griffith's earlier depiction of the same calamity, he and Breil used Grieg's "Hall of the Mountain King." "Reveille" is played when Lee orders his soldiers into battle, "Taps" when they don't come back.

Griffith knew the musical effects he wanted—even if they were obvious as well as objectionable. A title card reads THE FORMER ENE-MIES OF NORTH AND SOUTH ARE UNITED AGAIN IN COMMON DEFENSE OF THEIR ARYAN BIRTHRIGHT while "Auld Lang Syne" sounds beneath it. A menacing melody intrudes as "Negroes and car-petbaggers" arrive in town, along with sex-starved "mulattos." One of these takes more than a shine to the prim, pale Lillian Gish who tries in vain to escape his clutches, while Tchaikovsky's Fifth Symphony plays over the Klansmen riding hard to her rescue. Tchaikovsky's Fifth was a silent-picture favorite, probably because it goes from stirring march cadences to lush romanticism. Tchaikovsky gives way to Wagner's "Ride of the Valkyries," which was used half a century later to orchestrate the classic helicopter flyovers in Francis Ford Coppola's *Apocalypse Now*.

Birth of a Nation's postwar music leans toward bittersweet Americana. When Lee surrenders to Grant at Appomattox, "My Country 'Tis of Thee" (also known as "America") plays under it. *Birth of a Nation*'s final two reels are filled out with hymns, and it closes as a picture calling itself *Birth of a Nation* must, with "The Star-Spangled Banner." One of the more impressive aspects about the Breil-Griffith compilation is how precise they were about musical dates. Apart from Breil's original music, nothing composed after the Civil War found its way into the score.

Most of this music was prepared in time for *Birth of a Nation*'s New York premiere at the Liberty Theater in March 1915. Its remarkable commercial success gave Griffith the freedom and money—a budget four times *Birth of a Nation*'s negative cost—to film *Intolerance*. It also gave Breil the job of scoring *Intolerance*.

Griffith's *Intolerance*, at $1,900,000 by far the most expensive film project to that date, played across the country in 1917 and was judged a failure. (Fifty-six years later, in a famous poll of international film critics, it would place first as the "greatest film of all time.") Breil's original score is lost, but there's no evidence that it hurt the film's initial reception.

Breil's music career wasn't overly damaged by the failure of *Intolerance*. No one blamed him for what was seen as Griffith's excesses. Breil finally had a production at the Metropolitan Opera with his grand opera *The Legend* in March 1919. This wasn't a success either, and Breil spent several more years working on his opera *Asra*. On November 24, 1925, the opera had a single, poorly received performance in Los Angeles. Breil died of a heart attack there eight weeks later; he was fifty-five.

◦　　◦　　◦

Birth of a Nation's success inspired other filmmakers to hire musicians to assemble special scores. In 1915, music director George Beynon used much of Grieg's *Peer Gynt* suite to score Oliver Morosco's "picturization" of Ibsen's version of the same story, at the Broadway Theater in New York. A miscue in which "Dixie" was played by Beynon's pit orchestra, moments *before* the character called The Southerner is shot by Peer Gynt, brought gales of laughter from the audience. One poorly placed note, it was demonstrated, could destroy a picture's mood.

Also in 1915, Jesse Lasky signed opera star Geraldine Farrar to star in three films to be made in Hollywood over the course of eight weeks. Her fee was $20,000; she was also given use of a furnished mansion, servants, car, and a food allowance. The first picture was *Carmen*, filmed by Cecil B. DeMille. Bizet's operatic score was adapted for the film by Hugo Riesenfeld, born in Vienna in 1879; his adaptation was played at the film's American premiere at Symphony Hall in Boston.

Robert Hood Bowers (born 1877) had composed incidental music for dozens of plays and been a charter member of ASCAP when he compiled the well-received score for *The Daughter of the Gods* (1916). The picture showed off the physique of its star, former swimming sensation Annette Kellerman. George Beynon pronounced Bowers's orchestral accompaniment "the best" movie music up to that point.

It was stretching the truth to call these compiler-fitters *composers*. They knew music, how to extract the emotional effects they wanted from music libraries, and how to wield a baton in front of musicians— ergo, they were composers. It took a music personality of the stature of Victor Herbert, the dominant theatrical composer of his time, to attempt one of the first full-length, original motion-picture scores.

◦　◦　◦

Although Herbert is best remembered for his Viennese-styled operettas, he was actually Dublin-born. He arrived in New York with his wife, soprano Therese Furster, in 1887, after touring Europe as a cellist. By 1914 most of Herbert's great stage successes—including *Babes in Toyland*, *Mlle. Modiste*, and *The Red Mill*—were embedded in the American repertoire. He was fifty-five when he considered writing the score for *Fall of a Nation*—like *Birth of a Nation*, based on a novel by Baptist minister Thomas Dixon.

Dixon was basking in a sunburst of celebrity from *Birth of a Nation* when he approached Herbert in New York. He had been thinking of another story in combination with the emotional power of an orchestra. Herbert, determined to move away from the operettas that had made his name, liked the image of himself as a musical pioneer in a young medium, and consented to compose music for Dixon's new project. Herbert would remain at home in New York and compose while Dixon filmed in Hollywood, sending written scenes, or transcripts of already filmed scenes, back to Herbert as often as he could.

The two men began a correspondence that chronicles their respective creative travails—and their subsequent disenchantment with each other. Their letters provide an early example of a composer chafing under the demands of a filmmaker who could neither articulate what he wanted nor relinquish control of any aspect of the production.

Dixon's novel and photoplay—there is no extant print of the movie, though stills survive—were meant to warn Americans about "the twin perils of disarmament and woman suffrage." The complicated plot involved a New York congressman, a newspaper tycoon, a suffragist leader, and peace-advocating politicians. The thematic equation seemed to be suffrage equals a weakening of the nation's power. Astonishingly, Dixon agreed to a stipulation by Herbert that the Europeans invading America in the film not be identified as German. As a boy, Herbert had lived in Stuttgart; although in 1915 the United States was still observing the war in Europe from a wary distance, he was sensitive to making Germany the enemy.

But Dixon didn't keep his part of the bargain. Herbert perceived an anti-German tone in the scenes he received. And that was only one of the divisions between them. Dixon wanted Herbert to arrange for exhibition of the film at the Metropolitan Opera. Impossible. Dixon wanted musical sequences completed in two weeks or less; Herbert needed time to orchestrate his own compositions, a musical necessity that escaped Dixon's comprehension. Finally, Dixon wanted Herbert to come west, to be close to the filming, where the already overworked writer-producer-director could keep an eye on him.

Through all this, which took up the latter half of 1915, Herbert's letters were cranky and sometimes bitter. At the same time, he was proudly telling *Musical America*:

> The musical program will not be a mosaic or patchwork of bits of Wagner, Grieg, Beethoven, Schumann, Mendelssohn, Gounod, Verdi, Liszt, Bizet, Berlioz and other writers. It will be strictly new. . . .

In advertisements for the film, Herbert's name was displayed as prominently as Dixon's. *Fall of a Nation* opened on June 6, 1916, at the Liberty Theater on Forty-second Street west of Broadway, where *Birth of a Nation* had premiered. Many of the musicians who played at Herbert's stage shows served in the orchestra pit. The film did moderate business, but musically it got less attention than Jerome Kern's show *Very Good, Eddie,* which played nightly at the 299-seat Princess Theater, three blocks downtown.

ø   ø   ø

Released four days earlier than *Fall of a Nation* was the equally large-scale *Civilization.* Filmed by Thomas H. Ince, whose Los Angeles studio was dubbed "Inceville," *Civilization* was a pacifistic parable that's rather on the loony side. It, too, boasted a complete, original musical score by Victor Schertzinger (born 1890), who at the age of eight was playing violin in Victor Herbert's orchestra. A Pennsylvanian, Schertzinger received most of his early musical education in Brussels. He returned to the United States to give violin concerts, then toured Europe with John Philip Sousa's band, several of whose members came out of the Victor Herbert organization. Decades before anyone was referred to as bicoastal, Schertzinger served stints as music director for several Los Angeles theaters and as a Broadway conductor.

Schertzinger's score for *Civilization,* widely performed in even the smaller cinemas (a sound version was released in 1931), was only the beginning of a long Hollywood career. The composer of such standards as "Sand in My Shoes" and "Tangerine," Schertzinger wrote the songs for *The Love Parade* (1929), the first great Jeanette MacDonald–Maurice Chevalier picture, and directed more than a dozen movies, including a couple of Hope-Crosby *Road* pictures. But his great love remained music, his score for *Civilization* (which can be found at the Library of Congress, published by Leo Feist) his one ground-breaking achievement for film.

*   *   *

By 1919 moviegoers could sense the cinematic possibilities of sound. From Germany came the Tri-Ergon process, which converted sound waves to electric impulses that in turn were converted into light waves. Photographed on a one-tenth-of-an-inch strip spliced alongside the film, the light waves were "read" and turned back into sound, creating a soundtrack synchronized to the picture. It was hailed as a revolution. The problem, however, was that Tri-Ergon charged optical sound equipment makers a high fee for use of its patented design; nobody wanted to pay the Germans' prices. For the next seven years, Tri-Ergon's technology went unused in the United States.

So film composers' work continued to be realized through less sophisticated processes: music sheets, live orchestra, and conductor. Six or seven years before sound was placed on celluloid as a matter of course, the conductor still reigned. Why bother commissioning an original score by a Herbert or a Schertzinger if it couldn't guarantee box office? Audiences were said to be more comfortable with familiar musical selections anyway. In 1921 conductor George Beynon wrote, "The efficacy of the original score has not yet been found to transcend that of other scores. No matter how clever the composer may be, there is sure to be a monotonous sameness to his motifs which portray the various emotions of the picture." In his book on film music, Beynon paid scant attention to composers of original music but included an entire section, with photographs, on conductors-music directors. Emphasized was the musicianship of men like Jack Arthur, who supervised the music of the largest Toronto cinemas; Nat Finston, a violinist and concertmaster in New York and Boston, two decades before he became head of music at MGM; and Carl Edouarde, who conducted at the Strand Theater on Broadway.

Solo piano or organ remained the prime accompanying instrument. A keyboard "artist" like James C. Bradford could crank out several picture scores each year. A single violin, played with split-second rapport with the action on screen, could cover a lot of emotional territory. When an entire orchestra was in the pit, however, the drums took on added responsibility. "The trap drummer," composer Hugo

Friedhofer said, "was literally the sound effects man. They were quite extraordinary and ingenious, in the same way that the sound effects men from the old radio days were."

Murray Spivack (born 1903 in New York City) worked as a cinema percussionist before turning to sound recording in 1929. Known as a *boomboomnik* (Yiddish slang for drummer), Spivack was one of three drummers at New York's Capitol Theater. "[The orchestra] would play the first ten minutes of the picture, and then the organist would come in and play the balance of the picture, and then the orchestra would come in for the tail end, maybe the last five minutes of the picture, and that would be the show . . . prior to the feature you'd have an overture. And we'd play 'Poet and Peasant' or 'Light Cavalry.'"

◦   ◦   ◦

Many of the more interesting scores—some original, some new variations on the old musical thievery—accompanied pictures out of Europe. Hugo Riesenfeld wrote a score for Fritz Lang's *Siegfried*, with a generous helping of, naturally, Wagner. But Lang was known to loathe Wagner—he had vaulted backward past Wagner's version of the story to its source, the thirteenth-century epic *Nibelungenlied*, for his script—and commissioned Gottfried Huppertz to write a completely original score. Lang was livid when he learned that UFA, his Berlin-based studio, had released *Siegfried* abroad with Riesenfeld's Wagner-heavy music.

In France in 1922, Arthur Honegger, one of the notorious Les Six (a group of six modern composers who proclaimed themselves defiers of the musical establishment), composed a score for Abel Gance's *La Roué*. Two-and-a-half years in the making, eight-and-a-half hours cut to two-and-a-half and filled with grand and grandiose juxtapositions, *La Roué* was produced by Charles Pathé, who built the greatest film empire in France. Honegger would also score Gance's *Napoleon*, and, sixteen years later, Leslie Howard's film version of *Pygmalion*.

Honegger's fellow Les Six member, Darius Milhaud, wrote a score for Marcel L'Herbian's experimental film *L'Inhumaine*; the sets were designed by painter Fernand Leger, and playing piano in the film—indeed, making his Paris debut right there on screen—was twenty-three-year-old American composer George Antheil. Antheil's piano-pounding caused a riot on the order of the Paris premiere of *The Rite of Spring.*

The self-proclaimed "Bad Boy of Music," Trenton-born Antheil was influenced by what he'd heard of Stravinsky. "Bold, bumptious, and self-confident," according to Virgil Thomson, Antheil began giving piano concerts throughout Europe in 1921, when he was only twenty-one. He first arrived in Paris on June 13, 1923, with his companion, Boski (Elizabeth Markus, niece of the playwright Arthur Schnitzler), who later became his wife. He moved into the flat above Shakespeare & Company, Sylvia Beach's bookshop. The motherly Beach described him as a "fellow with bangs, a squashed nose and a big mouth with a grin in it." Within months he had charmed Beach's circle, including Joyce and Ezra Pound, and they praised his music lavishly.

Music critics would be less generous. After Leger designed the short film *Ballet Mécanique*—the actual filming was done by an American named Dudley Murphy—Antheil composed a score for it. In spite of, or maybe because of, Antheil's failure to properly synchronize it, the music was quickly unhitched from the film—ten minutes of giddy surrealism—and became notorious. *Ballet Mécanique* was "machine music," scored for sixteen player pianos, anvils, electric bells, car horns, buzzsaws, and airplane propellers. The January 21, 1926, edition of the Paris *Tribune* announced: "*Ballet Mécanique* to Wipe Out Big Orchestras and Audiences Too." When the piece was performed in Carnegie Hall on April 10, 1927, Aaron Copland was one of the pianists. One New York music critic, according to author David Ewen, declined to write a review, "claiming that the propellers blew away the notes he had made during the performance."

Antheil moved to Hollywood in 1934. He began to compose in a mellower mode and also began a writing career. He published articles in *Esquire,* turned out a syndicated lovelorn advice column and mystery novel under pseudonyms, and reviewed movie music for *Modern Music.* In the late '40s and early '50s, he became mentor to young film composers like Ernest Gold, and wrote film music (e.g., *The Pride and the Passion*) that contained little evidence of his early rebelliousness. In Hollywood he had turned into, in Virgil Thomson's words, the "Good Boy of Music."

Back in France, Les Six outsider Erik Satie—the "old man" the others admired—scored René Clair's twenty-minute comedy *Entr'acte*, which was filmed specifically to be shown between the acts of a Dadaist ballet. The film itself, like so much of Clair's work, is really more madcap than Dada. Running around in it are, among others, Frances Picabia, who wrote the script, composer Georges Auric, Marcel Duchamp, and Man Ray. Jacques Ibert (born 1890), older than the others, composed a score for Clair's magnificent 1927 comedy *The Italian Straw Hat* (based on the 1851 farce about the class pretensions of the Second Empire by Eugène Labiche and Marc Michel). For young French composers in the years just before and after the coming of sound, film was a wonderful new toy, a plaything that could carry their work to the masses with an alacrity that mere concerts could not. The tradeoff, of course, was that the films weren't theirs. No one spoke of Satie's *Entr'acte* or Ibert's *The Italian Straw Hat.*

In the USSR Eisenstein was making his models of montage, *Potemkin* (1925) and *October* (1928). These were scored in Germany by Edmund Meisel. Preparing his scores, Meisel screened a film over and over, assigning separate themes to individual silent sequences, then developed the themes into a musical whole that conveyed, at its best, the power of the film itself. Wolfgang Zeller scored *The Adventures of Prince Achmed,* a 1926 film by Lotte Reiniger, the pioneering animator known for her silhouette cartoons. Around the same time, Paul Hindemith was composing a piece for mechanized organ to accompany another cartoon figure, Felix the Cat. Hindemith wrote film music as early as 1922, when he was only twenty-seven, but little of it survives as film work; much of it found its way into later, longer "serious" pieces.

Until recently, Hans Erdmann's score for Murnau's 1922 *Nosferatu* was considered lost. Bram Stoker's widow had sued *Nosferatu*'s producers for copyright infringement—the film story was ripped off from *Dracula*—and all prints that could be found were destroyed. Fortunately, many weren't. Erdmann made several suites out of the score and, along with his books on film music, deposited copies at the Library of Congress (as required by U.S. copyright law), where they were discovered by musicologist Gillian Anderson. Although only parts of the score were found, Anderson and her arranger James Kessler were able to reconstruct the remainder using Erdmann's own notes.

•   •   •

In Europe the composition of a film score was considered an undertaking potentially worthy of the concert hall. In pre-Copland America, forever on the defensive for its lack of a history of serious composition, the film score was still viewed as frivolous. But a Promethean patriot like D. W. Griffith remained undaunted. After *Intolerance* and his association with Joseph Carl Breil, Griffith continued to commission film scores, though none proved as memorable. Carli Elinor took a music credit on a few more Griffith pictures. Louis F. Gottschalk (not to be confused with Louis Moreau Gottschalk, dead by 1870) wrote beautiful parts for violin and harp to accompany *Broken Blossoms* (1919). *Way Down East* (1921), less epic in scope than *Birth of a Nation* or *Intolerance* but just as closely observed, gave composer William Frederick Peters several classic sequences to score, including the justly famous rescue of Gish on an icy river.

Following standard musical training—violin lessons with his father in his native Ohio, study at the Leipzig Conservatory—Peters was working as house violinist at New York's Empire Theater by 1895, when he was nineteen. During a long stint as music director for actress Maud Adams, the original Peter Pan, Peters sidled his way into film scoring. He and Victor Herbert each composed separate scores for *When Knighthood Was in Flower* (1922), which featured the young Marion Davies and some of the most glorious medieval costumes yet photographed, and also *Little Old New York* (1923) with Davies again, this time in a Knickerbocker setting. Of course Victor Herbert's music has lived on; Peters, though a charter member of ASCAP and well-respected in his time, is largely forgotten. He died in Englewood, New Jersey, in 1938.

Way Down East, like some of the other more prominent pictures of the Silent Era, was rescored for sound in 1930 by forty-year-old New Yorker Louis Silvers. A vaudeville pianist who began his career writing for entertainer Gus Edwards, Silvers was already working with Griffith during the making of *Way Down East*, though it was the Peters score that was originally used. Silvers's score has a light-opera quality in its original passages, mixed with bits from the classics.

"There's No Place Like Home," "All Those Endearing Young Charms," "Rock a Bye Baby," and "Abide with Me"—each turns up and drives its point home.

Before rescoring *Way Down East*, Silvers was a prominent composer on Broadway. A tune of his called "April Showers" was used in the show *Bombo* (1921), sung by the energetic thirty-four-year-old Al Jolson. In 1923 Jolson signed with D. W. Griffith to make *Mammy's Boy*, capitalizing on his reputation for blackface minstrel songs. But Jolson, realizing that the silent film's accompanying music wouldn't include his voice, walked off the project. In New York he made a sound short for Lee DeForest. The result proved delightful, and he agreed to make another short, *April Showers*, for Warner Bros. By now Warners had established Vitaphone, the sound-on-disk system developed jointly by Western Electric and Bell Labs. Warners held yet another ace, the contracted services of Silvers. Together, Silvers and Jolson would make film history with *The Jazz Singer.*

◦   ◦   ◦

By 1923, Lee DeForest, already renowned for his work in developing radio, was beginning to harness some of his radio discoveries for film. He pioneered early amplification systems that could create enough sound volume to reach large numbers of people—a movie audience, for instance. Over the next three years, DeForest supervised the making of a thousand so-called Phonofilms, speeches by politicians and other public figures, as well as musical performances.

For bigger pictures, however, DeForest's method couldn't produce an appropriately big sound. So the old-fashioned live accompaniment had to do. Paramount/Famous Players led the pack in paying for original music for their more spectacular product. For DeMille's *The Ten Commandments* (1923), music director Irvin Talbot—he held that position at Paramount for forty-five years—arranged sheet-music cues derived entirely from the classics repertoire, for several thousand exhibitors to pass on to their orchestras. In 1923 the ubiquitous Hugo Riesenfeld moved to Los Angeles to score James Cruze's *The Covered Wagon*. Based on a novel by Emerson Hough, it maintained a surprisingly cohesive narrative as it followed a wagon train from Kansas City to Oregon. For this first great epic western, Riesenfeld even knocked off an exploitation song, "Westward Ho!," its sheet music subsequently found on thousands of pianos across the country.

For many musicologists, the most enduring big score for the silents was composed by an Iowan named Mortimer Wilson (born 1876). Wilson was educated at the Chicago Conservatory and in Leipzig before carving out a career as conductor-educator in Atlanta. In 1916 he moved to New York, where the cinemas were grander than anywhere else. Wilson saw the possibilities in writing for the medium, and was introduced to Douglas Fairbanks, who commissioned him to write music for his new picture, *Thief of Bagdad.*

SPECIAL SCORE FOR "THIEF OF BAGDAD" heralded a 1923 news clipping:

> For "The Thief of Bagdad" [Wilson] has evolved a theme character-istic of each of the principal characters—and separate motifs in keep-ing with the main situations. These he has woven into a colorful fab-ric of harmony to serve as background for players and action. He fol-lowed the production closely in order to absorb the proper atmos-phere and then, so that his closeness to unimportant detail might not influence his bigger conception, went to New York to do the actual composing. He returned to Hollywood with the finished score late last week. Music lovers pronounce this work a symphonic master-piece.

Recalling the score more than fifty years later, Hugo Friedhofer said it was "more or less in the quasi-oriental idiom of Rimsky-Korsakov." That's probably less of a putdown than it sounds. Few con-temporaneous composers could capture so many orchestral colors in their own writing as Wilson did.

After *Thief,* Wilson's next big film commission was to score Fairbanks's *Don Q.* During production, the *Los Angeles Times* described him as being holed up "in a stuffy little old studio" composing "eight or nine hours a day."

◦   ◦   ◦

Swashbucklers like *Thief of Bagdad* and *Don Q.* weren't the only big movies to get big scores. In 1917 the Irish-American, Maine-born John

Mortimer Wilson, c.1910
Courtesy UCLA Popular Music Library

Ford, after working variously as a prop man, stuntman, and actor (he was a Klansman in *Birth of a Nation*), had begun to direct features. When he got around to *The Iron Horse* in 1924, he was already, at twenty-nine, an old hand at westerns. *The Iron Horse* was an epic about the railroad crawling through the Old West, and Erno Rapee (born 1891 in Budapest) was given the job of providing the cinema music.

Rapee studied piano but quickly turned to conducting. In 1912 he toured Mexico and South America. The Hungarian Opera Company was then one of a dozen working opera companies in New York, and Rapee decided to stay in the United States when offered its directorship. Operas, then as now, took months to mount, so Rapee accepted steadier work as music director of the Rivoli Theater, which became the Rialto, the largest American cinema until the March 1927 opening of the Roxy. Rapee moved freely around the theater circuit, conducting here, adding a few musical patches there, and in 1924 published *Motion Picture Moods for Pianists and Organists,* which immediately replaced the Zamecnik volume as the cinema standard. "Adapted to Fifty-Two Moods and Situations," the book's heading announced. For a "picturization" of an "Aeroplane," Rapee suggested Mendelssohn's *Rondo Capriccioso*; for a Battle, Otto Langley's Agitato No. 3.

Meanwhile Rapee wrote a score for Douglas Fairbanks's *Robin Hood* (1922). For showings of *The Cabinet of Dr. Caligari* in 1924, Rapee ignored the familiar, heavier work of the nineteenth-century composers and drew musical selections from contemporaries like Prokofiev, Schoenberg, and Stravinsky. Apparently, the mordant chords of their works jarred audiences as effectively as the visual images did.

Rapee's most enduring film music was written in the waning days of the Silent Era. The film adaptation of the Maxwell Anderson–Laurence Stallings Pulitzer Prize–winning antiwar play *What Price Glory?* (1926) featured the song "Charmaine," written with Lew Pollack. Thirty years after the film's release, the Four Freshman had a hit with their version. *Seventh Heaven* (1927), the Janet Gaynor–Charles Farrell weeper based on the wildly popular 1922 Austin Strong play, contained "Diane," also with lyrics by Pollack. (Photographer Diane Arbus [born 1923] was one of hundreds of children named for the character, a Parisian street waif.) These songs were beautifully crafted, but they would have stood out anyway because they were sung on screen, in sync, while the remainder of the pictures was speechless.

Rapee never spent much time in Hollywood. He went to work for NBC in New York, conducting its regular Sunday night classical pro-

Erno Rapee
Courtesy ASCAP

grams beginning in 1934, and was musical supervisor at Radio City through most of the '40s.

⸱   ⸱   ⸱

Zamecnik scored German-born Erich von Stroheim's 1927 film *The Wedding March,* featuring Fay Wray and von Stroheim himself in full Prussian regalia. *The Wedding March* was accompanied in appropriately equipped cinemas by Zamecnik's score, recorded on DeForest's amplified disks. Sound equipment in theaters was still crude—sometimes it worked, sometimes it didn't—but synchronized sound was no longer a novelty with the public. Zamecnik turned out a full score for *Wings* (1927), the first Academy Award–winner for best picture, and one of the last major studio releases filmed entirely without speech.

In 1925 King Vidor directed *The Big Parade,* from a Laurence Stallings–Harry Behr script about a young American conscript learning the horrors of war. In filming its central battle scene, Vidor had a drummer beat a bass drum for the actors playing soldiers to walk in the same rhythm through the ominous, enemy-occupied woods. This is how music was often used during the Silent Era: off-camera, to provide a mood for the players while they acted. Before filming was completed, Cotton Club songwriter Jimmy McHugh was hired by MGM to write "My Dream of the Big Parade," a song whose sole purpose was to publicize the film.

A score for *The Big Parade* went out, cobbled together from original music by Dr. William Axt—we don't know where the honorific comes from, because Axt's formal education went no further than DeWitt Clinton High School—and David Mendoza. Both native New Yorkers, Axt (born 1888) and Mendoza (born 1894) probably met while conducting at the Capitol Theater. For a while Mendoza worked as concertmaster for the Victor Talking Machine Orchestra, Victor's house band. Axt was deeply involved with opera—he was conductor of the Hammerstein Grand Opera Company in New York—before working as a cinema conductor.

Axt and Mendoza also took a crack at music for *The Wind* (1927), my favorite of Lillian Gish's movies. Mendoza continued to work sporadically on movie scores until 1939, but his heart was in New York–based radio and theater music. Like Erno Rapee, he served as Radio City's music director. Axt scored *Ben-Hur* for MGM and eventually became head of its music department in the '30s. The picture that brought Axt to MGM's attention, however, was the John Barrymore swashbuckler *Don Juan*.

The premiere of *Don Juan* was an event orchestrated by Warners, which used its prized Vitaphone process for the first time on a nationally released feature-length film. Its narrative placed the infamous Spanish libertine in the court of the Borgias. At 126 minutes, filling approximately twelve reels, the film was synchronized to several disks that contained the sound—special effects like the swishing of swords and knocking on doors, as well as Axt's prerecorded music. The premiere was held at the Warner Theater, Broadway and Fifty-second Street, on August 6, 1926. The feature was preceded by a medley of musical shorts: the New York Philharmonic, opera singers, violin soloists such as Efrem Zimbalist and Mischa Elman, and the Cansino Dancers, led by Rita Hayworth's father, Eduardo Cansino.

Don Juan's young director Alan Crosland already had a few films under his belt, but directing a full-length movie with sound was new for him. The soundstage, previously unknown (because it was uncalled for), created headaches for the director, the sound technicians, and the actors, even if their speech wasn't being recorded. Nobody had yelled "Quiet on the set!" before Crosland; nobody had *had* to. Leading lady Mary Astor concluded that "Alan Crosland didn't have the strength of personality to hold the company together. He was a nice man. He'd walk around, well dressed, brushing a waxed mustache with a finger and saying, 'All right now, please, people—' but his crowds of extras were noisy and unruly."

Meanwhile, the movie studios could feel the demand for more and better sound films. Only sound, they felt, could help them compete with radio, which kept more and more people home at night. American movies, story-driven since the days before Griffith, were also competing with the likes of *Show Boat,* a musical play that managed to weave a cohesive narrative through some of the most beautiful songs ever heard in a theater.

Out of such marketplace desperation, Warners rehired Crosland to make *The Jazz Singer.* Jolson was the star. There was virtually no recorded dialogue, except for a brief moment or two between Jolson and his mama (Eugenie Besserer), and hardly any background music. It didn't matter. Like *Don Juan, The Jazz Singer* opened at the Warner Theater and astounded New York audiences with its picture-and-sound representation of life. The movie's artistic limitations were readily apparent, especially in its treacly story (though writer Samson Raphaelson would go on to become one of the movies' most important scenarists). But *The Jazz Singer* boasted one perfect thing: Jolson. No singer was better suited to sing to audiences from the screen; no other singer's personality was as big as those dimensions—30 by 60 feet—and still believable. Up there on the silver screen, Jolson sang "Dirty Hands, Dirty Feet," lyrics by Grant Clarke and Edgar Leslie and music by James Monaco, the Italian-born, Albany-reared composer who had worked his way up through Tin Pan Alley as a pianist. As soon as Jolson finished "Dirty Hands," he said right to the movie audience, "Wait a minute! You ain't heard nuthin' yet!," and quickly launched into "Toot Toot Tootsie," a 1922 hit credited to tunesmiths Ernie Erdman, Dan Russo, Ted Fiorito, and the venerable Chicago-based lyricist Gus Kahn. The other numbers were "My Gal Sal," the famous song by Paul Dresser, brother of novelist Theodore Dreiser; "Waiting for the Robert E. Lee," the 1912 standard by Lewis Muir and Wolfie Gilbert; Irving Berlin's "Blue Skies"; Louis Silvers's "Mother of Mine"; and the song that everyone associates with Jolson, "Mammy," by Joe Young, Sam Lewis, and the great Walter Donaldson.

There's no way to overstate the seismic effect *The Jazz Singer*, quaint as it now seems, had on the movie industry. Within weeks of its premiere, every studio revamped its production schedule. All over Hollywood, teams of carpenters and technicians were put on payroll to turn stages into soundstages—usually warehouse-like structures that could contain sound equipment and muffle external noise during filming. Musical sequences were filmed at night, when neighborhood traffic was at a minimum. Shooting *Rio Rita*, the second stage musical to be filmed (*The Desert Song* was filmed earlier at Warners), star Bebe Daniels recalled, "The thing that threw me at first working with sound was the absence of noise. We were used to the whirring of cameras and the small orchestra playing nearby to provide mood music while we worked in silent films." Lee DeForest, Daniels's second cousin, appeared on the *Rio Rita* set to personally reposition microphones.

The Jazz Singer contained performed songs—conducted by Lou Silvers and arranged under his supervision—but no underscore. That would be typical of the Hollywood studio pictures to come for the next eighteen months. Overnight, popular songwriters were more in demand than classically trained composers.

∘   ∘   ∘

After *Don Juan* and *The Jazz Singer*, no one wanted the old live accompaniment—the moviemakers even less than the audiences, because recorded sound gave them control they had lacked when relying on house keyboard players and cinema conductors for their music. While new sound films were being cranked out, the silents that were deemed profitable were given recorded scores; those already considered classics were given kid-glove musical treatment. Although Joseph Carl Breil was dead, his score for *Birth of a Nation* was recorded using Lee DeForest's sound-on-film process and sent out to the theaters accompanying a drastically edited version of Griffith's movie. The Lon Chaney *Phantom of the Opera*, originally scored for live accompaniment by its first cinema conductor, seventy-five-year-old Gustav Hinrichs, was rereleased in 1929 with a new score by Dutch conductor David Broekmann (1899–1958), who would also score Lewis Milestone's *All Quiet on the Western Front* that year.

So ended the silents and live musical accompaniment. Composers, conductors, and musicians who wanted a paycheck from the movie industry now generally had to go to California. Picture palaces stopped employing music directors and, of course, entire orchestras. Pianists had to find work elsewhere, and most of the mammoth cinema organs were removed and sold off, though naturally the market for a mighty Wurlitzer was limited—most auditoriums just weren't big enough to accommodate it, to say nothing of most living rooms.

For a while some movies occupied a no-man's-land, caught between their speechless filming and the need to outfit them with sound. A case in point is *Our Modern Maidens* (1929), Joan Crawford's sequel to *Our Dancing Daughters,* which was silent, and a precursor to *Our Blushing Brides,* which was filmed with sound. *Modern Maidens* was recorded by the Western Electric System and has a score pieced together by Arthur Lange. Forty at the time of filming, Lange had moved from Broadway musicals to Hollywood to work in MGM's music department. Over the titles we hear "I Love You," a hit lifted from the show *Little Jesse James* by Paul Whiteman–alumnus Harry Archer. The movie drops into an evening of youthful revelry; there's a Scott Fitzgerald Jazz Age tone, and the characters, despite their youth, are smart and cosmopolitan. "He's playing 'The Soap Song' from *The Barber of Seville*!" shrieks one character, as we're told by a title card. There's no speech, but there are crowd sounds, radio announcements, and an occasional whistle, in addition to the music. When Crawford drums at a party, we can hear the rim shot on the soundtrack. And when Crawford and Rod LaRocque make eyes at each other, the scene is washed by "If I Had You," the 1928 hit by British songwriters Reg Connelly and Jimmy Campbell. To moviegoers who also listened to the radio or owned a piano, the song did the work of a title card.

Within weeks of the release of *Our Modern Maidens* everybody was retooling soundtracks. Sound became the seat-of-the-pants element in movies. The stock market had collapsed on Black Thursday, October 24, 1929, and the plunge that followed sank people into despair as well as destitution. Movies were drawing larger audiences than ever because they were cheap and novel, an emotional and technological escape from harsh reality. Music was almost never used as background (a problem of verisimilitude—where was the music coming from?—that musicians like Arthur Lange wrestled with), but usually within the narrative, produced by radios, phonographs, or live performances.

French filmmaker René Clair, whose silent comedies are models of aural as well as visual wit, toyed with the musical problem in his 1931 comedy *A Nous la Liberté,* billed as *film sonore* ("resonant cinema"). The playful, dreamy score was by Georges Auric, another of Les Six and then just beginning his long film-scoring career. The movie focuses on an escaped convict who builds a phonograph empire, much like that of Pathé. Arthur Knight (in *The Liveliest Art*) described what happened when the convict's girlfriend sings to him from her window:

> Suddenly something goes wrong with the voice—it whines, and whirs, then fades away. A moment later, while the young fellow is still looking up at the window, the girl appears in the street, the song begins again and we discover that what we have been listening to all along is a phonograph record from another apartment.

A Nous la Liberté spoofed modern mechanization. The American movie that's most often compared to it is, of course, *Modern Times.*

◦　　◦　　◦

Modern Times was made eight years after *The Jazz Singer,* but its concessions to sound, like *City Lights* (1931) before it, were in an occasional recorded effect and in its music. Charlie Chaplin couldn't read or write music, but he regarded himself as a supreme creative and mimetic artist. At one Hollywood party, the story goes, Chaplin graced the other guests with an aria; when a guest expressed surprise that Chaplin could sing so beautifully, he replied, "I can't. I was only imitating Caruso."

The British music hall, where Chaplin trained as a comic, echoes through his movies. His 1914 one-reeler *Twenty Minutes of Love* had a comic rhythm loosely based on the then-popular two-step "Too Much Mustard." The 1917 *The Immigrant* was suggested by the wistful mood of "Mrs. Grundy." Chaplin wrote that "Auld Lang Syne" set the mood for *The Gold Rush* (1925).

But these were inspirations. When it came to composition, never mind orchestration, Chaplin needed help. He got it, though he tended to be stingy with credit. In 1992 musicologist Gillian Anderson found a score for Chaplin's *The Circus* (1928) credited to Arthur Kay, first head of music at Fox, at Chaplin's house in Switzerland. On *City Lights,* composer Arthur Johnston (who would go on to write such standards as "Pennies from Heaven") wove together several themes, the most promiment among them Jose Padilla's "Violetera." (Padilla, born 1889 in Granada, worked for years at the Moulin Rouge and at the Casino de Paris. His music was still an influence on Chaplin as late as 1952 in *Limelight*.) For the music in *Modern Times,* Chaplin had the help of a brash, frighteningly articulate twenty-four-year-old named David Raksin.

Known now as one of the greatest of film composers ("Laura," the theme to *The Bad and the Beautiful,* among others), Raksin had been aware of movie music since his early childhood, when his father—Israel Raksin, an occasional woodwind player for Leopold Stokowski and the Philadelphia Orchestra—conducted for the silents in Philadelphia. There the young, slender Raksin, wiry hair haloing his head, attended the University of Pennsylvania and emerged as a clarinetist and tenor saxophonist. A society dance band he had accompanied to New York failed to catch fire, and returned to Philadelphia; Raksin remained, lodged in a seedy hotel room north of Times Square. Eventually he landed a job as music arranger for Fred Allen's radio show. The show's pianist Oscar Levant, who had already been to Hollywood, took Raksin's arrangement of "I Got Rhythm" to George Gershwin. Impressed, Gershwin got Raksin a job at Harms,

Inc., a prominent Tin Pan Alley music publisher. Harms sent him to Boston to arrange music for the Dietz-Schwartz revue *At Home Abroad.* On August 8, 1935, Harms forwarded to Raksin a wire from his old friend Edward Powell:

> HAVE WONDERFUL OPPORTUNITY FOR YOU IF INTERESTED IN HAV-
> ING A SHOT AT HOLLYWOOD STOP CHAPLIN COMPOSES ALMOST
> ALL HIS OWN SCORE BUT CANT WRITE DOWN A NOTE YOUR JOB TO
> WORK WITH HIM TO TAKE DOWN MUSIC STRAIGHTEN IT OUT HAR-
> MONICALLY DEVELOP HERE AND THERE IN CHARACTER AND
> THEME . . .

The telegram was a musician's earnest variation on Herman Mankiewicz's famous 1926 wire to Ben Hecht (MILLIONS ARE TO BE GRABBED OUT HERE AND YOUR ONLY COMPETITION IS IDIOTS. . .).

Raksin was thrilled. He turned his *At Home Abroad* duties over to legendary Broadway orchestrator Hans Spialek, which was, Raksin said with typical self-deprecation, "a bit like having Babe Ruth batting for some promising rookie." Four days later he arrived in Pasadena. Immediately Raksin was put to work arranging sketches for the next morning's recording of Alfred Newman's music for *Barbary Coast*. Newman was turned off by Raksin's rookie enthusiasm—a bad sign, considering that Newman would conduct the recording of the music for *Modern Times.*

Raksin finally got down to work with Chaplin, who referred to the slight Philadelphian as "this infant." Although still in awe about working in Hollywood with perhaps the single most celebrated film star, Raksin spoke his mind. Callowly, he described Chaplin's music-hall approach as "vulgar." His frankness got him fired. Chaplin, "like many self-made autocrats," Raksin wrote, "demanded unquestioning obedience from his associates; years of deference to his point of view had persuaded him that it was the only one that mattered." But the next day Alf Reeves, Chaplin's "faithful manager," told him that Chaplin wanted to rehire him; Raksin had already proven himself too valuable in realizing Chaplin's musical ideas, many of which came to the star while sitting on the toilet.

Charlie Chaplin, Gertrud and Arnold Schoenberg, and David Raksin, 1935
Courtesy of and permission by David Raksin

Chaplin *was* musical. At lunch at Musso & Frank (at this writing, still a thriving Hollywood institution), Chaplin would order in song (to the tune of "When Irish Eyes Are Smiling"): "An I-rish stew/ with *veg-e-ta-bles . . .*" At the studio he "would whistle, or hum, or pick out on the piano" some notes he had brought with him. Raksin took these melodic threads to weave a carpet. For the tune that became "Smile," Chaplin wanted something akin to Puccini.

With all the music for *Modern Times* in place, Alfred Newman diligently rehearsed his orchestra. During the first recording session, however, Chaplin accused the musicians of laziness. Newman, even then fiercely protective of his people and unwilling to brook criticism from an amateur, stormed off the podium, promising to never work with Chaplin again. (He made good on the promise.) Edward Powell was forced to take over the recording sessions. Raksin sided with Newman, causing a second break with Chaplin that wouldn't be mended for another fifteen years.

The *Modern Times* music was the last of the great silent scores. For the song "Smile," Geoffrey Parsons and John Turner added lyrics ("Smile though you're heart is breaking") many years later. For Chaplin's next picture, *The Great Dictator* (1940), musical expertise was provided by Meredith Willson, whose Broadway musical *The Music Man* was still sixteen years in the future. Rudy Schrager handled the music on Chaplin's masterful *Monsieur Verdoux* (1947). In his autobiography Chaplin mentions none of them—neither Raksin, Powell, Newman, Willson, nor Schrager.

Chaplin's work as a film composer was, in a way, a miniature of the industry's determination to control all aspects of filmmaking as soon as it was feasible. In his music as well as in his movies, Chaplin was often the most maudlin of artists. But he could be counted on to cut his sentiment with insight and wit, musically as well as cinematically. In the nearly forty years since I saw *Modern Times* at the Queen Anne Theater, in my mind his comic gifts remain inextricably bound up with his music.

That's because the Silent Era was speechless but not silent.

TWO

Every Note . . . Is Like a Lover's Kiss

The Invasion of the Songwriters

Although *The Jazz Singer* was neither the first film with sound effects or a music track, nor even the first film with bits of dialogue, it was the first feature-length movie to include several songs inside a fictional narrative. "JOLSON SINGS!" cried the ads, and the obvious question was "Sings what?" Jolson was singing songs he'd already sung on Broadway and on the radio.

The songwriters hadn't necessarily set foot in Hollywood, or had even had much interest in pictures. After *The Jazz Singer*, however, Hollywood needed the song as an essential ingredient in its product. So it offered something no self-respecting songwriter could do without: money—a lot of money.

In his autobiography, Sam Coslow recalled sitting in his Manhattan office one day in early 1929 when his publishing partner Larry Spier dragged him across Times Square to the Paramount Theater Building to see an executive there. Warner Bros. was gobbling up music publishers and their catalogs, the executive told Coslow and Spier; MGM was about to buy the firms of Feist and Robbins, two of

36

Tin Pan Alley's oldest and most respected publishers. "We've had our eye on you two guys," the Paramount man said,

> and we like what we see. Now that talkies are here to stay, all the film studios are preparing big musicals. Al Jolson proved they're a gold mine. We need prolific songwriters, a catalog of songs to pick from, and music promotional executives.

After a brief consultation between the principals, Spier and Coslow, Inc., sold 80 percent of itself to Paramount, which changed the firm's name to Famous Music. Spier stayed in New York to oversee the publishing end; Coslow rode the Santa Fe Chief out to Los Angeles to write songs for Paramount Pictures. Coslow soon realized that no songplugger—the guy who got a song performed and publicized—could compete with the movies. Overnight the movies became the single most powerful songplugger imaginable. Tin Pan Alley, originally located on West 28th Street in New York, was now intimately linked to Hollywood, three thousand miles away.

Warners was first in the sound/music game, but the other studios were quick to exploit Tin Pan Alley and its ironclad licensing rules. It was a matter of economics. Naturally, a studio gearing up to present songs or familiar background music in its new sound features wanted to own the rights to that music, in order to minimize its costs. Hazel Meyer (in *The Gold in Tin Pan Alley*) put it this way:

> The system of planting nostalgic or otherwise appropriate songs in the fertile soil of Hollywood studios and coast-to-coast networks can reap a bumper crop of new records, performances and interest for a sleeping copyright. It is one reason why the movie-makers farsightedly paid millions of dollars to buy out, or into, several of the nation's top publishing outfits when films were equipped with sound.

The old-time "fitter," who raided music libraries for the cinema orchestras, now had more legally complicated responsibilities as he attempted to keep a picture's music in the family. But the surest way to secure music rights, to pay less and keep those rights in perpetuity, was to start from scratch and hire the composer and/or lyricist.

For an eighteen-month period, roughly from the middle of 1928 to the end of 1929, legions of songwriters, musicians, and arrangers arrived daily in Los Angeles. A handful of them accepted administrative assignments, forming and overseeing the new music departments created by the studios. Only a few were hired to write underscores, a strange new use of music that the musicians themselves argued about endlessly. Most of them, however, were contracted to write or play songs for the nearly one hundred musicals in preparation. By making musical pictures and exploiting the new developments in sound, the studios figured they were minting money. And for a year or so, they were.

Fox, owned by former nickelodeon showman William Fox before the company was joined to Joseph Schenck's Twentieth Century Pictures, provided plenty of money for a music department and musicals. Through 1929, its main musicals man was Arthur Kay. Formerly the conductor of the pit orchestra at Grauman's massive Million Dollar Theater in downtown Los Angeles, the very Prussian-mannered Kay (né Katzenbach) staffed Fox with local musicians.

For the early musical *Fox Movietone Follies of 1929* (which contained only a few sound sequences, and one scene in color), David Butler was hired to write and direct. Butler had been an actor with D. W. Griffith's troupe and had appeared in Fox's *Seventh Heaven* a year earlier. For the *Movietone Follies*, head of production Winfield Sheehan, a tough former police reporter, augmented Arthur Kay's staff with several music men. From France, Sheehan brought in the flamboyant Marcel Silver; but Silver was used to lavish stage productions and months of preparation, so Sheehan fired him in midproduction. Sheehan next hired songwriter Con Conrad (born Conrad K. Dober in 1891), the rakish New Yorker who'd had hits with "Margie" in 1920 and "Barney Google" in 1922. A hustling man-about-town, Conrad once promoted his bandleader friend Russ Columbo by engineering a phony romance between Columbo and Greta Garbo, a ploy that did nothing for her career, everything for his. Composer Archie Gottler and lyricist Sidney Mitchell were brought on board for the *Movietone Follies* and subsequent musicals as well. For a while this practice of putting songwriters and musical performers under contract for several pictures was seen as efficient and cost-effective. (In Chicago, Winnie Sheehan attended a production of the college musical *Good News* and became smitten with its eighteen-year-old ingenue Dixie Lee, a former "Ruth Etting of Tomorrow" contest winner; born Wilma Wyatt, Dixie Lee would appear in half a dozen Fox musicals in the next two years, and would become the first Mrs. Bing Crosby.)

Soon the Fox staff welcomed lyricist Wolfie Gilbert ("Waiting for the Robert E. Lee"), *Ziegfeld Follies* songwriter Dave Stamper, and composer Abel Baer ("June Night"). Of all the songwriters then under contract to Fox, however, the most important was undoubtedly one of *Good News*'s authors, Buddy DeSylva.

Buddy DeSylva (born 1895) and David Butler (born 1894) attended University of Southern California together. A dark-skinned beachlover, DeSylva played the ukelele (surely the '20s most socially ubiquitous musical instrument) for his friends at Ocean Park and at Catalina. Playing Vincent Rose's Puccini-derived tune "Avalon" on his uke, DeSylva came up with some lyrics—his first songwriting hit. Riding the trolley car, Butler and DeSylva concocted musicals, including a Prohibition comedy they called *Noah's Ark*; their dream casting had Fatty Arbuckle as captain of a houseboat anchored off Manhattan. Jolson, impressed by DeSylva's quickness with a lyric, persuaded him to return to New York, DeSylva's birthplace, "where the action was." At a going-away party for DeSylva, held in San Francisco, Butler brought a dapper, local violinist-composer named Joe Meyer who desperately wanted DeSylva to hear a tune he'd written; DeSylva listened reluctantly, and within half an hour had provided a lyric and title: "California, Here I Come." (Meyer subsequently went to New York, too, and composed "Clap Hands, Here Comes Charlie," "If You Knew Susie," and "A Cup of Coffee, a Sandwich and You.")

In New York, DeSylva met Lew Brown and Ray Henderson while working on the 1925 edition of *George White's Scandals*. According to Butler, Lew Brown was "strictly a gag man. DeSylva was the lyric writer and sometimes wrote tunes. Henderson was strictly a piano man, strictly the music." DeSylva was a year younger than Brown, who was born in Odessa, and a year older than Henderson. After several hits on Broadway, including *Good News* (1927), DeSylva, Brown, and Henderson went west to write songs for the movies.

Sunny Side Up was the first DeSylva, Brown, and Henderson score for Fox, and possibly the best. From it came "I'm a Dreamer, Aren't We All" and "A Talking Picture of You" (a lyric that would have been inconceivable just a few years earlier). David Butler directed, and Arthur Kay's orchestra played the tunes.

◦   ◦   ◦

Across town at Paramount, the creation of a music department was even easier. Paramount already had in place its so-called circuit staff, based in New York and playing in the orchestras of Paramount-owned cinemas on the East Coast. While conductor Irvin Talbot and vocal expert Max Terr stayed in New York to wrap up recording commitments, Paramount music director Nat Finston went to Los Angeles to assemble a music department. Former Paul Whiteman pianist Ray Turner and organist Sigmund Krumgold became the center of daily musical activity on the lot. The department was filled in by a recording supervisor, two music librarians, orchestrators John Leipold and Herman Hand, and a small platoon of music directors. The British-born Frank Tours (born 1877) proved to be the most versatile of these, assembling and conducting the orchestra for the 1928 Ziegfeld film production *Glorifying the American Girl.* Of the other more interesting music men, Hungarian-born Karl Hajos supplied music for *Morocco,* Marlene Dietrich's first American movie, and Jack King provided some underscoring and songs for several early Paramount sound pictures, including the marvelous "How Am I to Know?" (from *Paramount on Parade,* 1930). Back in New York, meanwhile, Jay Gorney, who would compose "Brother, Can You Spare a Dime?" a couple of years later, was installed as head of Paramount's Astoria studio.

A Paramount songwriters' building was quickly constructed to house the newly contracted musicians. Fred Ahlert (born 1892)—a Fordham Law graduate who spurned the law in favor of joining the popular dance band Fred Waring's Pennsylvanians—moved in and promptly wrote "I'll Get By" with Roy Turk (born 1892) for *Stepping High.* "Mean to Me" and "Walkin' My Baby Back Home" followed from the pair in short order. Sam Coslow joined two other Broadway songwriters, composer Richard Whiting and lyricist Leo Robin, to write songs for the Paramount musical *Dance of Life* (1929), an altered film version of the Broadway hit *Burlesque*. (Oscar Levant reprised his stage role as pianist.) Coslow's "True Blue Lou" became a hit when recorded by Ethel Waters, backed by Russ Columbo.

Whiting and Robin had arrived in Hollywood together before Coslow, and their work was already known to the general public. Whiting (born 1891 in Peoria, Illinois) attended prep school in Los Angeles, but spent most of his youth in Detroit. He became a song-plugger for Remick Music there and played piano at the Temple Theater, then one of the bigger vaudeville houses in the Midwest, where he met his bride, Eleanor. (Together they would become the parents of the singer Margaret Whiting.) Through the 1920s Whiting came up with one hit after another: "Ain't We Got Fun?" (written with Gus Kahn); "Sleepy Time Gal"; and, during a brief stint in New York, "She's Funny That Way" (written with Neil Moret), which contains what seems to be a message to Eleanor, "I'm only human, coward at best/I'm pretty certain she'd follow me west." After that, the family went to Hollywood.

Whiting's first Hollywood partner, Leo Robin, was born in Pittsburgh. (Many sources give Robin's birth year as 1900, but four to five years earlier is more likely.) He initially studied law, but the drama called, and he enrolled at Carnegie Tech to learn how to write plays. When Robin arrived in New York, he met his idol, George S. Kaufman, whom he resembled, and Kaufman steered him to song-writing after seeing Robin's sole published lyric, "My Cutie's Due at Two to Two Today!" Robin contributed the lyric "Hallelujah!" to Vincent Youmans's *Hit the Deck*. In late 1928 his publisher Max Dreyfus paired him with the already renowned Whiting for work at Paramount in Hollywood. The two songwriters met for the first time when their respective westbound trains—Robin's from New York's Penn Station, Whiting's from Detroit—arrived in Chicago and they each walked into the Sherman Hotel. "Mr. Robin," said the bellboy, "meet Mr. Whiting."

At Paramount they quickly turned out songs for *Close Harmony*, starring the baby-faced Nancy Carroll. This led to an assignment writing for Maurice Chevalier's first American picture, *Innocents of Paris* (1929). The film's smash hit, written with former Capitol Theater pianist Newell Chase, was "Louise" ("Every little breeze/Seems to whisper 'Louise'"). "Louise" proved so successful that it cemented Chevalier's relationships with Whiting and Robin, whom he persisted in calling "Rob*an*." Their work for *Playboy of Paris* produced "My Ideal," and they also turned out songs for director Ernst Lubitsch and his comic romp, *Monte Carlo,* starring the vivacious Jeanette MacDonald.

If you think of Jeanette MacDonald only as Nelson Eddy's romantic singing partner in several costume operettas, you don't know

Jeanette MacDonald, 1935
Courtesy the author

how glorious she could be. MacDonald was among the greatest of the early sound singers, surely the loveliest. With her limpid eyes and svelte figure, she was ripe for the movies in a way that more powerful singers —Ethel Merman and Mary Martin, to name two—were not. "The voice, never weighty but always true, was used with cunning grace," opera critic F. Paul Driscoll wrote.

For MacDonald in *Monte Carlo* (1930), Whiting and Robin wrote "Beyond the Blue Horizon," one of the first songs composed expressly to accompany the way a scene was shot. Lubitsch took pains to integrate the music with the dramatic (or comic) action, rather than to merely have a song played free-floating over the scenery or titles. MacDonald sings "Beyond the Blue Horizon" while riding on a train. Whiting's rhythms are timed to the click of the wheels, and Robin's lyric reflects MacDonald's state of mind—that of a princess who can envision a silvery future ahead of her.

After *Monte Carlo,* the Whiting-Robin team broke up without acrimony: Robin had to return to New York to tend to his sick mother; Whiting moved over to Fox. Lubitsch, meanwhile, had warmed to Robin more than to any other lyricist. When Robin returned to the West Coast, Lubitsch paired him with a gaunt Paramount pianist named Ralph Rainger (né Reichenthal)—like Robin, an escapee from law practice. Through the '30s, Rainger and Robin wrote some of the most memorable movie songs, including "June in January," "Easy Living," and "Thanks for the Memory."

Preceding *Monte Carlo* was the first MacDonald-Chevalier combination, *The Love Parade.* Though its staging may appear creaky now, its spirit is young and its music sublime. Lubitsch's songwriters were Victor Schertzinger—who scored *Civilization*—and Clifford Grey. Born in England in 1887, Grey, a former actor, came up through Broadway, and worked with Youmans and Robin on *Hit the Deck*; his most famous song is "If You Were the Only Girl in the World (And I Were the Only Boy)." For *The Love Parade,* Schertzinger and Grey provided "Dream Lover" and several other numbers, each incorporated into the film's romantic action.

Released near the end of 1929, *The Love Parade* came out in a silent version as well, to play in cinemas that still weren't wired for sound. But musically it opened new avenues for the movies, which had previously used songs the way theatrical revues did, as mere interludes separating barely connected or disconnected skits. The ravishing MacDonald, aided by Chevalier, would be at the heart of two more ground-breaking musicals in the next four years.

Over the Hollywood Hills, Universal had to make do without the brilliant services of a Lubitsch. Carl Laemmle, Sr., who had founded Universal Pictures in 1912, liked to put his relatives to work. ("Uncle Carl Laemmle/Had a very large faemmle," wrote Ogden Nash.) Although there's no evidence that Carl, Jr., had any strong taste for music, he knew pictures and knew how to delegate. He had served as executive producer on *All Quiet on the Western Front*. In late 1929, after the critical success of *All Quiet* seemed assured, Laemmle, Jr. was put in charge of the filming of *The King of Jazz*.

The King was Paul Whiteman. The corpulent, moon-faced bandleader, looking at the time like a taller Oliver Hardy, was seen as the perfect focus for a musical movie. His name evoked sounds of the concert hall—particularly New York's Aeolian, where his band had backed Gershwin in the premiere of the *Rhapsody in Blue*—as well as the '20s dance halls filled with frenzy and jazz. Whiteman was no jazz man. But *The King of Jazz* capitalized on his fame, and on his excellent capabilities as a boss who knew how to surround himself with able musicians. Among those who helped out on *The King of Jazz* were composer-conductor Ferde Grofé, who had orchestrated the original version of Gershwin's *Rhapsody*, and the three Rhythm Boys, Harry Barris, Al Rinker, and Bing Crosby, who had been part of Whiteman's act since 1927. The entire production, shot in 3-strip Technicolor, was "devised" by director John Murray Anderson. A Canadian with several years' experience directing musicals in New York, Anderson created an art deco design that is more arresting, in fact, than its music.

The King of Jazz features a fascinating version of *Rhapsody in Blue*, not just because it's so lively but because it's so much a product of its era. "Jazz was born in the African jungle," Whiteman intones, as a bass drum beats out a voodoo rhythm and a dancer's shadow simulates an African dance. The songs aren't any more sophisticated. John Boles and Jeanette Loff sing "It Happened in Monterey," composed by Mabel Wayne, a young Brooklynite and a rarity in Tin Pan Alley—a woman. Wayne had already worked up a few hits—"In a Little Spanish Town" and "Ramona" among them—when she came up with "Monterey." She seemed to specialize in Old California material, no matter who her lyricist was. ("Monterey"'s lyrics are credited to Billy Rose, although with Rose you could never be sure.) The Rhythm Boys perform "Happy Feet" with a lot of scatting; it's not much, but you can tell Crosby is going places.

Crosby was the great thing to come out of *The King of Jazz*. In his 1953 memoir *Call Me Lucky*, Crosby remembered the arduous production. "Picture technicians weren't developed the way they are now, and musical numbers took as much as a week to shoot." In Der Bingle's case, one reason was that he was jailed for driving "H.B.D."—Had Been Drinking—just weeks before the repeal of the Eighteenth Amendment. Sentenced to sixty days, Crosby was released for one day only to film the Milton Ager–Jack Yellen number "A Bench in the Park" with the Rhythm Boys.

Milton Ager had been a cinema pianist in his native Chicago before entering vaudeville and going to work for Irving Berlin. (Ager was the husband of *Variety* reporter Cecilia Ager and father of journalist Shana Alexander.) Jack Yellen was born in Poland and grew up in Buffalo, where he worked as a reporter while writing songs. Ager and Yellen wrote "I Wonder What's Become of Sally," "Ain't She Sweet," and "Hard-Hearted Hannah" before arriving in Hollywood. They followed up *The King of Jazz* with *Chasing Rainbows*, MGM's backstage musical entry for the year. *Chasing Rainbows* is thoroughly forgettable except for an Ager-Yellen song called "Happy Days Are Here Again." It became FDR's 1932 campaign song, even though lyricist Yellen was a diehard Republican.

Metro-Goldwyn-Mayer entered the songwriters' sweepstakes, too. Arthur Lange, then the most celebrated dance-band arranger in the nation, was hired by MGM, at $750 a week. On February 19, 1929, Lange (whose photographs show him wearing wire-rim spectacles, oiled hair, and an air of superiority) was met at the Los Angeles railroad

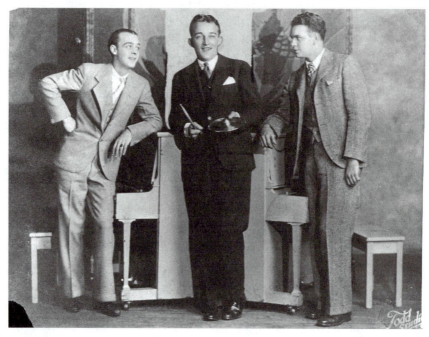

The Rhythm Boys: Harry Barris, Bing Crosby, Al Rinker, c.1930
Globe Pictures

station by songwriter Fred Fisher ("Chicago"). Set up in a bungalow at the Beverly Hills Hotel, Lange learned the next day that he'd been appointed head of music at MGM.

Fred Fisher, meanwhile, was the resident character on the lot. Irving Thalberg once passed him and asked his companion, "Who is that guy?" Told that it was the flamboyant Fisher, then past fifty and beholden to no one, Thalberg circled back, button-holed him, and asked him if he could write a symphony for a picture.

"Get me a pencil, boy," Fisher is said to have replied. "When you get me you get Beethoven, Mozart, and Chopin." Fisher's presence notwithstanding, the most valuable songwriters on the lot were the unlikely team of Ignacio (Nacio) Herb Brown and Arthur Freed.

Brown was born in New Mexico in 1896. When he was eight, his family took him to Los Angeles, where his father became a deputy sheriff. While at high school at Musical Arts, Brown took piano lessons from his mother. In the early '20s he began a tailoring business, then dabbled in real estate to cash in on Los Angeles's soaring property values. Songwriting was still a sideline. By 1921 he was occasionally writing with Freed, who was so different from Brown as to complement him.

Born in 1894 in Charleston, South Carolina, to a prosperous Jewish family, Freed attended Phillips Exeter Academy before entering vaudeville. A stint in Chicago as a songplugger introduced him to the Marx Brothers. (Years later, Freed would be instrumental in luring them to MGM.) In World War I, Freed wrote army shows. Then came the obligatory New York period and some writing with composer Lou Silvers. Freed had his first hit with "I Cried for You" (music by Gus Arnheim and Abe Lyman). Silvers, reestablished in Los Angeles and cranking out movie music like a one-man factory, persuaded Freed to come to the coast. After moving west, Freed ran the Orange Grove Theater in Hollywood—an early sign of his production-administrative capabilities. Signed by MGM in 1929, Freed was one of several writers paired with Nacio Herb Brown to write for Metro's first big talkie musical, *The Broadway Melody*. The picture was a smash, and out of it came, among other songs, "You Were Meant for Me." Working on *Broadway Melody*, Brown was just moonlighting—Irving Thalberg had persuaded him to take a leave of absence from his realty company.

It was a good thing, because Herb Brown became MGM's most dependable tunesmith, Freed the single most important producer of musicals in motion pictures. After *Broadway Melody*, which spawned a series of revue-like backstage movie musicals, Brown and Freed worked on *Hollywood Revue*. It included the first filmed performance of their "Singin' in the Rain," sung by dozens of studio stars wearing rain slickers beneath a soundstage downpour, while Brown accompanied them onscreen. Arthur Lange used an orchestra of fewer than twenty-five men, because the recording equipment couldn't handle any more sound without distortion. The film recording's clean sound had been pretested in the Metro short subject *Manhattan Serenade*, filmed to exploit Louis Alter's gorgeous melody of the same name (since used many times in the movies).

Fred Fisher also contributed songs to *Hollywood Revue*. A January 1930 squib from the *Long Beach Press Telegram* gives a fair rendering of Metro's well-oiled publicity machinery as well as Fisher's remarkable self-confidence:

"We need a snappy martial air to fill in this spot," remarked Harry Rapf, producer of the revue.

"What time can I play it for you?" asked Fisher.

"But Fred, you haven't written it yet," replied Rapf.

"What time can I play it for you?" repeated Fisher.

Within three hours he had returned with his music, arranged for the piano, a complete song, words and all. Dave Snell played it and Fisher sang it for the MGM executive. . . .

A few hours later the song had been orchestrated, a colored chorus had rehearsed it with Arthur Lange's orchestra and a "sound

Roy Turk, Fred Ahlert, Jack Benny, and Fred Fisher from MGM's *The Songwriters' Revue* (1930)
Courtesy of Academy of Motion Picture Arts & Sciences

track" was made that night. That's the story of "Strike Up the Band," Fred Fisher's latest hit.

Would that it were the Gershwins' "Strike Up the Band!"

The taciturn Herb Brown, dismayed by the decreasing quality of the studio's musicals, fled to New York. No longer thought of as a tailor or realtor with a piano-playing hobby, Brown joined Buddy DeSylva, also recently decamped from Hollywood, and Vincent Youmans to contribute to the show *Take a Chance*. Meanwhile, Freed planted his feet in Metro's Culver City cement—he didn't go anywhere else for another thirty-five years. Arthur Lange moved over to the newly merged RKO-Pathé but got caught in a power squeeze between David O. Selznick and William LeBaron. Soon Lange was out looking for a job again.

"By the end of 1929, you could shoot a cannon down any one of the studio streets and never hit a songwriter," said Hugo Friedhofer. Friedhofer was then arranging at Fox, having been invited down from his native San Francisco by George Lipschultz, who had taken over the studio's music department from Arthur Kay. In early 1930, the Fox music department included pianist-contractor Frank Tresselt and pianist-songwriter William Kernell—both men would remain after the merger with Twentieth Century five years later—and songwriter Jimmy Hanley. Born in Indiana in 1892, Hanley was a brash, likable guy who had composed, among many early hits, "Back Home in Indiana" (1917), "Rose of Washington Square" (1920), and "Second Hand Rose" (1921). Hanley tried to get Arthur Lange, who had conducted Hanley's show *Sidewalks of New York* on Broadway, hired at Fox.

But there was no money. Musicals had glutted the market, and the post-Crash atmosphere wasn't making it any easier. Every studio cut back its production slate. Lange found himself, two years after his arrival and at the age of forty-three, unemployable. "Once a person's relation with the industry is severed," Carey McWilliams wrote, "he is automatically excluded from the Hollywood community, with rare exceptions, regardless of his income or the size of his fortune." It was always thus, and remains true to this day.

McWilliams pointed out another shift that had occurred in Los Angeles in the years leading up to 1930. With the advent of sound, the movies had become an "indoor industry," requiring a greater degree of production control and sound-proofing, and creating a more marked division between the employed, who were inside, and the unemployed, who were outside.

Within months, Lange's life turned as arid as the southern California climate. His wife, Charlotte, charging desertion, obtained a divorce and custody of their two teenage sons. Lange, stumping for work, may have hired a publicist, because in the next few months several newspaper articles appeared that had the tinny ring of self-promotion. These were usually orchestrated to make it sound as if Lange were concerned with the greater musical good. Lange was quoted in the *Hollywood Daily Screen World,* July 8, 1931, as lamenting:

> In my opinion music has never "gone," has never been presented in a way to show what harmony can mean to a picture.
>
> Splendid musical pictures have been lavishly done, with gifted musicians in charge and players who were artists; but an atmosphere of pomp and ceremony, an over-effort has not been avoided, a sort of, "well, we must be impressive" manner of presentation that does impress instead of enthusing the average audience, and just misses charming them.

As a well-known bandleader and champion of jazz, Lange could get away with chiding his colleagues; but he was relatively safe anyway because by July 1931 musical production had dwindled to practically nothing.

A few months later a Reno, Nevada, newspaper covered another favorite issue of Lange's, one that had been vexing filmmakers for the past three years:

> The best brains in town are working overtime, trying to figure out the answer to the music problem. There is some use for music in pictures, undoubtedly a good use, but it remains to be discovered. Arthur Lange, who arranges the music you've heard in pictures starring Constance Bennett, Ann Harding and others in the RKO-Pathé fold,

has a unique idea. His theory calls for a strict line of demarcation between mood and action music. [Lange would] divorce the mood music from the screen, having it emanate from another part of the theater, through a different loud speaker. In that way, it would enjoy the same relationship with the talking picture that mood music, provided by orchestra or organ, provided for the silents. On the other hand, action music would continue to emanate from the screen.

Looking back on it nearly seventy years later, Lange's theory now seems terribly primitive. But the perception of unreality created by music coming off the screen along with the dialogue was tying producers in knots. They ducked the issue by keeping most non-musicals scoreless.

Fortunately, Lange didn't have to make a career of distributing philosophical press releases. In early 1932, William Fox fired Winfield Sheehan, enabling new music chief Ben Jackson to hire Lange. Back on his feet, Lange married Marjorie Joesting, a former Miss Washington. Within weeks, Sheehan was reinstated with much fanfare, while the studio police escorted William Fox's allies, including Ben Jackson, off the lot. By now non-musical films—that is, films in which song and dance didn't figure prominently—were beginning to appear with "mood music" or so-called underscores. Sheehan convinced music publisher Sam Fox to augment the department with men who could handle underscoring. Lange and Friedhofer were kept on, and Sam Fox (no relation to William Fox) hired Louis De Francesco as general music director, Dr. Edward Kilenyi as assistant director, and James O'Keefe as the new department head. This was a curious melange for a movie music department: De Francesco (born in Italy in 1888) had composed some music for early travelogues; "Doc" Kilenyi (born in Hungary in 1884) was renowned as George Gershwin's single most important teacher; and O'Keefe had worked as a recording manager for NBC radio and published several songs written with his brother Lester. None of them knew much about picture-making.

The result was that the old hands were called on repeatedly. Carli Elinor, who had compiled the first *Birth of a Nation* score for D. W. Griffith, was brought onto the Fox staff from the Carthay Circle Theater, where he'd been music director since 1925. Ray Heindorf, the lightning-fast arranger who had worked for Arthur Lange in

Manhattan, also came aboard. When Sheehan's film adaptation of Noel Coward's *Cavalcade* went into production in 1932, a recorded underscore was tested and found to have an enhancing effect. Louis De Francesco received the music credit, but it was Lange, working with Friedhofer and Heindorf, who actually scored the movie. False and static as it now seems, *Cavalcade* won the Academy's best picture for 1932. Critics invariably mentioned the music in their notices.

Then, that same year, the Depression intensified the need for entertainment, the more escapist the better. Some two years after movie musicals were pronounced DOA, they were coming back into vogue.

Metro-Goldwyn-Mayer needed Nacio Herb Brown back on the lot. Brown had discovered Broadway and Tin Pan Alley relatively late, and he was inclined to stay in New York. When Irving Thalberg failed to lure Brown back, he hauled out the heavy artillery—Freed—who persuaded Brown to return to Culver City. In 1933 they collaborated on songs for *Going Hollywood,* a pet project of William Randolph Hearst for his mistress, Marion Davies. In this West Coast variation on the backstage musical, Davies follows boyfriend Bing Crosby to the movie colony, determined to keep him from Fifi D'Orsay's clutches. Even under the guidance of director Raoul Walsh, the picture wasn't much. There was the title tune, and there was "Temptation," which Crosby, all got up as an unkempt wino, sang to a glass of tequila.

Nearing fifty, Brown retired to Mexico. But a few years of idle ranching went a long way, and he moved back to Hollywood in 1948. By that time Freed was the most respected producer on the Metro lot and the undisputed king of movie musicals.

Although it was the original talkie studio, Warners took a little longer than MGM, Fox, or Paramount did to construct a fully operating music department. Most of the studio's early musicals took their material and stars from Broadway and Tin Pan Alley.

On his broad shoulders, Al Jolson carried a series of *Jazz Singer* sequels. In *The Singing Fool* he sings "Sonny Boy" (DeSylva-Brown-Henderson) and "There's a Rainbow Round My Shoulder" (Billy Rose, Dave Dreyer); in *Mammy* he sings Irving Berlin's "Let Me Sing and I'm Happy." There were storylines, but they weren't the point. Story didn't

MGM songwriters, 1934: (*left to right*) Robert Katscher, Gus Kahn, Bronislau Kaper, publisher Jack Robbins, Arthur Johnston, Nacio Herb Brown (at piano), Harold Adamson, Burton Lane, Ned Washington, Arthur Freed, and Walter Jurmann
Photo by Tom Evans. Courtesy UCLA Popular Library

matter either in pictures starring Fanny Brice, Texas Guinan, or Sophie Tucker. Of these three, Tucker fared best if only because *Honky Tonk* (1929) positioned her as a chanteuse who, like a Fannie Hurst heroine, sacrifices herself for her daughter (Lila Lee); that Tucker sang "Red Hot Mama" and "Some of These Days" was just a bonus.

Warners proudly released *The Desert Song* (1929), adapted from the Romberg-Harbach-Hammerstein-Mandel blockbuster and attractive to cinema audiences as much for its color experiments as for its music. *The Desert Song* was a throwback to the Viennese operetta form that had begun to vanish a decade earlier. Mining the same lode, Warners released *Song of the Flame* (1930), more Herbert Stothart than George Gershwin, both of whom are credited, along with Harbach and Hammerstein. *Viennese Nights* (1930; scored by Romberg and Hammerstein again) at least offered the remarkably gifted Vivienne

Segal. *On with the Show* was stiff as a board, though it did have a surprisingly slender Ethel Waters singing Harry Akst and Grant Clarke's "Am I Blue?" Jerome Kern's *Sally* was released in 1929, but even Marilyn Miller singing "Look for the Silver Lining" couldn't disguise the fact that this was pretty much a filmed stage play.

All of these movies suffered from (for want of a better phrase) a lack of cinema. They had picture and voice and orchestra, but no movement. What Warners needed was a movie musical that showed things you couldn't see onstage. They got it, or began to get it, with the backstage musical entry *Gold Diggers of Broadway* (1929). The songs, including the weirdly Edwardian "Tiptoe Through the Tulips," were supplied by Al Dubin and Joe Burke. Dubin and Burke made a Mutt and Jeff pair. Dubin stood about five-eight and by 1929 weighed close to three hundred pounds; Burke was a foot taller and slender. Both men were Pennsylvanians, though Dubin was born in Switzerland in 1891.

Dubin was among the more interesting characters to come out of Tin Pan Alley—for his self-destructiveness as well as his talent. Alexander Dubin was the son of Minna and Simon Dubin, Eastern European Jews who had met in Berne where Simon was studying medicine. The family moved to Philadelphia in 1896, and Simon Dubin set up a gynecology practice. Yiddish, Russian, English, and German were spoken at the Dubins' house, where local anti-czarist Russian refugees congregated to argue politics. As a student at Perkiomen Seminary, forty miles north of Philadelphia, "Alick" Dubin played football and wrote verse, fiction, and song lyrics; Witmark published a couple of the lyrics. Lean and muscular, the teenage Dubin looked like he might have matriculated in Hell's Kitchen, with a face more Irish than Semitic. Already developing the appetites of Gargantua, he was expelled from Perkiomen for drunkenness. At twenty, Dubin was working as a singing waiter when he met Joe Burke; he moved in with the Burke family, establishing a pattern of emotional dependence on others that would last the rest of his life.

By all accounts, Dubin had the gripping persuasiveness of the addict determined to get his fix. He talked song publishers Jack and Irving Mills into letting him put lyrics to classic tunes like "Song of

India." In 1917 he began writing with James "Ragtime Jimmy" Monaco, whose music would become more popular during the next two decades. Then came army induction and artillery training at Camp Upton in Yaphank, Long Island, the instant military town immortalized by Irving Berlin, with a Wild West quality though it was less than two hours from Manhattan.

In 1921 Dubin married Helen McCloy and, at her behest, converted to Roman Catholicism. He supported his growing family—there were two daughters in quick succession—by writing with Burke, and with Jimmy McHugh and Sammy Fain. Prohibition, meanwhile, only seemed to wet his lips. Due to his drinking, Dubin was frequently in the doghouse. Temporarily, unhappily separated from Helen in 1925, he met Harry Warren at the Oyster Bar in Grand Central Station; Warren brought Dubin home to Forest Hills for a home-cooked meal. The Warrens quickly discovered that Dubin could eat as voluminously as he scribbled lyrics.

Harry Warren's path to Hollywood had been less rocky than Dubin's. The youngest of ten children, Warren was born Salvatore Guaragna in 1893. He learned to play the organ at his Brooklyn parish, which led to work playing piano at the Vitagraph film studio in nearby Flatbush. He played with increasing confidence while serving in the navy during World War I, stationed at Montauk Point. Upon his discharge, he married Josephine Veronica Wensler. (They would remain married for sixty-five years, until Warren's death.) A late bloomer by songwriter standards, Warren didn't publish his first song until 1922. He found work composing for several Tin Pan Alley publishing firms and with various lyricists; Gus Kahn was probably his favorite. Shortly after Warners bought the publishers Remick, Harms, and Witmark to build a music catalog, the West Coast office sent for Warren.

Warren arrived in California in early 1929 with lyricists Joe Young and Sam Lewis, who had enjoyed hits with Jolson's renditions of "Mammy" and "Rockabye Your Baby (With a Dixie Melody)." Lewis was portly and snapped his fingers as he spoke, as though he were marking off rhythm. With Young and Lewis, Warren was assigned to write extra songs for the film version of Rodgers & Hart's *Spring Is Here*. That's the way things were done out in sunny Los Angeles: once a movie studio had bought it, even a Rodgers and Hart show was no longer a Rodgers and Hart show.

"I couldn't stand it here then," Warren said in the early '70s. "I missed Lindy's. This place was nothing." Warren also chafed under the harsh demands and cavalier attitudes of the producers. One day, observing the filming of a musical number on a sound stage, Warren cried out, "They're singing the wrong lyrics!" Hal Wallis, then second-in-command to Jack Warner, said, "What difference does it make? Nobody knows what the right lyric is." When Warren protested, Wallis brushed him aside.

Warren returned to New York in late 1929 and resumed his Tin Pan Alley work. From this brief period came "I Found a Million Dollar Baby in the Five and Ten Cent Store," composed for Fanny Brice. But film musicals were becoming hot again just as the Depression had begun to bottom out. Grudgingly, Warren returned to Warners. Al Dubin, now nearly as wide as he was tall, had since brought his family west and had been writing with several composers, including Tin Pan Alley exiles Jimmy Monaco and M. K. Jerome. With Burke he had come up with "I'm Dancing with Tears in My Eyes (Cause the Boy in My Arms Isn't You)." Warners couldn't find a place for that one, but, published on its own, it became one of the biggest hits of 1930. In 1932 Joe Burke was let go—his last hit would be "Rambling Rose" some fifteen years later—leaving Dubin without a partner. That's when Harry Warren stepped in.

Darryl Zanuck, Warners' high-powered production chief before he took over the reins at Twentieth Century-Fox, had a set of galleys of a novel called *42nd Street,* by Bradford Ropes. Warren and Dubin worked off the galleys before a screenplay was drafted—director Busby Berkeley and star Ruby Keeler were signed without a script— and came up with the songs that helped to rescue the movie musical from its slumber.

Shortly before the production, Leo Forbstein took over as Warners' head of music. "Give me thirty-two bars of schmalz," Forbstein liked to tell his songwriters. Warren, who was enamored of Puccini but liked to begin his composing sessions by warming up with a little bit of

Leoncavallo's *Pagliacci*, gave him so much more. Forbstein's secretary told Al Dubin that her boyfriend was "getting to be a habit with me." Dubin, with Warren's lead sheet (where the melody is laid out) spread before him like a racing form, scribbled lyrics during his repasts; Warren remembered Dubin appearing with the lyric to "Shuffle off to Buffalo" scrawled on the back of a menu from San Francisco, where Dubin often went because the restaurants were better there.

The *42nd Street* songs, as well as those that followed by Dubin and Warren, were at once dramatic and idiomatic, show-bizzy and full of vim. Previously, the songs in even the frothiest movie musicals weren't especially danceable, and had little or no connection to the theatrical world's glitter and tawdriness, even when the stories revolved around show business. But these new musicals—*Gold Diggers of 1933, Footlight Parade, Wonder Bar, Dames,* and *Gold Diggers of 1935*—were different: "bawdy" and "naughty," as Dubin's lyric suggests. Ray Heindorf, brought over from Fox, made genuinely sexy arrangements of the songs. Young dance pianist Malcolm Beelby rehearsed the chorus girls as they pounded the dust right up from the floorboards.

A former Pittsburgh master of ceremonies named Dick Powell (born Richard Ewing Powell in 1904), owner of a pleasant, high nasal tenor, would catapult from ninth billing in *42nd Street* to first in *Gold Diggers of 1933*. Ruby Keeler projected a sweet naivete that was given roaring counterpoint by the public's knowledge of her offscreen marriage to Al Jolson. And Joan Blondell, fast becoming Jack Warner's favorite supporting dame, entered every scene chest and mouth first; her sauciness was as fresh and American as Dubin and Warren's songs. Dubin and Warren appear in *42nd Street* as fedora'd songwriters who argue when director Warner Baxer cuts their old-fashioned number, "It Must Be You," from his show.

Other songwriters on the Warners lot contributed tremendously to the resurgence of the musical. Lyricist Mort Dixon (born 1892), a former streetcar conductor and bank clerk who had made a fortune from his lyrics for "Bye Bye Blackbird" and "I'm Looking Over a Four-Leaf Clover," teamed at Warners with Allie Wrubel (born 1905), the former Paul Whiteman saxophonist from Connecticut. If Dubin and Warren helped make Dick Powell a star, Dixon and Wrubel kept him a star in *Happiness Ahead* (1934) and *Flirtation Walk* (1934). Richard

Whiting came over from Paramount and for a while wrote songs with petite scenarist Frances Marion. Soon a kid named Johnny Mercer, from Savannah, Georgia, by way of New York, arrived and became Whiting's regular partner. Veterans George Meyer and Edgar Leslie, writers of "For Me and My Gal," were frequently under contract.

But it was the Dubin-Warren team that set the pace. Warren's tunes danced by themselves, and Dubin married them to words and phrases that throbbed with urban energy. By the time of *Dames*'s pre-production, Warren and his wife, Jo, had settled into life in Los Angeles. Already grumbling about his lack of recognition, especially compared to the Broadway composers who controlled their own work, Warren crusaded with an almost missionary zeal for credit for his fellow musicians. (As arranger, Ray Heindorf received his first screen credit because Warren screamed at Leo Forbstein and Jack Warner.) Neither Warren nor Jo cared for Dubin's wife, Helen, whom they referred to as "The Irish Cop," the woman who insisted on Dubin's abstinence as she had insisted that he convert to Catholicism. In defense, Dubin's weight ballooned even more.

While working on the *Dames* songs, Dubin and Warren's office was being renovated. Unable to stand the racket any longer, Warren cursed the workmen and departed for the Warners commissary. One of the workmen complained to Dubin, "Who does that little kike think he is?" Delighted by this double ethnic misreading, Dubin waddled to the commissary and reported the remark to Warren, adding, "You should be glad, Harry, that I accept Jews!"

One of the other teams that worked on *Dames*, Sammy Fain (né Feinberg) and Irving Kahal, had several hits in the '20s before being called to Hollywood. Their first successful movie song was "You Brought a New Kind of Love to Me," first heard in *The Big Pond* (1930) when Maurice Chevalier sang it to Claudette Colbert. The song was reprised the following year in the Marx Brothers' *Monkey Business* (in which all four brothers take a crack at a Chevalier impersonation, mimicking its first line, "If a nightingale could sing like you"), along with a new Fain-Kahal song, "When I Take My Sugar to Tea."

Fain, a New Yorker, came up through well-traveled Tin Pan Alley ranks. Self-taught, he went to work as songplugger for publisher Jack Mills, and worked in vaudeville and radio. In 1927 he met Kahal, a Pennsylvanian who had come to New York with an art scholarship to Cooper Union. Kahal was singing with Gus Edwards' Minstrels when he and Fain began to collaborate. Their first songs had a conventional cast. "A New Kind of Love" was also conventional, but its up-the-down-staircase construction is so winning that it was immediately absorbed into the standard repertoire. Fain went on to become one of the most prolific Hollywood composers, especially in the '50s when his lush title tunes (e.g., "Love Is a Many-Splendored Thing") seemed to be everywhere; he died in 1989 at eighty-seven. Kahal was dead at thirty-nine, having written most of his lyrics for Warners and Paramount.

But there was a third author of "A New Kind of Love" and "When I Take My Sugar to Tea," a priest named Joseph P. Connor. Connor wrote music under the name Pierre Norman. Born in Pennsylvania in 1895, Connor first went west to attend college in Wyoming. His musical and theological studies ran along a parallel track, and his composing career is one of the oddest cases of moonlighting to come out of Hollywood. After *The Big Pond* Connor stayed at Paramount to compose for the fast-paced comedy *Laughter* (from an interesting Donald Ogden Stewart script that anticipates the '30s screwball comedies to come), then became a composer for hire at other studios. (He followed Fain and Kahal to Warners to help orchestrate *Footlight Parade*.) Connor never lost his professional connection to the East Coast, however, and when scoring work dried up he became a chaplain for the New Jersey State Police. He died in Teaneck in 1952, a priest whose estate had been swollen by royalties from "You Brought a New Kind of Love to Me," written with two Jews.

That Jewish songwriters were all over the motion picture industry is obvious. With a few notable exceptions, like Reverend Connor, Harry Warren, Richard Whiting, and Johnny Mercer, most of those who went west to write songs for the earliest talkies were Jewish. They were a dif-

ferent breed from the composers who scored silent movies for live performances.

The Silent Era musicians tended to be classically trained, often
receiving excellent music education in Europe, particularly in Germany
and Austria. As often as not, their keyboard technique came out of the
church and was transposed for the cinema. Their work was seen as gen-
teel, even if it was meant to accompany an entertainment as vulgar as a
movie.

By contrast, the Jewish songwriters came out of Tin Pan Alley,
where the two streams of show business and music came together. It
was only in show business that a Jew's religion—his "race," his identity,
his Jewishness—was of no concern. Amusement-seekers, as Parker
Tyler pointed out, worshipped only at the "universal church"; beneath
its roof, all that mattered was the testifier's ability to deliver entertainment. The testifier could be black, like Bert Williams, or Jewish, like
George Jessel (the original Jazz Singer on stage), as long as the people
stayed in their seats. Entrance to an elite college could be denied him;
most medical schools had black *and* Jewish quotas, and practice at certain law firms was out of the question—but not in the theater, particularly the musical theater, where the hook was (and still is) utterly demo-
cratic. Can you make the music? Can you make 'em laugh? That's all the
studio bosses wanted to know.

Part of the great wave of late nineteenth-century immigration that
deposited Europeans on the shores of New York Harbor, Jews brought
cultural traditions that added vitality to the great melting pot. In
Terrible Honesty, her book about New York in the 1920s, Ann Douglas
suggests that "Jewish music, with its Eastern and Mediterranean
sources, its complex rhythms and preference for minor keys, had something in common with the African-American sound." This connection
between the two musics may be forced, but Douglas's subsequent point
about language is not: that Jewish immigrants, living in the streets and
steeped in the Yiddish vernacular, "helped pave the way for the use of
the American vernacular in Tin Pan Alley lyrics." The peculiar idiom of
the tenement, where two or more languages were routinely spoken and
the struggle was to move up and out, translated into songs that were
raw and immediate. Americans identified with them—just as they
identified with the movies.

○ ○ ○

Irving Berlin came from the streets. He barely remembered the Russia of his infancy, but he grew up scrappy and ambitious on New York's Lower East Side—"Jewtown," as it was called. By 1911, combining his unschooled but highly sensitive ears with his gift for the idiomatic phrase, he was famous. Hurt by the crash of '29, the former singing waiter went to Hollywood solely to make money. He already had had "Blue Skies" sung in *The Jazz Singer*, and had written two songs for King Vidor's *Hallelujah*. In Hollywood, Berlin wrote "Marie" for Vilma Banky to sing in *The Awakening*; a decade later it became Tommy Dorsey's theme song. He wrote "Coquette" for Mary Pickford to sing to her security blanket in her Academy Award–winning performance in the picture of the same name. The title song for Joe Schenck's adaptation of Berlin's *Puttin' on the Ritz* became the lifelong theme of its star, Harry Richman, and subsequently provided Clark Gable with his most delightfully uncharacteristic moment, as a song-and-dance manager in *Dancing Lady*. With money in his pocket again, Berlin and his wife, Ellin Mackay, returned to New York. The next time he went west, he would make movie history with Fred Astaire.

Sam Coslow, though raised in Brooklyn rather than on the Lower East Side, had come out of the same tradition as Irving Berlin. Also like Berlin, he was a double threat—a tunesmith as well as a lyricist. At Paramount he remained on staff through several collaborators. One of them was Irving Berlin's former arranger Arthur Johnston.

Like so many musicians who came of age in the first two decades of the century, Johnston had played organ in his New York church and piano in various cinemas. For Berlin, Johnston served as amanuensis and arranger, turning the songwriter's one-fingered melodies into lush orchestrations. (Years later pianist Helmy Kresa would serve Berlin in the same capacity.) Emboldened by his former boss's journey west, Johnston went to Los Angeles at the end of 1929. In 1931 he helped Chaplin score the speechless *City Lights*, then went on staff at Paramount.

Paired with Coslow, the hard-drinking Johnston had been carrying the title "Just One More Chance" in his gin-soaked brain for a while. Coslow quickly set a lyric to it. Bing Crosby was the rising star on the lot, so Coslow and Johnston tried to persuade him to record it. No dice. The pot was sweetened when Mack Sennett, looking for a way into sound pictures, offered Crosby $750 to sing it in a short film. This time Crosby agreed. He subsequently sang "Just One More Chance" in *College Humor*, the movie that made him a star.

Coslow and Johnston continued to work together, off and on. Out of their collaboration came the great "Cocktails for Two," first sung by Carl Brisson in *Murder at the Vanities* (1934), months after the repeal of the Eighteenth Amendment. In *Murder at the Vanities* Coslow and Johnston chronicled another durable vice, "Marijuana." (Bette Midler repopularized the song in 1976.) Coslow and Johnston wrote "My Old Flame" for Mae West in *Belle of the Nineties*. Johnston would go on to compose "Pennies from Heaven" for the 1936 Crosby movie of the same name, with lyrics by the young Johnny Burke. By the late '30s, Burke would be Paramount's top lyricist.

                                    ๐   ๐   ๐

At Paramount before Johnny Burke, however, there was a tiny force of nature named Lorenz Hart. He had dropped out of Columbia's journalism school, was seven years older than his partner, Richard Rodgers, and from a more rough-and-tumble family. Rodgers and Hart were both Jewish and from upper Manhattan, but otherwise as different as collaborators could be. When they were first invited to Hollywood in 1930, they had been songwriting partners for eleven years, six of them with astonishing success.

Harry Warren's first Hollywood job was writing songs for the film *Spring Is Here*, adapted from Rodgers and Hart's 1929 Broadway musical. Interpolating other writers' songs into a film version of a musical comedy became standard practice in Hollywood; Rodgers never got used to it. *Present Arms*, Rodgers and Hart's 1928 show originally choreographed by the young Busby Berkeley, was filmed by RKO in 1930 as *Leathernecking*. Although the Broadway show contained their usual quota of wonderful songs, including "You Took Advantage of Me," *Leathernecking* was filmed without any of them. Curiously, the songless movie was scored by twenty-four-year-old

Oscar Levant and featured the first film appearance of Irene Dunne, then thirty-one.

Rodgers and Hart were first hired to compose for film by Jack Warner's First National Pictures (the first distribution arm of Warner Bros.). They were asked to write four songs for *The Hot Heiress*, with a script by their usual Broadway librettist Herbert Fields. "He Looked So Good to Me," since widely recorded as "He Was Too Good to Me," was dropped from the film before its release; their three other songs aren't among the boys' best. Disappointed by their initial brush with a big-studio musical, they returned to New York and wrote a Hollywood spoof called *America's Sweetheart*, which featured "I've Got Five Dollars."

But *America's Sweetheart* wasn't as commercially successful as their earlier musicals. So Rodgers and Hart signed another Hollywood contract, this time with Paramount Pictures. Their first assignment was to write songs for the film version of DeSylva, Brown, and Henderson's show *Follow Through*. All four of their songs were discarded before the film's release. Next came an Ernest Lubitsch project called *Love Me Tonight*. Although Lubitsch's stamp remains all over the finished film, he was forced to assume direction of *One Hour with You* from George Cukor, and Rouben Mamoulian took over for Lubitsch on *Love Me Tonight*.

Mamoulian's feeling for music, it turned out, ran deep. In *Love Me Tonight*, Parisian tailor Maurice Chevalier growls "Isn't It Romantic?" while his reflections play across a three-way mirror; the song moves from there into a moving taxi, where a passenger jots down the notes of the cabbie's melody, then through the French countryside in march time, then onto a violinist's strings, and finally into the bedroom of— Jeanette MacDonald! Framed by her moonlit window, dreaming of marriage, MacDonald has no way of knowing that the tune that has floated her way was begun by the very man she'll marry.

"Isn't It Romantic?" has since been heard in more movies than any other Rodgers and Hart song. "Mimi," stylistically similar to but better than the era's slew of songs named for women, became Chevalier's personal property once he wrapped his Parisian inflections around it. And the exquisite MacDonald sings the waltz "Lover" astride her horse, rhyming "glow" with "whoa!" as she tugs the reins. *Love Me Tonight*

Richard Rodgers and Lorenz Hart, 1930s
Courtesy Institute of the American Musical

combined gorgeous songs with an extraordinarily refined sense of cinema. Filmmakers as well as songwriters took note.

Like so many other New Yorkers, Rodgers and Hart didn't
respond well to the film capital; Rodgers in particular loathed
Hollywood. A dapper man with strict, almost Teutonic work habits—
Hart called him "The Principal"—Rodgers and his wife, Dorothy, rented a house at 724 North Linden Drive in Beverly Hills. Hart moved in
with them. Previously, Hart had joined them on their honeymoon in
the south of France. He was like an undomesticated pet, coming and
going at all hours, with or without a chorus boy in tow. Hart's homo-
sexuality was a discreet, downplayed thing; it was said (perhaps wish-
fully) by his relatives that he went out with men by default, feeling that
no woman could possibly desire what he saw in the mirror—a balding,
barrel-chested, five-foot homunculus with a perpetual five o'clock shadow and elevators in his bedroom slippers. At night Hart could be found
at the Club New Yorker in the old Christie Hotel on Hollywood
Boulevard, or at parties in Malibu, which already housed an exclusive

colony of movie people. By day, if he could be found at all, Hart occupied his Paramount "cell." He shared the space with Rodgers, of course,
but as usual couldn't be pinned down to work—not even at Paramount's
exorbitant salary. Sam Coslow remembered Hart

> dropping into my cubicle for an afternoon chat, mostly about the
> "good old days" back on Broadway, which he sorely missed. . . .
> Sometimes, when I was working against time, he would offer to help
> on my lines—for free. He would say, "What are you trying to come
> up with there? Can I hear it?" I would read my pencil-scribbled lyrics
> to him, and on more than one occasion he would pace up and down,
> digging for a good punchline for me, just as if he were collaborating
> on the song.

One month after *Love Me Tonight,* Paramount released the duo's
next project, the George M. Cohan vehicle *The Phantom President.*
Then Joe Schenk hired them to write for his United Artists production
Hallelujah, I'm a Bum (1933), a fascinating Jolson movie seen by too few
people. In S. N. Behrman's screenplay, adapted from an idea by Ben
Hecht and padded with recitative by Hart, Jolson is a Central Park bum
who helps a lovely amnesiac. The gem from the movie is "You Are Too
Beautiful": Jolson sings "And I am too drunk with beauty" instead of the
now standard "And I am a fool for beauty." The musical direction was
by Alfred Newman; Rodgers and Hart each have cameos.

But they didn't kid themselves. They still disliked Hollywood,
though Hart's partying tended to lighten his bleaker moods. In fact his
nocturnal wanderings didn't jibe with the Rodgers' more sedate, regu-
lated household, so Hart rented a house at 910 North Bedford, also in
Beverly Hills and now considered a landmark.

After *Hallelujah, I'm a Bum,* Rodgers and Hart were hired by
MGM, where they worked on several aborted projects. A collaboration
with Moss Hart on a movie musical for Jeanette MacDonald, to be
titled *I Married an Angel,* was scrapped by order of Louis B. Mayer who
was said to fear reaction from the Catholic Church; Rodgers and Hart
later turned the project into a Broadway musical, which was filmed in
1942—starring Jeanette MacDonald. Their songs for *Meet the Baron,*
an early Three Stooges romp, with Jimmy Durante, were thrown out.

Their work on *Dancing Lady* was hardly more rewarding. Nelson Eddy sang "That's the Rhythm of the Day," notable primarily for the verse phrase "On your toes!" which was to become the title of one of the duo's most successful Broadway musicals. Along with half the Metro music department, Rodgers and Hart contributed several songs to *Hollywood Party*, a couple of them aided by Durante's piano noodling. One of that movie's unused songs was called "Prayer," written for Jean Harlow; the tune was finally heard in MGM's *Manhattan Melodrama*. Metro's music publisher Jack Robbins liked the tune but urged Hart to come up with a more popular lyric for it. Hart sarcastically suggested "Blue Moon," a counterclockwise turn of the old Tin Pan Alley June-moon-spoon cliché. That was precisely what Robbins wanted. The rest is pop music history.

Rodgers and Hart stayed at MGM for one more project. It would be their most important and, though a commercial failure, elevate the standard for movie musicals once more. This was Lubitsch's version of Franz Lehar's *The Merry Widow*. In this film version, the music was Lehar's, the lyrics largely Hart's—some of his originals, some translations of the operetta's by Victor Leon and Leo Stein. Lyricist Gus Kahn, in the twilight of his long Tin Pan Alley career and newly settled in Beverly Hills, pitched in. The result—MacDonald and Chevalier appearing more attractive and singing better than ever—was sublime, though the film even then was considered something of an anachronism. *The Merry Widow* was an opulent, robust operetta that was just too remote to a moviegoing public still scarred by the Depression.

Next, Rodgers and Hart returned to Paramount to compose the songs for the latest Bing Crosby vehicle, *Mississippi*. By now Crosby was the studio's biggest star. Looking back, the most poetic musical comedy team of all time seems a poor fit with the early talkies' most influential singer. Crosby, playing a riverboat captain and discreetly girdled because of his ballooning weight, insisted on including Stephen Foster's "Swanee River" in the film. Forced to acquiesce to the star's demands and again reminded of their relative subservience, Rodgers and Hart pined for Broadway. One afternoon they opened the *Herald-Examiner* and found in O. O. McIntyre's column the airy query, "What ever became of Rodgers and Hart?" Rodgers knew as well as Hart did that it was time to go home. They returned to New York, and from there mailed back what would become the movie's greatest song, "It's Easy to Remember (And So Hard to Forget)." By the end of 1935, when *Mississippi* was released, Rodgers and Hart were staging one of their greatest Broadway hits, *Jumbo,* and never looked back.

With some sprinkled exceptions, Rodgers and Hart's greatest songs were first presented on Broadway. Ironically, Rodgers's music has reached millions through the film versions of the musicals he created with Oscar Hammerstein II, while Hart's lyrics, fusing searing wit to cooling passion, remain almost too clever, too inside, for the general public. But the duo's experience in Hollywood was typical of movie songwriters of the early '30s. They came for the musical possibilities offered by the talkies, and for the money offered by the studios; and they left because nothing belonged to them except the money. They came closest to creating film art with *Love Me Tonight.* Their work on *Merry Widow*—primarily Hart's lyrics—was nothing to be ashamed of, either.

●   ●   ●

The year before *The Merry Widow* was released, RKO sent into theaters a movie about an ape. It derived its power partly from the excellent special effects involving the ape, known as King Kong, partly from Fay Wray's fetching quality as the object of the ape's adoration—and partly from the empathic, wall-to-wall musical score by Richard Strauss's godson, an Austrian émigré named Max Steiner.

THREE

OPEN YOUR GOLDEN GATE
THE ÉMIGRÉ COMPOSERS

Max Steiner's name is familiar to many moviegoers who don't know anything about film composers. His music was the exemplar of the high-flowing, sweeping, Viennese tradition. With *Gone with the Wind* at its center, Steiner's movie career arced from his music for *King Kong*—widely regarded as the first complete original soundtrack, composed five years after the advent of sound—to the theme to *A Summer Place,* a huge hit in 1959. By then his composing style was falling out of fashion on the screen; in the concert hall, it had been out of fashion for the entire century.

Unlike so many other composers schooled in the Viennese tradition, Maximilian Raoul Steiner was actually born in Vienna, on May 10, 1888. Steiner's grandfather had owned the Theatre an der Wien, one of Vienna's more important theaters, which was subsequently turned over to his father. Studying with several teachers, Mahler among them, at the Imperial Academy of Music, Steiner proved to be a prodigy, winning the Academy's Gold Medal and composing an opera, *Beautiful Greek Girl.* When Steiner's father declined to produce it, Steiner took the opera to his father's rival, Karl Tuschl, who had just assumed stewardship of the Orpheum Theater. Sensing a marketing coup, Tuschl agreed to stage the work. The production brought the seventeen-year-old Steiner offers to conduct around Austria and Germany, with a side tour of Moscow thrown in.

In England, during the first decade of the twentieth century, London impresario George Edwardes was promoting a more sophisticated musical theater, steering it away from the Edwardian music hall and toward a continental style that derived much from Vienna—from Suppé, Offenbach, and Johann Strauss. Edwardes lured Steiner to London to conduct. Steiner's first show for Edwardes was *The Merry Widow*. After seven years in the pit of various London theaters, Steiner went to Paris to conduct at the Alhambra. It was 1914, the Great War had begun, and Steiner was detained as an enemy alien. Fortunately the duke of Westminster was a fan from Steiner's London days; it was through his generous offices that Steiner was permitted to emigrate to New York. He arrived in New York in December 1914 with thirty-two dollars in his pocket.

In New York, Steiner quickly found work with Flo Ziegfeld, who figured that a young man who had conducted for George Edwardes knew something about musical comedy. Steiner presided over the best in musical theater—the newer strains of Gershwin and Kern, as well as the Victor Herbert operettas that were closer to his own education—as an orchestrator and conductor.

In February 1927, Steiner conducted *Rio Rita*, the musical comedy that inaugurated Ziegfeld's capacious new theater, the Ziegfeld, on Fifty-fourth Street and Sixth Avenue in Manhattan. A couple of years later its composer, Harry Tierney, went to Hollywood to oversee the RKO film version. Tierney persuaded RKO chief William LeBaron to hire Steiner, a double threat as orchestrator-conductor, making him mighty attractive to a film studio geared up to make musicals.

The musical madness didn't last long. By late 1929, Tierney was one of hundreds of songwriters who found themselves out of work. But Steiner remained at RKO to handle various musical chores.

Shortly after Steiner went to work at RKO, the studio summoned former drummer-turned-soundexpert Murray Spivack. Checking in at the studio, Spivack shared "office space"—a tin shed—with Tom Mix's horse, Tony, one of the successors to his original "Tony." RKO's music head was Victor Baravalle who, like Steiner, had conducted in New York for Ziegfeld. Spivack claimed that a "domestic scandal" caused

Baravalle's dismissal. In any case, Baravalle returned to New York where he enjoyed a long career as a Broadway conductor. (He returned to RKO in the late '30s to handle musical direction for the last two Astaire-Rogers movies.) Max Steiner was then arranging music for a Bert Wheeler–Robert Woolsey comedy *Half Shot at Sunrise* (1930). With the head-of-music chair vacant, Spivack put in a word for Steiner to Lou Sarecky, assistant to William LeBaron. A former lyricist, LeBaron considered himself savvy about music; he gave Steiner the job.

Already routinely putting in twelve-hour days, Steiner brought in other composers and arrangers to help out, and kept the peachier assignments for himself. He provided some minor underscoring on *Check and Double Check*, an Amos 'n' Andy feature that included an appearance by Duke Ellington and introduced Kalmar and Ruby's "Three Little Words"; wrote patchily used music for *Cimarron*, one of sound's first big westerns; and composed a sonata for Katharine Hepburn and John Barrymore to play in *A Bill of Divorcement*.

Symphony of Six Million, a typical Fannie Hurst cryfest (rags-to-riches physician Ricardo Cortez struggles to save the life of dad Gregory Ratoff), gave Steiner room to compose. He began by under-scoring Ratoff's death, with results so pleasing to the producers that he was given the go-ahead to score the entire picture. In addition to composing original music, Steiner rearranged and re-orchestrated some familiar Jewish melodies so that they sounded brand-new. "Music until then had not been used very much for underscoring," Steiner said. "The producers were afraid the audience would ask 'Where's the music coming from?' unless they saw an orchestra or a radio or a phonograph."

Those two producers subsequently would give Steiner the chance to make movie music history. Pandro S. Berman was the young associate producer who, after becoming RKO's head of production, would bring Steiner on as music director for the early Astaire-Rogers movies. David O. Selznick would demand Steiner's music and musical guidance for the eye-popping Technicolor movies he would soon produce, *Becky Sharp* (1935), *Garden of Allah* (1936), *A Star Is Born* (1937), *The Adventures of Tom Sawyer* (1938), culminating in *Gone with the Wind* (1939).

These Technicolor pictures, however, came after *King Kong* (1933), which is widely regarded as the first underscore that not only greatly enhanced its film but, to observers, saved it. Steiner got carte blanche from producer Merian C. Cooper, who was willing to pay for whatever orchestrations and musicians the composer needed. Does any non-musician remember the *King Kong* music? Probably not. But Steiner's score, at its most effective, accomplished what a scoreless movie probably could not: it humanized the giant ape, whose simian-simple emotions were clarified by each chord.

The other venerated original Steiner score from this period was for John Ford's *The Informer* (1935). Before a scene of the Dudley Nichols script had been photographed, Ford and Steiner talked about the music. The result was a carefully worked out score, with a distinctive motif for each principal character. "A blind man could have sat in a theater and known when [the character] Gypo was on the screen," Steiner said. To many ears, the score is particularly annoying today, and I think it's because Gypo (played by Victor McLaglen) is barely more literate than King Kong; each chunky bar of music is meant to cue us to his inarticulate thoughts. What was essential to an audience watching an ape—to feel what he's feeling—becomes too much for an audience watching a hard-drinking Irish stoolie.

David O. Selznick may have felt the same way about *The Informer*—though he was based at RKO at the time, he had nothing to do with the production—or he may have already felt that Steiner's music was often too mimetic. In the scoring of his pictures, Selznick wanted more counterpoint—something other than what he termed "'Mickey Mouse' scoring: an interpretation of each line of dialogue and each movement musically, so that the score tells with music exactly what is being done by the actors on the screen." Claiming to be the first producer to have his films dramatically scored, Selznick conceded that much of that music had been "second-rate," including Steiner's, and he often argued for fuller use of the classical repertoire, which movie audiences responded to immediately. Selznick was larger than life and driven to perfection; if he couldn't always get perfection from the smaller, more retiring Steiner, he did his best to keep him operating at high speed. Addicted to Benzedrine, Selznick tossed some Steiner's way.

By 1935, Steiner was showing some unmistakable signs of paranoia. He was positive that everyone on the RKO lot hated his music, which he began to crank out with factory-like timing. In those days he usually nursed a glass of Scotch. "It is a hell of a feeling," Steiner wrote his music publisher, "for a composer of my standing and reputation and success to know automatically while I am writing that all of the music I am putting on paper is dead." This became an *idée fixe* for Steiner—that, given the apparently ephemeral, unrecognized nature of film music, his work would achieve little or no recognition. To counteract this, he arranged for Victor to make wax pressings of his own favorite movie themes. (Surely these are among the first unofficial soundtrack recordings.)

Steiner fancied himself a prankster. Murray Spivack was unable to intercept a letter that Steiner wrote to RKO's president Ben Kahane, stating that he was changing his office hours because he had accepted a day job as a "bed tester" at the May Company. This was only the latest in a series of incidents that irked Kahane. An agent named John Zanft tried to mediate between Steiner and Kahane, but the damage was done. Expressing neither embarrassment nor humility, Steiner was let go. Kahane replaced him with former Victor music director Nathaniel Shilkret, a pleasant little man who is remembered today primarily for composing the Sinatra song, "That Lonesome Road." Immediately, Selznick scooped up Steiner for himself. Meanwhile, head of sound Murray Spivack was also hired away, by newly amalgamated Twentieth Century-Fox, and replaced by Al Columbo.

Working for Selznick, Steiner suffered increasing eye trouble (possibly glaucoma). To get his work done, he took more Benzedrine. Selznick, who operated on an even higher octane level, showed Steiner how to inject it. (By then hip music lovers were singing "Everytime it rains/It rains bennies from heaven.") But the two men continued to have their differences, particularly about composition schedules: Selznick preferred his closely supervised pictures to be scored as photography went along, with his composer writing music based on the script and the "rushes" (the processed scenes of each day's shooting, now more commonly called *dailies*); Steiner preferred to see an edited work print, and only then begin to compose. Each man was hard-headed and stiff-backed.

With the understanding that he would occasionally work again for Selznick, Steiner accepted an offer from Leo Forbstein to join the Warners music department. Forbstein was just about everyone's favorite music chief because he ran interference with Jack Warner and left his composers alone. He had heard about Steiner's driving pace and idiosyncracies from his younger brother, Lou Forbes, Selznick's music chief. The odd aspects of Steiner's personality didn't disturb Forbstein as long as the man could get the work done.

Nearing fifty, Steiner worked only harder. There were Errol Flynn movies—*The Charge of the Light Brigade* and *The Green Light* (both 1936). Back at RKO, Steiner had done his first score for a Bette Davis movie, *Way Back Home* (1931) and again for *Of Human Bondage* (1934), while Davis was still coming into her own. On *Of Human Bondage*, Steiner's musical "limp" for Leslie Howard's crippled character Philip was a typical touch, an example of Steiner's Mickey-Mousing a character, heard as ham-handed by many. But Davis's movies became Steiner's favorite musical vessel. The melodramatics of, say, *Jezebel* (1938) and *Dark Victory* (1939) really got Steiner's blood racing. "Either Mr. Steiner is going up those stairs, or *I* am," Davis was reported to have said just before filming a scene in *Dark Victory*. Yet Davis, like most of the Warners team, leaned heavily on Steiner's music to create drama.

Meanwhile, Steiner's workaholism played havoc with his domestic life. Abandoned by his second wife, Audrey, he soon married Louise Klos, a harpist in the Warners orchestra, for whom he composed some brilliant parts. Photographs from this period in Steiner's life show him uncomfortable in forced repose, as if the stillness required for the camera shutter were more than he could bear. Hal Wallis, then the second most powerful man on the Warners lot, described Steiner as "a tiny, fast-talking, hypersensitive gnome with great wit and a strong streak of schmaltz" who "received visitors at his home on Sundays in white pajamas, smoking a large cigar, with rich strains of his latest score as background music."

Obsessives are frequently unaware of the picture they present to the world, and it was this obsessiveness that David O. Selznick wanted for *Gone with the Wind*. "My first choice for the job is Max Steiner," Selznick memoed his production manager Henry Ginsberg, "and I am sure that Max would give anything in the world to do it. I should think the approach should be through Forbstein and Forbes, but use your own judgment on this."

As Selznick predicted, Steiner fairly leaped at the opportunity to score the film. Fast as Steiner was, however, he had difficulty keeping pace with the rigorous production schedule for *Gone with the Wind.* For one thing, he balked at incorporating what Selznick called "the great Southern pieces" into the score. (In fact, the completed score was augmented by tunes from, or evocative of, the Old South.) For another, the scoring time, consisting of nearly three hundred distinct musical segments, was clocking in at three hours—a herculean assignment even for a musician as prodigious as Steiner. With plenty of help from orchestrators Adolph Deutsch, Hugo Friedhofer, Maurice DePackh, Bernard Kaun, and Heinz Roemheld, Steiner turned in his piano sketches which, Friedhofer testified, "were so complete they required a road map to find your way around them." The music—the last important component of the filmmaking process—was late.

Sensing disaster, Selznick commissioned an "insurance score" from Franz Waxman, who was already working for him on *Rebecca.* Waxman composed with less fuss than Steiner. Still, Selznick could tell that neither composer would meet his deadline. In a mayday wire to his chief backer, Jock Whitney, Selznick stated his regret that they had not hired Metro music stalwart Herbert Stothart, who had scored *David Copperfield* and *A Tale of Two Cities* for him. The upshot was that Stothart was discreetly consulted about working over Steiner's music.

The situation exploded in November 1939, some eight months after Selznick first approached Steiner about *Gone with the Wind.* "In case you don't know it," Selznick wrote to Jock Whitney, "the musicians out here are even more jealous of each other, and there are even more cliques among them than is true about producers, directors, actors, etc." Tipsy after a day at the studio, Stothart boasted to colleagues about being hired to "fix" Steiner's work. MGM vice-president Sam Katz "raised holy hell" about Stothart's sudden removal from his Metro assignments. And Stothart's boasting was reported to Steiner who, enraged, attacked the *Gone with the Wind* score with renewed vigor. Selznick couldn't have been more pleased. Nor could moviegoers who regarded *Gone with the Wind* as the greatest picture they'd ever seen.

Of all the music in *Gone with the Wind,* including "Dixie," surely the most famous and durable is "Tara's Theme," which evokes swooning romance as well as the pre-Reconstruction South. (So powerfully melodramatic is "Tara's Theme" that it served as the theme to *Million*

Dollar Movie, the New York–based show that televised the same movie each night of the week during my childhood.) This was Steiner's music through and through, despite all the help he had, and it was as colorful as the movie's Technicolor photography. When Scarlett O'Hara stands against the backdrop of the sunset and says, "Land is the only thing that matters," the score is as breathtaking as the sky. "Steiner is painting a picture with music," conductor John Mauceri said. By the time Steiner had completed the score for *Gone with the Wind,* he had made himself into a modern master.

At Warners, Steiner's work was orchestrated primarily by Hugo Friedhofer. A shiny-eyed, florid-faced man who sported a Van Dyke beard and double-breasted blazers, the San Francisco native had been let go from Twentieth Century-Fox after a mass dismissal in 1935. Friedhofer first worked with Steiner on the underscore for Selznick's American version of *Intermezzo* (1939). "Max had a way of pushing whole blocks of chords around," Friedhofer said. Typecast as an orchestrator by Leo Forbstein, Friedhofer desperately wanted to compose for the movies; but the Steiner-Friedhofer collaborations worked smoothly for Warners, so Forbstein declined to assign Friedhofer to his own picture. Meanwhile, Friedhofer knew how to make Steiner's big, blocky sound breathe.

Which isn't to say that Steiner's sound wasn't already cinematic. As an example of what Steiner could do with music that accompanied pictures, Friedhofer cited a tense scene from *The Letter* (1940): Bette Davis goes to see would-be blackmailer Gale Sondergaard, and the scene is played around a fluttering beaded curtain; Steiner persuaded the sound-effects department to mute the sound of the beads, then wrote music for an eighteen-piece percussion section to simulate the sound instead. "And of course it was one of those things that enhanced Max's reputation," Friedhofer said. "It was very, very effective in the picture."

On *Casablanca,* Steiner wanted to compose his own song for Humphrey Bogart's romance with Ingrid Bergman. But Steiner was, as usual, working off completed film rather than the script, and Herman Hupfeld's "As Time Goes By" was already in place. The song worked fine, but producer Hal Wallis didn't want to say that to his testy com-poser. Instead Wallis humored Steiner until Ingrid Bergman chopped off her hair for *For Whom the Bell Tolls*, making retakes unfeasible. Forced to accept the Hupfeld standard (introduced in a 1931 Broadway revue called *Everybody's Welcome*), Steiner cracked the tune open, put it back together, and folded it inside a globe of revolving themes—Moroccan, French ("La Marseillaise"), German, and Norwegian—in his underscore. Wallis insisted that "Perfidia" also be used in the back-ground. The overwhelming fondness many people feel for *Casablanca* is due in part to Steiner's music, which keeps the picture glowing in one's memory. Steiner was again greatly aided by Friedhofer's orchestrations.

◦   ◦   ◦

Around the time that Steiner arrived at Warners, in 1936, Hugo Friedhofer had begun to assist another studio composer from Vienna, Erich Wolfgang Korngold. Much has been written about Steiner and Korngold occupying the twin towers of Warners music, with Steiner seeing all music as filmic and Korngold seeing all film as music—or, to be more precise, as opera.

Considering Korngold's background, there was good reason for this. Korngold was born in Brno, Czechoslovakia, in 1897. His father, Julius, was one of Vienna's most prominent music critics, writing pri-marily for *Die Newe Frei Presse*. At age three, Korngold *fils* was already composing for piano. The story goes that Erich suffered through a childhood bout with measles and recovered with a full-blown musical talent. Whatever the source of his gift, Korngold, like Steiner, was a prodigy whose relationship with a musically sophisticated father seemed to trigger early and intense creativity. Not yet thirteen, Korngold completed his Opus 1, a Piano Trio; shortly after, the Imperial Opera premiered his *Der Schneemann* (*The Snowman*). A year later came the fourteen-year-old's *Schauspiel* Overture. Reviewing the overture in the *Boston Herald*, Philip Hale wrote that it "deserves an honorable place in the Museum of Infant Prodigies. If Master Korngold can make such a noise at fourteen, what will he not do when he is twenty-eight? The thought is appalling."

When his *Sinfonietta* was played by the Vienna Philharmonic on

November 28, 1913, the complex score, with a spine of ascending fourths, the "motif of the cheerful heart," was greeted with both cheers and derision. At the very least the music of Korngold "the Wonder Child" was alive with spontaneity. Some said his was a gift from the gods. "The boy has so much talent," Puccini said, "he could easily give us some and still have enough left for himself." Some said that this talent was actually the kowtowing of impresarios courting Julius Korngold's favor. By Erich's early twenties, however, a master like Richard Strauss had declared him a genius.

Even geniuses are permitted some normality. Korngold began a family. He married the daughter of Austrian actor Adolf von Sonnenthal and soon had two sons. Now a young father, he was squat and chunky, clothing himself in double-breasted suits and bowties and keeping his hair brush-cut. He demonstrated quiet wit when in public but preferred the companionship of his piano. Korngold continued to feed the voracious Vienna appetite for new works, including operas composed at an alarmingly fast rate. But he labored under the burden of childhood stardom and the shadow of his middle namesake.

Mozart had the luxury (if one could call it that) of early death. In his mid-thirties, Korngold seemed to be outgrowing the *wunderkind* label. He may have felt the need for a creative transfusion, or at least a return to fundamentals. He contributed new orchestrations for the waltzes of the Johann Strausses, Sr. and Jr., in a show first presented as *Waltzes from Vienna* in 1930, which landed on Broadway as *The Great Waltz* in 1934. That same year he accepted Max Reinhardt's invitation to orchestrate Mendelssohn for his Warners film version of *A Midsummer Night's Dream*. Hitler's tentacles were already curling toward Vienna, and Korngold accepted the invitation as much to investigate geographic alternatives as to meet new musical challenges.

In Hollywood, Korngold fell in love with the production-line methods of a movie studio. The very quality that made so many creative artists disdainful made Korngold grateful: no year-long schedules to compose, design, rehearse, and stage an opera; do the work, and ten weeks later, boom, there it is in front of an audience! "Writing for the films is like writing an opera, only it goes a bit faster," he said. Korngold's reputation had preceded him—everyone in Hollywood felt his presence as a "great" composer—but it was his light, glittery under-score for *Midsummer Night's Dream* that showed the factory foremen that he could do the job.

Korngold moved on to Paramount to write music for *Give Us This Night*, whose male star, Jan Kiepura, had sung Korngold's works in Vienna. (Kiepura enjoyed an astonishingly durable film career, singing from the beginning of sound to the early '50s in films made in a dozen countries.) *Give Us This Night* was light opera, meant to showcase the vocal and pictorial charm of Kiepura's costar, Gladys Swarthout. On the surface this seemed to be Korngold's cup of tea, but the brew was flat-ter than he could have anticipated. With Oscar Hammerstein provid-ing lyrics to Korngold's music, the music for *Give Us This Night* was rewritten (by many other hands) so many times that it was soon unrec-ognizable.

Korngold returned to Warners for *Captain Blood*. It was his first picture involving the young, swashbuckling, Tasmanian star Errol Flynn. In keeping with the ritual division of labor in film production, Korngold needed an orchestrator so he could concentrate on compos-ing. His copyist and amanuensis Jaro Churain, who had made it his business to look out for his fellow Czech while in Hollywood, recom-mended thirty-four-year-old Hugo Friedhofer. It took Korngold all of three weeks to compose his score. Apart from *Captain Blood*'s main title music, which was orchestrated by Warners ace music man Ray Heindorf, Friedhofer orchestrated the score, and few film scores are more rousing: trumpets go off like roman candles, drums roll across the sea. Because Korngold was borrowing freely from Liszt, he requested that his credit read "Musical Arrangements by Erich Wolfgang Korngold." Jack Warner and Leo Forbstein had a good laugh about that one.

After *Captain Blood*, Korngold scored four more pictures for Warners. One of these was *Anthony Adverse*, the bloated Hervey Allen bestseller. Korngold's music, bottom-heavy and straining for a Mahleresque profundity, won him his first Academy Award. He returned to Vienna with a new triumph.

Meanwhile, Errol Flynn was becoming the biggest action-adventure star on the Warners lot—indeed, in all of Hollywood. Not since Douglas Fairbanks's heyday had the town seen anything like

Flynn's athleticism, with his added sense of sybaritic danger. As Flynn's screen successes grew, the Warners producers trolled for new material in which he could duel, ride, jump around, and, when appropriate, make love.

In 1937, Flynn's newest swashbuckler, *The Adventures of Robin Hood,* was in preproduction—it would be the costliest Warners picture to date—and Steiner was slated by Leo Forbstein to provide its score. Forbstein took his cue from Jack Warner, who was delighted with Steiner's speed and the important tone he got into his scores. (Steiner had recently composed the commanding Warners fanfare that heralded every studio release before the titles.) But producers Hal Wallis and Henry Blanke wanted the extra bit of lustre they felt they could get from Korngold. They wired him in Vienna, where he was trying to complete his opera *Die Kathrin,* and asked him to return to California. Fortuitously the opera's premiere had to be delayed for eight months, so Korngold figured he could accept one more film assignment at no cost to his European career.

After arriving in Los Angeles, Korngold was taken to the Burbank studio and shown a work print of *Robin Hood.* On February 11, 1938, Korngold wrote to Wallis, "*Robin Hood* is no picture for me. I have no relation to it and therefore cannot produce any music for it. I am a musician of the heart, of passions and psychology; I am not a musical illustrator for a 90 percent action picture." Korngold professed to like the movie, but he undoubtedly wanted more aural space. *Robin Hood* required brisk tempos and, scene by scene, a lot of notes to accompany the action. Besides, Korngold didn't need the money and wanted to get home to Vienna.

Music chief Forbstein was dispatched to Korngold's San Fernando Valley house to change his mind. Still resistant, Korngold had packed his bags for a return trip to Austria with his family when he received word from his father that the Anschluss had been signed, placing all of Austria under German rule. The Korngolds' property and possessions had been seized by the Nazis. The family, including father Julius, managed to get safely out of Vienna. Korngold took the *Robin Hood* assignment on a week-by-week basis. Composing 73 minutes of music for 102 minutes of running time, he completed the score in seven nerve-wracking weeks. As usual, Friedhofer came in to orchestrate, with additional orchestrations made by freelancer Milan Roder, "a great big husky, pompous, Teutonic type" (according to Friedhofer). Long after the movie was released, Korngold told his friends that the assignment had saved his life.

In 1941, Korngold was assigned to score *King's Row* (1942), the blood-pumping, smalltown melodrama in which new amputee Ronald Reagan regains consciousness only to cry out, "Where's the rest of me?!" The screenplay was based on a novel by Harry Bellamann, a former member of the faculty of the Curtis Institute of Music in Philadelphia. An October 1941 squib in the *Los Angeles Times* suggested that Bellamann was heading to Hollywood "to help" Korngold with the score, prompting a rare outburst from Korngold: "I shall certainly be ready to 'head east,'" he wrote to Warners publicity director Robert Taplinger, "perhaps I could help *him* in writing his new book!"

Korngold completed the score, presumably without Bellamann's help, and the studio knew it had a winner. Written in B major, the title theme seems to be touring the entire town by double-decker bus, stopping here to watch the children frolic in pizzicato, parking there to peer through Ann Sheridan's window. "Erich Korngold's music is good and occasionally striking," Otis Ferguson wrote in *The New Republic*, "and it also occasionally seems he thinks *he's* making the picture." Moviegoers generally don't shun the overdone, not if it moves them to tears, and soon the studio was inundated with requests for Korngold's music. The Warners publicity department had to work up a form letter stating that the music was unpublished and unavailable for commercial distribution. "The Music Department feels that the work being done by its musical directors is, indeed, a contribution to creative musical endeavor," the form letter concluded. Grudgingly, the letter even once managed to mention Korngold by name.

In 1947 Korngold suffered his first heart attack. The attack came shortly after completing the score for *Escape Me Never*, a Korngold project if ever there was one (Errol Flynn portrayed a struggling composer!). Again the music harks back to Liszt and foot candles. At fifty, Korngold was regressing. He said he was retiring from films—and for a while he did, returning to Vienna and working on symphonic works and operas. Within a year he let it be known that he was again available for film work.

Max Steiner, meanwhile, sometimes worked on as many as twelve pictures in a year, for other studios as well as Warners. In a memorandum to Jack Warner's executive assistant Steve Trilling, Forbstein wrote:

> As you know we have been receiving as high as $3500 a week for [Steiner's] services on loanout and I am getting many calls every day for his services at other studios with price no object and I assure you that with the Warner spirit, if he lives for ten years, it will be a miracle. . .

Steiner was given a new Warners contract. He kept working, working.

The availability of his colleague Korngold was now met with startling indifference. Forbstein had just died, and Warners was giving the go-ahead to projects in a darker, more contemporary idiom. Steiner adapted beautifully to these subtle shifts and composed two of his better scores, for *The Treasure of the Sierra Madre* and *Key Largo,* at the age of sixty. In Vienna, Korngold concentrated on his Symphony in F-sharp, a genuine advancement in his music, which he completed in 1952. Three years later he took his last film assignment, *Magic Fire,* a Republic-financed biopic about Wagner, in which Korngold served more as music director-orchestrator than as composer. From Mendelssohn to Wagner, Korngold had played out his Hollywood career as the most fertile and febrile of the great nineteenth-century–influenced composers. Another heart attack killed him in 1957 in North Hollywood.

Steiner worked up to the last few years of his life. The theme to *A Summer Place* (1959), for which Ray Heindorf confidently supplied the underbeat, made him richer than ever, due in no small part to Percy Faith's chart-busting recording. In the next few years, Steiner scored product that, like *A Summer Place,* seemed to always star young blond men—Troy Donahue, Ty Hardin, James Franciscus—whose careers didn't stretch much beyond the onset of crow's feet. Steiner's own career dribbled to a halt with *Two on a Guillotine.* This would-be shocker was riddled with horror clichés, but producer-director

William Conrad (the square-jawed and -bodied actor who starred on TV as *Cannon*) blamed its box-office failure on Steiner's busy score. It was an ignominious end for the father of film composing, a man who took as much delight in the movies as in music. You can see it in Steiner's animated conducting in RKO's *The Half Naked Truth* (1932). Onscreen for less than a minute, the dimple-chinned little conductor appears to be having a ball.

Whenever Steiner and Korngold are compared, Korngold almost invariably comes out the winner. Korngold was, and is, taken more seriously by scholars. He's listed in several composers dictionaries—notably those by David Ewen, Rupert Hughes, and Deems Taylor—while Steiner's name is absent.

Steiner's prodigiousness worked against him: *how could all that music,* serious listeners demanded to know, *be any good?* A lot of it wasn't any good, of course. With so many assignments, it was inevitable that Steiner would recycle his themes. Compare, for instance, his "Resignation" theme from *Dark Victory* (1939) with his main title for *A Stolen Life* (1946). The description of these themes as "lush" wasn't always praise. Though he desired eternal fame, at least for his music, Steiner made no concessions to the concert hall. For years his *Symphonie Moderne* (sometimes referred to informally as "Theme for Max Rabinowitz"), from the 1939 picture *Four Wives,* was the only Steiner piece taken seriously enough to find its way into concert programs.

By contrast, Korngold was secure in his position as a composer of the world ("I am a musician of passions and psychology") and was adored by his employers, who could congratulate themselves on having bagged him in the first place. Even today scholars like to say that the music of John Williams is just warmed-over Korngold, who created all the ingredients of the swashbuckling film score long before anyone else.

That Korngold was a greater film composer than Max Steiner is a curious assessment, especially when one remembers how much help they each had from Hugo Friedhofer. Steiner, for all his Mickey-Mousing of his themes, seemed to understand the function of film music better than anyone. Korngold, meanwhile, wrote beautiful, stir-ring music that recalled nineteenth-century romantics like Mahler; but to call it original or innovative is to ignore the fact that Virgil Thomson was composing for films as early as 1936 (*The Plow That Broke the Plains*), Aaron Copland in 1939 (*Of Mice and Men*). Korngold arrived in Hollywood prepackaged as a "great" composer, but it was his reliability, not any advances he made in his music, that made him the darling of Jack Warner and Leo Forbstein. Although musicologists' appraisals and the series of RCA recordings produced by his son George did much to lift his work to the zenith of movie music, one suspects that Korngold composed way past his peak— somewhere around the age of twenty.

◦   ◦   ◦

For more than thirty years, Professor Arnold Schoenberg had been a practicing Protestant. But shortly after learning that the president of the Prussian Academy, where Schoenberg taught, was following the lead of Germany's new chancellor, Adolph Hitler, by calling for the suppression of all Jewish influence, Schoenberg reembraced the faith of his birth. In May 1933, Mr. and Mrs. Schoenberg took their infant daughter to Paris. But the asthmatic Schoenberg needed to live in a warmer climate than Paris, perhaps something Mediterranean. Desperate, he accepted a teaching job in Boston.

The Schoenbergs didn't last long there, either. In September 1934 they moved to Los Angeles, a climate much more hospitable to the Professor's health. Schoenberg had just turned sixty. His music was world famous but considered too difficult for most audiences. *Verklarte Nacht* (*Transfigured Night*), the 1899 string sextet composed in an almost Wagnerian idiom, was widely performed, but his compositions became increasingly complex and dissonant. Instead, Schoenberg's rep-utation rested primarily on his writings about theory, outlined in the *Harmonienlehre*, first published around 1911.

It was only natural that Schoenberg would take students, first pri-vately, then as a member of the faculties of the University of Southern California and the University of California at Los Angeles. Alfred Newman, in Los Angeles since 1930 and already considered one of the industry's three or four leading composers, signed up as soon as he heard the professor was in town.

Schoenberg never composed music for a movie, but it wasn't because Hollywood hadn't come calling. With a severity that bordered on the forbidding, Schoenberg didn't exactly put movie folk at ease. He looked forward to meeting Charlie Chaplin, then was appalled by what he perceived as the filmmaker's commonness. Hungarian composer Miklos Rozsa, new in town, ran into Schoenberg at the Crescendo Club, where musicians met once a month to listen to and discuss one another's work. Encouraged by the club's president to use only first names, Rozsa turned to Schoenberg and said, "Herr Professor, should I call you Arnold from now on?" "Herr Professor will do," Schoenberg replied.

The Schoenberg story that has made the rounds for years concerns MGM production chief Irving Thalberg. Apprised that the composer of *Verklarte Nacht* was teaching at USC, Thalberg sent word through Salka Viertel that he would like to discuss with Herr Schoenberg the possibility of his composing the score for MGM's upcoming production of *The Good Earth*. During the opening discussions, Schoenberg was amiable enough, even making a few accessible piano sketches for Thalberg to consider. But negotiations stumbled when Schoenberg demanded $50,000 for his work, then halted altogether when he insisted upon complete control of the dialogue, which he had imagined delivered in the half-sung, half-spoken *sprechstimme* style he had employed for years. Thalberg shrugged and gave his music department the go-ahead to use some Chinese folk songs that had been lying around.

Although he never received a paycheck from a film studio, Schoenberg's presence was powerfully felt in the Hollywood community. The other great German-Jewish émigré teacher in town was Ernst Toch. Like Schoenberg, Toch possessed a powerful intellect; like Schoenberg's, Toch's last days in Europe were fraught with tension and desperation.

In 1909, when he was twenty-one, Ernst Toch was beginning work toward a medical degree when he won the prestigious Mozart Prize for composition. Composing in a complex idiom that pushed the borders of tonality, Toch changed career direction. By 1933 he was a composers' composer, applying order and unity to works that were difficult but considered profound. Early that year he was working in his hideaway attic study when two Brownshirts came to the door looking for him. His wife managed to send them away, but the incident galvanized them into planning an escape. That spring, Toch attended an international music festival in Florence. There he observed sadly how far-reaching Hitler's influence had become. By prearrangement, he wired his wife I HAVE MY PENCIL—the signal to prepare for flight.

The Tochs made their way to London, where they remained for a year. Toch had composed two film scores in Berlin, and this experience led to work at London–United Artists, writing music for *The Private Life of Don Juan* (1934). New York City was the Tochs' next stop. There they were befriended by George Gershwin, who arranged for Toch to try scoring work at Warners. The Tochs moved out to Pacific Palisades, but the Warners job didn't pan out. Paramount, however, hired him on a film-by-film basis. "During the next ten years," Toch's grandson Lawrence Weschler wrote, "Toch would frequently supplement his meager royalties through studio work. Owing to the 'eeriness' of his modernist idiom, Toch was quickly typecast as a specialist of horror and chase scenes, and he was to have a hand in most of the mysteries coming out of the Paramount studio for the next several years."

Toch's scores for *Peter Ibbetson* (1935) and the Columbia picture *Ladies in Retirement* (1941)—each an oddly dark-toned entertainment that earned Toch an Academy Award nomination—sound more fitting for a composer of his international stature than less sober assignments like *Ghost Breakers* (1940). Commercial, showbiz Hollywood collided with *mittel Europa* when Toch's music credit for the Bob Hope comedy *The Cat and the Canary* (1939) appeared on the silver screen as Dr. Ernst Toch: *That* was respect.

Despite such credits, Toch concentrated on teaching, privately and at UCLA. Only slightly less intimidating than Schoenberg, he was venerated as a teacher because he was also a working film composer, and his students could hear how movies were affecting his work as well as theirs. Lawrence Weschler wrote that the "osmosis of Hollywood film scoring" was greatly responsible "for the slow bending of Toch's creative production during the late thirties and early forties into a more harmonic and tonal idiom."

Just before Toch began his tenure at UCLA, another Jewish composer arrived in Los Angeles. Mario Castelnuovo-Tedesco was Italian (born in 1895 in Florence), and had made a career in a more tonal, audience-pleasing style than either Toch or Schoenberg. By the time he was thirty he had gained an international reputation for his opera *La Mandragola*. In 1930 Toscanini conducted the New York Philharmonic in Castelnuovo-Tedesco's Symphonic Variations. During the '30s, the composer had begun to write books on music theory.

But Mussolini made life uncomfortable for Castelnuovo-Tedesco and his family. They eventually emigrated to Larchmont, New York, then to Beverly Hills. There was intermittent scoring work—notably on René Clair's *And Then There Were None* (1945)—but it was as a teacher that Castelnuovo-Tedesco made his mark. Through the late '40s and '50s, musicians like André Previn and Henry Mancini studied with him (each man regarded him as his most important teacher). After the war Nelson Riddle was a particularly promising student, and one could argue that Riddle's rich arrangements for Frank Sinatra had been directly inspired by his teacher. "He was a master orchestrator," music director-composer Saul Chaplin recalled. "Tedesco [*sic*] had endless tricks to make small orchestras sound larger. These were useful for scoring small pictures where the music budget never allowed a large enough orchestra." Tall, thin, white-haired, and invariably *sotto voce* in his instructions, Castelnuovo-Tedesco presented the appearance—thick-lensed eyeglasses, skewed necktie, ill-fitting pants—of the absented-minded professor. His eyesight was so poor that he could barely make out images on a movie screen, and driving in car-dependent Los Angeles was out of the question.

Castelnuovo-Tedesco and Toch were, with Schoenberg, the greatest teachers of film composers during the first quarter century of the sound film. As émigrés they had a certain cachet, even though Castelnuovo-Tedesco and Toch were less influential as composers and Schoenberg never composed for Hollywood. In his 1952 novel *Pictures from an Institution,* Randall Jarrell created a character, Dr. Gottfied Rosenbaum, who could have been a composite of these men:

> Long ago, Dr. Rosenbaum's settings of Brecht's most seditious poems—he specialized, in those days, in *Spreechstimme*—had left his audiences troubled and uncertain about the music, the police troubled but certain about the words; when the Germans went into Austria Dr. Rosenbaum escaped, as he put it, at the eleventh hour, by the skin of his teeth, without a garment.

Jarrell may have been thinking of Paul Dessau, who had composed music to Brecht but couldn't get his music accepted in Hollywood. (Even Dessau's score for the 1944 *House of Frankenstein* was thrown out.) Two other musical collaborators of Brecht's also may have served as models for Dr. Rosenbaum: Kurt Weill, who arrived in the mid-'30s, scored the comic melodrama *You and Me* for Fritz Lang, then turned his attention back to the theater; and Hanns Eisler, who got a fair amount of work, published *Composing for the Films,* an early critical treatise on the young profession, and, as an ardent Communist, eventually found himself nose-to-nose with the House Un-American Activities Committee.

Particularly before his arrival in Los Angeles in 1940, Igor Stravinsky's music qualified as decadent. He wasn't Jewish, but as a French citizen and musical revolutionary his works were condemned by the Nazis. During 1939, tubercular infections had killed his first wife and daughter, and his personal ties to Europe had come unraveled. He had long since turned his back on Stalinist Russia. He had visited Los Angeles before, liked it, and was close to a handful of southern California-based émigrés, notably Aldous Huxley. Stravinsky and his new wife, Vera, left Paris in March 1940 and arrived a few weeks later to stay.

Stravinsky had had a troubled history with Hollywood. In 1934, Warners released a mystery entitled *The Firebird,* in which a young woman's resistance to seduction and subsequent depravity is weakened after hearing a recording of Stravinsky's ballet suite. Unamused, Stravinsky sued for defamation of character. A Paris tribunal awarded him one franc for his pain and suffering. While still in Paris, Stravinsky was asked permission by the Disney company to use *The Rite of Spring* for its new animated production, *Fantasia.* When Stravinsky hedged at their insultingly low offer of a $5,000 flat fee, the Disney representatives reminded him that *The Rite of Spring* wasn't copyrighted in the United States—meaning they could legally use the music for nothing. Stravinsky took the money.

On one of his previous visits to Los Angeles, Stravinsky had been escorted around the Paramount lot by music chief Boris Morross, who was ardently campaigning for the studio to hire contemporary composers for contemporary pictures. Who was more up-to-the-minute than the great Stravinsky? Production chief Y. Frank Freeman wasn't interested.

In 1941, Columbia head of music Morris Stoloff persuaded Harry Cohn to let him hire Stravinsky to score *The Commandos Strike at Dawn,* an Irwin Shaw script about the Norwegian underground fighting the Nazis. Stravinsky, working from some Norwegian folk songs that Vera had discovered in a Los Angeles bookstore, completed the score with his usual speed. With some shame, Stoloff had to confess that there was still no movie—not a single frame of *Commandos* had been shot yet. Stravinsky was paid off, and Louis Gruenberg, a serious composer in his own right, was brought in to score the completed movie. Gruenberg's score was subsequently nominated for an Academy Award. Meanwhile, Stravinsky turned his rejected music into *Four Norwegian Moods.*

A similar fiasco occurred at Twentieth Century-Fox. Franz Werfel, author of the bestselling *Song of Bernadette,* recommended his friend Stravinsky to compose the score for the film adaptation of his novel. Production chief Darryl F. Zanuck probably would have declined Stravinsky's services out of hand, but Zanuck was away at war. So music head Alfred Newman signed Stravinsky, who went to work without much bother. That music, too, was rejected. Newman wound up composing the score himself, and it's widely considered to be one of his most beautiful film scores. Stravinsky, who wouldn't have been caught dead writing Newman's genuflecting woodwinds, turned his own "Apparition of the Virgin" music into the middle movement of Symphony in Three Movements. Nothing on his staff paper went to waste.

●   ●   ●

Whether or not they actually got screen work, Stravinsky, Schoenberg, Toch, and Castelnuovo-Tedesco kept their heads above water. Less-renowned émigrés weren't so fortunate. In Los Angeles, respected musicians who had fled Hitler often could find no work—no *composing* work, anyway—and exchanged woeful tales at the various salons around town. Many congregated regularly at the home of director Edmund Goulding. Goulding was British, homosexual, well-connected, and a specialist in the so-called "woman's picture" (e.g., *Dark Victory*) often starring Bette Davis. He was also a songwriter ("Ma'mselle") and con-sidered himself particularly sympathetic to the émigré musicians. Salka Viertel mixed European novelists, composers, and actors at her parties on Mabery Drive at the rim of Santa Monica Canyon, and sometimes found them living quarters nearby. "Here many European emigrants lived," David King Dunaway, a Huxley biographer, wrote accurately, "for its cover of sycamore and oak gave the canyon a Mediterranean air."

Viertel, along with director Ernst Lubitsch and agent Paul Kohner, conceived of the European Film Fund even before the United States entered the Second World War. Through the fund's influence, Warners and MGM agreed to hire émigré writers at approximately $100 a week. Émigré musicians received equivalent compensation; more often than not, their music was deemed unusable—if, in fact, it was heard at all. The system was so flawed that it made everyone uncomfortable. John Baxter wrote that "a musical academic like the Vienna Conservatory's Dr. Eugen Zador 'apprenticed' to Herbert Stothart at MGM. 'How on earth can I tell Dr. Zador what he does for a picture isn't right?' a technician told the *Times*. 'He has forgotten more about music than I will ever learn.'"

No one trusted these new arrivals; they were too damned *serious*. When a producer told composer-conductor Anthony Collins that he wanted music like *The Firebird*, Collins suggested he hire the compos-er himself—Stravinsky lived practically around the corner. "He couldn't do it!" the producer replied, betraying the prevailing industry scorn toward independent composers who worked in a contemporary, unro-mantic idiom. Upon his arrival in Los Angeles, Erich Korngold had been almost as famous as Stravinsky, but he knew how to charm and accommodate his producers; though his music wasn't really new, it didn't challenge the way Stravinsky's did.

Ernst Krenek, though "unimpeachably Aryan," had come under Nazi attack for writing decadent, Schoenberg-influenced music, particularly his 1923 jazz opera *Jonny Spielt Auf.* In Hollywood he simply couldn't find work. Determined to get Krenek a scoring assignment, George Antheil and Ben Hecht invaded Samuel Goldwyn's office and lavishly sang Krenek's praises. Goldwyn confessed he never heard of Krenek, so Antheil and Hecht began to argue about which Krenek hit was greater, *Rosenkavalier* or *Faust.* Goldwyn was intrigued. Unable to leave well enough alone, Hecht insisted that *La Traviata* was the greatest Krenek hit of all.

At that Goldwyn exploded: "Just bring that guy around here so's I can get my hands on him! Why, his publishers almost ruined me with a suit just because we used a few bars of that lousy opera!"

Krenek wasn't hired by Goldwyn or any other Hollywood producer, and eventually left town to teach at Vassar.

Being sponsored by an established film person like Antheil or Hecht was no guarantee of work; it was difficult enough just to get the composer to town. The Polish-born Alexandre Tansman had managed, at the behest of Charlie Chaplin, to get his family out of France. Once Tansman settled in Los Angeles, Chaplin had nothing for him to do. It took a while for Tansman to get his bearings. Finally, through the say-so of director Julien Duvivier, whom he had known in Paris, Tansman was assigned to score *Flesh and Fantasy* (1943), another of Duvivier's patented omnibus features that linked separate stories. Tansman wrote a marvelous score.

Hans Salter arrived earlier than Tansman, and though employed sooner, he had to fight for work. Born in Vienna in 1896, the son of a brewery manager, Salter tossed away a career in medicine to stay in music. In 1933, that most fateful year in German history, Salter was conducting at *Universum Film Aktien Gesellschaft* (UFA), Berlin's monolithic film production company, when he realized it was time to get out. Vienna, Paris, New York—Salter's road out of Europe was already well trampled.

Preparing for *100 Men and a Girl* (1937): (*left to right*) Joe Pasternak, Henry Koster, Charles Previn, Andres de Segurola, Deanna Durbin, Leopold Stokowski, Fred Hollander
Courtesy Melodie Hollander and Universal Studios

More fortunate than most, Salter had a job waiting for him in Hollywood: Joe Pasternak was producing at Universal after closing that studio's Berlin office, and he brought Salter into the music department. It was 1937; Salter was forty-one. He reported for work at the Universal lot in North Hollywood. But music chief Charles Previn, fearing that the newcomer was after his job, gave him nothing to do. The chill lasted for months. Salter had traded daily terror for daily anonymity.

Relations began to thaw when music recording was underway for *The Rage of Paris* (1938), a comedy starring Danielle Darrieux and Douglas Fairbanks, Jr. Previn sent an SOS to Salter because he needed a four-and-a-half-minute sequence scored *yesterday*. Salter looked only at the one sequence—he wouldn't see the entire film until thirty years later on television—composed the music, and turned it in, fully orchestrated. Previn took the music and rehearsed the Universal orchestra. After the sound was adjusted, Previn suddenly stepped down from the podium, handed Salter the baton, and said, "Hans, you're on your own." So Salter conducted the actual recording and won the respect of the musicians.

Although *Rage of Paris* was produced by Buddy DeSylva, who was remaking himself from songwriter into industry titan, the picture was really put together by screenwriter Felix Jackson and director Henry Koster. Like Salter, both men were Berlin refugees who had been brought aboard by Pasternak. Koster (né Kosterlitz) had been a cartoonist and journalist before getting his chance to direct; Jackson (né Joachimson) wrote, with and without Universal staffer Bruce Manning, some of the better light comedies the studio cranked out in the late 1930s and early 1940s. Jackson became the first husband of Pasternak's young discovery, Deanna Durbin.

Besides being crucial to Universal's solvency, Durbin's pictures provided Salter with steady employment. Salter also labored on the studio's bread-and-butter westerns and horror pictures, but the Durbin pictures—essentially domestic operettas that resolved in palatable moral lessons—were stuffed with the kind of music that Salter knew from his youth. Salter arranged and orchestrated the Strauss waltzes that swept through *First Love* (1939), a Cinderella story in which Durbin is an orphan taken in by her uncle. For the anomalously dark Durbin vehicle *Christmas Holiday* (1944), Salter was asked to orchestrate Wagner's "Liebestod" (from *Tristan and Isolde*) for Universal's orchestra.

"No siree. Can't be done," said Salter. "You can't reduce this music to nothing." In a rare and expensive capitulation to a staff musician's intransigence, Universal doubled its usual thirty-six-piece orchestra. Salter got the properly behemoth Wagnerian sound and received an Academy Award nomination.

o   o   o

Berlin was the film-making capitol of Europe in the '20s and early '30s, before the Nazis came to power. Picture people congregated at the Romanisches Café, drinking, trading stories and scripts. UFA was the largest film company, but there were more than three hundred other production companies of various sizes, some employing the most innovative filmmakers in the world.

Two particularly important musicians at UFA were from Silesian-Jewish families. Friedrich Hollaender was actually born in London (in 1896), where his father, Viktor, had been working as a musical director. Although his family operated the prestigious Stern Conservatory in Berlin, Hollaender probably picked up as valuable an education while apprenticing with Max Reinhardt. After a visit to America in the late '20s, he became enamored of film scoring, and upon his return to Berlin he landed a job at UFA. One of his assignments came from powerhouse producer Erich Pommer: *The Blue Angel* (1930), adapted from a Heinrich Mann novel and starring the unique, delicious Marlene Dietrich. Hollaender's music, including the song "Falling in Love Again," was orchestrated by a scholarly, birdlike young man named Franz Wachsmann.

Ten years younger than Hollaender, Wachsmann had attended the Dresden Music Academy before arriving in Berlin. Before joining UFA, he had played and arranged for the jazzy Weintraub's Syncopaters [*sic*], a name that subsequently tickled his American colleagues. If Wachsmann was less a melodist than most of his colleagues, he had a greater feeling for orchestral color; he sensed that film music required closer attention to orchestration if the music were to project any character.

Meanwhile, outside UFA's production walls, Berlin's popular songwriters were working at their pianos. Former medical student Walter Jurmann (born 1903), lean and Scandinavian-looking, had arrived from Vienna and was writing fox-trot songs with Fritz Rotter, one of the more important German popular lyricists of the '30s. Bronislau Kaper, a tall, bespectacled Warsaw native and a year older than Jurmann, was composing songs for tenor Richard Tauber to record. The two thirtyish men, Jurmann and Kaper, had just found each other and begun to collaborate when the Nazis began stepping on all of the arts. Jurmann loved American jazz and had no use for Hitler; Kaper's Jewish wife had already scuffled with some Brownshirts.

Jewish or Gentile, every man had his revelation, the moment when it became apparent that flight from Berlin was necessary and imminent. In 1933 Jurmann and Kaper slipped out of Berlin, as did Hollaender. Although his father, Viktor, was safe, most of Hollaender's family were rounded up and subsequently sent to concentration camps. For another year Franz Wachsmann remained in Berlin, until one evening he was accosted on the street by a gang of young Nazis and beaten nearly to death. There was no choice but to leave.

In Paris, Franz and Alice Waxman (né Wachsmann) found rooms at the Hotel Ansonia; Hollander (who had dropped the first *e* in his name) was already there; Billy Wilder arrived presently. Wilder directed his first movie in France in 1934, *Mauvaise Graine* (*Bad Seed*), and Waxman provided a jazzy score for it. Waxman also scored Fritz Lang's version of Molnar's *Liliom*. Berlin refugees were writing and filming on the run.

Also in Paris, Walter Jurmann and Broni Kaper were writing music for the film *Les Nuits Moscovites* (1934) when Louis B. Mayer happened to hear one of the songs they'd written for Jan "The Polish Ham" Kiepura. Mayer's representatives tracked down Jurmann and Kaper and offered them MGM contracts.

Separately, the other refugees also gravitated toward Hollywood. Hollander already had contacts at Paramount, and settled into the music department, soon joined by his father. The Waxmans arrived in Los Angeles when Erich Pommer, reestablished in Hollywood since the Nazis' seizure of UFA, invited Waxman to be music director for the film version of *Music in the Air*. Based on the Jerome Kern–Oscar Hammerstein musical comedy, the picture was partly adapted by Billy Wilder, his first American screen credit. It did little to revive the career of its star, Gloria Swanson, but Waxman proved reliable, and he soon found a staff position at Universal.

Within days of their arrival in Hollywood, songwriters Jurmann and Kaper were put to work. Kaper desperately wanted to score an entire film, but Mayer kept him hanging—he had Stothart and William Axt to rely on, and he wasn't convinced that a Polish songwriter could sustain all that music. Jurmann and Kaper added songs to *Escapade*, a 1935 remake of the German romantic comedy *Maskerade*, and for a while they served as song specialists for European-flavored pictures and comedies. For *A Night at the Opera* (1935), the Marx Brothers' first MGM movie, they composed "Cosi, Cosa," which Allan Jones sang. Joe Pasternak, who knew Jurmann and Kaper from their Berlin days, borrowed them to write songs for Universal's *Three Smart Girls* (1936), the modest musical that first showcased Deanna Durbin's talents. "All God's Chillun Got Rhythm" was sung by the great Ivie Anderson and Her Boys from Dixie in the Marxes' next MGM picture, *A Day at the Races* (1937); strip away Gus Kahn's ingenious minstrel lyrics and the tune is more boulevard than plantation.

Metro producers John Emerson and Bernard Hyman were looking for a story for Clark Gable. In a hallway they ran into screenwriter Robert Hopkins, famous for never setting pen to paper but blessed with a raconteur's ability to talk out remarkably formed ideas. "Two guys in San Francisco, one's a priest and the other guy runs a big saloon, and

Hollywood songwriters gathered in Gus Kahn's backyard, 1936: (*left to right*) Gus Kahn, publisher Jack Robbins, Jimmy McHugh, Johnny Mercer, Harry Warren (at piano), unidentified, Matty Malneck, Walter Jurmann, Bronislau Kaper, Harold Adamson, unidentified, Ted Koehler, Louis Alter
Photo by Tom Evans. Courtesy UCLA Popular Music Library

you end it with the San Francisco earthquake—bang!" Hoppie gave
Emerson an elbow in the ribs. "Do I have to tell you any more?" The
resulting Gable picture, *San Francisco* (1936), was presented with a
Jurmann-Kaper title song so endearing ("San Francisco, open your
golden gate"—lyric by Gus Kahn) that it remains the city's official
theme song.

Personally, Jurmann and Kaper were the best of friends; professionally, they began to slide away from each other. Taken more seriously as a composer, Kaper finally got his chance to score an entire movie
with *I'll Take This Woman* (Spencer Tracy falls hard and fast for Hedy
Lamarr). Soon he was scoring four or five pictures each year. Because
Herbert Stothart was really a music borrower, plundering nineteenth-
century classics for most of this themes, and Georgie Stoll more of a
conductor-supervisor than a composer, Kaper became Metro's original
composer of choice. He wouldn't relinquish that position for the next
twenty years.

Jurmann, still testing melodies on his grand piano in Beverly
Hills, continued to mine the fox-trot form that had made him financially comfortable. By 1941 the fire had gone out of Jurmann: perhaps
it was because Kaper had moved on, perhaps because Gus Kahn, his
favorite lyricist, had just died. Toying with the notion of producing, he
developed several screenplays, but he was much too diffident to get anywhere in an industry that responds mostly to aggressiveness. He had
somewhat better luck as an associate producer on Duke Ellington's
Jump for Joy (1941), with his old friend Ivie Anderson coming out of
semi-retirement to sing. Finally, Jurmann attempted a musical comedy,
Windy City, about the South Side of Chicago, which opened at the
Shubert Great Northern in Chicago in 1946. Expert Broadway contributions—Jo Mielziner designed the sets, Katherine Dunham choreographed—couldn't save it from condescending notices. ("Watery imitation Rachmaninoff," Cecil Smith called it.) At forty-three, Jurmann
stepped back more or less permanently from show business.
Meanwhile, in the year of *Windy City*'s failure, Kaper scored *Green
Dolphin Street,* and out of it came a jazz standard. It was only the first
of many hit movie tunes Kaper would compose over the next two
decades.

Although no longer working for movie studios, Walter Jurmann continued to socialize with his fellow émigrés. Songwriter Nicholas Brodszky ("Be My Love") introduced Jurmann to his future wife, Yvonne, a Hungarian dress designer, whom he married in 1950. Broni Kaper, whose father had been a businessman in Warsaw, immersed himself in American business, in real-estate investments, and the stock market. Freddy Hollander remained at Paramount where he composed such gorgeous songs as "You Leave Me Breathless" (for *Cocoanut Grove,* 1938), Alec Wilder's idea of an "adult, civilized, open, musical pop tune." Franz Waxman, scoring Universal's *Bride of Frankenstein* (1935), created startling effects by holding the right notes, and by keeping rhythm and orchestral color in kaleidoscopic motion. (The "Creation of the Female Monster" music cue tells the entire horror story in seven minutes.) Over the next decade Waxman would become Hollywood's resident longhair, founding the Los Angeles Music Festival in 1947, and a favorite model for a younger generation of film composers.

Hollywood was kind to these musicians. Whatever humiliations the movie industry imposed, it was better than living—or dying—in Nazi-occupied Europe. René Clair, perhaps the most aurally sophisticated of all the European émigré directors, encapsulated the dilemma they all faced: "In 1940 I had my choice between Hitler and Hollywood, and I preferred Hollywood—just a little."

٠   ٠   ٠

Long before Arnold Schoenberg had given America a thought, Russian musicians were arriving here by the boatload. Some were fleeing the Revolution of 1918–1920, but others came earlier. Heading west, they tended to make extended stops in Berlin, Paris, or London, before settling in New York; and then movie work drew them still farther west. They brought with them a muscular musicality comprised of unequal parts scholarship and arrogance.

At the age of five, Jascha Heifetz had made his debut in St. Petersburg; at eleven, he was playing violin with the Berlin Philharmonic; by the time he was twenty-four, he was an American citizen and internationally famous, unchallenged on his instrument. Marriage to silent screen actress Florence Vidor kept Heifetz in Los Angeles for extended periods, and he made himself the locus of serious musical activity there. Among his fellow Russian expatriates was Chaliapin's former pianist Max Rabinowitz (né Rabinovich), a virtuoso with huge hands who made his living by dubbing piano parts for the movies—or, even odder, by merely allowing his hands to be photographed in close-up for a piano-playing scene.

Several notches down on the virtuoso scale was Dimitri Tiomkin. Born in 1894, Tiomkin began his career as a pianist in St. Petersburg. He considered himself a romanticist in a long line of Russian romantic composers, and thought himself to be destined for greatness. He studied with Alexander Glazunov and made ends meet by playing piano for the silents, a job that included the occasional grunt or whistle. American music was everywhere in the city. At the St. Petersburg Cafe in early 1914, Tiomkin saw sheet music for "Alexander's Ragtime Band" and was astonished by its "swaggering" and "insolent" rhythm.

Tiomkin began to get concert bookings; one booking took him to Berlin where he settled for a few years. The Russian Revolution was in full swing, and Tiomkin had no reason to return to his homeland. His father was in Berlin, too, living with a second family and working as a bacteriologist, but after a sour reunion the two were estranged. One day in 1923 Emmanuel Bay, accompanist to violinist Efrem Zimbalist (and later to Heifetz), played for Tiomkin the Frank Silver–Irving Cohn song "Yes, We Have No Bananas." As American as baseball and burlesque, the song lodged in Tiomkin's brain. Wherever he went, he couldn't get America out of his ears.

Tiomkin sailed to New York, settling into a Seventh Avenue hotel, and soon partnered professionally with a pianist named Mikhail Khariton, a fellow Russian he had known in Berlin. They became a kind of Ferrante and Teicher of the vaudeville circuit, playing dual pianos to provide a "classy" break from the comedy acts. Tiomkin found the work lucrative. At the Russian deli in his West Side neighborhood, Tiomkin ran into fellow émigrés who thought he was a sellout: this is what an artist must do for money?

Meanwhile, a young Austrian choreographer named Albertina Rasch was adding her modish, highly stylized touch to Broadway shows. Her dance troupe was more show-biz than innovative. Tiomkin married Rasch, and their matrimonial partnership proved to be good business as well. When an opportunity came to play Gershwin's Piano Concerto in Paris, where Diaghilev held court over Russian émigrés and their acolytes, Rasch encouraged Tiomkin to do it. Tiomkin's audience included Prokofiev and the composer himself.

Tiomkin wasn't shy about his musical talent, while Rasch knew how to market herself. After inserting a miniature ballet into *Rio Rita* (1927), the Harry Tierney show that opened the new Ziegfeld Theater, Rasch set her sights on Hollywood. The second musical to be filmed, *Rio Rita* was successful enough to win Rasch an invitation to Hollywood to create similar miniature ballets. Rasch's promotional material offered producers "units of from six to twenty-four Rasch Girls . . . appearing in vaudeville feature acts, in Broadway revues, on the screen and in motion-picture prologues." Rasch knew how to promote "Dimi," too. For his part, Tiomkin played the Russian rube to the hilt, keeping a smile on his face and putting his company at ease with his self-consciously fractured, heavily accented speech.

Temporarily in Hollywood with Rasch, Tiomkin found work composing ballet music for MGM operettas—notably *The Rogue Song* (1930), based on Franz Lehar's work—and some underscoring for Universal's *Resurrection* (1931), based on the Tolstoy novel. These projects had Russian-flavored stories. If Tiomkin felt typecast, he kept his mouth shut to everyone except Albertina. After another long stint in New York, where Rasch choreographed Dietz-Schwartz revues, the Tiomkins moved permanently to Los Angeles in 1933. Tiomkin had been called west to score the all-star *Alice in Wonderland* (W. C. Fields portrayed Humpty-Dumpty). The Tiomkins rented a house from Buddy Rogers.

A year or so after *Alice in Wonderland*'s release, Tiomkin met film director Frank Capra. Columbia's resident genius, Capra had previously used house music director Lou Silvers to provide scores for his comedies. Capra didn't care for Tiomkin's quasi-English tunes in *Alice*, which sounded a little too Elgarish, but he maintained a friendship with the composer. In late 1936, after winning his second consecutive best-director Oscar, Capra thought Tiomkin was ready to compose for him.

The new Capra picture, *Lost Horizon*, was ripe for big musical themes; Tiomkin went all out. Morris Stoloff, who probably took more guff from his studio chief than any other head of music, had to fatten the payroll. To handle Tiomkin's music, nine orchestrators were hired. These men comprised an honor roll of great musicians. Among them were the Broadway orchestrator Robert Russell Bennett, who could write an instrumental part with one hand while calling his local bookie with the other, and William Grant Still, then just weeks away from becoming the first black musician to conduct a major American symphony orchestra. In addition to the orchestrators, Max Steiner was borrowed from Selznick to conduct a supplemented Columbia orchestra, and the Hall Johnson Choir was brought in to produce a heavenly sound. Max Rabinowitz, who had clucked at Tiomkin's vaudeville work when they were both based in New York, appeared in the film—face and torso as well as hands—as the piano-playing Seiveking.

Once he got a look at this veritable army, Harry Cohn sent for Tiomkin. Forcing the rookie composer to stand by, Cohn ranted at Stoloff: "Who does he think he is to have such a big orchestra and a chorus, too? Where does he think he is, Carnegie Hall?!" Tiomkin feared a greatly reduced orchestra, if not his dismissal. Suddenly Cohn asked about the beautiful blonde cellist, Helen Gilbert. Tiomkin praised Cohn's discerning eye for beauty, and the cost of the music was forgotten.

A few weeks later Helen Gilbert married double bassist Mischa Bakaleinikoff, who sat next to her in the orchestra. Bakaleinikoff came from a musical family. The oldest sibling, Vladimir, conducted the Cincinnati and Pittsburgh Symphony orchestras. Younger brother Constantin conducted the pit orchestras at the biggest Los Angeles cinemas—the Egyptian, the Mayan, the Million Dollar. Constantin, or Backy, as he was called, went to Paramount as a music director in 1932, then ended up at RKO, where he handled most of the B product for many years. In those days everyone knew the Bakaleinikoff brothers.

Between Rasch and Frank Capra, Tiomkin was getting some very personal career guidance. Before making *You Can't Take It with You* (1938) and *Mr. Smith Goes to Washington* (1939), Capra gave Tiomkin a copy of *What America Sings,* a book of Yankee hymns, Negro spirituals, and Revolutionary War ballads. Tiomkin fairly inhaled the songs. With a few pictures under his belt and an expanding knowledge of American music, Tiomkin was turning himself into an American composer.

Tiomkin kept himself freelance, untethered to any single music department. Fortunately he was a quick study. Scoring Hitchcock's *Shadow of a Doubt* (1943), Tiomkin reworked "The Merry Widow Waltz" into a jangling theme that signaled the lethal exploits of Uncle Charlie (Joseph Cotten). With its deceptively sinister score in place, the film was previewed in Long Beach. Tiomkin was positive it was a flop. Later, at Chasen's in Beverly Hills, he couldn't believe why the director would be smug and happy.

"Is calamity, Hitch. Audience laughing!"

"Oh, that?" said Hitchcock. "It was quite all right."

"But Hitch, when should be fear, terror, they going ha-ha."

"That was tension, Dimi. The laughs were a sign the picture had them on edge."

Tiomkin made himself indispensable by anticipating and delivering what an employer needed; sometimes he delivered too much. In 1945, David O. Selznick, having auditioned and dismissed at least six composers to write music for *Duel in the Sun,* hired Tiomkin. Selznick had previously produced some westerns, but this one starred his paramour, Jennifer Jones, and he wanted something special—an orgasm theme, for one. "I want a really good *schtup,*" Selznick told Tiomkin.

The poor composer just couldn't get it right. His other themes were fine to Selznick's discriminating ears, but, upon hearing Tiomkin whistle the orgasm theme, Selznick shook his head: "That's just not an orgasm." Tiomkin went at it like a fifty-minute man, composing a bombastic climax that came from the base of his spine. Hearing Tiomkin himself conduct the huge orchestra, Selznick found the new music too beautiful.

"I like it," he said, "but it isn't orgasm music. It's not *schtup.* It's not the way I f**k."

"My Selznick, you f**k your way, I f**k my way. To me, *that* is f**king music."

Selznick laughed. Tiomkin's music stayed in.

"Tiomkin was a lousy composer, but a wonderful dramatist," said the orchestrator Arthur Morton. Compared to those of some of his colleagues, Morton's appraisal may be downright tender.

"Then there is the spectacular Dimitri Tiomkin," wrote Vernon Duke, "who is in a class—or rather, Klass—by himself."

> His favorite procedure is to concoct a luscious ballad, aimed at Academy Oscar honors, and plug it to death through the entire length of the picture; the strain, which has often been familiar to the film patron in previous non-Tiomkin versions, becomes inescapable and is aimed straight at the patron's heart, while apocalyptic fanfares and percussive pyramids subdue the man's ears and actually make him long for the already memorized ballad's balm.

Actually, what Duke describes is the way much of the best film music works. Then again, Duke may have been venting his own frustration that "the False Dimitri" was so well paid for his labors, while Duke himself (né Vladimir Dukelsky) was not.

For Tiomkin in Russia, it was Irving Berlin's "Alexander's Ragtime Band"; for the White Russian Dukelsky, self-exiled to Constantinople, it was George Gershwin's "Swanee." Like Gershwin, the young Dukelsky (born 1903) wanted to write popular songs as well as serious concert works. After a requisite stay in Paris, he made his way to New York, where he sought out Gershwin and played his piano pieces for him. "There's no heart in it," Gershwin said. What a blow for the hopeful young Russian. Nevertheless, Gershwin encouraged him, telling him not to shy away from "going low-brow" if it was right, and gave him the name Vernon Duke—for his pop songs, of course.

With a lesson from the master and some burlesque accompaniment under his belt, Duke returned to Paris. There he received a commission to compose for the Ballets Russes de Monte-Carlo. He moved on to London where he began to compose for musical theater. By 1929 he was back in New York. Under the supervision of Jay Gorney, he provided some underscoring for a few early talkies made at Paramount's Astoria studios. Gorney's occasional partner Yip Harburg became Duke's most frequent lyricist, and in the early to mid-'30s Duke wrote the songs that remain his best-loved works: "I Like the Likes of You," "What Is There to Say?" "April in Paris" (Harburg's lyrics), "Autumn in New York" (Duke's own lyrics), and the incomparable "I Can't Get Started" (lyrics by Ira Gershwin).

In Hollywood, Duke's first important work came when he stepped in after George Gershwin's sudden death to complete the music for *The Goldwyn Follies* (1938). None other than conductor Serge Koussevitsky championed the "serious" works of Vladimir Dukelsky, but it didn't help him get the best scoring jobs—those were going to the house composers who could write fast, like Steiner, or to a self-publicizing freelancer like Tiomkin. With the remarkable song score for *Cabin in the Sky* (1943), Duke became a presence in Hollywood, though one doubts if the all-black musical would have been filmed had it not first been a Broadway hit.

On the West Coast, Duke had more time on his hands, and he began to write prose. The writing eventually produced an autobiography, *Passport to Paris* (1955), and an acidic survey of contemporary music, *Listen Here!* (1964). Undeniably pretentious, "a movie caricature of a Russian émigré" (said Jerome Moross) and a dandy, Duke was a wonderful writer whose prose was spiced by professional jealousy.

Hollywood had a way of mixing up the ridiculous and the sublime, especially when it came to the Russian émigrés. The Odessa-born and -educated Spitalny brothers, Leopold and Phil, were in town, excellent musicians both; yet Phil's fame rested with his All-Girls Orchestra. Rachmaninoff was right there in Beverly Hills, too, where he died in 1943.

The Hollywood movie people were at once excited and intimidated by Diaghilevian dialogs about the arts. Russians like Dukelsky, after all, had composed for the Ballets Russes (a high-flown tradition, by the way, beautifully satirized by Balanchine's dances in *On Your Toes*) and were said to know a great deal about theater as well. A master like Vladimir Horowitz was frequently asked to cut and paste his piano-playing to the needs of a film story. How could Horowitz, who was financially comfortable, ever say *yes*? How could the considerably less renowned Max Rabinowitz, always financially struggling, ever say *no*?

Daniele Amfitheatrof, part-Italian but born and raised in Russia, and the German émigré composer Hans Salter occasionally went to screenings together to hear each other's music. "We went to a preview once and there was a short ahead of the feature," Salter recalled. "And it said, 'Music by Daniele Amfitheatrof and Constantin Bakaleinikoff.' A *howl* went up in the auditorium and it set the mood for the whole preview. . . ." To American ears, the Russian names sounded exotic and a little intimidating.

◦   ◦   ◦

By the summer of 1944, the always intimidating Arnold Schoenberg was trying to figure out a way to keep his young family fed and clothed. That autumn he applied for a Guggenheim Fellowship:

> On September 13, 1944, I have become seventy years of age. At this date—according to regulations—I had to retire from my position as professor of music at the University of California at Los Angeles. As I was in this position only eight years, I will receive a "pension" of $38.00 (thirty-eight) a month, on which I am supposed to support a wife and three children (13, 8 and 4 years old).

The fellowship was denied. Schoenberg soldiered on, composing the brief *Accompaniment to a Cinematographic Scene* and his masterful *A Survivor from Warsaw* for speaker, men's chorus, and orchestra. He wasn't making money, but the best musicians in Los Angeles regarded him with awe.

The best of the musicians employed by the film studios were the members of the Hollywood String Quartet who recorded Schoenberg's *Verklarte Nacht,* augmented by viola and cello, in August 1950. The quartet, founded in 1937, was then comprised of Felix Slatkin, the concertmaster of the Twentieth Century-Fox orchestra; Eleanor Aller, the principal cellist in the Warners orchestra, married to Slatkin; Paul Robyn, principal violist at Warners; and, replacing Joachim Chassman after World War II, Paul Shure, the assistant concertmaster at Twentieth. For Schoenberg's sextet, violist Alvin Dinkin and cellist Kurt Reher (both frequently employed by Twentieth) were added. For the six, film studio work was lucrative but not terribly gratifying.

The sextet wanted Herr Professor to write the liner notes for their recording. Schoenberg demanded that they come to his Brentwood house and play *Verklarte Nacht* for him before he made a commitment.

When the six musicians arrived at the Schoenbergs', the temperature was more than a 100 degrees in the living room, with neither air conditioning nor fresh air. Schoenberg, who had been brought back from death one day in 1946 when his heart had stopped, entered dressed in a coat and scarf and silently sat down.

The sextet began the piece. Immediately Schoenberg interrupted the first run-through—they had been warned he might do this—to criticize it. Slatkin prevailed upon him to withhold criticism until the piece was played all the way through. The sextet began again. Their flawless rendition of *Verklarte Nacht* produced an effect that was tantamount to a knife through the soul. When they had finished, Schoenberg said nothing. Suddenly Gertrud Schoenberg entered carrying a tray of donuts and bourbon, and placed it before the six drenched, exhausted musicians.

"You will have your liner notes in the post on Monday morning," Schoenberg said.

FOUR

LONELY RIVERS FLOW
TO THE SEA

AARON COPLAND, JEROME MOROSS,
BERNARD HERRMANN; ALEX NORTH,
ERNEST GOLD, ELMER BERNSTEIN

In the early 1930s, a future documentary filmmaker named Pare Lorentz arrived in New York with a vague notion of becoming a music critic. Although he had studied music for years, he didn't play an instrument. Lorentz began to publish film criticism, and his articles were dotted with references to film background scores. Apart from René Clair and a handful of other filmmakers, Lorentz felt nobody was using contemporary music in its range of filmic possibilities.

This was when Max Steiner was just beginning his reign as the emperor of studio film scoring; when Erich Korngold was still testing Hollywood, before he became its darling composer; when younger, highly educated composers, reporting for work at a studio, were advised to listen to the sweeping, neo-nineteenth-century themes of Herbert Stothart. *The New Republic* film critic Otis Ferguson described the state of affairs:

> Fanfares, heavy orchestrations, lack of imagination obtrude on almost any film story you think of, yet anything in the way of delicacy and

restraint is ruled out of most productions on the ground of lack of appeal. . . .

And there is so little chance of a progressive, continuous, and memorable composition in furnishing chords now for a hurricane and next minute for Nelson Eddy, that the boys all too quickly find the easiest course to be that of swimming with the current, giving the boobs what they want, and overloading the microphone at every point of European action by sitting the brass section for the 1812 Overture no more than ten feet away from it. And if a composer does get a score he fancies he can work on in an original way, who is to blame him for pushing the music at the expense of theater continuity, using the main business of the picture itself as an excuse or suggestion for his themal development, until sometimes a country garden takes on the aspect of a mixture of a Legion convention and the Albert Hall.

Pare Lorentz shared Ferguson's view. By Christmas 1935, having published a fair amount of criticism, Lorentz was living in Sneden's Landing, New York, on the Hudson River. By day, he edited his first documentary film, *The Plow That Broke the Plains*, produced with money from the U.S. Resettlement Adminstration; by night he held forth until dawn on the poor quality of Hollywood pictures and the changing economy under the New Deal. Looking for a composer who was his own man and knew nothing of the Hollywood assembly line, Lorentz spoke to Aaron Copland, already renowned as one of the more interesting young American composers. For some reason, Copland and Lorentz couldn't come to terms. Roy Harris was approached, but he and Lorentz simply didn't like each other. Lorentz then consulted with young producer-director John Houseman, with whom he shared a pied-à-terre on Central Park South, and Houseman recommended Virgil Thomson.

Lorentz asked Thomson if he could compose music for a documentary, specifically one about the Dust Bowl.

"How much money have you got?" Thomson asked.

"Beyond the costs of orchestra, conductor, and recording," Lorentz said, "the most I could possibly have left for the composer is five hundred."

"Well, I can't take from any man more than he's got, though if you did have more I would ask for it."

The two men shook on it. "All these high-flyers talk nothing but aesthetics," said the relieved Lorentz. "You talk about money; you're a professional."

The Plow That Broke the Plains (1936) had been photographed under Lorentz's supervision by three great photograpers—Leo Hurwitz, Ralph Steiner, and Paul Strand. While Lorentz finished editing, Thomson boned up on cowboy songs that might help him compose music to accompany images of the devastated grasslands of the southwest. Given hardly more than a week to compose about twenty-five minutes of music, Thomson used the orchestrating services of the young Canadian composer Henry Brant, who had been recommended to him by George Antheil. Thomson composed at night; Brant would orchestrate his sketches the following day, with Thomson at his shoulder. "Brant was such a natural orchestrator that I even asked him once to salt up a passage with percussion. I did not, after one essay, depend on him for string chords or for phrasing, for though he could dispose these admirably, I did not like another's personality to color my sounds." The score was recorded by Alexander Smallens, presiding over thirty musicians culled from the New York Philharmonic and the Metropolitan Opera. The folk tune "Old Paint" ambles through the score; it was subsequently used by Copland in his score for the Agnes de Mille dance *Rodeo*.

Ornery as both men were, Lorentz knew he had a good thing going with Thomson. For Lorentz's next documentary, *The River* (1937), Thomson went to what he called "white spirituals," the Christian hymns of his Midwestern youth, even traveling to Washington, D.C., to consult with folk-song expert John Lomax at the Library of Congress. The working procedure for *Plow* was repeated for *River*—Thomson composing, Brant orchestrating, Smallens conducting.

After *The River* Thomson took a composing commission from Joris Ivens, who was filming under Ernest Hemingway's barrel-chested auspices *The Spanish Earth*, a documentary ostensibly about a Castilian irrigation project during the siege of Madrid. This time Thomson, working with Marc Blitzstein, plundered the private record collections of Gerald Murphy and Paul Bowles in Paris. Thomson and Blitzstein worked in the same way as Hollywood's old-time music "fitters," or suppliers, to piece together a score. They found several authentic Spanish recordings—Galician choral numbers, flamenco from Seville, among others. Today *The Spanish Earth* is remembered primarily for being a film project worked on (or over) by Hemingway, John Dos Passos, Archibald MacLeish, and an uncredited Lillian Hellman.

Lorentz, meanwhile, prepared his documentary *The City* for the 1939 World's Fair in New York. A forward-looking history of the American city—from the placid New England village to the smoke-choked industrial town to the newly awakened "Green City" of the future—the film was shot by Ralph Steiner and Willard Van Dyke, with a commentary written by Lewis Mumford and spoken by Group Theater stalwart Morris Carnovsky. Because Thomson was unavailable, who better to score such peculiarly American material than Aaron Copland? Ralph Steiner, not Lorentz, brought Copland onto the project. Copland soon learned how a film score can manipulate an audience that is already responding to visual images. His music for *The City*, at once bounding and energetic, poignant and warm in what has come to be regarded as the composer's unique style, suddenly made him viable as a Hollywood composer.

Aaron Copland had been rejected by Hollywood a couple of years earlier. Intrigued by George Antheil's writings about film composing, Copland allowed his friend, theater producer-critic Harold Clurman, then living in Beverly Hills, to make inquiries on his behalf. Of the music department heads who responded to Clurman, the most interested in Copland was Boris Morross of Paramount, who already had tried to persuade his bosses that contemporary pictures ought to be scored by the best modern composers—e.g., Schoenberg and Stravinsky—to no avail. Although no commission was offered by Morross, and though Antheil warned Copland that Hollywood was a "closed corporation," demanding prior film credits from its job applicants, Copland rode out to Los Angeles in spring 1937 to see for himself.

Like many New Yorkers getting their first look at the Hollywood community, Copland was perplexed by his friends' alienation—"[Clifford Odets and the Group Theater people] are fed up with Hollywood and yearning for the heat and grime of N.Y."—and by the lavishness of their personal properties. Although he felt welcomed by friends and colleagues, Copland discovered that he did need a film credit before anyone would seriously consider hiring him.

The City was that credit. Copland was in Woodstock, New York, working on his Sonata, when he received a telegram from producer Hal Roach asking him to score the film *Of Mice and Men* (1939). It's awfully late for a film composer to be brought onto a picture once principal photography has been completed—and it may be that Hal Roach had approached others first. Of his own talented music men, Leroy Shield had returned to Chicago; the light-fingered, Oklahoma-born Marvin Hatley was all wrong for such a grave story; and Arthur Morton, who had scored *Topper,* had recently gone to work for Alfred Newman. Copland flew to Los Angeles in October 1939 and saw the film; impressed by the quality of the production, he knew he had a lot to work with. Left largely to his own devices by director Lewis Milestone (first cousin to the great Russian violinist Nathan Milstein), Copland avoided the "full-blown symphonic music" that most film composers were encouraged to use, employed natural-sounding instrumentation— flutes and guitar, for instance, instead of piano and strings—and, contrary to industry practice, orchestrated his own work so that it would sound like his, not the orchestrator's. Much of the score sounded shocking to moviegoers' ears in December 1939, when *Of Mice and Men* was released. In particular, the single jagged chord that played under Lennie's crushing of Curly's hand was like nothing they'd heard before in cinemas.

Accepted at last as a film composer, Copland astonished his agent and colleagues by turning down Hollywood's next assignment and returning to New York. Although Copland had a reputation for thrift, for finding grant money and free lodging whenever possible, no amount of money was enough to keep him tethered to Hollywood. In New York he lectured at the Museum of Modern Art about his movie experience and got back to his Sonata.

But Copland returned to Hollywood the following year to score the film version of *Our Town* (1940). Producer Sol Lesser had made the invitation to him. Before traveling back to Hollywood, Copland read the Thornton Wilder play and set down some themes. Aware that this was a very different project from *Of Mice and Men*, Copland avoided percussion and most brass in favor of strings and woodwinds. Much of the score was composed in a drab United Artists office provided by Lesser. Copland's friend Jerome Moross helped orchestrate; Irvin Talbot came over from Paramount to conduct.

With his two very different but equally effective Hollywood scores, Copland had chiseled a crack in the romantic style of film scoring of Korngold and Stothart and their acolytes. Three years later, Copland returned for another project with Lewis Milestone—a Goldwyn production scripted by Lillian Hellman about how noble Russian villagers stood up to the Nazis. *North Star* (1943) was, by every possible reckoning, a disaster—the subject of particularly bitter feuds between Hellman and Milestone. Copland didn't return again to Los Angeles until 1949, to score *The Red Pony* at Republic. But his influence was felt all over town. Hugo Friedhofer made no bones about his worship of Copland, so apparent in his score for *The Best Years of Our Lives* (1946).

The Heiress (1949) was Copland's next assignment. Few Hollywood studio directors have been as intrusive as William Wyler— but then few directors knew as much about picture-making as Wyler, who eschewed whatever was fancy or fashionable for more direct effects. In this adaptation of Ruth and Augustus Goetz's play based on Henry James's *Washington Square*, Copland's music continually probes the character of protagonist Catherine (Olivia De Havilland), getting deeper inside her reactions than an old-fashioned film score would have done.

Just before the picture was released, however, Wyler expressed dissatisfaction with Copland's main title theme. This was a chronic problem with Wyler, who was almost completely deaf in one ear; more often than not, composers were frustrated by his seemingly arbitrary criticisms. Wyler had Nathan Van Cleave, who had orchestrated much of Copland's work, make a new orchestration of "Plaisir d'Amour," the nineteenth-century J. P. E. Martini waltz, which Copland had already woven into the middle of the score, and placed it behind the main title.

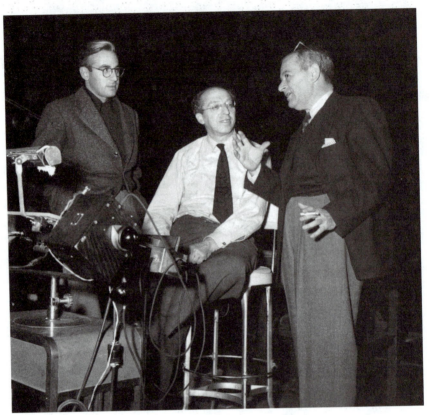

Augustus Goetz, Aaron Copland, and William Wyler on soundstage of *The Heiress* (1949)
Courtesy of Academy of Motion Picture Arts & Sciences and Universal Studios

(If you can't recall "Plaisir d'Amour," remember the melody of the Elvis Presley hit "Can't Help Falling in Love with You.") Copland, disgusted by Wyler's interference, refused to pick up the Academy Award for best scoring of a dramatic picture that he won a few months later. According to the composer, it was the only case of an Oscar-winning score being shorn of its overture.

This experience working on *The Heiress*—despite the great acclaim that greeted the score—made Copland turn his back on Hollywood. The feeling was probably mutual, because Copland's leftist leanings made him a risky hire during the '50s. Screenwriter Helen Deutsch remembered Copland telling Marc Blitzstein, "Marc, we have three strikes against us: one, we're communists; two, we're homosexuals; three, and worst of all, we're composers."

For New York–based Method director Jack Garfein, Copland scored *Something Wild* (1961), starring Garfein's wife, Carroll Baker, as a rape victim rebuilding her life. Copland's chief attraction to the project seems to have been that he could do his work on the East Coast. He never forgave Wyler's meddling. Yet such is the lunacy of moviemaking that Wyler himself requested Copland's services on *The Big Country* (1958). Fortunately for Jerome Moross—perhaps for all of us—Copland declined.

Born in Brooklyn in 1913, Moross was part of the notorious Young Composers' Group that included Arthur Berger, Henry Brant, Israel Citkowitz, Lehman Engel, Vivian Fine, Irwin Heilman, Bernard Herrmann, and Elie Siegmeister. The age limit for admission to the group was twenty-five—the exception being its leader, Copland, who was thirty-two when the group was founded. Miraculously, most of the YCG's regulars ultimately earned their livings through music.

Moross and Bernard Herrmann, two years older, had attended DeWitt Clinton High School, then at Fifty-ninth Street and Tenth Avenue, and discovered Charles Ives together. Ives, unknown to the public, was then in his mid-sixties and became a mentor to the two teenage composers. Moross graduated from New York University at eighteen, then attended Juilliard.

As fiercely intellectual as the other YCG members but quieter, Moross concentrated on ballet and theater scores beginning in 1934. At twenty-one he heard his music for the satirical revue *Parade* performed on Broadway. The dances were choreographed by Robert Alton, who would become an important part of the Freed Unit at MGM; director-to-be Charles Walters was one of Alton's dancers. Moross drew on peculiarly Americana themes for his ballet scores, *Paul Bunyan* (1934) and *Frankie and Johnny* (1938). CBS radio commissioned a piece with the stipulation that it include the "hobo" tune "The Midnight Special"; characteristically, Moross did as instructed, then just as characteristically turned it into *Ramble on a Hobo Theme*. Moross was quiet but he wasn't timid.

Jerome Moross, mid-1930s
Courtesy Susanna Tarjan

In 1936, after a stint as composer at the Chicago Opera, Moross needed money—he always needed money—so he traveled to Hollywood to work as an orchestrator. On his way there he stopped in Albuquerque, where the western vistas stunned him. In 1939 he met Hazel Abrams, who clerked at a Los Angeles bookstore when she wasn't working as a stand-in for actress Sylvia Sidney, and the couple married. Although he was making good money, Moross refused to settle in Los Angeles, returning to New York to present the ballet-opera *Susanna and the Elders* on Broadway in 1940. Subsequently, Moross would commute back to Los Angeles without giving up his New York apartment.

For most of the '40s, Moross was a well-paid Hollywood orchestrator. He worked with Adolph Deutsch on a couple of Warners melo-dramas, with Fred Hollander and Franx Waxman (when Waxman's regular orchestrator Leonid Raab was otherwise occupied), and then most notably with Friedhofer on *The Best Years of Our Lives* (1946) and *Joan of Arc* (1948). Like Friedhofer, Moross had to take below-the-line credits before he got his first scoring assignment: *Close Up* (1948) was an Eagle-Lion programmer written by John Bright and pop music maven Max Wilk. Drawing on some Liszt themes, Moross composed the "Little Mermaid" ballet for the 1952 Goldwyn release *Hans Christian Andersen*—but Frank Loesser, who had written all the songs for the film, lobbied successfully against Moross's credit.

Moross's relationship with Goldwyn was a durable one, and led Sam Goldwyn, Jr., to hire him to score the post-Civil War western *The Proud Rebel* (1958). Moross wove "Shenandoah" through his score as a motif. Ned Washington, everyone's first choice for cowboy movie lyricist since *High Noon,* wrote a lyric, "My Rebel Heart," to Moross's music, but it wasn't recorded.

Proud Rebel anticipated Moross's greatest score, *The Big Country* (1958). After Copland turned down Wyler's offer to score the western, Sam Goldwyn recommended Moross. The result is arguably one of the two or three greatest western movie scores. Most of the orchestrations were by Bernard Mayers, with help from Gil Grau, Sandy Courage, and Conrad Salinger. The nearly symphony-sized orchestra included concertmaster Anatole Kaminsky; guitarist Laurindo Almeida; oboist and frequent composer Gerald Fried; violinist Alfred Lustgarden and cellist Edgar Lustgarden; trumpeter Uan Rasey (whose smoky solos would float through the music in *Chinatown* seventeen years later); pianists Ray Turner, John Crown, and John Williams; and Dominic Frontiere (on accordion!). These were some of the best musicians in Hollywood, and producers Wyler and Gregory Peck were lucky to get them—the industry-changing musicians' strike was only weeks away. An expert male chorus was on hand to record the wordless main title theme, but Moross decided it sounded overblown. Not surpising, the music displeased Wyler, who harangued the composer until he could see the difference the score made during a screening.

Every composer who works in Hollywood gets typed. *The Big*

Country and *The Proud Rebel* got Moross the job of scoring the Panama & Frank western, *The Jayhawkers* (1959), released by Paramount and now remembered for containing what is essentially the theme used for the Universal TV series, *Wagon Train*. Moross didn't realize he was repeating himself until he looked at the *Jayhawkers* music again. Paramount grumbled about legal action, then shrugged it off, figuring they could use a similar favor someday from Universal.

The most majestic of Moross's scores was surely *The Cardinal* (1963). Moross was given the job by Ingo Preminger, Otto's brother and the real music lover of the two. Starring Tom Tryon (before he remade himself as bestselling novelist Thomas Tryon), *The Cardinal* ran nearly three hours, and followed the young prelate as he loved and suffered in Rome, the deep South, Boston, and Vienna. The soundtrack is heavy with churchbells and themes that billow like chasubles, but it's also filled with Moross's unique brand of Americana. Just when the picture threatens to become irretrievably humorless, along comes a bluesy clarinet to recapitulate the gorgeous main theme, or a revue-like number performed by "Bobby" Morse and his Adorabelles. (I'm not making that up.) The main title theme became known as "Stay with Me," with lyrics by Carolyn Leigh added after the film's release.

The Cardinal was Moross's last great film score. He composed music for the odd medieval drama *The War Lord* (1965). Hans Salter was brought in by Universal to score the battle scenes, and the score ended up suffering from a pompous style that Moross and the filmmakers had been trying to avoid. *Rachel, Rachel* (1968), directed by Paul Newman, was a pleasing experience because he could do everything in New York; but in Hollywood the music was mixed down to a hush—you had to strain to hear Moross in it.

Moross worked energetically until his wife, Hazel, died; then he seemed to lose the will to go on. His last big project was a one-act opera, *Sorry, Wrong Number,* based on the play by Lucille Fletcher, the first wife of his longtime friend Bernard Herrmann.

That Bernard Herrmann had friends is, at first blush, curious. Reputed to be the most irascible, caustic, and outspoken of film composers, Herrmann could berate a meek third violinist for playing a B-natural instead of a B-flat, then head upstairs and yell at Darryl Zanuck for some slight he had suffered. Herrmann was an equal-opportunity cur-mudgeon. Even at a tender age, in German class at DeWitt Clinton, Herrmann grabbed the staff paper that the younger Jerome Moross had been composing on, studied the score, then tossed it back. "Dishwater Tchaikovsky!" he pronounced it. When he and Moross were part of the Young Composers' Group, they would listen to their fellow members' compositions, of which Herrmann invariably said, "It stinks!" He was twenty-one at the time.

Bernard Herrmann was born in New York City in June 1911. At thirteen he won a $100 composition prize—a small fortune in 1924. Like Moross, "Benny" Herrmann studied first at New York University, then at Juilliard. At eighteen he conducted his own *Americana* ballet. At twenty-one he began to compose symphonic music for the radio. The following year he was routinely conducting on CBS. He often kicked off his radio concerts playing one of Castelnuovo-Tedesco's Shakespearean overtures; after one broadcast, Toscanini called to praise him. "Young man, that was very good," said the maestro, who soon brought him over for some work at NBC, too. Herrmann also provid-ed the background music for the Columbia Workshop radio plays.

One of the Columbia radio executives was Davidson Taylor, who introduced the young Herrmann to the even younger Orson Welles. Their first collaboration was on the Mercury Theater of the Air's *Macbeth*. According to John Houseman, Welles arrived at the only rehearsal accom-panied by "an elderly gentleman in kilts—with a bagpipe"; in other words, Welles's idea of the perfect music for *Macbeth*. Welles ignored Herrmann's music and said to the bagpiper, "Every time I raise this hand, you come in and play!" Herrmann didn't take this lying down—batons and scripts flew through the air—and Dave Taylor had to play peacemaker.

Welles was only the biggest and most theatrical of Herrmann's antagonists. Houseman reported: "[Herrmann's] relations with his orchestra (which included such world-famous players as Harry Glanz on trumpet, Mitch Miller on oboe) were erratic, to say the least. I remember that one night, after a particularly stormy session, he flung his baton across the studio, dismissed the orchestra, then turned to me, gray with fatigue and fury. 'I've known it all along!' he muttered sav-agely. 'There's a strong fascist element in the woodwinds!'"

Herrmann's activities were hardly confined to radio. In the mid-

'30s he composed the dramatic cantata *Moby Dick,* introduced by Sir John Barbirolli conducting the New York Philharmonic. He seems to have begun his opera *Wuthering Heights* around this time, although it wouldn't be completed for another decade. (Herrmann could quote whole chunks of the Brontës' novels.) His reputation for explosive fury—David Raksin called him "a virtuoso of unspecified anger"—preceded him wherever he went. Houseman maintained that Herrmann's inability "to be civil to the wives of board members," and an ongoing feud with Arthur Judson, who managed the Philharmonic and also served as president of the powerful Columbia Concerts Corporation, "kept him permanently out of symphonic jobs in this country."

Herrmann and Welles understood each other, after a fashion, so it was only natural that Herrmann would join Welles while the latter prepared *Citizen Kane* (1941) at RKO. For a while Herrman bunked with Franz and Alice Waxman. He composed music cues as sequences of the film were completed. Veteran soundman James G. Stewart, then only vaguely aware of Herrmann's fiery reputation, voiced his opinion that one of the music cues wasn't working; the full symphonic thunder of Herrmann's rage poured on Stewart. Decrying his incompetence—in fact Stewart was at least as responsible as Welles was for the magnificent, innovative use of sound in *Citizen Kane*—Herrmann went to fetch Welles. Instead of siding with Herrmann, Welles agreed with Stewart. The music cue in question was redone.

Herrmann never did settle down. But he came to understand why some music works in a scene and some doesn't. And he had Welles's cooperation, for Welles often timed his montages to Herrmann's music rather than the other way around.

The late orchestrator Christopher Palmer deftly analyzed Herrmann's "Theme and Variations," which scores the deteriorating relationship of Kane (Welles) and his first wife in a montage of scenes set against the couple at the breakfast table: "Herrmann accompanies each scene by a mini-variation on a slow waltz theme, the variations becoming increasingly dissonant and less waltzlike as the atmosphere between the two becomes increasingly chilly. The reason for Kane's loss of interest in his wife is, of course, his overweening ambition, and the music tells us when the Kane theme finally appears in the last two variations of the waltz theme turned upside down. In other words, as Kane makes plain where his true interests lie, so the music strips the mask from its features, too."

Needing a fictitious opera as a vehicle for Kane's second wife—or, to be more precise, a "difficult" opera that RKO didn't have to pay for— Herrmann composed an opera called *Salammbo,* after Flaubert's second book. (In *Raising Kane,* Pauline Kael wrote that screenwriter Herman Mankiewicz wanted to use Massenet's 1894 lyric comedy *Thaïs,* which, ironically, had been written for the Sacramento-born soprano Sybil Sanderson, at one time William Randolph Hearst's fiancée. *Thaïs* was scrapped because RKO would have had to pay for it.) Composed deliberately in a late-nineteenth-century, Franco-Oriental style but, as Christopher Palmer pointed out, "incorporating twentieth century touches of harmony and orchestration," Herrmann's recitative and aria provided the musical excerpt that conveyed the soprano's lack of talent. There had, in fact, been two operas based on *Salammbo*—one by the French composer Reyer, first performed in 1890, the other left unfinished by Moussorgsky. The text for Herrmann's *Salammbo* was pieced together by John Houseman, using bits from Racine's *Athalie* and lines from *Phèdre.* "For the film," Palmer wrote, "Herrmann engaged a light soprano [Jean Forward], her best efforts proving so unavailing against the Straussian power of the orchestra as to give the impression that she was floundering in quicksand."

Citizen Kane wasn't wholly completed before Herrmann, intrigued by the medium, accepted another RKO assignment, *All That Money Can Buy* (1941). The story was essentially "The Devil and Daniel Webster"—the film is often referred to, in fact, by the title of the Stephen Vincent Benet story. Employing Herrmann was probably a conscious attempt to exploit some of *Citizen Kane*'s cinematic tricks. Certainly Walter Huston as the Mephistophelean Mr. Scratch is hard to forget. *All That Money Can Buy*'s score, woven through a quilt of New Hampshire folk melodies, is lighter than *Kane*'s, and won Herrmann an Academy Award. Fine as it is, there was a widespread feeling in the film community that the Oscar was really for *Kane.*

Herrmann and Welles were still not finished working together. Herrmann scored *The Magnificent Ambersons* (1942), a fascinating score that was sadly cut along with much of the picture. *Jane Eyre* (1943) was somewhat more complicated. John Houseman and British writer-director

Bernard Herrmann recording music for *All That Money Can Buy* (1941)
Photo by Ernest Bachrach. Courtesy of Academy of Motion Picture Arts & Sciences

Robert Stevenson were paired by David O. Selznick to adapt the Charlotte Brontë novel; when they turned in their working draft, however, they were startled to discover that Selznick had bowed out of the project. But not quite. Turned over to producer William Goetz, the Houseman-Stevenson script was put into pre-production at Twentieth Century-Fox, and Aldous Huxley was brought in to enhance the dialogue. Meanwhile, Selznick, incapable of keeping his mitts off even those projects he had rejected, went to lunch with Orson Welles, who said that

Herrmann was the man they needed for the music. The Mercury Theater had presented its version of *Jane Eyre* four years earlier, with Herrmann's background music. Herrmann's admission to the Twentieth Century-Fox lot introduced him to Alfred Newman, beginning a twenty-five-year friendship between the two thorny composer-conductors.

Then came *Hangover Square* (1945). The "Concerto Macabre" was the high point of this longhaired variation on Jack the Ripper, made spookier by Herrmann's strange sonorities, and by Laird Cregar, who had gone on a crash diet to play the demented pianist. (Cregar died at thirty-eight, immediately after principal photography was completed.)

Herrmann took a break from his Hollywood work in the mid-'40s to return to New York. For a long time Herrmann lived on East Fifty-seventh Street in Manhattan with Lucille Fletcher and their two children. He composed music for Norman Corwin's V-E Day radio special, "On a Note of Triumph" (May 8, 1945). The Johnny Bond Trio sang "Round and Round Hitler's Grave," written by Corwin, Woody Guthrie, Millard Lampell, and Pete Seeger. Hermann distilled his *All That Money Can Buy* score into an orchestral suite, *The Devil and Daniel Webster*. A chunk of *Citizen Kane* became the ballet suite *Welles Raises Kane*. He completed *Wuthering Heights,* which turned out to be way too costly to produce. "The Fantasticks" was a song cycle for four voices and orchestra, and "For the Fallen" was a tribute to the war dead. Away from the movies, Herrmann wasn't idle.

Herrmann returned to Fox to score *Anna and the King of Siam* (1946)—some four years before Rodgers and Hammerstein transformed the story into *The King and I*—then moved on to *The Ghost and Mrs. Muir* (1947). In story terms the romantic fantasy seems far from Herrmann's style, yet much of the score is delightful and sounds downright Hitchcockian, eerie and insolent. Perhaps Herrmann protected his sound by routinely orchestrating his own work (though Twentieth employed the best orchestrators in the business). With *The Ghost and Mrs. Muir*, Herrmann perfected what Christopher Palmer called "the distinctive Herrmann 'sound': the steely spaciousness of his string lines, his evocative use of low woodwind sonorities, which often involve unusual combinations—it is quite common for a Herrmann score to call for two or more English horns, alto and bass flutes and as many as four bass clarinets."

Many moviegoers hold special affection for *The Day the Earth Stood Still* (1951), maybe because it was the first major studio science-fiction movie they saw. Herrmann's score employed the theremin, an electronic instrument developed in Russia by Leon Theremin, whose high-pitched, quavering sound has since become a staple of horror and sci-fi film soundtracks. Film scholar Leonard Leff gave a succinct description of the theremin: standing about as high as an old-fashioned floor radio, "its high-pitched sounds were produced by a player's running his hands over two tuning rods; the closer the hands to the instrument, the more intense the vibrato and the volume of sound." Paul Shure (born 1921), the assistant concertmaster of the Twentieth Century-Fox orchestra and, in his spare time, the Hollywood String Quartet's second violinist, played Herrmann's theremin lines on the soundtrack.

A series of Fox assignments through the mid-'50s threatened to type Herrmann as a master of exotica. *The Snows of Kilimanjaro, White Witch Doctor, Beneath the Twelve Mile Reef,* and *King of the Khyber Rifles* all came within a two-year period. He shared scoring responsibilities with Alfred Newman for the high-profile CinemaScope production of *The Egyptian* (1954), because Zanuck was in a hurry to get it out. *Prince of Players* (1955) was also CinemaScope, and featured Richard Burton as Edwin Booth doing Shakespeare. For Herrmann, this was the period during which he began his most important and productive collaboration, with director Alfred Hitchcock.

Without breaking with Twentieth, Herrmann was hired to score Hitchcock's black comedy *The Trouble with Harry* (1955) for Paramount. Herrmann's unique style was a perfect fit for Hitchcock's wry combination of black humor and suspense. Herrmann subsequently distilled his music into an eighty-page orchestral score, lasting approximately eight minutes, entitled "Portrait of Hitch."

The Man Who Knew Too Much (1956) featured Doris Day singing "Que Será, Será (Whatever Will Be, Will Be)," which became a hit. The picture also contains Herrmann's one film appearance, conducting the London Philharmonic in Arthur Benjamin's "Storm Clouds" cantata, its climax covering the crucial gunshot at Albert Hall.

The Hitchcock-Herrmann collaboration reached its apogee with

Vertigo (1958). Of all Hitchcock's movies, *Vertigo* seems to hold more moviegoers in a vise-like grip. Perhaps it's because, as Hitchcock himself suggested, we see Kim Novak perform what is in effect a striptease in reverse, "forced to make up, not take off." Along with Jimmy Stewart, we observe Novak's doppelganger and try to get beneath her facade; we're guided through sequences entirely without dialog by Herrmann's hypnotic, spiraling music, which provides an emotional base and retains the story's essential mystery.

No Hollywood picture demonstrates more vividly than *Psycho* (1960) the charge that music can inject into a screen image. After viewing his own pre-score cut of the movie, Hitchcock was reportedly unhappy with the film; there was even talk of cutting it into sections for his TV series. But Herrmann asked for time to see what he could develop.

Once having seen the film, it's easy to recall Janet Leigh driving away from jeopardy (and toward her doom); without Herrmann's frantic chords, the sequence would be reduced to Leigh grimacing and occasionally checking her rear-view mirror. And in the notorious shower scene, the stabbing sounds on the soundtrack, with their repeated D-naturals rising and falling in volume, have been likened to psychotic bird-calls: they pierce psychic armor that we didn't know we had.

"Hitchcock very rarely deals with character portrayals," Herrmann said years later, "or has little or no interest in people's emotions, but deals in situations generally that are of a suspenseful nature—his interest in music is in relationship only to how the suspense can be heightened." Viewed without Herrmann's music, *Psycho* would be a curiosity piece—loaded with horrific images, to be sure, but lacking the gripping terror that makes it a classic.

Meanwhile, other projects had called to Herrmann. There had been a televised *Christmas Carol* (December 23, 1954) that starred Fredric March as Scrooge and Basil Rathbone as Jacob Marley. Other TV work followed, including scoring work for *The Twilight Zone, Have Gun Will Travel,* and Hitchcock's television show, which was introduced each week by its creeping Gounod theme. In the year of *Vertigo,* Herrmann also began a long-running collaboration with producer Charles Schneer and visual wizard Ray Harryhausen. *The Seventh Voyage of Sinbad* (1958) was the first of these, but the most characteristic Herrmann score for Schneer may be *The Three Worlds of Gulliver* (1960).

In the mid-1960s, Herrmann scored *The Birds* and *Marnie*—the infamous Tippi Hedren phase of Hitchcock's career. But their collaboration came to a heartbreaking close on *Torn Curtain* (1966). Hitchcock, determined to remain current, wanted music that rocked in a hip, European way. Herrmann turned in a score that was grand and detailed, lush with French horns. Immediately Herrmann was paid off and fired, and British composer John Addison was commissioned to provide what National Public Radio producer Andy Trudeau has called "a non-score."

The greatest of director-composer collaborations was over. Though hurt, and more curmudgeonly than ever, Herrmann continued to speak of Hitchcock as the Master. Herrmann salved his wounds by working on an operatic version of Israel Zangwill's 1894 story *The King of Schnorrers*. (Around 1967, a recording of Herrmann's opera was produced by John Rubinstein.)

In the late '60s Herrmann moved to England with his second wife, where he felt more appreciated as a conductor; for years the Los Angeles music establishment had, he felt, ignored his conducting abilities. Moreover, England was comfortable. He had his collections of first editions—he particularly treasured Henry James and the painter-memoirist James McNeil Whistler, two expatriates who loved life in London—and original music scores, and didn't have to think about what was in the pages of *Variety*.

By then, fortunately, Herrmann had been taken up by a younger generation of filmmakers. François Truffaut brought him on to two Hitchcockian pictures. Hitchcock acolyte Brian DePalma hired him for *Obsession* (1969) and *Sisters* (1973). Summoned back to Los Angeles to view a rough cut of *The Exorcist* (1973), Herrmann was told by director William Friedkin, "I want you to write me a better score than the one you wrote for *Citizen Kane*." "Then you should have made a better movie than *Citizen Kane*," Herrmann replied, and departed. (Lalo Schifrin was subsequently hired to score *The Exorcist*, but Friedkin condemned Schifrin's work as "big, loud, scary, wall-to-wall accent." Instead a score was assembled from what Hugo Friedhofer referred to as "Polish avant-garde," with Mike Oldfield's "Tubular Bells" used as a central theme.)

Martin Scorcese hired Herrmann to compose what turned out to be his valedictory score, for *Taxi Driver* (1976). Arriving in Los

Angeles, the ailing Herrmann was sixty-four but appeared twenty years older. Yet he managed to gather his energies to produce a beautiful musical summing-up: from the percussive, banging-on-the-door opening, to the bluesy closing theme played by saxophonist Ronny Lang that drifts through the cosmetic New York night. Herrmann died on Christmas Eve 1975, the night he completed *Taxi Driver*'s recording, almost thirty-five years after *Citizen Kane*.

Herrmann was deeply mourned. This was a man who, when invited by his friend Franz Waxman to hear him conduct Beethoven's *Eroica*, snapped, "Who's interested in your idea of the *Eroica*?" Beneath the gruff exterior, there may even have been a gruff interior—but beneath that was a delicate musician whose sensibilities are still evident in his movies and recordings.

"For all of his facade as a curmudgeon, he was really a cuddly teddy bear," said David Benesty, who sang the role of Tiny Tim in Herrmann's '50s TV version of *A Christmas Carol* and became reacquainted with the composer in the 1960s. "He had a wonderful, sensitive quality." Herrmann spoke with growly New York diction—he said *wid* for *with*, and his *r*s tended to vanish inside a sentence—that made him sound like an irked Henry Miller. He never did suffer fools, gladly or otherwise.

◦   ◦   ◦

Virgil Thomson was interested in scoring Pare Lorentz's 1940 movie, *The Fight for Life*, which documented birth in a Chicago hospital. But Lorentz assigned the score to Louis Gruenberg, who also tried Hollywood and maintained a significant presence there for a dozen years. So Thomson went to France for a while. With several new compositions completed, he returned to New York and accepted the *Herald Tribune*'s offer to write a music column, for which he was well paid to voice his opinion.

Thomson didn't give up on film, however. In 1948 the already legendary documentary filmmaker Robert Flaherty had him score his *Louisiana Story* (1948). Accompanying images of oil-rigging and Cajun life on the river, the score pumped *La Mer*-like orchestral color into indigenous folk tunes. Sponsored by Standard Oil, *Louisiana Story* is among the most listenable, as well as watchable, "industrials"—a documentary that purports to show how business is conducted and, in the process, vividly depicts a way of life. The score was nominated for an Academy Award but failed to win it. Thomson was annoyed by the explanation given by someone in a Hollywood music department: the Philadelphia Orchestra's recording of his music had been "unprofessional"—i.e., it hadn't been sweetened in the standard movie music way by heightening the sound of the first violin. "Hollywood," said Thomson, who had to content himself with the Pulitzer Prize, the only one yet awarded for a film score.

With Thomson and Copland as examples, serious younger composers no longer disdained film work. After 1942, when he was appointed director of music for the Office of War Information, Oklahoma music teacher Gail Kubik (born 1914) scored the documentaries *The World War* and *Air Pattern Pacific*. He provided the music for William Wyler's documentary *Memphis Belle* (1944), about the famous B-17's mission over Germany. This led, years later, to Kubik's commission to score Wyler's 1955 *Desperate Hours,* an underrated score that the composer subsequently rewrote as "Scenario for Orchestra."

Robert McBride (born 1912), was steeped in the Southwestern and Mexican music of his Tucson boyhood when he arrived in New York and began to compose for Martha Graham. In the late '30s, McBride wrote much of the music for the *March of Time* newsreels, the two-reelers underwritten by *Time* magazine that lasted until television co-opted its brand of quick-cutting visual reportage and barking narrations.

Another Martha Graham composer, Alex North, also initially worked on documentaries and industrials. North came relatively late to Hollywood—he was 40—but changed the rules anyway. Though a native Pennsylvanian rather than New Yorker, Alex North came out of the same Manhattan-educated line as Copland, Moross, and Herrmann. Born December 4, 1910, North was one of four sons of a Russian immigrant blacksmith. His eldest brother taught him piano, and his playing eventually brought him to the Curtis Institute, and then, when he was twenty-one, to the Juilliard School in New York.

Given his age and geography, North could easily have been a

member of the Young Composers' Group. Modern dance and theater were his compositional workshops. In November 1935, North and Jerome Moross orchestrated and played the two piano parts of Hanns Eisler's music for Brecht's *Mother* (an early version of *Mother Courage*); out of North's work came his "Negro" cantata that he also titled "Mother." (The Russian Revolution and the blues were items in North's bag of tricks.) Between 1935 and 1939, North composed for modern-dance choreographers Martha Graham, Hanya Holm, and Agnes de Mille. In 1939 he went to Mexico with former Graham dancer Anna Sokolow, with whom he was involved, and her troupe; when he returned to America, he seemed fully formed as a composer. Writing in *Music in America*, Elie Siegmeister praised North by saying that he was already attempting to "bring jazz and classical music together."

In 1941 North married Sherle Hartt. Within months he was in the Army, and was eventually promoted to captain. A civilian again, he received two important commissions in 1946—one from Benny Goodman, for whom he wrote "Revue for Clarinet and Orchestra" (Goodman soloed, Leonard Bernstein conducted), another from the *Herald Tribune*, to collaborate with former folk singer Millard Lampell on a cantata based on the Nuremberg Trials. By 1948 North had two children and had won a Guggenheim Fellowship, a meaningless award to Hollywood but one that enabled him to compose what he wanted to in New York. At this point North could have gone on like his idol of the moment, the Mexican composer Silvestre Revueltas, composing for the concert hall and the theater. But then came a play that changed many lives, including North's.

Death of a Salesman opened on Broadway on February 10, 1949, with incidental music by North. Director Elia Kazan had already established himself in Hollywood: Alfred Newman had scored Kazan's first movie, *A Tree Grows in Brooklyn*, as well as *Gentleman's Agreement* and *Pinky* (a fine score); David Buttolph had handled Kazan's quasi-documentary thriller *Boomerang*, and Herbert Stothart scored the dreary *Sea of Grass*. These were all studio-controlled assignments. For *A Streetcar Named Desire* (1951), financed by Warners, Kazan had more autonomy, and he engaged North because of his work on *Death of a Salesman*. Composing in a driving, jazz idiom that he had shaped for years, North changed Hollywood film scoring with *Streetcar*. He got considerable help from veteran orchestrator Maurice DePackh. That same year it seemed a given that North would also score the film version of *Death of a Salesman*. But the movie was so clumsy and depressing that its impact on the screen was minimal.

Warners, impressed by North though also a bit intimidated—some of his music had been censored for being too "carnal"—negotiated with him to score the period actioner *Distant Drums*. North didn't care for the material—in 1840, stolid soldier Gary Cooper stages a daring raid on a Seminole fort to rescue his men—and Warners tried to strong-arm him into accepting an insultingly low fee. North hadn't yet learned how to fight Hollywood-style. "I used to say to Alex North, 'That's your problem, kiddo, you're not arrogant enough,'" David Raksin said. When negotiations with Warners broke down, Elia Kazan wrote sympathetically: "Dear Alex, Warner Brothers are Warner Brothers. Can I say less!!??? They should be allowed to swim in their own shit and choke to death on it. You should never do pictures you despise—that's the long and short of it. . . ." Max Steiner, arrogant enough and not inexpensive, eventually wrote the *Distant Drums* score.

But North learned quickly. He worked with Kazan again on *Viva Zapata!* With one foot semi-permanently planted at Twentieth Century-Fox, he roamed through several studios during the '50s. With a penchant for what Murray Spivack called "freak instruments," he was also versatile. He could write boppy music for *Go Man Go*, the story of the Harlem Globetrotters, then quickly pivot and score *Desiree*. He got rich from the royalties on "Unchained Melody," written for the prison picture *Unchained* (1955). After that the steamy Southern gothic—*The Rose Tattoo* (1955), *The Long Hot Summer* (1958), and *The Sound and the Fury* (1959)—became his bailiwick.

In April 1959, North signed to compose the score for *Spartacus*, with Kirk Douglas producing and starring, and young director Stanley Kubrick replacing the veteran Anthony Mann. North was paid $25,000 for the score, which turned out to be among the most-beloved of all movie music. For years North received mail describing the effect the music had on his correspondents. The beautiful, angular "Love Theme" has been widely recorded, notably by jazz artists Yusef Lateef and Bill Evans (overdubbing himself on three pianos).

The score for *The Misfits* (1961) was well reviewed. But North was still getting queries about *Streetcar*, composed a decade earlier. It was the combination of *Streetcar*'s notoriety and *Spartacus*'s pre-Christian Roman setting that got North his biggest job, *Cleopatra*.

In August 1961, producer Walter Wanger sent North a welcome-aboard letter, and included "lyrics to a song that was supposed to have been sung by Caesar's troops":

Men of Rome, keep close your consorts,
Here's a bold adulterer.
Gold in Gaul you spent in dalliance,
Which you borrowed here in Rome.

By October 13 North had completed several musical pieces, including an imitation of a Gregorian chant and his own "very lush . . . romantic theme." For entertainment purposes within the movie, North, working off his research of the period, requested: eight double-reed pipes (flutes), four parallel flutes and four angular flutes; two harps, one portable shoulder harp, one large floor harp; one long-necked lute; three percussionists playing cylindrical or barrel-shaped drums, crotoles (finger cymbals), bells, tambourines, and sistra (metallic frames that suspend jingling rods and loops); and, "if possible," artificial hand- and foot-clappers made of bone or ivory. In the Los Angeles of 1961 there wasn't a huge call for instruments like these; but many were found and duly rented. (A rental contract from Drum City, on Santa Monica Boulevard, ran to three pages of instruments alone.)

North bickered frequently with director Joseph Mankiewicz, and he couldn't negotiate a soundtrack album with the studio to his satisfaction. Ted Cain, handling business affairs for the Twentieth Century-Fox music department, summarily canceled North's contract more than a year after he had begun work on the project. North's agent, Nat Goldstone, wrote in frustration to Richard Zanuck to intercede. With Alfred Newman absent from the music department, the negotiations dragged on. Either through Zanuck or Cain, North was permitted to complete his work.

Nearly five years in the making, including a year and a half of North's life, *Cleopatra* was gleefully excoriated when it was released in 1963. Mankiewicz, probably unsuited to the project from the outset, had said he was aiming above "the *Taras Bulba* crowd," suggesting character rather than grandiosity. It didn't come out that way. "All is monumental—but the people are not," Judith Crist wrote. "The mountain of notoriety has produced a mouse."

By virtue of his *Cleopatra* employment, however, North was able to command astronomical fees for the rest of his career. During the next twenty years he composed for movies, his most important score was probably for Mike Nichols's adaptation of *Who's Afraid of Virginia Woolf?* (1966). North introduced the picture with a harpsichord and woodwinds that nuzzled one another, surprising moviegoers who were expecting the old musical fireworks, particularly in a movie about embattled, hard-drinking spouses.

In a letter to North, composer Robert Emmett Dolan gave a dead-on analysis of the *Virginia Woolf* score. In *The Heiress*, Aaron Copland didn't cite or quote music of the period so much as provide his impression of the period, using contemporary dissonances to underline conflict; in *Virginia Woolf*, North faced the reverse problem. His solution was to compose a glittering quasi-baroque theme to counterpoint the characters' troubles and suggest that they really were meant for each other.

Inevitably, television offers proved inviting. In 1965 North provided music for the TV series *The Long Hot Summer*—he had, after all, scored the movie—with Lionel Newman conducting each week. As independent as he had become, like all movie music men, North occasionally had the humbling experience of being reminded that he was only the composer. His entire score for *2001: A Space Odyssey* was thrown out and replaced by music by the Strausses, Richard and Johann, and by Khachaturian.

North remarried in 1972. He and his second wife, Annemarie Hoellger, had a son, Dylan. An Emmy for the 1976–77 miniseries *Rich Man, Poor Man* was a welcome award—he had never won an Oscar. That was rectified a decade later when the Academy of Motion Pictures Arts and Sciences presented North with a 1985 honorary Oscar, the first ever presented to a composer, "in recognition of his brilliant artistry in the creation of memorable music for a host of distinguished motion pictures." That same year North's work in *Prizzi's Honor* showed that he could at seventy-five still convey musical wit and depth. Between them, North and the film's even older director John Huston gave the lie to the shibboleth that Hollywood is only for the very young.

.   .   .

On April 2, 1940, the New York *Herald Tribune* announced: "Broadcast Music thinks it has a real find in Mr. [Ernest] Gold, an eighteen-year-old Viennese refugee." Three years earlier in Vienna, Gold had become smitten by Max Steiner's music for *Garden of Allah*. Within another year the Anschluss had forced his family to flee Austria for New York. The *Herald Tribune* article promoted Gold's song "Here in the Velvet Night" (lyrics by Gold's manager, Don McCray), the first song placed in BMI's song catalog in its bid to compete with ASCAP. Gold's "Practice Makes Perfect" had won a BMI song competition, and that, too, was getting a lot of airplay, along with public-domain songs such as "Jeannie with the Light Brown Hair" and a lot of Latin music, because radio station owners were boycotting all ASCAP material.

In its war with ASCAP, BMI did a lot of good for Gold. At twenty, he was able to get some of his concert pieces, including his precocious *Pan American Symphony*, performed. But these were, for the most part, negatively reviewed—one piano concerto was dismissed as "movie music." When Gold moved to Los Angeles in 1945, he was interviewed by Columbia music head Morris Stoloff, who took a look at the concerto and laughed—it *was* movie music, an unabashed appeal to listeners' emotions. Stoloff put him to work scoring *Girl of the Limberlost* (1945). Later, Gold took minor assignments at Universal, RKO, and Republic. Slender and spectacled, with a dimpled chin sometimes obscured by a goatee, Gold looked every inch the bright young composer. He studied with George Antheil, who still published widely but again accepted scoring assignments. Through Antheil, Gold would eventually break into the front rank of film composers.

In 1949 Gold became engaged to a young singer named Marni McEathron, known professionally as Marni Nixon. Only two years out of L.A.'s Dorsey High School, Marni Nixon was attending University of Southern California and already working in opera and motion pictures. Nixon sang Gold's songs in and around Los Angeles. They were married in spring 1950 and began a family, producing two children, Andrew and Martha, over the next four years.

In the early '50s Gold was relegated to assignments on B pictures.

The 1953 *Jennifer*, starring the usually interesting Ida Lupino, was musically memorable for the Matt Dennis–Earl Brent song "Angel Eyes." Meanwhile, Gold was frustrated in his concert career by repeated rejections from a Los Angeles–based conductor (unnamed by him in correspondence, but probably Alfred Wallenstein). Still feeling his way around the seemingly lawless entertainment business, he served as musical director for Kathryn Grayson's 1954 Las Vegas act. It was money, and it got him out of town.

Dejected by his Hollywood experiences, Gold took his family to New York, where he hoped to be taken more seriously. In an April 1954 letter to *Los Angeles Times* music columnist Mildred Norton, Gold wrote

> After nearly ten years in Los Angeles, during which time I wrote practically only chamber music (for obvious reasons), I have decided to follow the example of no less than *fourteen* (14!) musician friends of mine, and put 3000 miles between the City of Angels and myself. I'm returning only occasionally for picture scores—like many other self-respecting composers.

Gold seemed to want approbation from classical musicians and critics without burning his bridges to Hollywood. Who could blame him?

At the same time, Gold's wife, Marni Nixon, was becoming known to the film studios for her chirpy, ultra-clear voice. Nixon had already dubbed Margaret O'Brien's brief singing in Joe Pasternak's syrupy *Big City* (1948). She also sang in movies as a member of the Roger Wagner Chorale, perhaps the most illustrious classical singing group based in Los Angeles. (Marilyn Horne was a member; Salli Terri sang and arranged.)

Gold returned to Los Angeles when Ingo Preminger hired him to orchestrate George Antheil's music for the medical melodrama *Not as a Stranger* (1955). Although this was orchestrating, not composing, it was work for his old mentor Antheil and a high step up—in production values, if not story quality—from the B pictures he had done earlier. Sidney Cutner pitched in on the orchestrations for the Stanley Kramer production. Paul Sawtell was contracted to conduct the soundtrack.

Bobby Helfer, later of MCA music, managed the orchestra, which consisted of such world-class musicians as violinist Anatole Kaminsky and flautists Martin and Sylvia Ruderman. The soundtrack was recorded at the Goldwyn Studios in Hollywood.

Not as a Stranger made Gold viable as an "A" music man—as an orchestrator, at least, if not necessarily as a composer. Meanwhile, Marni Nixon grabbed a plum job ghosting for Deborah Kerr's vocals in the screen version of *The King and I* (1956). Gold accepted another orchestrating asignment from Antheil, who was scoring Kramer's *The Pride and the Passion*. At the same time he composed his own jazzy score for *Man on the Prowl* (1956), played by the Los Angeles Philharmonic and the local concert pianist John Crown and the Twentieth Century-Fox composer-pianist Lou Maury. Gold had written in a jazz idiom before—for *Man Crazy* (1952) and for *Affair in Havana* (1957; John Cassavetes as a composer suffering through an illicit romance; astonishingly, Burton Lane is credited as screenwriter). For Billy Wilder's *Witness for the Prosecution* (1957), Gold conducted Matty Malneck's score, then took on more scoring work himself for Warners' *Too Much Too Soon* (1958), based on Diana Barrymore's chest-beating memoir.

George Antheil became too sick to handle the next Kramer picture, *The Defiant Ones,* so the assignment went to Gold. Although he had carte blanche, Gold shrewdly used jarring rock 'n' roll, initially heard as source music from a portable radio, to accompany the posse chasing shackled prisoners Sidney Poitier and Tony Curtis.

By the time Antheil died in New York in February 1959, Gold and Marni Nixon were at the center of musical activity in Hollywood. Though still frustrated by the serious music scene there, Gold had proved that he could handle just about anything—even jazz. Kramer signed him to score his most pretentious project to date, *On the Beach* (1959). At least Gold's score is somewhat more restrained than the self-important storytelling. Some of the musicians on the soundtrack were Bob Bain (guitar), Benny Carter (tenor sax), Shelly Manne (drums), Red Mitchell (bass), Gus Bivona (clarinet), who had played for many years with the MGM orchestra, and pianist Johnny (John) Williams, then twenty-seven and just beginning to hit his stride as a jazz orchestrator. In addition to these sterling jazzmen, Gold was given use of a sixty-five-piece orchestra, which whirled and wept its way through the traditional Australian favorite, "Waltzing Matilda."

Gold handled the music for Kramer's next picture, *Inherit the Wind.* Then came Otto Preminger's *Exodus* (1960), about the establishment of Israel as an independent state. This wasn't a Kramer project but, given its scope and its thundering self-importance, might as well have been. The dusty epic had just enough star-power to bring in large audiences. Gold gave the picture everything he had, finally winning an Academy Award for the score.

Exodus's title tune hit the top of the charts in Ferrante & Teicher's dual piano rendition. Paul Francis Webster, then trailing only Ned Washington and Johnny Mercer as the movies' reigning roving lyricist, was asked by Chappell Music to supply words. When Webster was told that Preminger had to okay the lyrics, he walked away. In a curious business twist, Chappell got usable lyrics from Pat Boone, who had enjoyed huge hit recordings singing Webster's lyrics to "April Love" and "Friendly Persuasion." Boone's Dot recording didn't go platinum, as Ferrante & Teicher's did, but the song was very popular.

Gold returned to work for Kramer for another self-important film, *Judgment at Nuremberg* (1961). More interesting was *Pressure Point* (1962), produced by Kramer but directed by let's-try-anything Hubert Cornfield. The film is about a lizardy white racist, portrayed by Bobby Darin, baiting psychiatrist Sidney Poitier. Gold used a cembalet, which mimics the sound of a harpsichord, as well as stereo harp and electronic violin for *Pressure Point's* jarring score. *A Child Is Waiting* was the next Kramer project, followed by the most expensive comedy made up to that date, *It's a Mad Mad Mad Mad World.* The assignment seemed to affirm Gold's good fortune. Marni Nixon had just dubbed for Natalie Wood in *West Side Story* and would soon dub Audrey Hepburn in *My Fair Lady.* A third child, Melani, was born to Nixon and Gold in September 1962.

A three-hour-plus comedy, *Mad World* required a lot of notes. The 280-bar title theme was surely the longest composed up to that point. The score was as pushy and frenetic as the comedy stars—Milton Berle, Phil Silvers, Sid Caesar, Buddy Hackett, Terry-Thomas—who run through this marathon treasure hunt. In an odd but commercially successful marriage of music and artist, the soundtrack was re-recorded by Arthur Fiedler and the Boston Pops.

Then came *Ship of Fools* (1965). Like most Kramer pictures, it had ambitions way beyond its reach. But *Ship of Fools* may be Gold's best score. It contains a shimmering main theme, and three original songs with German lyrics by actor-writer Jack Lloyd (born 1922 in Duisburg, Germany). John Simon, writing about *Ship of Fools,* said that the "score unremittingly fills your nostrils with acrid exhalations"—but the music is telling and lovely where the script is not. Much of it sounds as if Gold was drawing on wisps of half-remembered melodies from his Vienna childhood.

The Academy ignored Gold's contribution to *Ship of Fools.* After that, things slowed down for him, as well as for Kramer. Frank DeVol, master of domestic/comic jingle music, scored Kramer's *Guess Who's Coming to Dinner?* (Gold should have got down on his hand and knees to thank him.) In 1968 there was another Kramer assignment for Gold, the misconceived *Secret of Santa Vittoria,* earning Gold the best score nomination he'd deserved for *Ship of Fools.*

There the collaboration took a ten-year break. Kramer took on the youth generation in *R.P.M.* (*Revolutions Per Minute,* 1971) and *Bless the Beasts and Children.* For these, he hired a younger team, Perry Botkin, Jr., and Barry DeVorzon. Botkin had grown up in the Hollywood music scene, learning guitar at his father's knee, while DeVorzon came out of Brill Building rock 'n' roll songwriting of the late '50s. (In the mid-'60s, DeVorzon produced the hits "Never My Love" and "Along Comes Mary" for The Association. They were the kind of tuneful, unthreatening rock tunes that Establishment Hollywood could latch onto.)

Meanwhile, Gold's life was changing. By 1972, Gold and Marni Nixon were divorced. It was rumored that, as part of their settlement, Gold had turned over to Nixon all of his rights to the *Exodus* theme. Nixon moved to Seattle to sing with the Seattle Opera. Their son, Andrew, still in his early twenties, was becoming one of the most versatile session guitarists in Los Angeles.

There was one last Gold-Kramer collaboration, *The Runner Stumbles* (1979), that did little to help either of them. Before Gold turned sixty he was hauled onto a pedestal as a grand old man of movie music. He was even honored with a star on Hollywood Boulevard's Walk of Fame—the first composer to receive such recognition. Yet one suspects that Gold hungered for the kind of peer approval that didn't come out of awards or box-office grosses.

◦   ◦   ◦

Elmer Bernstein appears to have had considerably less ambivalence about his livelihood. The son of Russian and Austrian immigrants, Elmer Bernstein was born in New York one year after Ernest Gold. His film career began a few years later than Gold's—which probably helped, in the long run, to get his concert hall aspirations out of his system. At this writing he still composes. Along with John Williams and Jerry Goldsmith, Bernstein is one of three film-scoring elders who have managed to turn out interesting work for a wide spectrum of projects, year after year.

While Bernstein was attending Juilliard on scholarship in the late '30s, Aaron Copland introduced him to composer-teachers Israel Citkowitz, Roger Sessions, and Stefan Wolpe, who taught him about composing and arranging. Bernstein worked briefly as a concert pianist and then as a radio composer. He served in the Air Force during World War II, wrote shows there, and married in 1946. A solo piano recital at Town Hall in 1950 was his final New York appearance before Sidney Buchman and Buddy Adler persuaded him to come to Hollywood—specifically to Columbia Pictures. Bernstein was set up in an office next to George Duning, Columbia's durable house composer, and the brilliant orchestrator Arthur Morton.

Bernstein participated in only two Columbia projects before the work dried up: *Saturday's Hero* (1951), a Buchman production, and racetrack melodrama *Boots Malone* (1952). By the time Bernstein had scored them he found himself, like writer Lampell, blacklisted—or graylisted, because he was still too green to have established himself in Hollywood. The McCarthy blacklist was already sweeping through the industry.

Columbia President Harry Cohn had long resisted the fear of employing people named by the House Un-American Activities Committee (HUAC) as Communists, but several incidents burned him. Columbia contract player Larry Parks, who had made a lot of money for the studio with his impersonation of Al Jolson, was pressured into naming names or going to jail; his career was effectively finished. Cohn advised his writer-director Robert Rossen to cooperate with HUAC, but Rossen refused to name names, repeatedly invoking the Fifth Amendment, and he was released from his contract. Most devastating to Cohn was the loss of Sidney Buchman, who had been Bernstein's champion at the studio. Determined to keep Cohn out of the troubling proceedings, Buchman not only refused to name names but refused to cite the Fifth. "It is repugnant for an American to inform," Buchman said. After some legal wrangling, Buchman was fined $150 for contempt and given a one-year suspended sentence. Cohn stayed away while Buchman cleaned out his desk. Bernstein, whose leftist sympathies were known around Columbia, had to go too.

At RKO Bernstein scored *Sudden Fear* (1952), a Joan Crawford suspenser. He was particularly proud of some swank source music that he tagged "Hysteria"; emanating from a radio, the music pours out like shells from a Tommygun and hints at his jazz work to come. But it was as if Bernstein were starting all over. The best assignments he could get were pictures like *Cat Women on the Moon* (1953), a 3-D black-and-white howler, produced by Three Dimensional Films; and two quickies for Republic pictures—*Make Haste to Live* (1954), a thriller about the sudden reappearance of a publisher's dead husband, and *The Eternal Sea* (1955), with the craggy Sterling Hayden as aircraft carrier captain John Hoskins. Pictures like these were considered "programmers"—second features tacked onto the A product to make a double bill—and unlikely to win Bernstein's music much attention. It was actually a step up when he served as Agnes de Mille's rehearsal pianist on the film version of *Oklahoma!*

By now Bernstein's graylisted status was fading; at least he had shown that he was employable. Over at Paramount, Danny Kaye was making what would prove to be his greatest picture, *The Court Jester* (1955). The music director was Vic Schoen, a dance-band leader who really knew more about making records than about film scoring. The musical muscle on the project, however, was Danny Kaye's wife, Sylvia Fine. The gatekeeper of Kaye's musical numbers in virtually all of his pictures, Fine was especially adept at creating his inimitable, express-train patter. On *The Court Jester,* Fine had the lyric-writing help of Sammy Cahn—their cowritten credit sequence of Kaye performing

"Life Could Not Better Be" is among the screen's musical delights—but she needed musical help as well. Paramount music head Roy Fjastaad asked Bernstein to lend a hand. For six weeks, Bernstein worked uncredited on the score, tying up half a dozen disparate comic and romantic themes.

Then came a call from Agnes de Mille's uncle, epic film producer Cecil B.

Bernstein was initially assigned to sprinkle songs and dances around Victor Young's score for *The Ten Commandments*. But Young, de Mille's usual composer, was ailing after an enervating Broadway experience, so Bernstein composed the entire score. The job placed him back on producers' first list of composers.

Even before *The Ten Commandments* was released, Bernstein moved on to *The Man with the Golden Arm* (1955). Much of the notorious jazz score was arranged by Shorty Rogers who, along with drummer Shelly Manne, appeared as himself in the picture. Bernstein's work on *Sweet Smell of Success* (1957) isn't so overtly percussive—and the picture itself is much better. Of the scores that followed in the next decade, *The Magnificent Seven* (1960) solidified Bernstein's "A" ranking—it followed Moross's *Big Country* score as a model of "western" music, and in the process made Bernstein rich when Philip Morris used the main-title theme for its Marlboro commercials. *Walk on the Wild Side* (1962) was notable for Saul Bass's striking title sequence featuring silhouetted cats, accompanied by the music (according to Christopher Palmer) "padding and prowling (double bass solo), stalking and finally scrapping (big brassy flare-up at the end)." *To Kill a Mockingbird* (1962) is many listeners' favorite Bernstein score, quietly evocative of humid nights and fireflies. "I decided to focus on the kind of particular and peculiar magic that is the imaginative world of the child," Bernstein said. "Simplicity was the keynote."

In the early '60s, the frenzy for an exploitable title song had not yet abated. Because of his big, jazzy scores, Bernstein wasn't immediately thought of as a great melodist. But title themes for *Love with the Proper Stranger* (1963; Jack Jones sang Johnny Mercer's lyrics on the soundtrack) and *Baby, the Rain Must Fall* (1964; Glenn Yarborough had the hit recording) proved that Bernstein could handle those demands if he had to.

For *The Great Escape* (1964), Bernstein resurrected a theme he'd first conceived as a teenager, a jaunty, insolent march, primed by tubas and clarinets, that's more comic than heroic. (It's first cousin to the "Colonel Bogey" march.) *The World of Henry Orient* (1965) was scored for director George Roy Hill, a fine amateur musician in his own right, but the music that most moviegoers remember from it is the deliberately awful piano concerto, composed by Kenneth Lauber, that Henry Orient (Peter Sellers) pounds away at. *Thoroughly Modern Millie* (1967), Bernstein's next score for Hill, won him an Academy Award, but an entire platoon of musical talent also worked on the film: André Previn scored the musical numbers; Cahn and Van Heusen wrote the "Tapioca" dance number and the title song.

Between these two films came my own favorite Bernstein score, *Hawaii* (1966; based on the James Michener novel). Bernstein did some research and discovered that nineteenth-century Hawaii "had no melodic instruments, except for a little nose flute that produced about three notes. They had a lot of percussion instruments like gourds and small drums, and they had chants, basic two-or-three note chants rocking back and forth between these notes." With such limited resources, Bernstein was forced to come up with sweeping melodies that were exotic and Ravelian (cf. *Daphnis et Chloe*) in texture. The powerful orchestrations were by Leo Shuken and Jack Hayes.

During the 1960s Bernstein divorced and then married for a second time. His children, particularly his son Peter and daughter Emilie, began to show a special interest in his work. (Eventually they each served an apprenticeship orchestrating his compositions.) There was also plenty of television work. *Johnny Staccato* (featuring John Cassavetes as a jazz musician) and *The Big Valley* were just two out of many series that Bernstein worked on. The television music some of us remember best, however, is his elegiac theme to the documentary series *Hollywood and the Stars*. It evoked a "feeling of nostalgia for all the lost glamour and romance" of a bygone era and spawned countless imitations, none as succinct as Bernstein's.

In the early '70s, Bernstein, then president of the Composers and Lyricists Guild (formerly the Screen Composers' Association), spearheaded the members' strugggle to retain greater copyright percentages for their works. (Henry Mancini was routinely given a better share, but few composers had his leverage.) A class-action suit wasn't settled until 1979. Meantime, Bernstein recorded film scores—his own and other composers'—on his Film Music Collection series, modeled on the RCA series begun by George Korngold and Charles Gerhardt. And no film composer, including the tireless George Antheil and the articulate David Raksin, has done more to promote understanding of the profession. Bernstein's journal *Filmmusic Notebook,* which routinely included long interviews with other composers, was published during the '70s.

Near the end of the decade Bernstein scored a series of comedies, beginning with *National Lampoon's Animal House* (1978), *Airplane!* (1980), and in 1981 *Heavy Metal's* experimental use of the Ondes Martenot, the eerie-sounding electronic instrument (developed by Maurice Martenot and musical cousin to the theremin). *Trading Places* (1983) and *Ghostbusters* (1984) followed, although much of Bernstein's score for *Ghostbusters* was snuffed to make room for Ray Parker, Jr.'s hit title song.

Although it's well beyond the timeframe of this book, Bernstein's score for *My Left Foot* (1990), the story of writer Christy Brown's early years fighting cerebral palsy, is worth mentioning. In scoring the film, Bernstein made good on a promise he'd made twenty years earlier in Dublin to Noel Pearson. "When you do get to produce a movie," he'd said then to Pearson, the director of the Abbey Theater, "I'll do the score for you for nothing." Pearson did—and so did Bernstein. Like Christy Brown, Bernstein's music for *My Left Foot* struggles awkwardly to find the right chord; once found, the music resolves itself with exhilaration. Again he employed the Ondes Martenot, played by Cynthia Millar, a favorite Bernstein musician.

Two years later, Bernstein adapted Bernard Herrmann's score from the 1962 *Cape Fear* for Martin Scorsese's remake. At seventy, the composer who had been guided as a young man by Aaron Copland was reworking music by a Copland disciple of a previous generation.

o   o   o

"Myself," Virgil Thomson wrote, "till I was twenty-five or six, I had a glutton's appetite for sound. After that, my need was more for giving out than taking in." From Copland to Elmer Bernstein, these men began "giving out" by composing to documentary film images, theater pieces or ballet, before making their way to Hollywood. Ernest Gold's Austrian childhood notwithstanding, theirs has been a distinctly American music—at times Ivesian, at other times jazzy and propulsive, occasionally banal and almost never dull.

FIVE

WORK LIKE A SOUL INSPIRED

FRED ASTAIRE AND THE
GREAT SONGWRITERS

In 1932, when Adele Astaire left show business to marry Charles Cavendish, the young British peer she had captivated along with the rest of London, her brother, Fred, had to rethink his career. Fred Astaire's initial attempt to go out on his own was in the New York stage production of Cole Porter's *Gay Divorce*. Critics missed Adele; one critic suggested Fred seemed so uncomfortable that he kept glancing toward the wings, hoping his sister might be there.

This is part of the power of art: to transform what was seen as a limitation—a man suddenly alone—into an asset. Fred Astaire, alone or partnered, was probably the movies' greatest dancer; he was also their greatest singer. More than anyone else, including Bing Crosby, Astaire introduced the best songs by the best writers, and delivered them with an easy, direct connection to the audience that, in turn, made the writers write their best.

Such apparent ease doesn't come easily, of course. A great deal of work went into the transformation of Frederick Austerlitz, Jr., brewer's son, to Fred Astaire, impeccably dressed song-and-dance man gliding down the avenue.

By the age of six, Fred was accompanying his sister to dance school in their native Omaha. Adele soon danced her way past her teachers. In 1905, needing money but also determined to provide Adele with opportunities unavailable in Omaha, Mrs. Austerlitz took the children to New York. Later that year Fred and Adele Austerlitz—though younger, the boy was billed first in theatrical tradition—appeared on the vaudeville circuit as miniature newlyweds. Photographs of the period show little Fred in what would become his signature garb: top hat, white tie, and tails. During their first or second vaudeville tour, Fred and Adele were given the surname Astaire, which may have come from an Alsatian uncle, or may have simply been their mother's diminution of Austerlitz.

As teenagers, the Astaires attended the earliest American shows of Jerome Kern at the same time that the teenage George Gershwin saw them. They idolized Vernon and Irene Castle, the husband-and-wife dance team who popularized the Turkey Trot, the Castle Walk, and the Hesitation Waltz. Irene's leggy, boyish figure helped mold a new perception of female beauty through the 1920s. The Castles appeared in *Watch Your Step* (1914), the first complete musical score by Irving Berlin. "Syncopated Walk" was part of that score, and syncopation became the key word associated with Berlin, who had become famous at twenty-three for "Alexander's Ragtime Band." Vernon Castle not only danced like a dream but also played drums and sang.

In New York and on the road, Fred and Adele kept experimenting. Operetta and the revue were still the prime sources for the standard American musical; in the best musical comedy, like Jerome Kern's, these were squeezed together into something new. *Very Good, Eddie* (1915) and *Leave It to Jane* (1917) were more intimate and plot-integrated than most previous musicals. Absorbing these and the Castles' performances, Astaire wanted to create his own "outlaw" dance idiom by making an amalgam of the styles—tap, ballet, and ballroom—he grew up with. These were the years, the critic Elizabeth Kendall has suggested, when Astaire and

> other smart dance arrangers began to melt down those musical comedy poses, those kicks and asymmetric poses from the Charlestons and popular dances, into a style as precise as classical ballet, as

moderne and asymmetrical as Cubist or Futurist painting, as rhythmically compelling as African tribal rites.

In those same years, George Gershwin worked as a songplugger at Remick. Now and then the Astaires dropped by his office. "We would tell George how much we wanted to do a musical comedy," Astaire recalled in the early 1970s, "and he'd say, 'Why, so do I! And someday I'm going to write one for you.' To all three of us, musical comedy was a big step up from vaudeville acts and songplugging." Gershwin was nineteen, Fred eighteen.

Before Gershwin could make good on his promise, the Astaires appeared in Jerome Kern's *The Bunch and Judy* (November 1922, lyrics by Anne Caldwell). In 1923, the Astaires played London for the first time, in *Stop Flirting,* a revue that featured songs by several writers. At that time the London–New York axis was well traveled, but London had never seen anything quite like the Astaires—particularly Adele, who was just elegant and distant enough to make Englishmen swoon. *Stop Flirting* also gave Fred Astaire his first Gershwin tune, "I'll Build a Stairway to Paradise," to sing in a show.

Producing *Lady, Be Good!* in 1924, Alex Aarons knew he was taking a chance by allowing Fred and Adele to carry the show, and by allowing young George and Ira Gershwin to write the entire score. Before the show opened, the Gershwins' "The Man I Love" was dropped because Adele couldn't sing it convincingly—she was a daring flapper, not a quavering voice of vulnerability. Still working on their "Fascinatin' Rhythm" dance routine during Philadelphia tryouts, the Astaires couldn't come up with an exit step. George Gershwin sat down at the piano, took them through the number, then at the last measure called out, "Now travel with that one," getting them offstage in a routine so virtuosic that it guaranteed applause.

Vincent Youmans and Arthur Schwartz enjoyed a similar rhythmic rapport with the Astaires. In the 1930 Youmans show *Smiles,* Astaire sang no fewer than five songs (Ring Lardner contributed lyrics), and Adele introduced Walter Donaldson's "You're Driving Me Crazy." In *The Band Wagon* (1931), Schwartz provided the great dance numbers for the Astaires and the magnificent Tilly Losch.

But it was with the Gershwins that the Astaires were most closely in step. From the next Gershwin-Astaire collaboration, *Funny Face* (1927), came "'S Wonderful," "My One and Only," and "He Loves and She Loves." Alex Aarons, producing the Gershwins' *Girl Crazy* in October 1930, asked Astaire to come to the theater to help out with the choreography on "Embraceable You," to be sung and danced by the nineteen-year-old Ginger Rogers. Rogers was a younger version of Adele Astaire's goddessy flapper but more approachable. Meeting for the first time, Astaire and Rogers rehearsed the "Embraceable You" routine in the lobby because the stage was so crowded.

In 1932, after several long stays in England, Adele Astaire married Lord Cavendish and retired from show business. This was part of a ritual reciprocity of the day—a female star of the theater was coveted by society, and in turn coveted society's acceptance. Even more so than Fred, Adele had successfully remade herself—from Midwestern brewer's child into Lady Cavendish. There was nothing deceptive about it; rather, it was a beautifully sculpted image, chiseled by years of putting on the Ritz and traffic with the aristocracy of London and New York.

Professionally abandoned by Adele, Fred worked to refine his own image, taking ever greater risks in his dance routines while projecting a deliberately narrow persona, one that kept him in a dinner jacket. Astaire's solo act, Ann Douglas suggested in *Terrible Honesty*, "was a creamy embossed calling card, printed perhaps on Tin Pan Alley presses, but meant and ready to lie on the silver salvers of Fifth Avenue's best families."

No songwriter combined Tin Pan Alley and Fifth Avenue more authentically than Cole Porter. Porter was just beginning to hit his stride in 1932 at forty, when he wrote the songs for *The Gay Divorce*, the show Astaire had chosen to test his popularity apart from Adele. It was appropriate that the show had been adapted from a book by the young Dwight Taylor (who in turn had adapted an unproduced play by his stepfather J. Hartley Manners). "Of all the younger men of the Twenties," publisher John Farrar wrote, "Dwight Taylor knew the most people in the interlocking hierarchies of theater, writing, journalism and Society." (Taylor's father, producer-playwright Charles Taylor, had been producing Broadway hits since the turn of the century; his mother, Laurette Taylor, was the Irish colleen who snares an English nobleman in the 1912 *Peg o' My Heart*, J. Hartley Manners's wedding present to her.) Shuttling between Fifth Avenue and Times Square, the Taylor-Manners clan wasn't unlike the Astaire siblings—theater folk with the trappings of the high-born.

The Gay Divorce wasn't a smashing success, but the show did respectable business. It introduced Porter's "Night and Day," an ersatz Moroccan rhythm married to a lyric that Porter claimed was inspired by dining next to Mrs. Vincent Astor: irritated by the sound of a broken eaves spout during a rainstorm, Mrs. Astor exclaimed, "That drip drip drip is driving me mad!" Astaire sang "Night and Day" and the lovely "I've Got You on My Mind."

Astaire stayed for six months in *The Gay Divorce*. When he left there was movie interest in the property. Encouraged by his agent Leland Hayward, Astaire went to Hollywood to see about making it. He knew he'd have to position himself to star or he wouldn't get to dance the way he wanted to.

Before he could star on his own, however, Astaire found supporting work at MGM, through Louis B. Mayer's son-in-law David O. Selznick. Selznick had assigned Richard Rodgers and Lorenz Hart to write a song for the new Clark Gable–Joan Crawford picture, *Dancing Lady* (1933). Rodgers and Hart came up with a number called "That's the Rhythm of the Day." Selznick wanted the song to be made "a little better"; bristling, Richard Rodgers explained that you can't make a song better—it's either good or it's no good. The song was passed off to Nelson Eddy. Something else was needed—and clearly not from Rodgers and Hart. During this crisis screenwriter Allen Rivkin attended a party hosted by Fox story editor Leonard Spiegelgass, and heard twenty-one-year-old Burton Lane play "Everything I Have Is Yours" on the piano. Rivkin told Selznick about Lane and his partner, Harold Adamson, and the two were quickly signed. In *Dancing Lady* Astaire, playing himself, performs in two Lane-Adamson numbers, "Heigh-Ho, the Gang's All Here" and "Let's Go Bavarian." They were his first Hollywood numbers.

His next role was in *Flying Down to Rio*, made by RKO. Astaire was paired with his old New York acquaintance Ginger Rogers, though they weren't the stars—Dolores Del Rio and Gene Raymond were.

While in town to compose the songs, Vincent Youmans stayed at the famous Garden of Allah apartments (home to other New York exiles Dorothy Parker, Robert Benchley, and Scott Fitzgerald); at this time, he began to show the symptoms of the tuberculosis that would eventually kill him. Edward Eliscu, who had written with Youmans on Broadway, arrived to write the lyrics; lyricist Gus Kahn was also on hand to help. Out of the Youmans-Eliscu-Kahn collaboration came "The Carioca," the first memorable Astaire-Rogers dance number.

Astaire and Rogers's work in *Flying Down to Rio* stood out from the rest of the cast, and they were quickly signed for starring roles, in

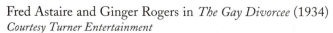

Fred Astaire and Ginger Rogers in *The Gay Divorcee* (1934)
Courtesy Turner Entertainment

the film version of *The Gay Divorcee*—an unaccented *e* was added to the name, presumably to soften the idea for the Hays Office. Of Porter's songs, only "Night and Day" was retained. House songwriters Harry Revel and Mack Gordon contributed two songs. RKO sound chief Murray Spivack bought two more songs, "The Continental" and "A Needle in a Haystack," from Con Conrad and Herb Magidson. "The Continental" crystallized the sparkle of the Astaire-Rogers team and won the first Academy Award for best song in 1934.

RKO's musical director at the time was Max Steiner, whose considerable musical theater experience and keen sense of timing perfectly complemented Astaire's talents. From New York, Steiner imported Edward Powell and Robert Russell Bennett to orchestrate the film. One night Steiner went to the Colony Club, on the Sunset Strip, where a black-haired young Chicagoan named Hal Borne presided at the piano. Steiner wasted no time hiring him. Hearing Borne work out a tune on the RKO soundstage, Astaire turned to Steiner and said, "We've got a piano!" Because of union regulations aimed at keeping Easterners from taking jobs away from local musicians, Borne could rehearse with Astaire and even appear on camera, but he couldn't record until the union's one-year probationary period was over. RKO dance director Dave Gould hired Astaire lookalike Hermes Pan, a young Southerner, to help with choreography. Pan soon became Astaire's choreographer and doppelganger.

RKO bought the Jerome Kern–Otto Harbach musical *Roberta* specifically for Irene Dunne, who could sing, and for the Astaire-Rogers team. The movie version brought Kern permanently to Los Angeles—he had been there off and on since 1930 but hadn't been inclined to give up his Bronxville house. With his adored wife and daughter, Kern unpacked his massive collection of books, set up his inspirational bust of Wagner next to his piano, and went to work on a couple of new songs. When Kern needed new lyrics to replace Oscar Hammerstein's on "I Won't Dance," producer Pandro Berman brought in the young, no-nonsense Dorothy Fields.

From a family steeped in musical theater, Fields was still in her early twenties when songwriter J. Fred Coots ("You Go to My Head") introduced her to his friend Jimmy McHugh. McHugh was already an established songwriter and, according to Fields's recollection, didn't think much of her talent. But a few weeks after their first meeting, McHugh called and asked if she'd like to collaborate on songs for New York's famous Cotton Club. Out of that period came "I Must Have That Man" and "I Can't Give You Anything But Love." Fields and McHugh moved their operations to Hollywood. But each of them kept returning to New York, and each worked easily with other partners.

Fields sat next to the notoriously crusty Jerome Kern on the piano bench and wrote out her lyrics. "I Won't Dance" worked fine, of course, because its mock petulance was the perfect signal for Astaire and Rogers to do just that—dance—with a quote from "The Continental" thrown in for good measure. But it was Fields's lyric for "Lovely to Look At," written to accompany the title character's fashion show, that made everyone take notice. Irene Dunne sang this one; some years later, Astaire would record it and make it his.

To adapt *Roberta* for the screen, Pandro Berman called on the young New York playwright Allan Scott. Like Dwight Taylor, Scott had the right pedigree for the series: Amherst, Oxford, Broadway. Scott built up Astaire's role and created one for Rogers out of wholecloth. He also happened to live a couple of blocks from Kern, a close proximity that was rare in sprawling Los Angeles. "Kern just never stopped," said Scott, who worked on the script at Kern's house. "I mean, he could write a song every five minutes." If Kern felt that Scott or Fields didn't like the tune he was working on, he would stop and turn the bust of Wagner to face away from him.

After the *Roberta* songs were completed, RKO asked Kern to write songs for Lily Pons to sing in the upcoming *Love Song*. To everyone's surprise, Kern requested Fields as his lyricist. Together they wrote a song called "I Dream Too Much," which seemed so promising that it became the movie's title.

While Kern and Fields were writing for Lily Pons, Astaire was getting songs tailor-made by a songwriter who had rejected him and his sister many years earlier. As if to compensate for that mistake, Irving Berlin wrote his heart out on *Top Hat*.

Berlin, like Astaire, coveted upper-class respectability. A child of New York's Lower East Side ghetto, Berlin had knocked on society's door when, as a young widower, he courted Ellin Mackay, the patrician Long Islander whose father was dead set against her marrying a Jew. (She married Berlin anyway.) Appropriating material from black music and dance, Berlin scored early with "Alexander's Ragtime Band." In 1930 Harry Richman introduced "Puttin' on the Ritz," a song that gathered all the cross-cultural materials that went into Berlin's and Astaire's art. "Berlin owed his career," Ann Douglas wrote, "as did Astaire and many others among his most talented white and black peers, to his instincts for creative slumming." In the original version of "Puttin' on the Ritz," Berlin's lyric invites the listener to Lenox Avenue, the major Harlem thoroughfare where the party appears to be going on right in the street. Such a lyric for some listeners—who couldn't believe that a musically uneducated white man, even one raised with Jewish music and the sounds of the streets, could put such syncopation into his songs—supported the widespread canard that "a little colored boy" wrote most of Berlin's songs.

At RKO, Berlin and Astaire recognized each other immediately. They had a great go-between in songwriter Dave Dreyer ("Me and My Shadow"), who had been a staff pianist at Irving Berlin Music and eventually became head of the RKO music department. While Berlin wrote the music and lyrics to the *Top Hat* songs—including the stupendous "Cheek to Cheek" and the most famous of Astaire's patented dressing-for-the-evening numbers, "Top Hat, White Tie, and Tails"—the script was being prepared by Dwight Taylor and Allan Scott. Berlin was used to writing upward of two dozen songs for a single show; for a movie he had to keep his productivity in check.

"Irving was so fecund," Allan Scott said, "and there were wonderful things that we just couldn't use. I remember him during *Top Hat* singing something called 'White Christmas.' We knew it was a wonderful song, but we had no way we could use it." Consulting the screenplay, Berlin would read an exchange of dialog: "Isn't it a lovely day?" asks Astaire's character, Jerry Travers. "Yes, to get caught in the rain," cracks Ginger's character, Dale Tremont. Set to Berlin's music and lyric, "Isn't It a Lovely Day?" became an instant classic.

Famously hard-bargaining—later it would turn into chronic litigiousness—Berlin wanted a flat $100,000 from RKO for his *Top Hat* work. Producer Pandro Berman countered by offering a $75,000 fee against 10 percent of the gross over and above $1,250,000—a box-office figure unlikely to be reached by any film, let alone *Top Hat*. When the grosses came in at more than $3,100,000, Berlin ended up netting far more than his requested fee.

Thanks to its great succes, Berlin was hired to write songs for the next Astaire-Rogers teaming, *Follow the Fleet* (1936). The film took Astaire out of the monkey suit and put him in a gob's uniform. "Let's Face the Music and Dance" was Irving Berlin's dance dream (just as "You and the Night and the Music" was Arthur Schwartz's). "I'm Putting All My Eggs in One Basket" was a typically indirect but heart-felt declaration of commitment: Fred Astaire wasn't the type to come out and say "I love you."

In the wake of *Follow the Fleet*, Berlin took on other movie projects, primarily at Twentieth Century-Fox. At RKO, Astaire and Rogers appeared in *Swing Time* (1936). The movie was directed by George Stevens. With Max Steiner's dismissal from the studio, Nathaniel Shilkret had taken over the musical direction. The Kern-Fields songs included the pared-down polka "Pick Yourself Up," "A Fine Romance," the magnificent homage "Bojangles of Harlem," "Never Gonna Dance," and the Oscar-winning "The Way You Look Tonight"; not a clinker in the bunch. The "Pick Yourself Up" number, in which the little dance corral can't contain the dancing stars, is the one that so perfectly defines them: the initially glacial, suspicious Rogers is eventually won over by the emotionally clumsy but otherwise graceful Astaire, who turns the tables on her as they get to know each other through the dance. But even standing still, or as still as he was capable, when Astaire sings "The Way You Look Tonight" to the shampoo-headed Rogers, you believe every note, every sigh.

Astaire went into the recording studio for Brunswick. He had recorded sporadically since the early '20s in London, and there were some recording dates with society bandleader Leo Reisman. Now, as a bona fide movie star, he recorded his movie songs for Brunswick with Reisman, then with Johnny Green, and finally with English bandleader-composer Ray Noble. These were great recordings because they captured, on disk, Astaire's relaxed but eager-to-please singing style, as well as the elaborate courtship, performed by his feet. The Brunswick sides were recorded right after the films' principal photography and weeks before their release dates; the disks were in the stores days before the films were in the theaters. To those moviegoers—and from 1935 to 1937 there were millions each week—who had heard the recordings beforehand, Astaire was a familiar friend, not superior to you, not even more confident, just more graceful and probably better dressed.

☙   ☙   ☙

After spending years on *Porgy and Bess,* George Gershwin glanced over his shoulder and saw his old musical comedy rivals gaining on him. Cole Porter had written the songs for MGM's *Born to Dance* (1936), which included "Easy to Love," "I've Got You Under My Skin," and the unused "It's De-Lovely." At Fox, Irving Berlin was already discussing the possibility of a film biography of himself. Richard Rodgers and Larry Hart had returned triumphantly to Broadway, turning out one amazing song after another. After concentrating on the operatic form, Gershwin wanted to return to the more stripped-down, popular song, where he could get loose in three minutes or less.

The Gershwins had had one stint in Hollywood when they worked on *Delicious* (1931) for Fox. David Butler was the director; Hugo Friedhofer had orchestrated most of George Gershwin's score, which included his "New York Rhapsody," otherwise known as "Rhapsody of the Rivets." (The piece drifted its way into Gershwin's Second Rhapsody, commissioned and premiered by Serge Koussevitsky conducting the Boston Symphony Orchestra in 1932.)

When the Gershwins arrived at RKO to work on *Shall We Dance?* (1937), it was a new opportunity for them as much as it was for Astaire and Rogers. The general feeling was that, in the few years the Gershwins had been away from Hollywood, George's melodic lines had become longer and roomier, and Ira's lyrics had deepened. Ira dipped repeatedly into his notebook for inspiration. For "Let's Call the Whole Thing Off," for example, Ira had recorded that his brother-in-law English Strunsky had bought a tomato factory in New Jersey and had to force himself to say tom*ay*to instead of tom*ah*to so that the farmers could understand him.

George Gershwin and Ginger Rogers on an RKO soundstage of *Shall We Dance?* (1937)
Photo by John Miehle. Courtesy Academy of Motion Picture Arts & Sciences and Turner Entertainment

By almost any reckoning, *Shall We Dance?* is a falling-off from *Swing Time,* with a less cohesive storyline. But the collection of songs is unbeatable: "Beginner's Luck," "Slap That Bass," "They All Laughed," "Let's Call the Whole Thing Off," "They Can't Take That Away from Me," and "Shall We Dance?"—all of them belonging to Astaire. Shilkret conducted again, with Mark Sandrich directing Astaire and Rogers for the fourth time.

Shall We Dance? was released at the end of April 1937. Less than three months later, George Gershwin was dead of a brain tumor. The entire nation seemed to be in shock. Gershwin's obituary shared page-one space with Amelia Earhart's disappearance: the latter was a presumed death that intrigued; the former was a confirmed death that devastated.

Around Thanksgiving of that same year, the Astaire-Gershwin

collaboration *Damsel in Distress* was released, directed by George Stevens, with musical direction by the recently returned Victor Baravalle. Songs like "A Foggy Day" and "Nice Work If You Can Get It" were in the same league as the *Shall We Dance?* songs, but the picture was less watchable. Costar Joan Fontaine, although easy to look at, neither sang nor danced, and her rapport with Astaire wasn't apparent onscreen.

Like the rest of the country, Ira Gershwin took George's death hard. For months he kept to his house, unable to work, unable to listen to music, spending time only with his domineering wife, Lee. Then, one day Ira put on the *Shall We Dance?* Brunswick recordings that Astaire had made with Johnny Green. Astaire's singing coaxed Ira out of his grief and sent him back to work.

Irving Berlin, of course, never stopped working. His songs for *Carefree* (1938), the penultimate RKO teaming of Astaire and Rogers, included "I Used to Be Color Blind" and "Change Partners." Arlene Croce reminds us that as Astaire became a star, critics increasingly referred to him as insouciant. Is it mere coincidence that Sans Souci was the Times Square supper club owned by Vernon and Irene Castle before World War I?

The Story of Vernon and Irene Castle (1939) ended the Astaire-Rogers partnership. Allan Scott was signed to write a script based on a rather poetic treatment by Oscar Hammerstein; but the widowed Irene Castle was so interfering that Scott bowed out. The movie goes to great lengths to follow the Castles' lives closely, yet everything about it is bleached out. The Castles' music directors, for instance, were black—James Reese Europe, probably the first so-called jazz artist to play Carnegie Hall, conducted their shows for years—yet the movie makes them white. In this case the movie suffers from lack of courage—a far cry from Astaire's 1936 blackface tribute to Bill Robinson, which was at once audacious and humble.

After *The Story of Vernon and Irene Castle,* Astaire and Rogers went their separate ways for a decade. (They would not be reunited until the 1949 *Barkleys of Broadway,* and then only because Judy Garland was too ill to costar.) Through the '40s, Rogers became one of the dominant female movie stars, winning a best actress Oscar in 1940 for RKO's *Kitty Foyle.*

●   ●   ●

Unlike Rogers, Astaire couldn't be separated from his music. He sang more Cole Porter—"Begin the Beguine" and "I Concentrate on You"— in MGM's *Broadway Melody of 1940.* Paramount's *Second Chorus* (1940), with songs by a platoon of writers, was seen as a long step down for Astaire. One of the songs, "I Ain't Hep to That Step but I Dig It," was by Astaire's pianist Hal Borne and Johnny Mercer. Astaire, who probably would have been content to write songs if he'd lost the use of his legs and voice, had also written with Mercer. "I'm Building up to an Awful Letdown" is probably their most famous collaboration, though it wasn't written for the screen.

Things began to look up for Astaire when he moved to Columbia, who paired him with Rita Hayworth in *You'll Never Get Rich* (1941) and *You Were Never Lovelier* (1942). The first had songs by Cole Porter, which got no airplay because of an ASCAP-BMI fight; the second had songs by Kern and Mercer, and they're among their best. The orchestrations for these were made mostly by the brilliant Conrad Salinger, and they make a tremendous difference in Astaire's musical energy.

Hayworth made a difference, too. With her long legs, broad shoulders, and willing attitude, she made a great partner to Astaire. As a kid in vaudeville he had frequently run into her dancer father, Eduardo Cansino. A common history wasn't what made them click, though. Hayworth possessed a natural sensuousness that seemed out of Rogers's range. She may not have been a greater partner to Astaire than Rogers, but in their two movies together Astaire looks at Hayworth with sexual desire rather than professional interest. He seems to want her.

Between the two Hayworth pictures, Astaire appeared in *Holiday Inn.* The teaming with Bing Crosby, the movies' other peerless recording artist, was inevitable. They were buoyed by the great Berlin score, by the smart musical direction of Robert Emmett Dolan, and by Paul Weston's dance band arrangements, which turned all of soundstage New England into a year-round nightclub. Berlin had persuaded Mark

Harold Arlen
Courtesy ASCAP

Sandrich that there was a movie to be made centered around holidays—
that is, Berlin's songs about the holidays. Crosby handled the bulk of
the singing, including "White Christmas," which soon became the
best-selling record and sheet music of all time, as well as the lovely "Be
Careful, It's My Heart." Astaire sang "You're Easy to Dance With"—
no lie, since it was addressed to costar Virginia Dale. That Crosby and
Astaire played rivals for the affections of the same woman (Marjorie
Reynolds) was seen by some as symbolic. In *Holiday Inn* Astaire lost the

battle. Stranded on a desert isle, however, which one would you rather spend a year with?

Astaire returned to RKO for *The Sky's the Limit* (1943). Johnny Mercer was on hand again, this time working with Harold Arlen, the bluesiest of all the great white songwriters. As a wartime romance, *The Sky's the Limit* has a drab, gray tone, but no one who has seen it can forget Astaire's ferocious, bar-demolishing dance to "One for My Baby," nor his heartfelt response to Joan Leslie in "My Shining Hour." A listener can only weep that Astaire didn't record more Arlen—say, the Arlen-Harburg "Buds Won't Bud" (from *Hooray for What?*).

Then came a long, involuntary break. At forty-four Astaire must have wondered if he was finished. For years his recording career had been hinged on his movie career, and that too had gone flat. It would be years before Astaire would again sing Cole Porter onscreen. Never again would he work with Jerome Kern, who suffered a fatal cerebral hemorrhage in November 1945 during a trip to New York, where he had contracted with Rodgers and Hammerstein to write a musical about Annie Oakley. At Metro, under Arthur Freed's aegis, Astaire got to sing Harry Warren onscreen: *Yolanda and the Thief* (1945; lyrics by Freed); *The Barkleys of Broadway* (1949; lyrics by Ira Gershwin); and *The Belle of New York* (1952; lyrics by Johnny Mercer). From this last picture emerged "I Wanna Be a Dancin' Man," which took its place alongside Astaire's other show-business-is-in-my-blood declarations. Otherwise the songs weren't up to Warren's (or Astaire's) best. An early recording of the Warren-Dubin "We're in the Money," with Leo Reisman's band, suggests that Astaire could have been a great Warren interpreter if the two men had caught each other a little earlier.

Harry Warren had once chided Irving Berlin, who uncharacteristically had gone hitless for a year or two, by asking him what happened to "the little colored boy" who wrote all those great songs. "He died," Berlin said.

But Berlin was back in form by the time he accepted the assignment to compose the songs for the Annie Oakley musical—it would

Fred Astaire and Judy Garland in *Easter Parade* (1948)
Courtesy Turner Entertainment

become his greatest show, *Annie Get Your Gun*. And all the songs for Paramount's *Blue Skies* (1946), which reunited Astaire and Crosby, were his. Crosby's original costar was the tap specialist Paul Draper. Draper continually derided leading lady Joan Caulfield during rehearsals. Unwilling to stand the strain on the set, Crosby arranged for Draper's dismissal and brought in Astaire. In "Puttin' on the Ritz," Astaire danced with eight duplications of himself, each one filmed separately, then spliced together. Astaire changed Berlin's lyric from "Lenox Avenue" to "Park Avenue" where "Rockefellers walk with sticks or um-ber-ellas." The alteration permanently gilded Astaire's "creamy embossed calling card."

Another Berlin project, *Easter Parade* (1948), cemented Astaire's relationshiop to Arthur Freed, who would produce the few interesting Astaire musicals to come. In the next decade, Astaire would memorably handle songs by Burton Lane and Alan Jay Lerner (*Royal Wedding*), by Arthur Schwartz and Howard Dietz (*The Band Wagon*), and by Cole Porter (*Silk Stockings*).

"I'm dancing and I can't be bothered now," Astaire declared in *Damsel in Distress*. Dancing alone or with a partner, the man was his own master. When singing, however, the greatest screen interpreter of popular songs had the inestimable help of our greatest songwriters. There was no one they'd rather have written for.

SIX

OR WOULD YOU RATHER BE A MULE?
PARAMOUNT PICTURES

After appearing in Paramount's revue *The Big Broadcast* (1932), that featured radio stars like Burns and Allen and Kate Smith, Bing Crosby's popularity soared. He returned to New York, starred in the Chesterfield Hour on radio, and played the Paramount Theaters in Times Square and in Brooklyn. Everybody wanted to write for Crosby, who was recording for Brunswick at the time. Sam Coslow and Arthur Johnston knew they were lucky when they were assigned by Paramount to write songs for the upcoming Crosby production, *College Humor* (1933).

If studios have personalities, then Paramount's in the 1930s was collegiate. Where MGM was like an opulent boudoir, carefully reflecting its great female stars like Garbo and Crawford, and Warners a grimy back alley in its musicals as well as its gangster dramas, Paramount was a college campus.

To promote *College Humor,* the magazine of the same name and Paramount Pictures jointly sponsored a Miss College Humor beauty contest. The winner was a sparkling, creamy-skinned girl from Tucumcari, New Mexico, named Bessie Patterson. Patterson had previously won a "Typical Western Girl" contest; her prize this time was to appear in a Crosby picture.

College Humor made Crosby a movie star. Patterson didn't appear in it, but she was given a bit part in his 1935 movie, *Rhythm on the Range.* Crosby introduced her to a young songwriter named Johnny Burke, who was then writing songs with Arthur Johnston for Crosby's next project, *Pennies from Heaven,* which was to be produced at Columbia. Johnny Burke and Bessie Patterson fell in love.

Burke had already tried marriage. He was game again, but Bessie Patterson was young and relatively unformed. Perhaps playing Pygmalion to her Galatea, Burke persuaded her to enroll at the University of Southern California. In June 1939, five years after winning the Miss College Humor contest and arriving in Hollywood, and hours after receiving her baccalaureate, Patterson married Burke in Mexico; by then, Johnny Burke had become indispensable to Crosby.

Born in Northern California in 1908 and raised in Chicago, where his father was a building contractor, Johnny Burke served as dance pianist for the University of Wisconsin college orchestra. Later in New York, he spent a few happy years working as a staff pianist at Irving

Bessie Burke, Midge Polesie, Herb Polesie, Dixie Crosby, Johnny Burke, Bing Crosby, Westwood Marching & Chowder Club, 1939
Courtesy Terry Polesie

Berlin's publishing firm. A slight, good-looking man, Burke was called to Hollywood in the first wave of songwriters' migration. He was signed by Fox. His early efforts were hardly distinguished. "The Boop-Boop-a-Doop Trot" was something he worked up for Dixie Lee, the future Mrs. Crosby, while she was singing and dancing at that studio. When his contract wasn't renewed, Burke returned to New York. Paired with considerably older composer James "Ragtime Jimmy" Monaco, Burke concentrated on lyric-writing. The Burke-Monaco songs got them back to Hollywood, and a contract at Paramount.

To be sure, there were other songwriters that were important to the studio. Leo Robin and Ralph Rainger, two quiet, intellectual men, were active on the lot. Robin and Rainger wrote "Love in Bloom" for Crosby and Kitty Carlisle in *She Loves Me Not* (1934); it became Jack Benny's theme song after Benny hauled out his violin and joined a supper-club orchestra on the tune. For *Easy Living* (1937), one of the best comedies of the '30s, Ralph Rainger composed a skippy, terrific title tune, to which Robin added lyrics later. "Thanks for the Memory" was part of the '38 edition of *The Big Broadcast* series, and it stunned everyone involved in the picture. Apparently, director Mitchell Leisen was having trouble setting the right tone for a scene between the amicably divorced couple Bob Hope and Shirley Ross; Robin and Rainger attempted to convey that the two were still in love without saying so, while maintaining a light tone. When Leisen heard "Thanks for the Memory," he pronounced it unfunny, but he was so moved he knew he had to use it. Staff composer Freddy Hollander broke down when he heard it. Shirley Ross sang it, and it was all she could do to keep from crying on camera.

Through the '30s the Robin-Rainger collaboration was the most dependable at Paramount, but there were others active on the lot as well. Lewis Gensler, who had written "Love Is Just Around the Corner" (from the 1934 *Here Is My Heart*) with Robin, later became a producer. London-born Harry Revel, composing to Mack Gordon's lyrics, served not only as a composer but as onscreen pianist in *Sitting Pretty* (1933). Sam Coslow was still active. But Rodgers and Hart had fled, winding up the Hollywood phase of their career by writing for the Paramount

Ralph Rainger
Courtesy ASCAP

production *Mississippi* (1935), in which Crosby introduced "It's Easy to Remember."

Time and again, Crosby showed that he could sell a song like no one else. No single song proved this as clearly as "Sweet Leilani," a quasi-Hawaiian number written by Crosby's pal Harry Owens. Although he had a helluva time pronouncing the title, Crosby wanted the song for his new Paramount picture *Waikiki Wedding* (1937). The song was interpolated into a score that included Robin and Rainger's

"Blue Hawaii." In the movie the song was travestied, or so Owens thought, when it was sung over a sequence in which a squealing pig got loose. Nevertheless, Crosby's Decca recording clung to the Number One spot for three months—a testament to his incomparable stature as the most popular of record-making movie stars.

Crosby owned the controlling interest in Del Mar, the paradisia-cal racetrack not far from the California-Mexico border. "Where the turf meets the surf" was the motto coined by Midge Polesie; Midge's husband Herb had written *East Side of Heaven* (1938), a Crosby vehi-cle with songs by Johnny Burke and Jimmy Monaco. Burke flew a light plane between Hollywood and Del Mar, shuttling friends back and forth during the racing season. "We'd get in the plane and fly over the grandstand," director David Butler remembered, "and he'd tip the wings. Everybody would get up and wave their handkerchiefs to him as we left." Solo, Burke was darkly brilliant; coupled with Bessie Patterson, however, he was absolutely golden and could do no wrong. Hearing a solo by Bob Crosby's trumpeter Billy Butterfield, composed by bassist-arranger Bob Haggart, Burke added a lyric to the tune that became "What's New?" That was a few hours' work tossed off between Paramount assignments.

o   o   o

In late 1939, the Paramount lot welcomed a new composer, a tall, pleas-ant-looking man who was nearly bald though he was only twenty-six. Jimmy Van Heusen was such a carefree, this-is-the-life bachelor that wealthier, more celebrated men envied him.

Born Edward Chester Babcock in 1913, he went to work as a radio announcer in Syracuse, New York. Edward Chester Babcock was no name for an announcer, so he was inspired to take his new name when he looked out the station window and saw a billboard advertising Van Heusen shirts. Van Heusen worked his way down to Manhattan and scuffled for a while. At one point he ran the elevator at the Park Central Hotel for sixteen dollars a week. A deft pianist with a style that wasn't derived from any identifiable source, Van Heusen produced tunes that seemed almost prearranged, arriving full and swinging on the music stand. (In this way, his closest antecedent is probably Jimmy

McHugh.) Alec Wilder said, "I well remember a thin young man sitting outside an arranger's office, endlessly playing the piano during the late thirties." In those years Van Heusen worked at Remick Music publishers under the supervision of Mousie Warren, Harry's brother. Van Heusen supplemented his Remick income by playing in the city's prominent whorehouses. (Years later, Van Heusen was one of the few movie-industry figures to appear publicly at the funeral of Polly Adler, New York's most notorious madam.) The whorehouse playing earned him a reputation as a swordsman, but those tunes were the thing that made musicians and producers take notice.

Swingin' the Dream (1939) was a weird Broadway experiment, a jazz take on *A Midsummer Night's Dream,* featuring the likes of Louis Armstrong and Benny Goodman, that was roundly panned. Van Heusen was working with the celestially inclined lyricist Eddie DeLange, however, and they came up with the beautiful "Darn That Dream." The song, if not the show, won him the invitation to Paramount.

Van Heusen wasn't long in Los Angeles before Johnny Burke latched onto him. Perhaps Burke was feeling that Jimmy Monaco— twenty-five years his senior, and enjoying his first hit when Burke was all of three—was too old-fashioned for him. David Butler said, "There was a little feeling about Burke and Van Heusen, because Jimmy Monaco and Burke were partners, and Burke pulled away from Monaco and got Van Heusen. Jimmy Monaco felt very bad about it. But he came up with 'Six Lessons from Madame La Zonga' right after that and it was a big hit." It was such a big hit, in fact, that it inspired the title of a Lupe Velez picture at Universal. Crosby was loyal enough to Monaco to name a prize racehorse Madame La Zonga, but not so loyal that, relying on his sensitive musical antenna, he didn't immediately turn to the new Burke-Van Heusen team.

Burke the Irish poet was on a roll. He and Van Heusen quickly came up with the marvelous "Imagination," for Mary Martin to sing in *Love Thy Neighbor* (1940). The picture was another attempt to exploit the studio's radio properties (in this case, Jack Benny and Fred Allen). Then came the Hope-Crosby *Road to Zanzibar.*

Burke and Monaco had written the songs for the first Hope-Crosby *Road* picture, *Road to Singapore* (1940). No single song from it is especially memorable, but the comedy, originally conceived for Paramount contract stars Fred MacMurray and Jack Oakie, went over nicely. For the next picture in the series, *Road to Zanzibar* (1941), there was no question that Burke would write with Van Heusen. Because Paramount executives didn't want to offend any potential film market, Zanzibar was selected—"for political good will," Crosby wrote—as the nominal setting for the Hope-Crosby safari romp. Burke was instructed to write a song "in a language at which no nation could take umbrage." (Burke used the Esperanto he had studied in college.) The film, also directed by Victor Schertzinger, is an improvement on *Singapore*. "It's Always You" is introduced by Crosby, singing to Dorothy Lamour in a canoe on an African lake; Crosby paddles his hand through the water to the sound of a harp, and the melody begins. (Victor Young was the musical director.) It was the first of the marvelous Burke–Van Heusen tunes that Crosby introduced on the screen.

It helped, of course, that Crosby was such a quick study. David Butler said, "He was the fastest man I ever saw with learning a song. He'd get a song, and come over and say to Johnny Burke, 'Play it.' Johnny would play it a couple of times. [Crosby would] start humming it, and then the third time he'd sing it—he'd know it perfectly." When Burke wasn't available, Troy Saunders would provide Crosby with a low piano track; later, pianist-songwriter Joseph Lilley was his piano man.

The Crosby gems by Burke and Van Heusen began to accumulate. In *Dixie* (1943), he sang "Sunday, Monday, or Always"—his timetable for romance. *Going My Way* (1944) put Crosby in a collar—he was a *tough* priest, mind you—and let him sing "Swinging on a Star." The seed of the song sprouted when Burke heard Crosby admonish one of his sons for behaving "like a mule." The onscreen object of Crosby's lesson in song—" . . . or would you rather be a mule?"—were the members of the Robert Mitchell Boys' Choir. But for the Decca recording, the Choir was replaced by the Williams Brothers (including Andy Williams, then fifteen). On the Decca album of 78s released a few months later, an insert offers a tiny photograph of the songwriters: Van Heusen looks young and geeky with only a tuft of hair at his crown; Burke, brought low by a beetling brow, appears to be aging rapidly though he's only thirty-six. The album notes stated, "After eight years, Johnny Burke is still writing for Bing. He is married, has three wonderful children—twin girls and a boy." Van Heusen's entire bio is twin-klier: "Bachelor—with a home in Hollywood—and a Tarzana, California ranch round out the picture of Jimmy Van Heusen, music maker."

Swinging for back-to-back homers, the same team made *The Bells of St. Mary's*, adding Ingrid Bergman to the mix. Its song, "Aren't You Glad You're You?," was a companion piece to "Swinging on a Star." Crosby sang it to the forlorn young Joan Carroll, and it brought her out of the doldrums. Johnny Burke had a sixth sense about what Crosby would respond to and put across.

The Burkes socialized with the Crosbys and pals from radio days: the Johnny Mercers, Hope, Jerry Colonna, Crosby's shadow Barney Dean; Van Heusen hung out with Sinatra and a younger, club-crawling element. Sinatra liked Van Heusen next to him the way he liked to be next to the band when recording—to let the swing rub off on him. Van Heusen was cool, unbothered, unburdened by artistic angst. He kept himself fortified with vitamins, ostensibly to counteract the effects of his prodigious drinking. Crosby, often clinging to the wagon by his fingertips, would tell friends, "When the sun goes down I run away from Van Heusen like the plague."

Within the Crosby circle of Paramount performers and musicians—they formed the core of the Westwood Marching and Chowder Society, which performed semi-annual shivarees for its members—the great beauty was Bessie Burke. Phil Silvers, who was more in Sinatra's crowd, and Van Heusen wrote a song for her, "Bessie with the Laughing Face." A year later Silvers sang it at Nancy Sinatra's birthday party, and that's how Sinatra co-opted it for his new daughter, as "Nancy with the Laughing Face."

Every now and then, Burke and Van Heusen unhitched themselves from Crosby, and vice versa. Always the studio's favorite singing star, Crosby had an easy time with the Harold Arlen–Johnny Mercer songs written for him. In *Here Come the Waves* (1944), he sang "That Old Black Magic," which was originally sung by Johnny Johnston two years earlier in Paramount's *Star-Spangled Rhythm*. (Mercer claimed the lyric jumped off from Cole Porter's line "Do do that voodoo that you do so

Invitation to Westwood Marching & Chowder Club party, 1938
Courtesy Terry Polesie

Johnny Mercer, unidentified, Bing Crosby, Dixie Crosby, Herb Polesie,
David Butler, Bessie Burke, Westwood Marching & Chowder Club party,
1938
Courtesy Terry Polesie

Tommy Dorsey, Herb Polesie, Ozzie Nelson, Pat O'Brien, Westwood
Marching & Chowder Club, 1938
Courtesy Terry Polesie

well.") Also in *Here Come the Waves,* Crosby and Sonny Tufts sang "Ac-
cen-Tschu-Ate the Positive," which Mercer got from the evangelical
rhythms of a Harlem preacher he had heard. Mercer was colloquial in
a different way from the urban Jewish lyricists: rural and sunbaked
rather than urban and nocturnal, repeatedly using words like *son* and
boy and non-words like *whoo-ee,* the cries of a super-relaxed singer who
only sounded as though he were improvising.

David Butler and John Scott Trotter, Westwood Marching & Chowder Club, 1938
Courtesy Terry Polesie

Johnny Burke, Perry Botkin, Bing Crosby, Jimmy Monaco (at piano), Victor Young (side of picture), Westwood Marching & Chowder Club, 1939
Courtesy Terry Polesie

Program for 1940 edition of Westwood Marching & Chowder Club
Courtesy Terry Polesie

Mercer's easygoing Southern style, companionably escorting all comers down the road, may obscure the immeasurable contribution of Harold Arlen. At once formal and bluesy, Arlen somehow made his best songs sound spontaneous. (Alec Wilder points to Arlen's father, whose cantorial music, by definition, demanded constant improvisation.) In the early '40s at Paramount, Arlen (with Mercer) wrote "Hit the Road to Dreamland," sung by Mary Martin and Dick Powell in *Star-Spangled Rhythm* after they realize they've been out all night and ought to turn in. In the 1945 *Out of This World*, the title tune apparently poured forth from Eddie Bracken's throat, although it was Crosby's voice that emerged.

But Arlen and Mercer didn't belong to Paramount the way Burke and Van Heusen did. At their best, Burke and Van Heusen knew how to swing poetically, occasionally overdoing it ("Polkadots and Moonbeams") but more often conveying the sweet rush of romance, at once painful and exhilarating. In *And the Angels Sing* (1944; the title came from Johnny Mercer's lyric to Ziggy Elman's revamping of an old

Jewish tune), the love-perplexed Dorothy Lamour sings "It Could Happen to You." Burke's lyric for "Suddenly It's Spring" was cut from *Lady in the Dark* (1944)—Ginger Rogers danced to just the melody— but the song quickly became a standard. Best of all was "Like Someone in Love," which Dinah Shore sang in *Belle of the Yukon* (1944; the title role belonged to Gypsy Rose Lee). Burke and Van Heusen had an even bigger hit from that picture, "Sleigh Ride in July," but "Like Someone in Love" is the song that proved so sturdy. The melody's long, light lines are married to Burke's cataloging of romantic symptoms ("Lately I seem to walk as though I had wings/Bump into things/Like someone in love"). The images are ones that Burke reached for time and again— moonlight, weather, music heard or overheard—but they're often glimpsed through self-deprecation or bafflement. Burke sorely wanted Broadway respect. Toward that end, he and Van Heusen worked up a musical comedy called *Nellie Bly,* a strange homage to, and parody of, *Around the World in Eighty Days.* Produced by Eddie Cantor and Nat Karson, with Paramount music man Joe Lilley conducting, *Nellie Bly* opened on Broadway on January 21, 1946. It closed after a meager sixteen performances.

Burke and Van Heusen set up their own publishing company, managing to exploit their old Tin Pan Alley and newer Crosby contacts. They also signed younger songwriters. Mel Tormé and Bob Wells took a $75-a-week advance from them; one of the things Tormé and Wells came up with, deep in the middle of a Burbank, California, summer, was "The Christmas Song."

Burke worked slowly, painstakingly, to achieve his effects. Van Heusen, much more relaxed, often left his piano to lie back on a couch, a patch of melody gestating in his head. The *Road* franchise resumed with *Road to Utopia* (1946), which included "Welcome to My Dream" and "Personality." Then came *Road to Rio* (1947), which featured the gorgeous "But Beautiful." Burke's lyric in the bridge queries, "Who can say what love is?/Does it start in the mind or the heart?" Although there would be several more songs for Crosby, notably for the film version of *Connecticut Yankee,* "But Beautiful" was the last great Crosby–Burke–Van Heusen collaboration.

In May 1948, the Burkes separated. The period that followed was uneasy. Crosby was still with Paramount, but nothing was quite working out as before. For *Here Comes the Groom* (as usual in his non-*Road* roles, Crosby is a father or father-figure), Crosby and Jane Wyman sang "In the Cool, Cool, Cool of the Evening," by Mercer and Hoagy Carmichael. In fact neither Mercer nor Carmichael, who had gone back twenty years together, was still on the lot—the song had been written earlier for an unproduced Betty Hutton picture. A second Crosby-Wyman pairing, *Just for You* (1952), used Harry Warren and Leo Robin. Burke and Van Heusen wrote songs for Crosby's next picture, *Little Boy Lost,* but the story was too soggy to inspire them.

That same year Burke and Van Heusen prepared their second Broadway collaboration, *Carnival in Flanders.* Troubled from the out-set, the show couldn't be saved even by Preston Sturges, who was

Johnny Burke & Jimmy Van Heusen, late 1940s
Courtesy of Academy of Motion Picture Arts & Sciences

brought in at the last minute to fix it. It closed within a week. But out of it came "Here's That Rainy Day," widely regarded by professional musicians and listeners alike as the team's masterpiece. "It has great weight and authority," Alec Wilder wrote, "and must have been a song written under extremely intense circumstances."

It was. On and off the Paramount lot, it was felt that Burke and Van Heusen had been together too long. Burke remarried and kept thinking about Broadway, where he'd been denied success; Van Heusen didn't seem to care about all that. When Burke and Van Heusen were commissioned to write a title song for Otto Preminger's *The Man with the Golden Arm* (1955), they were unaware that the picture would be injected with such a jazzy, overpowering score by Elmer Bernstein. Sinatra recorded the title song, but it didn't make it into the finished film, and Sinatra's record went unreleased. In fact the song isn't bad. Van Heusen's tune sounds appropriately woozy; and with phrases like "paradise was just a false alarm," there are signs of the old Burke, quick and poetic.

Van Heusen, already part of Sinatra's pack, hooked up with Sammy Cahn, who had been writing lyrics for Sinatra since *Step Lively* (1944), Sinatra's second picture. Cahn had had a profitable, pre-Hollywood collaboration with Saul Chaplin, and was still writing with Jule Styne, but unhappily. If there was anything furtive about this new collaboration, it doesn't seem to have hampered their productivity. Van Heusen and Cahn wrote "Love and Marriage" for Sinatra, playing the Stage Manager, in the 1955 TV production of *Our Town*. They were on their way as a team.

That same year, Cahn and Van Heusen were knocking their brains out to come up with a title song for Sinatra's new comedy, *The Tender Trap*. One afternoon Burke dropped by. It was embarrassing for Cahn, who had often squirmed at Burke's fondness for telling jokes about an implicitly Jewish character named Meyer. And now Burke was in a position similar to that of his former partner, Jimmy Monaco. Compared to the swinging, thriving Van Heusen, Burke felt old. While Van Heusen was rolling out one song after another for Sinatra, who had stepped into Crosby's old post as the most popular recording artist of the day, Burke was writing for Paramount's new version of Rudolf Friml's warhorse, *The Vagabond King*. At the same time, he kept up a sideline writing as K. C. Rogan—an acronym composed of the names of his three children, Kevin Curtis, Rory, and Regan—supplying lyrics to themes by Schumann and Rossini.

By the end of the 1950s, when Van Heusen and Cahn had become Sinatra's regular writing team, Burke was living more or less permanently in New York. He poured most of his energies into a new musical for Broadway, composing the music as well as words. He still showed flashes of his old touch when he provided words to Erroll Garner's "Misty" ("I'm as helpless as a kitten up a tree"). His show *Donnybrook!*, starring Eddie Foy, Jr., was finally produced in 1961. Three years later, Burke died in his sleep, probably of a stroke, at his apartment at the Parc Vendome on West Fifty-seventh Street.

Ray Evans & Jay Livingston
Courtesy ASCAP

o   o   o

Unlike Burke or Van Heusen, Jay Livingston and Ray Evans spent little time working in the Tin Pan Alley grind; instead they came up mostly through the theater. In a way, they are emblematic of movie songwriters whose work plowed deep into the culture (the Christmas perennial "Silver Bells") but who remained anonymous to the general public. Unlike most songwriting teams, Livingston and Evans usually worked jointly on music and lyrics. Although they didn't seem to have a distinct style, musically or lyrically, they could handle just about any assignment.

Jay Livingston was born Jacob Harold Levison in Pennsylvania in 1915, seven weeks after Ray Evans's birth in Salamanca, New York. They met at the University of Pennsylvania. After graduation they joined a band—Livingston on piano, Evans on clarinet and saxophones—that was booked on the Cunard Line. Back in New York, Evans took a job as an accountant, while Livingston wrote arrangements for NBC radio. Writing together, they managed to get a song, "G'Bye Now," into the popular Olsen and Johnson show *Hellzapoppin'* (1938; most of the show's songs were written by Sammy Fain and Irving Kahal).

It hardly boosted their careers. A couple of years passed. Ole Olsen asked Livingston and Evans to drive his car out to Hollywood; they did, and stayed. They found a few songwriting jobs, notably "The Cat and the Canary" for PRC's low-budget *Why Girls Leave Home* (1944). Johnny Mercer, impressed by their work, introduced them to Buddy DeSylva and got them hired at Paramount. Their break came when Victor Young, who had scored the still-underrated weeper *To Each His Own* (1946), declined to write a title tune for it. The boys did it without much fuss. It wasn't sung in the picture, but Eddy Howard's recording of it went gold.

"Buttons and Bows" was their next big hit. It was pushed hard by Dinah Shore's record, shrewdly released by Capitol weeks before the picture, *The Paleface* (1948). Bob Hope sang it in the movie. Three years later, Hope's costar Jane Russell sang it with him, along with Roy Rogers, in *Son of Paleface* (1952), a funnier movie.

Between these films, Livingston and Evans wrote a song for an Alan Ladd movie called *Captain Carey U.S.A.* (1950). Sung only in Italian in the movie, "Mona Lisa" was used as a warning to the Italian underground that Nazis were nearby. The song was then pitched to Capitol artist Nat "King" Cole, who initially declined to record it. Someone at Paramount persuaded Cole, then living a few blocks from the studio in exclusive Hancock Park, to listen to the songwriters' demo version. Cole agreed to make the record but, displeased with it—the recording was made in April 1950 under Nelson Riddle's baton—left it on the shelf. But two months later it was finally released as the B side to a song called "The Greatest Inventor of Them All."

Meanwhile at Paramount, Bob Hope, sans Crosby, was turning out some minor comedy classics. *The Lemon Drop Kid* (1951) was taken from a Damon Runyon story about a hapless Broadway bookie. For a Christmas sequence, Livingston and Evans wrote a song called "Tinkle Bell"; when Lynne Livingston advised her husband that the word *tinkle* might be misconstrued, the song became "Silver Bells."

By 1955, nearing the end of a decade-long stay at Paramount, Livingston and Evans stuck a toe in television. *Satins and Spurs* (1954) was the first television "spectacular"—conceived by NBC executive Pat Weaver, produced by Max Leibman, and starring Jay Livingston's sister-in-law Betty Hutton, who sang the team's songs. (Hutton played a rodeo queen in love with journalist Kevin McCarthy.) The reviews were so hostile that Hutton retired for a while from show business. Despite its poor reception, Livingston and Evans maintained their television contacts and eventually composed the themes to *Bonanza* (1959)—yes, there are published lyrics—and to *Mr. Ed.* Their 1957 title tune "Tammy" (for *Tammy and the Bachelor*) was done at Universal, where the young Henry Mancini provided the orchestrations. The connection to Mancini would resume in the 1960s when the duo provided lyrics for Mancini's TV theme to *Mr. Lucky*, and for his film song "Dear Heart."

Livingston and Evans departed Paramount with a bang. "Whatever Will Be, Will Be" was written for Hitchcock's remake of *The Man Who Knew Too Much* (1956). Songs weren't normally part of Hitchcock's arsenal, but Paramount demanded one because Doris Day was starring, and everyone would expect her to sing. The song originally had Italian lyrics, and then was recast in Spanish as "Que Será, Será." Paramount insisted on using English lyrics because the Motion Picture Academy wouldn't permit a non-English title to be submitted for award consideration.

Whatever the title, Doris Day hated it—"It's a kiddie song," she said—but manager-husband, Marty Melcher, disagreed. Day had no idea what a smash the song, which conveys a pretty banal philosophy, would become. Due to its immense popularity, she reprised it in the 1960 *Please Don't Eat the Daisies* and the 1966 *Glass Bottom Boat,* both made at MGM.

○   ○   ○

Songwriting teams like Livingston and Evans were relatively stable. Other composers and lyricists turned out some equally great songs at Paramount but changed partners as readily as they changed clothes.

Hoagy Carmichael, looking out the window of his Paramount office, thought, *Who's that little character swinging his coattails and whistling? I never saw anybody so self-assured.* It was Carmichael's first look at Frank Loesser, who had an unnerving air of self-confidence. Loesser drank upwards of ten cups of coffee a day, moved around on his toes, and now and then took a poke at any producer who annoyed him. "At first the kid shook me up," Carmichael said, after he was paired with Loesser. "His exuberance and his zany talk were too much for me. Frank didn't seem serious enough about the matter of writing songs." Carmichael eventually saw how wrong he was. "Two Sleepy People," from *Thanks for the Memory* (1938), was a prime example of Loesser's lyric-writing (to Carmichael's music)—conversational, clever, and managing to convey adoration without spelling it out.

The following year Loesser worked with Paramount house composer Freddy Hollander on *Destry Rides Again* (1939). Hollander had composed "Falling in Love Again" for Marlene Dietrich, and now the Hollander-Loesser team came up with a jaunty number for the German bar girl, "See What the Boys in the Back Room Will Have."

Loesser was feeling his oats—no major songwriter, by most accounts, was so cocky yet so lovable—when Paramount made the unforgivable sin of loaning him out—to B-studio Republic, of all the humiliating places. There was no mystery to the deal. Republic contract songwriter Jule Styne had been assigned to compose a few songs for the new Judy Canova movie, *Sis Hopkins*. Styne, figuring he needed a word man who hadn't been writing only about cowpokes and the prairie, asked for a "top" lyricist. So music co-head Cy Feuer borrowed Loesser from Paramount music head Louis Lipstone, paying an enormous premium for Loesser's services. When told about the deal, the short-tempered Loesser hit the roof. The idea of being trapped on Poverty Row was an affront to him.

Working on the *Sis Hopkins* songs in the Republic songwriters' barracks, Styne played Loesser a melody on the piano. Loesser quickly slammed the door shut and ordered Styne to stop. "Don't you ever play that for anyone else!" he barked. "We'll write that song at Paramount!" Styne and Loesser completed their *Sis Hopkins* assignment. A few weeks later the process was reversed—Styne was loaned to Paramount, where he played the same forbidden tune for Loesser. "Again," Loesser kept insisting, "again." When he seemed to have the tune lodged in his head, Loesser went away for a few days. He returned with the lyrics that became "I Don't Want to Walk Without You, Baby" from *Sweater Girl* (1942).

For Loesser, Paramount was where he did his undergraduate work. At the time he had the energy of an entire pep squad. It's apparent even in an innocuous picture like *Happy Go Lucky* (1943), in which he and Jimmy McHugh turned out "Murder, He Says" for the rotor-motored Betty Hutton, "Let's Get Lost" for Mary Martin (made famous again by jazz trumpeter Chet Baker), and "Sing a Tropical Song," with which the Andrews Sisters began a whole cycle of pop calypso songs.

After his Paramount contract ended, Loesser went freelance. At Warners he teamed with Arthur Schwartz to write the lyrics for "They're Either Too Young or Too Old" and other songs for *Thank Your Lucky Stars* (1943), another in the series of wartime revues that every studio produced. As Paul Fussell has pointed out, the most popular songs during World War II were not of patriotism so much as deprivation, usually of the sexual variety. Like Sam Stept's "Don't Sit under the Apple Tree" or Johnny Mercer's "Dream," "They're Either Too Young or Too Old" told of the effect war was having on the singer's romantic life. Narrators in song were forced to do without—till then, compelled to dream, to be presented with would-be partners who were clearly unsuitable.

"They're Either Too Young Or Too Old" was hardly Loesser's only war-related song. In 1944 he left Hollywood to go into the army. This brought him back to New York. Infantry public relations officer E. J. Kahn, Jr., on leave from *The New Yorker*, wanted Loesser to write a song for the Infantry—"maybe about a hero," Kahn said. "Get me a hero," said Loesser. Kahn submitted a list comprised mostly of wonderfully unwieldy, melting-pot names. Loesser dismissed them as too tough to rhyme; but then he came to the name Rodger Young. The resulting song, "Rodger Young," did all right in 1945, but not as well as Loesser's "Praise the Lord and Pass the Ammunition." The two war songs—one uncharacteristically treacly, the other wry and mordant in the more familiar Loesser style—were the first ones he'd composed the music for as well as the lyrics.

By the late '40s, Loesser returned to Hollywood, although he began to spend less time in town. He handled music and lyrics for another Betty Hutton picture, *The Perils of Pauline* (1947). There was a mini-scandal in the industry when his adorable patter song "Baby, It's Cold Outside" (from MGM's *Neptune's Daughter*, 1949) won the Academy Award; his rivals protested that Loesser and his wife Lynn had been performing the number at private parties for years, therefore it obviously hadn't been written for the movies. The Academy was unmoved. *Where's Charley?* (1949), produced by former Republic music head Cy Feuer, was his first musical comedy, and *Guys and Dolls* (1950) moved him six furlongs ahead of the pack.

Once Loesser, like Cole Porter, had begun to write music *and* lyrics, his gifts seemed outsized for the movies. He interrupted his work on the musical comedy *The Most Happy Fella* to take an assignment from Samuel Goldwyn—the suggestion may have come from music director Walter Scharf, who had been at Republic when Loesser was there—to write the songs for the Danny Kaye musical *Hans Christian Andersen* (1952). Loesser completed his song score, which included such immediate standards as "Wonderful Copenhagen," "Thumbelina," and "Inchworm," then went home to New York. Paramount Pictures was lucky to have had him for a while.

。　　。　　。

In 1967, after swinging hard on "Street of Dreams" at the Sands Hotel, Sinatra declared to his audience, "That's by the late Victor Young!" Young had been dead for a decade, but Sinatra's typically generous attribution made it sound as though Young had died the day before yesterday.

Young's Paramount career overarched all the composers and songwriters who passed through its gates. His life was too brief. Yet he filled it with the lushest music—his underscores and songs are equally beautiful, composed of long melodic lines—that outlives the work of more renowned composers. His show business career began with "Sweet Sue" and ended thirty years later with "Around the World in Eighty Days."

Victor Young was born in Chicago in 1900. His Polish-Jewish parents reversed the migratory trend by sending him to live with rela-

Victor Young
Courtesy ASCAP

tives in Warsaw. For about fourteen years, Young grew up there. During World War I he was interned by the Russians in Kiev; escaping with the aid of a Bolshevist officer, he managed to climb into a cattle car heading back to Warsaw, but he was captured en route and then detained by the Germans. Released at the end of the war, at seventeen, he returned to Warsaw and to the violin that he loved.

Young was already composing on the violin when he married his Polish childhood sweetheart, Rita. Her took her back to Chicago, where Victor became music director at the Central Park Theater. Squat and granite-jawed, his sweet music belied his pugnacious appearance. In Los Angeles, Young investigated musical opportunities for the silents. Then he went to New York, working as a violinist and arranger for Ted Fiorito's orchestra. Many years later a Paramount publicity bio said that Young had turned down a $500-a-week vaudeville contract "because he regarded popular music as unworthy of his violin," but Young seems to have embraced pop music early and enthusiastically. "Sweet Sue (Just You)," published in 1928, was as pop as a pop song could get—no more than a jig.

Over the next few years Young turned out several more tunes that became pop standards. With lyricist Sam Lewis (born 1885) he wrote "Lawd, You Made the Night Too Long" (subsequently transposed into "Sam, You Made the Pants Too Long") and "Street of Dreams"; after moving to Hollywood in 1933, with Ned Washington he wrote "Ghost of a Chance" (Bing Crosby was given a cut as co-lyricist) and "A Hundred Years from Today."

Paramount would be Young's home base for two decades, through the music administrations of Nat Finston, Boris Morross, Louis Lipstone, and Roy Fjastad. Perhaps because he was an excellent violinist, Young composed in broad melodic lines that lent themselves to brief, hummable songs. He made it seem easy. "[Paramount's] chief composer was Victor Young," Miklos Rozsa recorded of his own arrival at the studio in the early '40s, "a kind and charming man whom I liked very much, but who wrote in the Broadway-cum-Rachmaninoff idiom which was then the accepted Hollywood style." Rozsa realized that the Paramount brass had come to expect "hit tunes" as well as effective, dramatic underscoring; Young had spoiled them.

And what tunes! The title tune for 1944's *Love Letters*—a Jennifer

Jones–Joseph Cotten wartime melodrama—was still being successfully recorded twenty years later by Ketty Lester and Elvis Presley. It earned Young his first Academy Award nomination. (The lyrics were by "Body and Soul" lyricist Edward Heyman.) That same year, Young's gorgeous "Stella by Starlight" was introduced in the suspenser *The Uninvited*; the song has been used in the movies many times since, notably in Jerry Lewis's *The Nutty Professor* as the theme for Stella Stevens's character, Stella Purdy. Young's theme to *Golden Earrings* (1948), with or without Livingston and Evans's lyrics, sounds so authentically gypsy that many listeners still believe it comes from an old Central European folk tune. Young was loaned out to Goldwyn to score 1949's *My Foolish Heart*, very loosely based on J. D. Salinger's story "Uncle Wiggily in Connecticut."

Young had a long association with director Cecil B. DeMille, beginning in 1940 with *Northwest Mounted Police*, continuing through *Reap the Wild Wind* (1942), *Samson and Delilah* (1949), and *The Greatest Show on Earth* (1952). DeMille was demanding and irascible. "[DeMille] had certain things that he hated worse than anything, which was diddle-y diddle-y music," editor June Edgerton remembered. "And every picture, Victor said, 'I'll never do another picture with him again. Never!' But of course he always did." DeMille was already thinking about remaking *The Ten Commandments*. Young wanted no part of it.

In the early '50s Young stepped up his activities away from Paramount. The Robert Mitchum Korean War film *One Minute to Zero* was scored at RKO by Constantin Bakaleinikoff but included Young's beautiful "When I Fall in Love (It Will Be Forever)." Young took the obligatory stab at TV scoring and came up with the theme to *Medic* (1954), the early realistic medical drama narrated by Richard Boone. For Fox, Young scored the ham-handed Bogart picture *The Left Hand of God* (1955); the star is clearly nearing the end and doesn't seem to have his heart in it, but Young's love theme shimmers. "Around the World in Eighty Days," given a gentle shove into standardsville by Sinatra's fine Capitol recording, was composed for the 1956 Todd-AO movie of the same name. The title song "Written on the Wind" (Universal, 1956), with lyrics by Sammy Cahn, was in the mode of lush, soupy title tunes; this one made a neat fit with Douglas Sirk's widely admired melodrama.

In March 1955, Young was writing songs with lyricist Stella Unger for their upcoming Broadway musical *Seventh Heaven* when he told the Chicago *Sun-Times*: "Writing a movie score is like a boy sitting in the balcony seat with a girl. He must be forceful enough to impress the girl—but not loud enough to attract the usher!"

Unable to say no to DeMille, Young tentatively agreed to score *The Ten Commandments* after all, though the assignment would have to wait until he returned from New York where he was overseeing the Broadway production of *Seventh Heaven*. (Gloria DeHaven and Ricardo Montalban starred, with a very young Chita Rivera in a supporting role.) The musical flopped, and Young arrrived back in Hollywood too sick to work. The job was turned over to Elmer Bernstein, who inherited Young's two marvelous orchestrators, Sidney Cutner and Leo Shuken. Young, meanwhile, didn't last out the year. That November he died in Palm Springs, at fifty-six.

"When Victor talked to you," Peggy Lee wrote, "he spoke as if he were measuring off bars of music. He would move his hand from left to right, making little strokes like gentle karate chops. . . . He used to say, 'The bass line is the roadbed, Peg.'"

In the summer of 1960, under the aegis of director Bernard Girard and producer Robert Lewis, Paramount tentatively planned a biopic of Young. The filmmakers must have figured that Young's early adventures, fleeing the Russians only to be captured by the Germans, were the stuff of compelling screen biography. And all that overpowering music to underscore it! But the movie was scrapped, probably wisely. The studio orchestras had vanished; rock 'n' roll was taking over. Hollywood rarely got musical biographies right, anyway: for every *Yankee Doodle Dandy* that worked, there were twenty *Rhapsody in Blue*s that didn't.

Young had no peer at Paramount. That is, even the better house composers like Fred Hollander and Gerard Carbonara lacked Young's range. But some extremely gifted musicians passed through the studio gates. One of these was Miklos Rozsa, who had arrived in Hollywood in 1940 sponsored by his frequent London-based employer and fellow Hungarian, Alexander Korda.

Although his scores for Korda pictures, including *The Jungle Book* (which was one of the first soundtracks released on record, in an album of 78s), were well known, it was Rozsa's concert works that generated excitement among musicians. Producers and executives remained indifferent.

Billy Wilder, scheduled to begin a new picture in late 1942, had hoped to use composer Franz Waxman. But Waxman was under contract to rival studio Warners. Wilder asked Paramount to secure the services of his second choice, Rozsa. Wilder and his collaborator Charles Brackett had transposed a Lajos Biro play, *Hotel Imperial,* to Rommel's campaign in North Africa and titled it *Five Graves to Cairo.* "My contract with the picture was for four weeks, which left me about three weeks to write some forty-five minutes of music," Rozsa said.

Aware that he had to prove himself on this, his first Hollywood studio assignment, Rozsa tackled the score. The studio's music director, Louis Lipstone, hated the score and its "dissonances."

"What dissonances?" Rozsa wanted to know.

"In one spot," the music director said, "the violins are playing a G natural and the violas a G sharp. Why don't you make it a G natural in the violas as well—just for *my* sake?" Billy Wilder, pleased with the music, told the music director that he wasn't serenading customers in the *kaffeehaus* any longer and ought to leave the music to the composers.

This hardly endeared Rozsa to Lipstone. Fortunately, Rozsa enjoyed a separate concert career—with greater success than any other composer frequently employed by the studios—in what he called his "double life." (Rozsa scored the 1947 *Double Life.*) Some of the finest American and European concert halls hosted his music. "In my naivete I imagined that all this prestige would enhance my reputation in Hollywood—that there would be cries of 'Hail, Rozsa!' when I walked into the studio the next day. Nothing of the sort: film people didn't listen to the radio and the musical directors wouldn't have gone to a concert if you paid them."

Although he lay low, Rozsa came in for more criticism from Lipstone, who believed Rozsa was writing "Carnegie Hall" music that had no place in a film. For Rozsa's next assignment, Billy Wilder's *Double Indemnity,* the music director instructed him to listen to Herbert Stothart's music for *Madame Curie,* and eagerly awaited the first preview when production chief Buddy DeSylva would have his ears

Miklos Rozsa, 1970s
Courtesy Institute of the American Musical, Inc.

assaulted—and presumably have Rozsa fired. When the preview screening was over, however, DeSylva praised Rozsa's score as "hard-hitting" and only wished there were more of it. "By this time [Lipstone] was grinning from ear to ear and put his arm around DeSylva, saying, 'I always find you the right guy for the job, Buddy—don't I?'"

The *Double Indemnity* score attracted producer David O. Selznick, who hired Rozsa to score Alfred Hitchcock's *Spellbound* (1945). Hitch wanted a "big sweeping love theme" for stars Ingrid Bergman and Gregory Peck, plus music that connoted the paranoia at the heart of the movie. In order to capture the film's dark psychological mood, Rozsa suggested that he compose for the theremin, the electronic instrument famous for its haunting glissandi; he later recalled his employers' reaction to the idea: "Hitchcock and Selznick hadn't heard of the theremin and weren't quite sure whether you ate it or took it for headaches, but they agreed to try it out." Of course Rozsa was also writing for piano and orchestra, but the theremin added novelty to a Hollywood film score.

After *Spellbound's* first preview, in Pasadena, where it was accompanied by a temp track, Rozsa came up with the love theme, now among the most popular themes from the movies. Suddenly the composer was bombarded by Selznick's memos instructing him how to compose for the movies. For a scene in which Bergman silently passes Peck's room, Selznick wrote to Rozsa, "Be sure to sell Ingrid's love when she sees the light under the door (cymbals)." Not knowing what "cymbals" meant exactly, Rozsa did it his own way. Later, excerpts from the popular score were published by Chappell Music as the Spellbound Concerto, which Rozsa pointed out isn't really a concerto at all.

Spellbound was distributed by Selznick rather than Paramount. Rozsa was insulted when, a year later, he was invited by Selznick to audition for the job scoring *Duel in the Sun*. (Rozsa was well beyond the auditioning stage of his career.) Instead, Rozsa returned to Paramount to work for Billy Wilder on *The Lost Weekend* (1945), a job that illuminated the difference a composer could make.

For *Lost Weekend*, Rozsa turned again to the theremin, an instrument beautifully equipped to suggest the delirium suffered by its dipsomaniacal protagonist. When his scoring was completed, Rozsa received a call from Selznick's office to scold him for using the instrument again—as if its employment in *Spellbound* constituted a monopoly held by Selznick. *Lost Weekend's* preview contained a "jazzy, xylophone Gershwinesque" temp track, pieced together by members of the Paramount staff, that led the audience to expect a comedy. Once recorded onto the soundtrack, Rozsa's music again drew the ire of Louis Lipstone; this time only the support of Charles Brackett kept Rozsa's music in. At the 1945 Academy Awards, Rozsa's *Lost Weekend* score lost—to his own *Spellbound*, a weaker score by his own admission. But Lipstone had to eat crow.

After receiving his first Oscar, Rozsa shuttled between Paramount and Universal, in his film noir phase (*The Killers, Desert Fury*) At the end of the '40s, he landed a staff job at MGM. For more than a decade his muscular, symphonic lines were put to use for the studio's A product, notably the quasi-Roman epics *Quo Vadis* (1951), *Ben-Hur* (1959), and *King of Kings* (1961). When such pictures were in vogue, as Rory Guy wrote, Rozsa and Alfred Newman "seemed to vie for the title of God's kapellmeister."

Victor Young had also done his bit as God's choirmaster in several pictures. Thankfully, Paramount had never run strong in the biblical department—DeMille was the primary agent of such balderdash—and stuck to what it did best, comedy and suspense, even after the 1958 studio orchestra strike. The studio never did find any composer to replace Young.

In 1961, Paramount sold the rights to its *Road* pictures to United Artists. Crosby and Hope were in their late fifties; Dorothy Lamour, though only in her mid-forties, was deemed too old to carry the leading lady role. Playing herself in *Road to Hong Kong* (1962), she appeared onscreen for only a couple of minutes while deferring to the younger Joan Collins. This time Van Heusen and Sammy Cahn supplied the songs. But something fundamental was missing—a certain sweetness, perhaps, as well as the looseness that the younger men had had in spades. Hope's character was named Chester Babcock—after Van Heusen, of course. Like most inside jokes, it signified that the door was closing forevermore.

SEVEN

I RECALL PICNIC TIME WITH YOU

COLUMBIA PICTURES

Of all the movie studios operating at the beginning of sound, Columbia Pictures was the last to set up a working music department. Even the equally compact RKO had employed influential music directors by 1931 or so. Columbia didn't really enter the music fray until late 1933.

This was an odd situation for a former songplugger like studio chief Harry Cohn. Before he was twenty, Cohn was singing as the "Edwards" half of Edwards and Ruby, the "Ruby" half being a piano man named Harry Rubinstein. (The piano man would keep the name Ruby and subsequently team up with a former dancer named Bert Kalmar.) For Harry Ruby, the partnership was fraught with so much humiliation that after Cohn ascended to the presidency of Columbia Pictures in 1932, he refused to sign a songwriting contract at the studio.

Harry Cohn was notoriously difficult to work for. Stories abound about this most hated and feared of all movie moguls. (My favorite: writer Norman Krasna, determined to be released from his Columbia contract, rewrote his will to stipulate that his ashes be thrown in Cohn's face.) A mass of contradictions, the barely literate Cohn enjoyed his most durable rapport with writers; a songplugger for years, he seems to have possessed no deep knowledge of music. But in early 1934 help was on the way when the former Paramount orchestra concertmaster Morris Stoloff arrived at Columbia to help out with the Grace Moore picture *One Night of Love.*

Grace Moore's career had already risen and fallen several times by the time she arrived in Hollywood in 1929. Before entering the operatic world, the often blonde, Tennessee-born soprano had appeared in a few editions of Irving Berlin's *Music Box Revue* on Broadway, introducing "What'll I Do?" in 1924 and, in a duet with Oscar Shaw, "All Alone." Some observers have referred to Moore as beautiful; certainly she was striking in a cool, severe way. One way or another she got to financier Otto Kahn, who arranged for her to study opera. In 1928, she made her debut at the Metropolitan Opera in *La Bohème,* and traveled to Hollywood the following year at the behest of Irving Thalberg.

Moore rode in a Pullman car paid for by ardent admirer L. B. Mayer, from New York to Los Angeles. (Her entourage included singer-comedienne Beatrice Lillie, who had been signed by Fox.) Moore reported to Thalberg at MGM, ready to become a movie star. Although synchronized sound was new to Hollywood, there had in fact been many films made featuring opera stars. As far back as 1908 Enrico Caruso had appeared in short films. Soprano Anna Case, who had hailed from Clinton, New Jersey, and sang at the Met, was billed as "the Most Beautiful Woman in Grand Opera" and made films in the 1920s. Geraldine Farrar (*Carmen*) had her turn, along with Giovanni Martinelli (*Pagliacci*). Around the time Moore arrived in Culver City, Fox imported Irish tenor John McCormack to Hollywood to star in *Song o' My Heart* (1930). On a relatively clear soundtrack, McCormack sang "Rose of Tralee" and "I Hear You Calling Me." But the picture is remembered more for introducing Maureen O'Sullivan to screen audiences than for McCormack, who was built like a fireplug and had no camera presence.

Grace Moore had a different problem: she was inclined to obesity. MGM cast her in Romberg's *New Moon* opposite Lawrence Tibbett, who strained to lift her. Distressed by the studio's treatment of her, she rapidly gained more weight. After her third film, she was let go, and returned to New York, her career in tatters. Her price, she soon discovered, was half of what it had been before she had gone to Hollywood.

Against the odds, Moore managed to revive her operatic career. New acclaim took her west again, to the Hollywood Bowl. At a party thrown in her honor by director Edmund Goulding, Moore was approached by Harry Cohn, who wanted to sign her to a hefty $25,000 contract. Moore hedged and waited to see if Thalberg would cast her opposite Maurice Chevalier in *The Merry Widow*, then in preparation at MGM; when the role went to Jeanette MacDonald, Moore signed with Cohn.

Now that Columbia had her, Cohn and his producers didn't know what to do with her. Although svelte once again and apparently blonder than ever, Moore had talents that seemed more in tune with an earlier era. Cohn dumped Moore on the young, inexperienced, aspiring producer Everett Riskin, brother of screenwriter Robert Riskin, figuring he would eventually throw up his hands. (Surrender by a Columbia employee usually preceded permanent obeisance to Cohn, which is the way Cohn wanted it.) But Riskin had his writers rework a familiar story about a beautiful young soprano chafing under her demanding Italian coach. An adaptation was prepared, at least partly based on a novel by Dorothy Speare, a dark-haired and very tall soprano who had been coached in Milan and fictionalized her experiences there. Soon *One Night of Love* was in pre-production.

Moore went to see Harry Cohn about the music. In his book on Cohn, Bob Thomas reconstructed the meeting this way:

"Harry, darling, I must sing *Butterfly*."

"That old thing?" Cohn buzzed the music department on his intercom. "Find out how much they want for 'Poor Butterfly,'" ordered the former songplugger, thinking Moore wanted to sing the 1916 Raymond Hubbell tune.

"No, no," Moore corrected. "I mean the *Butterfly* by Puccini."

"You mean he stole it?" said Cohn, shocked.

In the film, Moore got to sing *Butterfly* and several other classics, including the "Habanera" from *Carmen* and Tchaikovsky's "None But the Lonely Heart."

Lou Silvers came over from Fox with his arranger Rex Bassett, and they handled much of the music for *One Night of Love*. Victor Schertzinger directed and, as usual, contributed a song (the title song, with lyrics by Gus Kahn). Opera specialist-violinist Dr. Pietro Cimini was brought in to advise on the arias. Morris Stoloff, who had been signed away from Paramount, conducted the orchestra. During much of the filming, Moore behaved in prima donna fashion. Once she flatly refused to sing the arrangement made for her of Puccini's "Un Bel Di," returned to her dressing room and locked the door, leaving the sixty-plus orchestra members idle on the sound stage. At Cohn's instruction, the gentle Stoloff went to Moore and, speaking through the closed dressing room door, informed her that hourly wages for the Columbia musicians would come out of her salary as long as she refused to sing. Moore grudgingly reappeared and gave a fine performance.

One Night of Love outgrossed MGM's *Merry Widow* and practically everything else that year. Moore lost 1934's best actress Academy Award to Claudette Colbert (for Columbia's *It Happened One Night*) but received the Gold Medal from the Society of Arts and Sciences in New York for "raising the standard of cinema entertainment." Schertzinger and Silvers received the first best-scoring Oscar. The title tune lost the best-song Oscar to "The Continental" by Con Conrad and Herb Magidson from RKO's *The Gay Divorcee*.

Still, *One Night of Love* was so well loved that it triggered a three-year spate of movies featuring opera stars. Jan Kiepura moved from Europe to Hollywood with his wife, soprano Marta Eggerth. The slightly cross-eyed, lovely mezzo soprano Gladys Swarthout was given a Paramount contract, while Metropolitan star Lily Pons (then married to conductor André Kostelanetz) warbled for RKO. Tenor James Melton signed at Warners and, between arias, introduced Warren and Dubin's "September in the Rain" (in *Melody for Two*, 1937). Nino Martini's most acclaimed appearance was in Rouben Mamoulian's *The Gay Desperado* (1936), underwritten by United Artists. Baritone Nelson Eddy had been in films since 1931, but the 1935 *Naughty Marietta* launched his durable teaming with Jeanette MacDonald. (Cartoonist Al Capp nailed down the tone of their duets as "depraved sincerity.")

As early as 1935, *Charlie Chan at the Opera* and the Marx Brothers' *A Night at the Opera* were parodying the genre with a vengeance. Apart from the teenage Deanna Durbin (who was a movie musical genre unto herself), it would be another eight or nine years before operatic stars reappeared on screen, most of them in films produced by Joe Pasternak's unit at MGM. Kathryn Grayson, Patrice Munsel, and Mario Lanza starred in more tightly construct-ed stories, with heldentenor Lauritz Melchior singing in supporting roles. Of all these stars, Lanza appeared latest, though he was dead at thirty-eight; *The Great Caruso* (1951), coming near the beginning of Lanza's film career, was probably the last successful studio-made opera movie. The better opera movies that followed—say, *Diva* (1982), featuring the statuesque Wilhemenia Fernandez, or *Meeting Venus* (1991)—came mostly from Europe and tended to underplay their operatic components.

As for Grace Moore, she appeared in a few more semi-operatic Columbia movies, most of them produced by Everett Riskin. If any of them is remembered, it's probably *I'll Take Romance* (1937), and then only for its lovely title song, by Oscar Hammerstein and George Jessel's protégé Ben Oakland. Hammerstein and Oakland were reteamed for another Columbia project, *The Lady Objects*, but Moore was finished in Hollywood. Her presence, slender or not, simply couldn't attract movie audiences. Still, her concert career thrived through most of the '40s. In 1947 she died in a plane crash on a Copenhagen runway; she had just turned forty-six.

o   o   o

In 1936, Morris Stoloff took command of Columbia's entire music department. The Philadelphia native was pleasant, hard-working, and diplomatic. A violinist by training, he could analyze a score with light-ning speed. His wife, Elsa, had been a soprano; together the Stoloffs attracted musicians from all over Los Angeles to their house. Harry Cohn persisted in calling him "Stoller." An excellent conductor, Stoloff occasionally took on the oddball assignment, like ghosting William Holden's violin-playing in *Golden Boy* (1939).

Over the years Stoloff brought in adept arrangers and orchestra-tors. Conrad Salinger and Paul Mertz worked on the two Astaire-Hayworth pictures made at Columbia, *You'll Never Get Rich* (1941) and *You Were Never Lovelier* (1942). Mertz also composed Jean Arthur's piano "impromptu" in *Mr. Smith Goes to Washington* (1939). For years Columbia's orchestra was overseen by Rudy Polk, a violinist associated with Jascha Heifetz. Dimitri Tiomkin often worked for director Frank Capra, the studio's most-successful director. Mischa Bakaleinikoff handled the musical direction for most of the studio's B product.

Composer-arranger Saul Chaplin was invited aboard after a debilitating break with lyricist Sammy Cahn.

> Working in the Columbia Music Department during the '40s was an education for me—thanks to my able tutor, Morris Stoloff. He introduced me to every facet of music in films: music editing, music mixing, recording, rerecording, preparing a film for scoring, tempo click tracks.... I learned what to ask for to achieve a particular result I had in mind. And I got lots of experience. It was not uncommon for me to find myself working on as many as five pictures at the same time. For one, there would be vocal arrangements to make; for another, a song to be rehearsed; for another, a new song to be written; for another, scoring; and a fifth, rerecording.

Columbia wasn't MGM, of course, and it lacked Warners' and Paramount's rich histories of early movie musicals. After *One Night of Love*, its next path-breaking musical movie was, oddly enough, *A Song to Remember* (1945), a biography of Chopin.

Stoloff hunted high and low to find the right pianist to actually make the Chopin recordings that actor Cornel Wilde, playing the Polish composer-pianist, would fake. Stoloff invited Arthur Rubinstein to Columbia, where Harry Cohn shouted out, "Hiya, Ruby!"; Rubinstein withdrew from consideration. After Stoloff had Vladimir Horowitz on the hook, he and Cohn's executive assistant Sidney Buchman deliberately kept Cohn away from the maestro. Following a Hollywood Bowl recital in memory of Rachmaninoff, however, Horowitz was offended by a fan's innocent query—"You were marvelous, darling, but why do you play that dreary stuff?"—and it took all of Stoloff's diplomatic powers to keep him from bolting. That's when Cohn buttonholed Horowitz, causing Stoloff and Buchman to hold their breath. "Jeez, your piano playing tonight was great!" said Cohn. "Some of that slow stuff I don't understand, but that brrrrrr up and down the keys is colossal!" Horowitz let out his magnificent whinnying horse laugh, and everyone relaxed. But Horowitz, too, dropped out when he learned that the Chopin pieces would have to be edited to fit the film story.

Stoloff eventually procured the services of Jose Iturbi, the skilled Spanish pianist (born 1895) who was underrated by the music community because he appeared so often, and with such evident satisfaction, in mediocre pictures. Shrewdly, Stoloff also hired Miklos Rozsa, who had rescored Schubert for the Korda picture *New Wine* (1941), which Rozsa so hated that he refused his credit. Although Rozsa didn't care for the Chopin script either, he couldn't pass up the challenge. He waded through the shimmering Chopin pieces and made his selections; if nothing appropriate turned up, he wrote musical patches "in the style of."

This didn't mean that Cornel Wilde had to just show up. Sammy Cahn reported standing in Morris Stoloff's office when he saw a notice on the bulletin board: "Cornel Wilde is to be at the studio to learn the Polonaise from 2 to 3, the Etude from 3 to 4, the Concerto from 4 to 5."

Despite the jerry-rigged music, *A Song to Remember* was a resounding box-office success. The Iturbi 78-rpm recordings outsold even the Andrews Sisters' hit, "Rum and Coca-Cola," and sheet music sales of Chopin's piano pieces enjoyed a resurgence that hadn't been seen in decades. Stoloff had again shown Harry Cohn that he could piece together a commercial movie about classical music.

Of course *A Song to Remember* is a little ridiculous, particularly if you want the facts. "I saw recently what was supposed to be a screen biography of a real person—Frederic Chopin. Showpan, they called him," the acerbic critic James Agate recorded in his massive diary, *The Ego*:

> There is no possible film story of that real historical personage—so they made one up, in glorious Technihorror. It was a jumble of nonsense from beginning to end. For example, the film suggested that Chopin toured Italy, Austria, Hungary, Holland, and Denmark to help the starving Poles. Actually, being hard up, he toured Liverpool and Glasgow to help himself!... They showed us Chopin composing at the age of ten the D Flat Valse which is known as Opus 64.

None of this mattered to audiences. What mattered was that Cornel Wilde, in a supernova impersonation, was playing—or pretending to play—all that wonderful music. For the record, the director of *A Song to*

Remember was Charles Vidor, a dapper Hungarian who was Harry Cohn's best buddy, then later, as with so many Cohn employees, his arch-nemesis.

Before things went sour with Cohn, however, Charles Vidor was often called on to handle the films that starred Columbia's brightest light, Rita Hayworth. After her two films with Astaire—the first with songs by Cole Porter, the second with songs by Jerome Kern and Johnny Mercer—Hayworth was ready for another musical: *Cover Girl,* which was produced by composer Arthur Schwartz. Jerome Kern was rehired, and Ira Gershwin served as his lyricist for the first and only time. Musically, Kern and Schwartz were sympatico; in fact Schwartz's own style suggests that he could have composed the melodies for "A Sure Thing," "Make Way for Tomorrow," or "Long Ago and Far Away." Stoloff used Saul Chaplin to orchestrate the film, with Carmen Dragon helping on the arrangements.

Chaplin had initially been hired as a vocal arranger, but his long association with Phil Silvers, who was co-starring in *Cover Girl* with Hayworth and Gene Kelly, convinced Stoloff that he could supervise the music. Arranging "Put Me to the Test"—the lyric had been scrapped from the Gershwins' *Damsel in Distress* seven years earlier—Chaplin had to edit the song to fit Kelly's dance routine, and needed to add two lines of his own. Stoloff, knowing Kern's temper, told Chaplin to see if he could get new lyrics from Ira Gershwin.

The next day, Chaplin arrived at Gershwin's house to find, seated around the living room, producer Schwartz, Yip Harburg, Leo Robin, Johnny Mercer, Oscar Levant, and playwright Marc Connelly. Stuttering, Chaplin managed to explain to the entire group what he needed. Gershwin prevailed upon his pals to stay and help them. "Lines started coming at me like buckshot," Chaplin wrote. "The biggest contributor was Yip Harburg. He sprouted couplets like a fountain." In the end, Gershwin came up with the two lines.

Kern wasn't particularly pleased with either Chaplin's arrangement of "Put Me to the Test," or with Gershwin's two additional lines. When the number was screened for him, Kern sat stonefaced through it, then said, "If it works at the preview, keep it in; otherwise throw the damn thing out!" Kern was notoriously, fiercely protective of his music. A tune he called "Midnight Music"—Kelly sang it to Hayworth at midnight—was matched with Gershwin's lyric "Long Ago and Far Away," much to Kern's chagrin.

In any case, the *Cover Girl* songs are gorgeous, and the movie managed to integrate music and dance with the story of Brooklyn nightclub owner Danny McGuire (Kelly) holding fast while the love of his life, dancer Rusty Parker (Hayworth), wins a cover girl contract and flirts with fame in Manhattan. Ghosting for Hayworth's vocals was Martha Mears. (Five years later Mears, playing a nightclub singer, introduced Victor Young's "My Foolish Heart" in the Goldwyn movie of that name.) Fortunately Hayworth herself didn't have to sing to generate heat.

So winning was the *Cover Girl* team that Harry Cohn bought the screen rights to Rodgers and Hart's Broadway success, *Pal Joey*. The idea was for Kelly to reprise his role as Joey, with Hayworth playing the innocent young Linda. But MGM refused to release Kelly, and the property languished for another thirteen years, when it was made with Frank Sinatra as Joey, new Columbia star Kim Novak as Linda, and Hayworth as the world-weary Vera.

In the 1940s, the fortunes of Columbia Pictures were closely bound up with the stardom of Hayworth. If the musical pictures showed her off to marvelous advantage, it was *Gilda* (1946) that made her a superstar. Put together by screenwriter-turned-producer Virginia Van Upp, *Gilda* doesn't make a whole lot of sense. But when Hayworth, in a black strapless gown, does a tipsy striptease while singing "Put the Blame on Mame," nothing else matters—not logic or coherence, and certainly not leading man Glenn Ford. Vidor directed and Stoloff conducted, as usual. The former dance-band pianist Marlin Skiles (born 1906) worked on the vocal arrangements. Hugo Friedhofer, at last escaping his orchestrator's cubbyhole at Warners, was brought in to compose the underscore. (Earlier in the year, Stoloff hired Friedhofer to make an arrangement of "The Anniversary Waltz" for *The Jolson Story*. Stoloff took one look at Friedhofer's arrangement and correctly noted, "You worked a lot of Jewish weddings when you were a cello player," because he had spotted the "schmalzy" cello obligato in the score.)

Once again, it wasn't Hayworth singing in the movie—this time it was Montreal-born Anita Ellis, older sister of Broadway musical star Larry Kert. (Ellis would dub Hayworth again in *Lady from Shanghai*.) "Put the Blame on Mame" sounds like an old burlesque number. In fact, it was written for *Gilda* by Doris Fisher and Allan Roberts, both Columbia contract songwriters. Doris Fisher (born 1915), daughter of songwriter Fred Fisher, began her career as a singer with Eddy Duchin. Roberts, ten years older, came to Hollywood through the offices of producer Mike Todd. Roberts, working at his piano, and Fisher wrote some of Columbia's more popular songs, including "You Always Hurt the One You Love," "Into Each Life a Little Rain Must Fall" (both 1944 hits for the Mills Brothers), and "That Ole Devil Called Love." Occasionally Roberts collaborated with fellow New Yorker Lester Lee, who wrote for Hayworth in her later Columbia films.

$$\circ \qquad \circ \qquad \circ$$

Largely wary of musicals, though, Columbia generally kept relatively few songwriters under contract at any given time. Far and away the most industrious of these few was Sammy Cahn.

Sammy Cahn and Saul Chaplin had gone west in April 1940 in search of work. Although their catalog contained "Rhythm Is Our Business," "Until the Real Thing Comes Along," "Dedicated to You," and "Bei Mir Bist Du Schoen," they couldn't find work as songwriters. Both men were in their late twenties and full of moxie, especially Cahn, who sold a song using his already patented style: feet apart in a boxer's stance, hand out, head thrown back. But 1940 was a period of retrenchment for movie musicals. The second phase of important Hollywood musicals had ended, and of all the 1939 blockbusters—including *Gone with the Wind, Wuthering Heights, Mr. Smith Goes to Washington, Ninotchka*—only Metro's *The Wizard of Oz* contained original songs, and these were by established Hollywood writers.

The only job Chaplin and Cahn could find was with B-studio Republic Pictures, who hired them to write a script for Bob Crosby and His Bobcats. The screenplay for *Rookies on Parade*—comprised mostly of vaudeville sketches they knew from the Catskills—also became a songwriting assignment so Republic could save some dough. While Chaplin and Cahn were writing for *Rookies on Parade*, Morris Stoloff was apprised of their imminent availability and arranged for them to come to Columbia.

Most of Chaplin and Cahn's Columbia songs were written in an eighteen-month period for B-unit producer Irving Briskin, "a tall, amiable, rather gruff man." Several potential projects, including one with Hayworth who was to star in *Eadie Was a Lady,* were shelved. They managed to get songs in Columbia's *Time Out for Rhythm* (1941; Rudy Vallee, Glen Gray and His Casa Loma Orchestra doing "Boogie Woogie Man"), *Blondie Goes Latin* (1941), and *Two Latins from Manhattan* (1941), but their timing was off. There was a preponderance of Latin-flavored pictures, because Hollywood was looking to South America for a new audience to replace the European audience, lost to them since the Nazis had occupied so many countries.

A more immediate problem for the songwriters, however, was that ASCAP songs were getting no airplay that year, due to the union's recent tussle with the National Association of Broadcasters and ASCAP's new rival, BMI. Because Chaplin and Cahn were both ASCAP members, nothing they wrote got on the radio. Unable to plug its own product, Columbia didn't renew their contract. The ambitious, aggressive Cahn had seen it coming, but the more retiring Chaplin had not. When their manager informed Chaplin that Cahn was going out on his own, he was devastated.

Chaplin was scooped up by Columbia for his solo services; Cahn partnered with Jule Styne at Republic. One of their first collaborations, "I've Heard That Song Before," was sung by Martha O'Driscoll (ghosted by Margaret Whiting) in the 1942 *Youth Parade.* The way Cahn told (ad nauseum) the story of its composition, Styne sat down at the piano one day and played the first few bars of a melody that had been rolling around in his head for a while.

"It seems to me I've heard that song before!" shouted Cahn.

Annoyed, Styne said, "What are you, a tune detective?" Cahn explained no, that was the lyric he imagined with the melody. It was the beginning of a collaboration that would last, off and on, for more than a dozen years.

Little of the Cahn-Styne collaboration survives as Columbia film work. There were songs for Kay Kyser's band in *Carolina Blues* (1944), the Hayworth semi-musical *Tonight and Every Night* (1945), and *Tars and Spars* (1946), the Coast Guard musical that introduced Sid Caesar to screen audiences. But the duo's greatest value to Columbia lay primarily in their social availability to Harry Cohn. With the assistance of the frenetic, eternally ad-libbing Phil Silvers, Cahn and Styne wrote an entire evening's show for Cohn's fiftieth birthday party. (The high point of the evening, by most accounts, was the surprise appearance of Al Jolson, who sang "Rockabye Your Baby" to Cohn.) Cahn became Cohn's regular opponent in gin rummy, one of the few activities that relaxed the executive. Unlike Cohn's other opponents, Cahn never lost on purpose, and he maintained his batch of IOUs until he was ready to cash them in with the boss.

Sensing that the gruff Columbia chief was cheating himself out of music fees, Cahn encouraged him to buy Crawford Music so the studio could have a publishing arm. Once that deal was made, Cahn recommended that Jonie Taps, a songplugger then working at music publisher Shapiro, Bernstein in New York be hired to run the newly acquired company.

> Jonie Taps is best described as a very short squattish man who has a laugh as loud and explosive as it is unexpected. A squat Babe Ruth. Fastidious dresser in the true music-man sense: white on white Cye shirt, Mele handsome shoes, Sulka tie, monograms, custom-made suits—all standard for the top man in the music business down to the errand boy.

At first, Jonie Taps resisted meeting Harry Cohn. When he finally did, the two men quickly became confidants. Taps not only took over Crawford Music; he became *the* musicals producer on the Columbia lot.

Cohn benefited from his new music interests, but his boorish, controlling behavior antagonized valuable players like Cahn and Styne. An attempt to keep the songwriters tied to a five-year contract drew Sammy Cahn's undying enmity. After the gentler, more forgiving Styne failed to patch relations between Cohn and Cahn, the songwriters decamped to Warners, bouncing back and forth between that studio and MGM over the next few years.

Twirling through a few of Cahn & Styne's Columbia assignments was the girl-next-door starlet Janet Blair (born Martha Janet Lafferty in 1921). Originally signed by the studio to ghost for Rita Hayworth, she photographed so rosily that she won roles for herself. She introduced Cole Porter's "You'd Be So Nice to Come Home To" in *Something to Shout About* (1943). The year before that, Blair appeared as Rosalind Russell's younger sibling in *My Sister Eileen*; in a 1955 remake, the story received a complete song score by Leo Robin and returning Broadway conqueror Jule Styne. The underscoring of the second version was done by a crewcutted, former dance arranger named George Duning.

⚬ ⚬ ⚬

Born in Richmond, Indiana, in 1908, Duning was educated in Cincinnati. In his early twenties he joined bandleader Kay Kyser. Along with Van Alexander, Duning wrote arrangements that gave a harder swing to a band that had previously sounded "sweet" in a soft, Lombardo-like style. Duning also played piano and trumpet for Kyser, and arranged most of the music for Kyser's popular Lucky Strike radio show, a deliberately goofy quiz program that came to be called "Kay Kyser's Kollege of Musical Knowledge."

By the early '40s, Kyser's program was minimizing music in favor of knockabout antics, and the whole enterprise was wearing thin on Duning. When Kyser's band appeared in Columbia's 1944 *Carolina Blues*, Morris Stoloff recognized Duning's arranging talents, and signed him to work at the studio.

In those days, Hollywood musicians congregated each Sunday at Beverly Hills High School to play and discuss each other's latest work. There Duning met Arthur Morton, who showed him his variations on music by Vittoria, the sixteenth-century Spanish composer, which he'd initially orchestrated for Alfred Newman in *The Hunchback of Notre Dame* (1939). In town for eight or nine years by then, Morton was already deeply involved with the movie industry as well as its music. He had arrived from Minneapolis to write songs, and subsequently became a composer for Hal Roach; *Topper* was an early credit. His older brother Lawrence followed and was soon the country's leading critic of film music; and his father-in-law, Sam Hellman, was then working on the script of *My Darling Clementine* for Fox. Morton and Duning became drinking buddies.

Duning arranged music for several Columbia movies, then went into the navy. It was only when he returned from the sea in 1946, that he really got going as a composer. Dick Powell wanted him for the rainslicked melodrama *Johnny O'Clock* (1946). Then came a gaggle of underscores, sometimes as many as eight in a year, a work schedule approaching Max Steiner's. This was mostly on Columbia's B-plus features, which were still being conducted primarily by Mischa Bakeleinikoff.

Every now and then, Duning was given an assignment of more than passing interest. *To the Ends of the Earth* (1948) was an astonishingly effective score for another Dick Powell tough-guy programmer. *Shockproof* (1949), a film noir showcasing Cornel Wilde and his wife, Patricia Knight, gave Duning the opportunity to compose in bittersweet colors. *Johnny Allegro* (1949), which mashed *Gilda* and *The Most Dangerous Game* together in a plot about a counterfeit ring, was in a similar key. Duning had a gift for making heavy melodramatics play lighter.

Duning was kicked upstairs for *Jolson Sings Again* (1949), an unnecessary but eventually lucrative sequel. Saul Chaplin had left the studio, hired away by Johnny Green at MGM, leaving Stoloff in need of an all-around music man for the studio's more expensive product; Duning was the man. The sequel focused on Jolson's "second" marriage (in reality it was his fourth) to a nurse, and on his comeback as he approached sixty, ignited by the surprising success of the earlier *Jolson Story*. (In one vertigo-inducing scene, Larry Parks as Jolson meets Larry Parks the actor who will portray him in the movie.) Again, Jolson's voice came out of Parks's mouth. For their work on the sequel, Duning and Stoloff were nominated for a best scoring of a musical Oscar. (They lost to MGM's *On the Town.*)

In 1950, Duning's music was given first-class treatment in *No Sad Songs for Me.* In this weeper, starring Margaret Sullivan as a terminally ill young wife planning for her family's future, Duning got to try out some sweeping themes. Stoloff conducted a forty-three-piece orchestra for those themes, as well as for the Brahms Symphony No. 1, also used in the picture.

By then Arthur Morton was aboard. (After ten years at Twentieth, Morton had made the mistake of asking Alfred Newman for a raise.) Duning loved the way Morton orchestrated, especially for brass. They had adjacent offices on the lot and drank together at Naples tavern across the street, where Raoul the bartender kept them sufficiently oiled.

Three 1953 productions bolstered Duning's position at the studio. *Miss Sadie Thompson* and *Salomé* were Rita Hayworth projects. Jo Ann Greer dubbed her in *Miss Sadie Thompson,* a semi-musical, Technicolor remake of the Somerset Maugham story, "Rain," though neither Greer nor Duning is credited on the Mercury soundtrack album. For the dance sequence in *Salomé,* Duning asked Stoloff to hire Daniele Amfitheatrof, who had more experience composing for that kind of thing.

Duning composed and pulled together various musical elements for the big-budget Pearl Harbor picture *From Here to Eternity.* To test the all-important sound of Pruitt (Montgomery Clift) playing "Taps" for his murdered friend Maggio (Frank Sinatra), half the Columbia music department, including members of the Los Angeles Philharmonic, trekked out to a distant canyon with a carload of bugles. After a grueling afternoon of acoustical experiments, they thought they had the sound they wanted and drove back to the studio to plan the elaborate recording process. "Are you nuts?!" screamed Harry Cohn when he heard about the costly outing. Cohn dictated that the recording be made there on the soundstage, with a lot of vibrato, from a single bugle. "And you know what? Cohn was right," said Arthur Morton. Trumpeter Mannie Klein played "Taps" with the kind of schmalz that made audiences cry—exactly the effect that was called for. (By that time Klein's wife, Marion, was the Columbia orchestra contractor, hiring musicians and planning the orchestra's recording dates.)

The song "Re-Enlistment Blues" is by Fred Karger and Bob Wells, as is the title tune, written expressly for the movie but before principal photography had begun. Duning incorporated it into two jukebox scenes, and in the scene when Lorene (Donna Reed) brings Pruitt home to her apartment. Sinatra's Capitol recording of the song, arranged and conducted by Nelson Riddle, sent the song through the roof. Within a few weeks, "From Here to Eternity" found its way into Columbia's *It Should Happen to You;* Peter Lawford's character plays a recording of it while trying to seduce Judy Holliday. (*It Should Happen to You* was scored by Freddy Hollander, who was undoubtedly instructed to exploit the tune.)

After *Eternity,* Duning took a breather. *On the Waterfront* (1954) was a Columbia anomaly—a Sam Spiegel production first, a Columbia Picture second—and the music came from well out of the reach of the Music Department. In New York, after principal photography was completed, Sam Spiegel asked Leonard Bernstein to take a look at a rough cut. Elia Kazan has written:

> It was down to length but clumsy and uneven in details. Sam had been talking to Lenny Bernstein, and something about his apologetic tone angered me further.... "This is a great picture," I shouted—the first time this had occurred to me. Bernstein agreed with me and we had a composer.

This was a monumental decision for Bernstein, whose one previous movie studio residency, at MGM for *On the Town,* had sent him rushing back to New York.

Fortunately, Bernstein didn't have to contend with studio types, just Spiegel and Kazan—strong egos, to be sure (like Bernstein's), but far outside the Hollywood mainstream. Although Bernstein's *On the Waterfront* score has its passionate detractors, it remains one of the most beautiful and powerful suites from the movies. Just as Bernstein sounds as if he owes a lot to Copland in general, his *On the Waterfront* sounds as if he has listened specifically to *Quiet City,* the incidental music that Copland composed to accompany a 1939 play by Irwin Shaw.

On the Waterfront moves from its broad opening theme, wide as the Hudson River, to the menacing percussiveness that anticipates so much of *West Side Story,* and then to the achingly sweet love theme sent airborne by flute. In his book *Film Music,* Roy Prendergast criticizes much of the Bernstein score for being "intrusive and inept-sounding from a dramatic standpoint"; Prendergast finds Bernstein's music needlessly jagged, and covering dialog that you should be able to hear. I can't help feeling, however, that this was an audacious, and successful, experiment: when the music drowns out a conversation, as in the anguishing scene when Marlon Brando confesses to Eva Marie Saint that he unwittingly set up her brother for execution, the music tells us everything we need to know—and perhaps more eloquently than speech could. Like most serious, non-Hollywood composers, Bernstein tended to orchestrate his own work; for *On the Waterfront*, he may have received assistance from Sid Ramin and Irwin Kostal.

Ramin and Kostal also worked on *West Side Story* (1961), a very bad picture despite all the talent that went into it. Apart from that, Bernstein never again had anything to do with movie music. Columbia Pictures and Harry Cohn were grateful for the box-office receipts and awards earned by *On the Waterfront*, but they left Bernstein to preside over his New York musical domain.

In Los Angeles, Columbia pictures were still scored by the old system: composer, music director, orchestrator, music cutter, studio musicians, etc. *The Eddy Duchin Story* (1955), was a natural for Duning, whose experience with Kay Kyser's band lent the movie more swing than anyone could have expected. Carmen Cavallaro played the soundtrack piano. For *Picnic* (1956), Duning ingeniously combined a lush melody of his own—it evokes dewy meadows, warm nights, and the flush of new romance—and grafted it onto the 1934 hit "Moonglow," credited to bandleader Will Hudson and his co-leader and lyricist Eddie DeLange. Duning and Arthur Morton made the combined "Picnic" and "Moonglow" themes weightless so that the music drifts over the action like cumulus clouds across a cerulean sky. As usual, Stoloff conducted, and American record buyers responded by making "Moonglow and Theme from 'Picnic'" the seventh best-selling record of 1956. Stoloff, the fifty-eight-year-old former violinist who had begun his West Coast career with the Los Angeles Philharmonic, suddenly found himself on the charts next to Elvis Presley ("Don't Be Cruel"), The Platters ("Great Pretender"), and Gogi Grant ("Wayward Wind"). Not bad for a Philadelphia fiddler.

Duning had too many scores to compose before he could slow down, but he must have enjoyed his colleagues' approval. André Previn wrote that the *Picnic* score "really knocked me out." There were encomiums from Johnny Green and director Josh Logan, who didn't deny how important Duning's contribution had been to *Picnic*. Hugo Friedhofer wrote to Duning, " . . . if you don't pick up the Award for this one, it will be the most flagrant miscarriage of justice since [Alex] North lost on 'Streetcar' to you-know-who [Franz Waxman won for *A Place in the Sun*]."

Shortly after the film's release, Steve Allen lobbied to provide lyrics to the *Picnic* theme. Record producer Bob Thiele, then concentrating on pop material but soon to become one of the most important jazz producers in the business, lived next door to Allen in Manhattan. Knowing Allen had written lyrics, Thiele persuaded the McGuire Sisters to record them. Released on the Coral label, the single became an instant hit. Steve Allen also penned words to Duning's title themes for *Bell, Book and Candle* (1958) and *Houseboat* (1958), a loanout of Duning's services to Paramount. (The Oscar-nominated song from *Houseboat*, however, was "Almost in Your Arms," by Livingston and Evans.)

During this period, the Duning score that made his colleagues really sit up was *Cowboy* (1958), a lively, semi-jazz work that underscored Frank Harris's autobiographical story of a writer (Jack Lemmon) trying to negotiate the alien West. Columbia star Glenn Ford played Lemmon's trail boss, and the picture is more interesting than it sounds.

Columbia Pictures was thrown into turmoil with the death of Harry Cohn at sixty-seven on February 27, 1958. Morris Stoloff, twenty-three years in the same office as head of music at the studio, remained like a rock. He managed to keep most of his composers, even though the studio musicians, at Columbia as elsewhere, were out on strike.

George Duning had already scored several pictures for Richard Quine (a former juvenile performer at MGM who occasionally wrote lyrics), and now he wrote appropriately soupy music for Quine's *Strangers When We Meet* (1960). He also composed a theme for *Song Without End* (1960), Columbia's D.O.A. attempt to remake Liszt as it had so successfully remade Chopin. The Liszt works were ghosted by Cuban pianist Jorge Bolet. Duning's music was excluded from *Song Without End*'s Academy Award, which went to Stoloff and his co-music director Harry Sukman. A former concert pianist who had been on staff at Paramount for years, Sukman (born 1912) did the lion's share of musical work on the picture, and then recorded *The Franz Liszt Story* on Liberty Records.

For Stoloff the Academy Award for *Song Without End* was, at best, bittersweet vindication. (It was his third for music direction.) The studios' defeat of their striking musicians, at the end of 1958, had provided ostensible cause for Stoloff's dismissal a year later, but it's probably fair to say that Stoloff was swept out with the wave of Harry Cohn loyalists by Cohn's successor, Abe Schneider. Stoloff sued Columbia Pictures for breach of contract; his attorney, Frank Mankiewicz, negotiated a $50,000 out-of-court settlement.

By the time the check cleared, Stoloff was on to other, if not greener, pastures. He brought Harry Sukman with him to Warners to co-music direct *Fanny* (1960), Josh Logan's dramatic film version of the Harold Rome musical. (The scoring is the best, perhaps the only worthwhile, element of the movie.) Sukman began to take television work, eventually scoring hundreds of episodes of *Bonanza, Dr. Kildare,* and *Gentle Ben.* Stoloff, then in his mid-sixties and wealthy, enjoyed a semiretirement. He spent his last years listening to the music he had grown up with—Fritz Kreisler, Leopold Auer—reminiscing about the Harry Cohn days at Columbia, and still shaking his head in disbelief at the financial returns from "Moonglow" and "Picnic."

George Duning, meanwhile, was such a quick and inventive composer that he had no trouble finding work in either movies or television. At the beginning of the '60s he scored three Dean Martin pictures in a row, the comedies *Who's Got the Action?* (1962) and *Who's Been Sleeping in My Bed?* (1963)—both Jack Rose productions at Paramount—and the Lillian Hellman melodrama *Toys in the Attic* (1963), which yielded a lovely title tune. *Any Wednesday* (1966) may be the score that sifts Duning's musical qualities down to essentials: light, melodic, hummable, and unobtrusively working to embellish comedy that only occasionally plays on its own feet.

Produced at Warners, *Any Wednesday* was one of the mid-'60s comedies that, though it had recently been a Broadway hit, felt left over from an earlier era. (Deft, light composer-conductors like David Rose and Frank DeVol handled similar assignments at the time.) In 1967, *The Graduate* changed the rules for film scores by showing how commercial a compiled song score could be, thereby minimizing the services of the studio-trained composer. The consistent money was in television anyway, so Duning went to work for Aaron Spelling, scoring *Mannix, The Big Valley,* and many other shows.

EIGHT

SHE GAVE YOUR VERY FIRST KISS TO YOU

ALFRED NEWMAN AND TWENTIETH CENTURY-FOX

Louis Silvers was running the Fox music department in 1935. In the widespread practice of the time, Silvers signed most of the A pictures himself, whether or not he had done any actual composing; the B pictures were usually signed by the Russian composer Samuel Kalen, who liked to write high brass parts that drove the soundmen crazy. "Don' pinch mit the climaxes," Kalen told the soundmen.

Fox was still a primitive factory. Alfred Newman came with the new regime, Twentieth Century Pictures, formed in 1933 by Joseph Schenck and Darryl F. Zanuck, respectively, the former head of United Artists and the former production chief at Warners. In 1935 when Zanuck became production chief of the newly amalgamated Twentieth Century-Fox, he imposed a keen story sense on the studio's product, which in turn demanded better integrated and more varied music. It was Schenck who had initially lured Alfred Newman to Hollywood in late 1929.

It may be doubly important that Newman, born in March 1901, was the eldest of ten children: it enabled him to eventually employ two of

Alfred Newman
Courtesy ASCAP

his brothers, Lionel and Emil, at Twentieth Century-Fox; and it gave him an authority he might have lacked had he been a younger sibling. The Newmans were Ukrainian Jews who lived at the threshold of poverty; his father worked as a New Haven produce dealer. A piano for the music-loving Alfred was out of the question, but his mother arranged for him to practice on a friend's.

By the time he reached his eighth year, Newman was a good enough pianist to play Beethoven's sonatas for money. The money went largely untouched by his parents, who had quietly saved enough to send him to study with Sigismond Stojowski, the great Polish pianist who had been living in New York since 1905; based at the Musical Art Institute, he also taught Oscar Levant, who was even younger than Newman and equally prodigious. Through Stojowski, Newman was sponsored in concert by no less a personage than Paderewski. But when the family money ran out, Newman was forced to go to work as an actor-musician-conductor on the vaudeville circuit, which at least provided an occasional paycheck. He was twelve years old.

Fortunately, Newman worked for the best. He made an early tour with Gus Edwards, part of which required him to appear on stage as Little Lord Fauntleroy. At eighteen, he conducted on Broadway for the first time, leading the orchestra for the first edition of the *George White Scandals,* a smash hit, with music by Richard Whiting. Then came that rarest opportunity for any musician, let alone a minor: he was invited to guest-conduct the New York Philharmonic.

Newman quickly established himself as an able conductor who could also compose when necessary. He was in the pit orchestra for the Gershwins' 1927 *Funny Face,* which inaugurated the Alvin Theater, and then composed music to accompany Douglas Fairbanks's silent *Robinson Crusoe* (1928). Out of that orchestral score came a melody that, ten years later, was transformed into the popular song "Moon Over Manakoora." (The lyrics were by Frank Loesser when it turned up in the 1937 film *The Hurricane.*)

After the enervating poverty of New Haven, followed by the job-to-job scuffling in the New York theater world, Newman probably wanted to settle down. So when United Artists' Joe Schenck offered him a job in Hollywood to supervise Irving Berlin's music for *Reaching for the Moon,* Newman quickly headed west.

Although nominally a United Artists employee, Newman was frequently loaned to Samuel Goldwyn, who shared the UA studios. Goldwyn took a shine to Newman and depended on him for musical counsel. In 1931 Goldwyn hired Newman to score *Street Scene,* the King Vidor film version of Elmer Rice's play. The main theme, then often referred to as "Sentimental Rhapsody," was the very model of the symphony-of-the-city theme—Gershwinesque, all right, but darker, dusky without being jazzy. "Street Scene," as it came to be called, would be part of Newman's musical arsenal for the next twenty-five years.

For Goldwyn and UA, Newman hired the best musicians and orchestrators he knew from New York. Edward Powell, known to his friends as the Great Engineer for the way he built a piece of music and set it in motion, was Newman's regular orchestrator at Goldwyn, and remained with him through their entire Twentieth Century-Fox careers.

In addition to conducting, the thing he loved best, Newman was getting a double education in composing on the run for various producers, and in Hollywood egotism. With Charlie Chaplin he worked smoothly as a conductor on the music for *City Lights* (1931), disastrously on *Modern Times* (1935). He composed the drumroll-and-fanfare signature theme that appeared under the logo of Twentieth Century Pictures; it was subsequently transferred to Twentieth Century-Fox to herald its A releases, and has since become one of the most recognizable pieces of film music. Newman also composed an equally effective fanfare to accompany the famous Selznick logo of his shingle in the foreground and Tara-like office facade in the background; this five-second patch of music had been used earlier in his score for *Dancing Pirate* for RKO (1936). Also for Selznick, Newman composed a muscular, brass-heavy score for *Prisoner of Zenda* (1937), cutting the brass with the lush strings that would become his trademark. There were memorable scores for big pictures like *Gunga Din* (1939) and *The Hunchback of Notre Dame* (1939). *Wuthering Heights* (1939), with "Cathy's Theme" at its erotic center, made producers realize that Newman had become a fine film composer as well as conductor. Later that same year he was locked into working solely for Twentieth Century-Fox when he was named its general music director.

Before Newman became Fox's musical chief, Twentieth Century-Fox had a staff scoring its musicals and coaching the stars. Shirley Temple went through a series of vocal coaches; the longest-lasting was probably Enrico (Ric) Ricardi, who owned the popular Santa Monica nightclub the Horn. Another early coach for the cute-as-a-button starlet was pianist Jule Styne. Studio boss Joe Schenck was in Miami Beach when he saw wide-eyed actress Andrea Leeds's nightclub act; impressed by her singing, Schenck was told that she'd been coached by the Chicago-born Styne. Schenck offered Styne $350 a week plus travel expenses to come to the West Coast. Styne was given an office next to Russian composer-arranger Sam Pokrass, who worked primarily with the Ritz Brothers and, if requested, would play piano standing on his head. Styne worked with Temple on *Heidi* (1937), and *Rebecca of Sunnybrook Farm* and *Little Miss Broadway* (both 1938).

Styne probably enjoyed no assignment more than working with Alice Faye. Born Alice Jeane Leppert in New York in 1915, Faye was in residence at Fox by the mid-'30s. Stanley Green wrote, "Between 1938 and 1943, the blonde, throaty-voiced singing actress with the snub nose, pouting lips, and hourglass figure was Fox's reigning singing star." The hourglass figure made her look sensational in period musicals like *Alexander's Ragtime Band* (1938).

At the time, Irving Berlin was in his Fox phase. The best Berlin musical of the period—perhaps the best Berlin on film until *Easter Parade,* in fact—was *On the Avenue* (1937), with Faye, Dick Powell, the icily exquisite, non-singing Madeleine Carroll, and the hyperkinetic Ritz Brothers. Faye and the Ritz Brothers did "He Ain't Got Rhythm," and Faye and Powell sang "I've Got My Love to Keep Me Warm." Arthur Lange, still a presence on the lot, handled the music direction.

When the idea of a Berlin biopic first came up, it was 1937 and Berlin was not yet fifty. But Berlin's Russian-Jewish, Lower East Side roots made him squirm—he didn't hide them so much as de-emphasize them—and he objected to Zanuck about being the sole focus of a screen biography, to be titled *Alexander's Ragtime Band.* Gradually an amalgam of music men, including the recently deceased George Gershwin (1937), was worked out, and the fictional composer's early years were moved from the Lower East Side to San Francisco. Alfred Newman served as music director; Alice Faye sang the title song. Of twenty-one other musical numbers, there were a few beauts: Faye sang "All Alone" and "Remember"; Faye and Ethel Merman sang "Blue Skies"; Merman roared out "A Pretty Girl Is Like a Melody" and "Heat Wave" (which Marilyn Monroe would caress in Fox's 1954 *There's No Business Like Show Business*).

Faye was the first and greatest in a series of voluptuous singing stars at Fox. Betty Grable followed and, with those magnificent gams, proved to be more popular during World War II; but Grable was always less readable and approachable than Faye, who radiated a natural warmth. Later, June Haver—also blonde, handsomely constructed and easy to listen to—was added to the Fox line-up. But Faye remained the greatest. She handled not only Berlin songs but the songs of the resident studio songwriters. In *Sing, Baby, Sing* (1936) alone, Tony Martin sang "When Did You Leave Heaven?" (by Richard Whiting and Walter Bullock) to Faye. Faye sang the marvelous "You Turned the Tables on Me"—music by Louis Alter, lyrics by Sidney Mitchell—and the title song by Jack Yellen and Lew Pollack.

In 1938, the studio was preparing a John Barrymore programmer called *Hold That Coed.* For the movie, Lew Pollack had written a few songs with contract lyricist Sydney Clare (best remembered for "On the Good Ship Lollipop"), but was unavailable to complete a song needed at the last minute. Jule Styne got the call and turned out a song with his sister, Claire Bregman (mother of bandleader Buddy Bregman).

At Fox, Styne had taken a young pianist named Walter Scharf under his wing. Scharf had played for Vincent Lopez and Rudy Vallee, and was known to be a fun-loving guy with a taste for gambling. On days when they were expected to be on the studio lot, Scharf and Styne would drive out to Santa Anita in time for the first race; sometimes they were joined by a popular bookie named Harry Gordon. Harry's brother, the three-hundred-pound lyricist Mack Gordon, had been on the Fox lot since 1936, when he and his composer partner Harry Revel had come over from Paramount. Of all the lyricists who regularly received a Fox paycheck, Mack Gordon was the greatest.

Mack Gordon was born Morris Gittler in Warsaw in 1905. His family came to the United States around 1908, and Gordon attended public schools in Brooklyn and in the Bronx. Gordon, then as slender as a door, worked in vaudeville as an actor, later as a lyricist. In 1929 he met Harry Revel, a London-born, European-trained pianist who had worked in quasi-Hawaiian bands, light opera, and revues for French impresario André Charlot (who subsequently became a character actor in Hollywood). Gordon and Revel began to write songs together. As a team they contributed to the 1931 edition of the *Ziegfeld Follies*, and were soon invited to Paramount. Gordon was reluctant to move his first wife, Rose, and two toddlers to Los Angeles, but Revel and the Paramount salary helped change his mind. At Paramount, the slight

Mack Gordon and Harry Revel writing for *Sitting Pretty* (1933)
Courtesy Academy of Motion Picture Arts & Sciences and Universal Studios

Revel and the increasingly hippo-shaped Gordon just got better and better. "Did You Ever See a Dream Walking" was written for *Sitting Pretty* (1933). "Stay as Sweet as You Are," a song virtually owned by Nat Cole since the 1950s, showed up in 1934's *College Rhythm* when Lanny Ross sang it.

The songwriters jumped to Fox in 1936. Gordon and Rose divorced that year. Gordon took on still more weight, and so did his lyrics. In Fox's *Wake Up and Live* (1937), the always believable Alice

Faye sang "There's a Lull in My Life"—she's backed by Ben Bernie's Orchestra—and the lyric escorts you right into the void; that wasn't the old Mack Gordon.

Everyone changed partners in 1939. Gordon married actress Elizabeth Cook, and he ended his partnership with Revel, apparently without acrimony. Darryl Zanuck, perhaps concerned by rising costs after Alfred Newman's appointment as music head, cut the music department in half. In addition, Shirley Temple ended her stay at the studio with *Young People* (1940), a highly fictionalized recap of her career that Zanuck himself had cooked up; her days as a box-office draw for *any* studio were over. Jule Styne was let go, with parting advice from Zanuck to concentrate on songwriting, not vocal coaching. (Styne took the advice.) Revel, teamed with lyricist Mort Greene (born 1912), found work at RKO; after partnering with Paul Francis Webster, the assignments came from Universal. But his work was never again as inspired as it had been with Mack Gordon.

Gordon, meanwhile, stayed on the Fox lot, where he was partnered with a new arrival from Zanuck's old studio. Harry Warren, at the peak of his powers, was due for another sturdy, productive collaboration. Three years earlier, Warren's longtime partner, Al Dubin, plagued by drink and obesity, had begun to unravel. During the filming of *The Singing Marine* (1937), Dubin took a powder, and Johnny Mercer, then twenty-seven, was called in to complete Dubin's lyrics. After surgery to remove a fistula, Dubin became addicted to morphine. When Richard Whiting died in February 1938, Warners pushed hard for Whiting's regular lyricist Mercer to partner with Warren. Humiliated, Dubin left town suddenly and took up residence at the Taft Hotel in New York.

Though left high and dry at Warners, Warren had little trouble writing with Mercer. Among many songs from this brief period had come "Jeepers Creepers," which Louis Armstrong sang encouragingly to a racehorse in *Going Places* (1938), and "You Must Have Been a Beautiful Baby," with which Dick Powell serenaded Olivia De Havilland while rowing on Central Park lake, in *Hard to Get* (1938). Then Mercer took a more lucrative Paramount contract.

Hired by Fox, Warren was immediately partnered with Mack Gordon. Gordon's lyrics were less propulsive than Dubin's and a touch more poetic. Where Dubin rhymed for dance, Gordon rhymed for emotional expressiveness. Dubin's words evoked the American streets, the more urban the better, where romance was sex and sex was bawdy; Gordon's words evoked a more interior and tender locale, even when actual places like Chattanooga or Kalamazoo were part of the scheme. Gordon's most characteristic lyrics—to Warren's tunes, anyway—stated a romantic or pre-romantic condition in the first line or two, then amplified that condition through the balance of the song: "I Know Why (And So Do You)"; "You'll Never Know (How Much I Care)"; "The More I See You (The More I Want You)"; and so on. Other lyricists listened and learned. Sammy Cahn, hardly prone to praise his rivals, said, "I found the work of Mack Gordon very attractive to my ear." Of course Harry Warren's music helped make it attractive. It didn't get any better than "At Last," a typically elegant song (that has enjoyed renewed popularity due to the Etta James recording).

The Warren-Gordon songs from the years 1940 to 1945 were handled by a small cadre of Fox's musical stars. *Down Argentine Way* (1940), which Alice Faye had to bow out of after an attack of appendicitis, made Betty Grable a star and introduced Carmen Miranda to American audiences. Miranda did her special thing again in *That Night in Rio* (1941), where she performed "I Yi Yi Yi Yi." Fox released two pictures showcasing Glenn Miller and his band: *Sun Valley Serenade* (1941), followed by *Orchestra Wives* (1942). Musical leading man John Payne carried the hokey story in the first flick, with former ice-skating champ Sonja Henie going around the rink with him. George Montgomery portrayed a trumpeter in *Orchestra Wives,* with Carole Landis plucked from Fox's stable of full-figured blondes in a secondary role (and Dale Evans, recently arrived in Hollywood, in a bit part). The Glenn Miller movies experimented with new stereophonic recording processes that made the Warren-Gordon songs sound especially vibrant; some of the stunning arrangements were made by Miller's respected arranger Bill Finegan, known for his complex style.

Weekend in Havana (1941) had John Payne showing Alice Faye a good time in you-know-where, with Carmen Miranda supplying the headgear. In *Iceland* (1942), Payne was involved with Henie again—Henie's musical coach at the studio was a pianist-conductor named Jack Pfeiffer—but it was Joan Merrill, backed by Sammy Kaye's Orchestra, who sang "There Will Never Be Another You" to ex-fiancée Payne.

Helen Forrest, backed by the Harry James Orchestra, introduced "I Had the Craziest Dream" in *Springtime in the Rockies* (1942)—Payne, Grable, and Miranda were the featured players this time. Faye sang "You'll Never Know" to faraway boyfriend Payne in *Hello, Frisco, Hello* (1943), and again in *Four Jills in a Jeep* (1944). Dick Haymes, a fine singer but a constipated screen presence, sang "The More I See You," implicitly about costar Grable, in *Diamond Horseshoe* (1945).

Each of these great songs had had to be auditioned for Zanuck, who considered himself a pop music expert. While Warren played piano, Gordon would sing, adding a trombone chorus with his voice. "That sonofabitch could sell me anything," Zanuck said of Gordon.

By early 1943, Warren had begun to work occasionally with Leo Robin, whose longtime partner Ralph Rainger had died in a plane crash in October 1942. Gordon wanted to produce—and became part of a short list of producing lyricists that included Buddy DeSylva, Arthur Freed, and, later, George Jessel. After Warren went over to MGM, Gordon began to prepare *Three Little Girls in Blue* (1946). The story was a Zanuck favorite, a remake of *Three Blind Mice* and *Moon Over Miami,* in which three sisters set out to snare husbands in turn-of-the-century Atlantic City. (The plot was used again for the 1953 film *How to Marry a Millionaire.*) Gordon took a new partner, Russian-born (1910) pianist Josef Myrow, who composed "You Make Me Feel So Young" for the movie. But Gordon also turned to old partner Warren for one more tune, which became the sublime "This Is Always." In addition to his producing responsibilities, Gordon still wrote the lyrics.

After *Three Little Girls* was finished, Gordon continued to write with Myrow. Within a couple of years he was headed once more for divorce court. Elizabeth Cook Gittler said to the *Los Angeles Times*: "When I told him I was lonely, he told me to listen to his songs. When I objected, he told me to see a lawyer."

⁂

While Gordon and Warren were writing all those terrific songs at Fox, Al Dubin was scrambling for a living and for some sanity. In 1941 he asked Warners to be put back on the payroll. Warners took him on, but dropped him down from $1350 a week to $500. His new contract, drafted with his specific problems in mind, said in part:

In the event the Composer suffers or asserts any incapacity within the purview hereof, Producer shall have the right to investigate the nature of and extent of such incapacity by its own physician or otherwise, and Composer agrees to lend his assistance to any such investigation and agrees to submit to any and all physical examinations requested by Producer.

Dubin signed the contract, but his return to Warners was brief. Convinced he was dying in a hotel room on Cahuenga Boulevard, he sent for his estranged wife, Helen, who in turn summoned a priest. Songwriter Dave Franklin—coauthor of "The Merry Go Round Broke Down" and "The Anniversary Waltz," and not incidentally Jewish— arrived at the hotel just in time to see the priest depart. Franklin didn't know what to make of it.

Stage Door Canteen, the last movie to include new songs by the great Al Dubin, New York City, 1943.
Courtesy the author

Dubin rallied. Soon he was healthy enough to crisscross the country every few weeks—always by train; he was afraid to fly—to tend to his two sets of families. On one of those trips he got lucky when producer Sol Lesser hired him and Jimmy Monaco to write eleven songs for *Stage Door Canteen* (1943), United Artists' entry in the armed forces musical series. Dubin was working almost at his heyday salary again. The two songwriters, aging hypochondriacal Monaco and obese junkie Dubin, made quite a pair.

In February 1943 Dubin, at last divorced from Helen, married young Edwina Perrin in Tijuana. Perrin wanted desperately to become a movie star. It wasn't going to happen. The marriage was over almost immediately, and a divorce was granted Perrin in July of that year.

Dubin fled back to New York and moved into the Empire Hotel. He agreed to write songs with Burton Lane for Olsen & Johnson's *Laffing Room Only* (1944), but he completed only one song, "Feudin' and Fightin'," before abandoning Lane. On February 8, 1945, Dubin collapsed in the street and, lacking identification of any kind, was taken to Roosevelt Hospital, where a Paulist priest administered last rites. In an eerie precursor to Jerome Kern's death, a piece of paper with Gerald Marks's name was found in Dubin's clothes; Marks ("All of Me") was called by the hospital, and arrived to find Dubin in a coma. Within an hour or so, Dubin was dead. ASCAP arranged for the body to go to nearby Riverside Mortuary. Instead, Helen Dubin, who had heard about her former husband's death on the radio, had the body shipped back to Los Angeles and buried at Holy Cross Cemetery. A few months later Dorothy Shay, "the Park Avenue hillbilly," had a hit with Dubin & Lane's "Feudin' and Fightin'."

o   o   o

Upon his promotion to head of music at Fox, Newman instituted some immediate changes. Prior to Newman's promotion, Silvers had overseen the music, while James O'Keefe and Frank Tresselt handled business affairs. With Newman's ascension, O'Keefe was let go, while Tresselt focused exclusively on the studio orchestra as its contractor. Newman, who did not stint when it came to making the pictures sound good, increased musical spending substantially; Ted Cain was brought in to keep the costs under control. Newman hired an Englishman named Charles Dunworth, a cellist, who quickly instituted the so-called "Newman system" of scoring right on the sound stage—a red grease pencil was used to mark the film itself, making easily viewable, five-foot streamers on the screen to cue the conductor. David Buttolph (born 1902) had been hired by Lou Silvers as an orchestrator, but Newman, needing composers, switched his responsibilites, along with Cyril Mockridge (born 1896), a quiet Brit who showed a mouthful of beautiful teeth whenever he deigned to smile. Urban Thielman was brought in to replace Mockridge as studio pianist.

Newman was now free—or freer, anyway—to compose and conduct. Right out of the box, his score for *The Grapes of Wrath* (1940) attracted a lot of attention. But it was his music for *How Green Was My Valley* (1941), greatly enhanced by Cyril Mockridge's Delius-inflected additional themes, that qualified as the first of Newman's truly beautiful scores. *The Song of Bernadette* (1943) brought him his third Academy Award, his first for a dramatic score.

"[Newman] was, of course, talented," editor Robert Tracy said in the 1970s.

> He was also a little Caesar. He was brutal with an orchestra on the stage if they didn't perform precisely. He was very strict. He knew what he wanted, and he wouldn't settle for anything less. His hours were the thing as disliked as anything, as I recall, because he never started recording until four in the afternoon, and he would go until four the next morning if he felt like it, or if he didn't run out of J&B Scotch. In those years it was hard to come by.

Murray Spivack said that Newman knew how to handle himself—with his musicians and with the executives. "He had a certain bravado about him, he wouldn't take anything from anybody." But Newman, according to Spivack, treated his musicians well. "He was a very, very strict conductor, very meticulous, but at the same time he treated his musicians as though they were really musicians and not just a bunch of workaholics." When Newman's orchestra worked late, as they often did, he would order dinner catered by Chasen's—for *everyone*. But the price of his respect could be high. Newman would not be spoken back to. He referred to anyone who displeased him as "lard-ass."

Newman didn't talk back to studio chief Darryl Zanuck—Bernard Herrmann was the only composer who got away with that—but tried to educate him musically. "Darryl's idea in the very beginning," Hugo Friedhofer recalled, "was that kind of association where a situation on the screen would remind him of a certain pop song title. And that was the way it would be. Or else he wanted music you could tap your feet to. But Alfred, little by little, sort of broadened [Zanuck's] musical horizon."

Zanuck adored Newman's "Street Scene" and permitted—no, encouraged—its inclusion in several Fox pictures. *I Wake Up Screaming* (1941) was a strange thriller that somehow featured Metro's "Over the Rainbow" as well as "Street Scene" in its score. Cyril Mockridge composed the threading underscore, and if his two bosses wanted "Street Scene" in there, so be it. The pattern was repeated for *The Dark Corner* (1946), which is often mistakenly credited as the source of "Street Scene." The justifiably famous *Kiss of Death* (1947), with a score credited to David Buttolph, placed Victor Mature in jeopardy in New York City, while *Cry of the City* (1948) did much the same, only less effectively; both featured the well-worn theme.

Newman may have become self-conscious about inserting the theme into so many scores, even if it provided instant identification with New York for movie audiences. On September 17, 1948, Zanuck's memo to Newman addressed the point: "Dear Al: Do nothing but continue to use 'Street Scene' wherever it fits." Zanuck let Paramount use the theme for *My Friend Irma* (1949), where it helped establish the Manhattan locale in about two bars of music. The theme's grandest use came in *How to Marry a Millionaire* (1953), right after Newman's fanfare and the stairway-to-the-stars "extension" he'd composed to denote CinemaScope; onscreen, Newman himself conducts the Twentieth Century-Fox orchestra in a concert prelude to the story proper.

By some accounts, Newman had lobbied to use "Street Scene" in Otto Preminger's *Laura* (1944), even though he'd declined to assign himself to score the picture. For better or worse, Edward Powell talked him out of "Street Scene" this time. But who would write the music? The assignment had also been turned down by Bernard Herrmann, who figured if it wasn't good enough for Al Newman, why should he bother with it? Meanwhile, producer Preminger toyed with the idea of using "Summertime" as a theme, but Ira Gershwin killed that notion when he refused to grant the rights.

Next on the factory list was the young staff composer-orchestrator David Raksin. Raksin had been on the Fox lot for about three years, mostly orchestrating alongside his old friends but occasionally composing as well. He'd worked on Fox programmers like *Dr. Renault's Secret* (1942) and wrote the ballet music for *The Gang's All Here* the following year.

"I remember the day, down in the old Lasky room at Fox," said editor Robert Tracy, "when a young fellow came in in a pair of tennis shorts, with a tennis racquet. I didn't know who he was. We were timing a picture, and this fresh young guy came in, and [Lou] Silvers started to chew him out and tear him apart. . . . It turned out to be David Raksin."

When the *Laura* assignment fell to him, David Raksin was thirty-three. He was professionally respected but personally miserable—for one thing, his marriage was in jeopardy. The rumor was that *Laura* was also in jeopardy. In mid-production Otto Preminger had taken over its direction from Rouben Mamoulian, who couldn't abide him. (Who could?)

At the first rough-cut screening that Raksin attended, Zanuck presided. Zanuck wanted to trim a scene in which Dana Andrews, as the investigating detective, wandered through Gene Tierney's (Laura's) apartment. "But if you cut that scene," young Raksin piped up, "nobody will understand that the detective is in love with Laura." "Who is that?" Zanuck asked an assistant. Raksin was permitted to make his case to the boss—not only for retaining the scene, but for music that would tip the audience to Dana Andrews's feelings, which were stirred by an oil portrait of Laura. Zanuck capitulated. Later, Raksin was berated by Al Fisher, a music-department representative whom the musicians had dubbed Hingehead for his yes-man obsequiousness toward Alfred Newman. "I hope you realize what you've done," Fisher said ominously.

Then Raksin had to deal with Preminger. Preminger now wanted to use Ellington's "Sophisticated Lady" as the main theme. Laura was sophisticated, went Preminger's argument, and this would drive the point home without spelling it out: "This girl is a whore!"

"By whose standards, Mr. Preminger?" said Raksin.

Preminger turned to Alfred Newman and said, "Where did you *find* this fellow?"

Raksin was given the weekend to come up with a suitable theme, otherwise "Sophisticated Lady" would be used. He went home and wrestled with several melodies. He was also descending into a well of sorrow as he coped with a surprise letter from his wife that effectively ended their marriage. When Raksin hit bottom, he came up with the first phrase of "Laura"; the rest was easy.

A week into the scoring, Raksin was working only on the second reel (out of approximately eight), and he already had the main theme coming out his ears. So he tried something different. Alfred Newman came by and, at Raksin's agitated behest, took a look at the newly scored scene. To the quizzical Newman, Raksin said, "I don't know what's the matter with it, but somehow it isn't of a piece with the rest of the stuff I've written so far." "Well, I can tell you, since you ask," Newman replied. "Where's that beautiful tune?" Newman pointed out that Raksin, composing carefully and working over his main theme, may have wearied of it—but the audience hadn't.

The score for *Laura* and the title song (lyrics added later by Johnny Mercer) were instant classics. They helped make the movie just about everyone's favorite romantic detective story; the ever-deepening mystery that's really absent from the plot is provided by Raksin's music, conducted by Alfred's brother Emil. As with so many themes that catch the public's fancy, everyone had a theory about where "Laura" came from. Raksin received one letter from an American soldier, stationed in Belgium, who said he recognized the "Laura" theme from Beethoven's Ninth Symphony. Tickled, Raksin wrote back, "What I did was to take the slow movement of the Ninth, the one before the Scherzo. I found a section where the celli were in a tenor clef, then turned it upside down and pretended that the music was in *alto* clef. Having done that, I then took every third note and put them together to form the new theme now known as 'Laura.' How you figured that out for yourself is beyond me...." Closer to home, some ears picked up a similarity to Fred Hollander's theme composed for *Here Comes Mr. Jordan* (1941).

Whatever the wellsprings of its source, part of the marvelous mystery of "Laura" is the way it sounds eternally suspended in mid-air. Raksin was pleasantly surprised when the first Mrs. Preminger, the Hungarian actress Marion Mill, said accurately and in her thick German accident, "De tune ends on de dominant!"

Raksin went to work again for Preminger on *Fallen Angel* (1945), an attempt to duplicate *Laura*'s success. Dana Andrews was aboard in a twist on a familiar thriller plot in which the mistress, not the wife, is murdered. It's lurid, certainly, and Alice Faye is in the wrong movie. But out of that score came "Slowly," a languid blues favored by jazz players. (Dave McKenna and Milt Jackson have each recorded fine versions.)

Preminger was the director on Raksin's last big Fox assignment, *Forever Amber* (1947). The novel by Kathleen Winsor was considered scandalous at the time—it portrays a beautiful, conniving courtesan (Linda Darnell) in the court of Charles II—though the film version was something less than sexy, never mind scandalous. Yet audiences, then and now, seem to enjoy what Raksin called "every high-cholesterol minute." In scoring this 140-minute "historical" romance, Raksin did a smart thing by settling on a Handelian style that audiences associated as English, rather than on the more authentic but less evocative musical styles of Charles II's time. By turns pompous, witty, and bawdy, it's a magnificent score, and suggests that Raksin also could have handled the Biblical epics that were so fashionable in the '50s.

But Raksin chose not to. He moved to RKO, where he scored *The Secret Life of Walter Mitty* (1947), with Emil Newman conducting again. Then he arrived at MGM, where his music got only more elastic. Raksin was invited by writer-director Abe Polonsky, a childhood pal of Bernard Herrmann's and Jerome Moross's, to score his *Force of Evil* (1948). Polonsky said he wanted something along the lines of Alban Berg's *Wozzeck*—ah! a film director who loves twentieth-century opera! So Raksin happily invited Polonsky out to his Northridge ranch to further discuss the score. With a record on the phonograph in

Franz Waxman and orchestrator Edward Powell listening to playback during recording session for *The Virgin Queen* (1955)
Courtesy John Waxman

the background, the two men talked for awhile until Polonsky, annoyed, barked, "What's that crap you're playing?!" "That's *Wozzeck*, Abe," said Raksin.

A few years later, Metro was making *Tribute to a Bad Man,* a western-sounding title that eventually was nixed for the much better *The Bad and the Beautiful* (1952), courtesy of publicity whiz Howard Deitz. Bernard Herrmann was interested in the scoring assignment, but his old friend John Houseman, who produced, knew Herrmann was wrong for it and said so. So Herrmann recommended Raksin. Houseman signed Raksin and requested "a siren song." Working in a studio penthouse claimed by Kay Thompson whenever she was on the lot, Raksin composed and delivered the siren song for the main-title sequence that became known as "Love Is for the Very Young," but Houseman and director Vincente Minnelli were uncomfortable and silent upon hearing it. Fortunately, Betty Comden and Adolph Green happened to be on the lot and immediately pronounced the theme beautiful. Raksin subsequently conducted the MGM orchestra—an orchestra not quite up to the level of Alfred Newman's at Twentieth, but damn good. It included such remarkable musicians as saxophonist Gus Bivona and trombonist Si Zentner.

While Raksin was composing at Twentieth Century-Fox, he had the services of at least four fine orchestrators: Edward Powell, Herbert Spencer, Arthur Morton, and Maurice DePackh. (Earle Hagen, composer of "Harlem Nocturne," was also orchestrating the B product at the studio.) Spencer's office held what his colleagues referred to as "the woodwind piano" because its sound lent itself to imagining how the woodwind section would play. DePackh was known as a musician who could sniff out an instrument; he'd hear a piano line, point his nose, and say, "That should be an English horn!" Working off the composers' sketches, which could be as limited as a single piano line, these men conceived and wrote out the instrumental parts on as many as thirty staves, in effect creating orchestral color and texture—the very sound produced by the orchestra. For their models they took such masters of musical color as Ravel and Respighi.

Of the studio composers, David Raksin, who had worked for years as an orchestrator, turned in particularly detailed sketches, practically orchestrating himself as he went along. On the other hand, Alfred Newman, always pressed for time, always handling several projects at once, gave his orchestrators sparse sketches. Newman would compose, then one or sometimes two of the staff orchestrators working in tandem would create the complete score that Newman took into the recording studio to conduct.

Instead of scaling back his activities, Newman became only more industrious in the late 1940s. He could go from the contemporary melodramatics of *Gentleman's Agreement* (1947) to the swooning, stirring *Captain from Castile* (1947). *A Letter to Three Wives* (1949) had a theatrical main-title theme, and the famous musical transitions from one wife's story to the next are nudged along by the Brahms Piano Concerto No. 2 in B Flat Major. *All About Eve* (1950) opens with a proscenium-wide pageantry that anticipates William Walton's score for *Richard III*, and its pseudo-Shakespearean grandeur helps fool you into believing that the trashy backstage story that follows is high art.

Newman probably worked on as many as thirty Fox pictures between *All About Eve* and *The Robe* (1953), the first CinemaScope feature. Much of *The Robe*'s score mixes Hebrew-chant–like rhythms with brass figures that herald Roman might, and vocals ascending to a Christian heaven. (Carole Richards was the offscreen alto soloist; at Metro, Richards often ghosted for Cyd Charisse.) *The Robe* wasn't the first Roman epic of the '50s—*Quo Vadis,* scored by Miklos Rozsa, preceded it by a couple of years—but it got the most attention.

The Egyptian (1954) followed in its wake. Zanuck felt that Franz Waxman was the man for the job; but Waxman was assigned instead to *Prince Valiant,* another CinemaScope production, so Newman divided *The Egyptian* scoring chores between himself and Herrmann because Zanuck wanted to release the picture as soon as possible.

As CinemaScope gained ground, and musicals made something of a comeback to compete with televison, Newman maintained an expert staff of musicians. David Buttolph had moved over to Warners in 1948, but Cyril Mockridge could still be depended on. (His score for 1954's *Woman's World* amounts to the perfect soap-opera music.) Hugo Friedhofer, having broken through as a composer, returned to the studio in 1950. Waxman and Herrmann were on and off the lot. Daniele Amfitheatrof composed and conducted for Fox's B unit. Sol Kaplan, an excellent pianist, was around to score *Niagara* (1953) until he was blacklisted. Les Clark wrote some songs, but mostly he handled dance music for musicals stars like Dan Dailey. Tall, reedy Ken Darby had come over from RKO in 1950 to serve as vocal arranger, replacing Charlie Henderson who left to create Las Vegas nightclub acts. (Composer of "Deep Night" with Rudy Vallee, Henderson had served for years as a Fox songwriter, and subsequently published *How to Sing for Money.*) Beginning with *David and Bathsheba* (1951), Darby served as choral director on most Newman-scored pictures.

By the mid-1950s, Newman had earned all the trappings of success. His brother Lionel was on the lot as music director-arranger, "a man who knew everything before everyone else" (according to Henry Ephron). Brother Emil was also frequently back on the lot to conduct. (Another brother worked as a film composers' agent, and another, a physician, was the father of Newman's nephew, Randy.) Five of Newman's seven children were born during his third marriage (to Martha Montgomery), and two of them, David and Thomas, would eventually take up their father's line of work. They all lived in a house designed by Lloyd Wright, son of Frank Lloyd Wright and a respected architect in his own right. Thomas Newman recalled, "[My father] worked an awful lot and his habit was to work late at night and sleep in the morning and maybe get to work around 10:30 or 11:00, but he worked out of the house. So as I walked up from the hill where the school bus let me off, I'd always hear him plunking on the piano."

Newman also served as music director for the 1945 Rodgers and Hammerstein musical *State Fair*, their only production written directly for the movies. In fact Newman and Rodgers went as far back together as 1929, when he was conductor for the Rodgers and Hart shows *Heads Up!* and *Spring Is Here*. It seems odd that the acidic Rodgers would permit his middle-period work to be filmed at Twentieth, considering that, just before shooting began on *State Fair*, Darryl Zanuck had demanded Rodgers and Hammerstein's immediate presence in Los Angeles: after traveling all the way across country with their wives to meet with the great man, they spent twenty minutes listening to Zanuck talk about his war experiences in North Africa before they were dismissed; that was all. It was "a matter of pride and muscle," Rodgers wrote. "He had paid us a lot of money and had acceded to our working conditions, but he wanted the satisfaction of being able to make us do as he wished."

Yet even after that experience, Rodgers and Hammerstein sold most of their musicals to Twentieth Century-Fox. Part of the reason may have been Zanuck's unbridled enthusiasm: "*State Fair* is the most popular musical we have had in years and the business nationwide is just sensational. There are two reasons for its success: the wonderful score and the great charm of the piece as a whole." It also helped that

Spyros Skouras, the New York–based president of the studio, knew how to sell Rodgers and Hammerstein.

Oklahoma! (1955) had been released by Todd-AO, with Jay Blackton, the original conductor on Broadway, supervising the music, and the picture had done very well. (That year Blackton was nominated for best scoring of a musical picture for both *Oklahoma!* and *Guys and Dolls.* "Too bad, Jay, you're competing against yourself," Newman said sympathetically. Blackton won anyway for *Oklahoma!*)

But the subsequent Rodgers and Hammerstein musicals went to Twentieth Century-Fox. So Newman, usually aided by Ken Darby, supervised their music for *The King and I* (1956), *Carousel* (1956), and *South Pacific* (1958). (*The Sound of Music* was also distributed by Twentieth, but Newman, nearing the end of his career, was on another assignment; its musical direction was handled by Saul Chaplin, Irwin Kostal, and Sid Ramin.)

Billy Bigelow in the film version of *Carousel* was originally going to be portrayed by Frank Sinatra. As usual, Sinatra brought Nelson Riddle onto the picture as his arranger, and an entourage accompanied him to Maine for a few weeks of filming. According to Henry Ephron, who produced for Twentieth Century-Fox, Sinatra's songwriter sycophants laughed uproariously at everything Sinatra said. (Sammy Cahn is the implied offender.) Legend has it that Sinatra couldn't tolerate the bucolic Maine coast, far from Jilly's and Toots Shor where the action was. But what made Sinatra bolt was Spyros Skouras's decree that *Carousel* would be shot in 55mm as well as 35mm, requiring longer, more elaborate set-ups and much more time on the set—anathema to Sinatra. Gordon MacRae was brought in to replace Sinatra. The kicker was that, after losing Sinatra, the 55mm footage was scrapped because it required too many theaters to install equipment they couldn't afford.

Deeper into the '50s, Newman began to pour the majority of his energy into composing. Gradually he was stepping back and allowing his brother Lionel to handle some of the more important musicals. *Gentlemen Prefer Blondes* (1953) was supervised by Lionel, *There's No Business Like Show Business* (1954) by Lionel and Alfred. Another

Monroe picture, Billy Wilder's sniggering screen version of *The Seven Year Itch* (1955), opened with a main-title theme that sounded suspiciously like *A Letter to Three Wives*. But who was going to say anything? Musically, Newman was the boss; Zanuck, the only man who could control him, had left in 1956, becoming an independent producer while cavorting in France.

From this period, up through the end of his Twentieth Century-Fox contract in 1959, Newman composed at least two scores that stand with his—or with any composer's—best. The music for *Anastasia* (1956) gets right to the rich ambiguity of the story, as well as under the skin of Ingrid Bergman's tortured, manipulative pretender. Some serious listeners have claimed *The Diary of Anne Frank* (1959) to be Newman's masterwork. "Few scores have more poignantly, more exquisitely drawn the tragedy and heroism of this young woman, her family and friends in the face of relentless evil," Jack Smith declared in *Films in Review*. I prefer *The Best of Everything*, which is lighter and maybe even more interesting despite, or because of, the sudsy material; or even *Airport* (1970), Newman's last score, done for Ross Hunter at Universal. Newman was arrogant but never pompous.

After Newman left Fox in 1959, he continued to work there now and then. *How the West Was Won* (1963), done at MGM, required a massive amount of scoring and supervising. But he was not a healthy man. Speaking in a cigarette voice, he looked grayer and more simian than ever. With Ken Darby's considerable help, Newman took on the scoring of *The Greatest Story Ever Told* (1965), but bad health and director George Stevens's cavalier handling of the music combined to make it a rotten experience. Like so many movies Newman wrote music for, *The Greatest Story Ever Told* is practically unwatchable, but much of the score is heavenly.

Composing in solitude, Newman ranked with the best. It was as Twentieth's conductor, however, presiding over the "Newman strings," that he made such powerful music. And it was his long tenure at Fox, as composer-scholar Fred Steiner suggested, that enabled "difficult" composers like Herrmann, North, and Raksin to thrive in the Hollywood system.

NINE

WALTZING IN THE WONDER OF WHY WE'RE HERE
THE FREED UNIT AT MGM

By the late 1930s, songwriter Arthur Freed had told Metro boss Louis B. Mayer that he wanted to produce pictures. Mayer had good reason to listen to Freed, whose songs, written with Nacio Herb Brown, had made Metro's early musicals successful. After seeing the original *Broadway Melody* (1929), everyone was singing "The Wedding of the Painted Doll" and "You Were Meant for Me"; after *Hollywood Revue of 1929,* "Singin' in the Rain" became a standard. Seven years later in *Broadway Melody of 1936,* "I've Got a Feeling You're Foolin'" was a hit, and "You Are My Lucky Star" would pay dividends to Freed's descendants. Freed and Brown had provided still more songs for *Broadway Melody of 1938,* though the most memorable number from that picture, "You Made Me Love You," written by Jimmy Monaco and Joe McCarthy, was already in the standard repertoire.

As an introduction to that song, fifteen-year-old Judy Garland sang "Dear Mr. Gable" to a photograph of Clark Gable. The special material had been written for her by a tall, square-jawed young Texan named Roger Edens who had spent years working on Broadway in various capacities, most importantly as vocal arranger and pianist for Ethel Merman. Watching and hearing Edens work behind the scenes on various MGM soundstages, Freed developed a respect for the Broadway exile. Edens seemed to have an instinct for what show music could be put across to a movie audience, and what could not; it was a matter of presentation, of what the camera, as well as the microphone, picked up. Supporting MGM's ace tap dancer Eleanor Powell on *Born to Dance,* for example, Edens had helped stage the extravagant battleship number "Swingin' the Jinx Away"—"an embarrassment of bad taste," he admitted, but gobbled up by audiences.

After the release of *Broadway Melody of 1938,* Arthur Freed persuaded Louis B. Mayer to buy *The Wizard of Oz,* because Freed as a boy had loved the L. Frank Baum book, first published in 1899, and its many sequels. Mayer, feeling that Freed at forty-four was still too green to produce, lured Mervyn LeRoy over from Warners' to oversee the making of *Wizard.* Although LeRoy took plenty of credit for the finished product—"I found myself at MGM and L. B. Mayer asked me what I wanted to make," LeRoy wrote—people on the lot knew that Freed was responsible for the purchase of the property, hiring songwriters Harold Arlen and Yip Harburg, much of the casting, and keeping a close ear to the arrangements. Roger Edens, a decade younger than Freed but just as experienced and usually in sync with the child star Garland, also monitored the arrangements by Murray Cutter.

Wizard's conductor was Herbert Stothart, the Teutonic Wisconsinite who had gone from Broadway to Metro, bringing with him a bombastic style—wall-to-wall music, most of it peeled from nineteenth-century classics—forged in the silent era. Stothart was the most prominent of Metro's musical old guard, which included composers William Axt, Dave Snell, and Edward Ward. Freed, in his own thinking about movie music and movie musicals, would cross from the Stothart side of the bridge to the Edens side.

As a reward for his quiet but all-important contribution to *Wizard,* L. B. Mayer handed Freed his own production. Stella Adler was Freed's assistant at the time. For the film version of *Babes in Arms,* the first teaming of Mickey Rooney and Judy Garland, Freed promptly cut most of the Rodgers and Hart Broadway score, retaining only "Where or When" and the title number. He interpolated Eubie Blake

MGM luncheon (probably) honoring Herbert Stothart, mid-1940s. That's
Stothart smiling at camera; Metro music head Nat Finston two men down
the table, leaning back; Franz Waxman next to Finston; Bronislau Kaper at
end of table, putting food in his mouth.
Courtesy John Waxman

and Noble Sissle's "I'm Just Wild About Harry"; "Ida, Sweet as Apple
Cider" by Eddie Leonard, the pro-baseball player turned minstrel songwriter; Arlen and Harburg's "God's Country"; and "I Cried for You"—
Freed's lyric set to music by Gus Arnheim and Abe Lyman. In addition,
Brown and Freed wrote "Good Morning" for the film, and Edens wrote
the specialty number "Daddy Was a Minstrel Man." *Babes in Arms* was
the first Metro picture directed by Busby Berkeley, who had brought
from Warners his elaborately synchronistic, saucy precision. Edens,
then thirty-four, supervised the musical adaptation, with orchestrations
by MGM staff arrangers Leo Arnaud and George Bassman. Big-
haired, ever-smiling Georgie Stoll conducted, but it's widely agreed
that musically Edens was the boss.

*   *   *

In 1937, while *Broadway Melody of 1938* was being prepared at MGM, a young German pianist named Magdalene "Lella" Simone began work as a rehearsal pianist at Metro. Simone was like dozens, perhaps hundreds, of Europe's forced émigré musicians who fled oppressive regimes, except that she was female and blessed with a striking Marlene Dietrich-like beauty.

Born in Berlin on August 26, 1907, Lella Simone had been a true piano prodigy, giving concerts as early as 1923. Before she was twenty she had married and divorced, leaving a son in the custody of her former husband. Lella's father, Samuel Saenger, was Jewish, but it was actually her marriage to a Jewish banker named Theodore Simon that prompted her to flee Germany with him in 1933. For a while the Simons lived in New York, staying at the Plaza and getting by on cred-

Lela Simone, early 1940s
Courtesy Tomas Firle

it and their wits. Otto Klemperer helped out by introducing her as a concert soloist. But there wasn't enough work, and the Simons soon had to vacate the great hotel. After a year in San Francisco, they moved to Los Angeles. Increasingly estranged from her husband, Lella found her way to MGM where she was hired as a rehearsal pianist by music chief Jack Chertok.

After fully displaying her chops, Lella graduated from rehearsal pianist to soloist with the MGM Orchestra, which was often led by Herbert Stothart or Georgie Stoll. One day during filming of *Ice Follies of 1939,* one of Metro's more bizarre stories of backstage life (Lew Ayres and Jimmy Stewart appear on ice skates!), she was given one hour to master a formidable Franz Waxman piece that was dizzy with sixteenth notes. She vaguely knew Waxman from Berlin, but so great were the demands on him that he couldn't give her more time. Lella shrugged, studied the piece in the allotted hour, then played it perfectly. Standing at the back of the soundstage, the dazzled Roger Edens said, "Who is that girl?!" After that day he wouldn't forget her.

In 1939 American naturalization enabled Lella to become a a fulltime Metro employee; after her divorce from Simon in 1940, she became known as Lela Simone. She worked hard to get her son, Tomas, to the States, though he was safe with his father; her parents, then living in France, were considerably more vulnerable. Meanwhile, at Metro Lela Simone showed there was nothing she couldn't do: piano teacher, vocal coach, preparer of music cues, music editor, translator (German, French, English), and sounding board.

In 1940 Simone had not yet been officially assigned to work with either Edens or Freed, who were busily completing *Little Nelly Kelly,* a new Garland vehicle full of Brown-Freed songs and a lot of blarney. Edens worked up a new arrangement of "Singin' in the Rain"; the orchestrations for it, and for the George M. Cohan songs included in the score, were made by Conrad "Connie" Salinger. If, in the musicals unit beginning to form around the literary-minded Arthur Freed, Edens was the heart, then Connie Salinger was the soul. With his pencil he did more than anyone else to create the sound of the MGM musical, particularly the Freed musical, in its heyday.

Salinger did it elegantly. Upon graduation from Harvard, Salinger sailed to Paris. There he studied with Paul Dukas (*The Sorcerer's Apprentice*), and with Charles Koechlin, described by Virgil Thomson as "ever curious about novelty and warm toward youth." Under their tutelage, Salinger composed. But he seemed to find his center in other men's compositions. He went to New York and found work arranging for Harms, Inc., and for Paramount-Publix, at the Paramount Theater. Salinger became known around town as an ace orchestrator whose style was constructed around sensual vocal space. In 1938 Alfred Newman, then working at United Artists, called Salinger west; Edward Powell, another supremely gifted Broadway arranger, was already there to greet him. But Powell took more readily to arid, staunchly anti-cosmopolitan southern California than Salinger did. Within a few months Salinger returned to Manhattan.

Something about the movies, however—or, more to the point, movie music—had bitten Salinger. Too proud to return to Hollywood immediately, he remained in New York for a while. Then, quietly, Salinger accepted an offer to arrange the music for the radio program of his friend Robert Emmett Dolan, which was broadcast from Los Angeles. He took a couple of jobs at Metro that worked out nicely, then orchestrated the marvelous Kern-Mercer songs for Columbia's *You Were Never Lovelier*. Salinger settled more or less permanently at Metro in 1943. He was forty, much admired, fiercely private, homosexual before it was politically advisable to admit it, and prone to drink away his cares.

In the early '40s, Freed and Eden began working on a series of musicals. First came *Strike Up the Band* (1940), perhaps the least appealing of all Judy Garland–Mickey Rooney movies. (Despite the Gershwin title, Edens wrote most of the music, with Georgie Stoll conducting.) Next came *Babes on Broadway*, which is easier to sit through, less because of the script or Berkeley's direction than because the songs are just better. With music by Burton Lane and lyrics by Freed's much younger, bespectacled brother Ralph, "How About You?" ("I love potato chips, moonlight and motor trips") is one of the cleverest, sweetest songs to come out of the movies. Connie Salinger's arrangement showed his touching rapport with singers—in this case, Garland and Rooney—that would make his arrangements and orchestrations so prized at Metro.

Lady Be Good (1941) had virtually nothing to do with the 1924 Gershwin show of the same name; it introduced the Kern-Hammerstein "The Last Time I Saw Paris" that caused such a fuss when it won the Academy Award for best song. (Kern himself protested because Hammerstein, upset when Paris fell to the Nazis, had wired him the lyric, and the resulting song wasn't written for the movie. Yet it beat out "Blues in the Night," the Arlen-Mercer song that Kern admired.) *Ziegfeld Girl* wasn't much better, although Nacio Herb Brown–Gus Kahn's "You Stepped Out of a Dream" became a classic. (It was one of Kahn's last completed lyrics before his death in 1941.) At this point Salinger, burning midnight oil as he orchestrated much of the studio's musical fare, became indispendable to Freed. Edens in turn became Freed's associate producer. Together, Freed and Edens brought in Lela Simone. She was as literate as Freed, as musical as Edens, and had a steeliness that enabled her to do much of the dirty work.

The Freed Unit was in place. Always an eagle-eyed talent scout, Freed negotiated with David O. Selznick for the services of Gene Kelly, then just months out of his starring role on Broadway as *Pal Joey*, to costar with Garland in *For Me and My Gal*. (Salinger and Edens both worked on the music.) He brought former stage designer Vincente Minnelli on to direct Lena Horne's sequence in *Panama Hattie*, then signed him to direct all of *Cabin in the Sky*, with its Vernon Duke–John Latouche songs, including "Taking a Chance on Love," supplemented by the music of others (for example, Arlen and Harburg's "Happiness Is Just a Thing Called Joe"). *Cabin in the Sky*, which Minnelli had also directed on Broadway, wasn't like any mainstream studio picture produced before—an all-black cast in a Faustian musical drama, with slinky temptress Lena Horne providing aural (and visual) counterpoint to Ethel Waters, the embodiment of soulfulness.

By the beginning of 1943, when the music for *Girl Crazy* was recorded, there was no smarter, more sophisticated musical platoon in the movie business than Freed's. When Garland sang "Embraceable You" with a toy grand piano as a prop and a male chorus backing her, you knew you were in the hands of experts. Together, Roger Edens and Connie Salinger—one arranging vocals and supervising, the other orchestrating—were remaking the way music was presented in a movie musical, using lusher arrangements played by smaller orchestras.

Not that they did it alone at Metro. In 1943 Garland also appeared in *Presenting Lily Mars,* the first Metro production by Joe Pasternak, the Hungarian with the Louis Armstrong voice who had defected from Universal. Pasternak had worked as a busboy in the Paramount commissary in the early '20s; a decade later he was producing German-language musicals at Universal's Berlin studio, until the war brought him back to Los Angeles. Like Freed, Pasternak prided himself on knowing talent. He couldn't bring over discovery Deanna Durbin, who had been Universal's most valuable property. But eventually he brought over Nicholas Brodszky, a composer who could write lovely three-minute songs, and Henry Koster (né Hermann Kosterlitz), an underrated director of musicals. Pasternak's films had a heavier, more operettaish flavor than Freed's story- and dance-driven movies. Opera stars Lauritz Melchior, Ezio Pinza, and, notoriously, Mario Lanza all made pictures under Pasternak's banner at Metro.

The other important musicals producer on the lot was Jack Cummings, who was said to have to work even harder than his colleagues because he was L. B. Mayer's nephew. Born Jacob Kominsky in New Brunswick, Canada, in 1900, Cummings took over the *Broadway Melody* series beginning with the 1940 entry. Cummings probably had a sharper ear than either Freed or Pasternak. On MGM's Stage One, during recording, Cummings appraised orchestrations by standing next to the cello section, as though taking the orchestra's temperature, and days of labor often had to be scrapped because the producer didn't like what he heard. In 1943, Arthur Freed turned over to him a project called *Bathing Beauty*; Cummings, enlisting the bands of Harry James and Xavier Cugat for musical support, turned a handsome swimming champion named Esther Williams into a star.

Across the lot Conrad Salinger, virtually alone, arranged and orchestrated the Ralph Blane–Hugh Martin songs for Freed's production of *Meet Me in St. Louis* (1944). The movie, based on Sally Benson's stories about growing up in turn-of-the-century St. Louis, has its share of detractors ("saccharine," "plotless"), but few movies gave us so many memorable songs. The title song went back decades, of course, written by Tin Pan Alley lyricist Andrew Sterling ("Wait Till the Sun Shines,

Nellie" and many, many songs with railroad motifs) and composer Kerry Mills. "Have Yourself a Merry Little Christmas" was written expressly for Garland to sing to younger sister Margaret O'Brien, but some original lines—especially "Faithful friends who were dear to us/Will be near to us no more," and "It may be your last/Next year we will all be living in the past"—were deemed ghoulishly pessimistic by Garland, and altered by just a word or two. "The Boy Next Door" has become a favorite among jazz musicians for its subtle chord changes. "The Trolley Song" was written after Freed insisted on a song about the trolley ride itself; stumped, Ralph Blane went to the library and, looking through a picture book about St. Louis, found the caption "Clang Clang Clang Went the Trolley." Salinger's arrangements of these songs conveyed the color and background of St. Louis just as well as the photography did. And his orchestrations were something revelatory for a movie musical: he used thirty-six to thirty-seven instruments, considerably fewer than the usual studio aggregation, combining to create a musical persona for every character in the script.

Songwriters Martin and Blane had met in New York in the mid-'30s. Martin from Birmingham, Alabama, and Blane (né Hunsecker) from Broken Arrow, Oklahoma, each sang with the Kay Thompson Singers in 1938 (in *Hooray for What?*, starring Ed Wynn). In 1941, under George Abbott's auspices, they wrote the Broadway musical *Best Foot Forward*. After dashing off "Wish I May, Wish I Might" for the 1943 Metro version of the show, the two Southern boys were invited to write the songs for *Meet Me in St. Louis*.

Meet Me in St. Louis was also the second Metro picture for Martin and Blane's previous boss Kay Thompson. Born in St. Louis—various sources give her birth year as 1912 or 1913—daughter of a jeweler, the willowy, dynamic Thompson was a piano prodigy and an athlete. In many early photographs, her face and figure combine to give the impression of a fair-haired Bea Lillie. She first went to California in 1929 and worked as a diving instructor before getting hired as occasional guest vocalist with the Mills Brothers—on radio, that is, where their racial differences were less important than their stylistic ones. In New York, Thompson joined Fred Waring's Pennsylvanians as arranger-singer—his radio program billed her as "comic vocalist"—then took a shot at her own radio show, "Kay Thompson and

Company," on CBS, costarring a young comedian named Jim Backus. The show flopped, but it brought her to the attention of the Metro music men.

Thompson had the discipline of a glee-club director and the sensibility of a party girl. She was fun and could talk to anybody. At social gatherings, she often joined Salinger, Simone, and Edens, the Freed Unit trio that had come to be known on the lot as The Royal Family. They drank together. Edens and Salinger, both gay and erudite, adored Thompson's dry cocktail laughter; her jazzy musical ideas were just a bonus.

In contrast to the happy fraternizing of Thompson and crew, Freed kept himself aloof from the rest of the group. As a lyricist he had had the touch of a businessman. From "Singin' in the Rain" to "Good Morning," his words stroll through their clichés with a shrug; they're cued to cheerful romantic sentiment ("You Are My Lucky Star," "All I Do Is Dream of You") without achieving much depth, or even cleverness. Freed's writing lacked the dazzle and specificity of his brother Ralph's lyrics for, say, "How About You?" or "You Leave Me Breathless."

Overseeing other people's writing, however, Freed was an intuitive, merciless editor who wasn't inclined to wrestle with complexity. "When he was disgusted with something," Lela Simone told Rudy Behlmer, "he just said, 'Look here, guys, let's cut it out. Finished.'"

Nor was he particularly warm. "He wore armor, armor," said Irving Brecher, who worked for seven months on the screenplay for *Meet Me in St. Louis*. Lela Simone described Freed as "very closed. He was only open when he was mad, which was rather often." Stocky, well-dressed, often with a cigarette jammed between pudgy fingers, he's seen in many photographs looking off into the middle distance. Asked to evaluate something out of his field of interest—choreography, for instance—he would jingle the coins in his pockets and look down. "Although he knew perfectly well what he liked and did not like," Alan Jay Lerner said of Freed, "what he wanted and what he did not want, his method of conveying it was so circuitous that the mind grew vertiginous with his non sequiturs and it took patience, respect, and maniacal determination to ferret out nuggets of information." Lerner remembered confronting Freed in his office:

> LERNER: Did you read the script?
> FREED: Yup. I spoke to Oscar [Hammerstein] yesterday.
> LERNER: Do you think the part is big enough for Chevalier?
> FREED: I thought you were going to be at Ira's [Gershwin] last night.

Or at the MGM commissary, Freed and Lerner had just sat down and were studying the menu when an agent approached with beautiful young Romy Schneider in tow:

> AGENT: Arthur, I'd like you to meet Romy Schneider. She's out here to make a picture.
> *Freed does not hear and looks up at Romy Schneider.*
> FREED: I'll have the cheese omelette.

Unimpressed by celebrity itself, Freed openly admired talent, especially if it combined literary and musical gifts. To Freed, Oscar Hammerstein was an Olympian. Just before the first production of *Oklahoma!* was mounted, Freed tried to put Hammerstein under contract as his associate producer, the position that Edens subsequently filled. Freed, known for his powers of persuasion, managed to lure several other people west. Betty Comden and Adolph Green, the lyricists-librettists whom he referred to as "The Kids," weren't inclined to return to Hollywood after they had appeared briefly as part of The Revuers (Judy Holliday, John Frank, and Alvin Hammer were the others) in *Greenwich Village* (Twentieth Century-Fox, 1944)—the satirists' total contribution had been edited down to a single line uttered by Betty Comden to Don Ameche: "Here's your hat, sir." After their shows *On the Town* (music by Leonard Bernstein) and *Billion Dollar Baby* (music by Morton Gould) were produced on Broadway, everyone wanted Comden and Green—as writers, however, not as performers. Freed brought them back out by offering lavish salaries and relative independence. Composer Gian-Carlo Menotti accepted Freed's invitation and completed two original screenplays but, discovering that he wouldn't have the last word on how his material would be used, departed without rancor. Freed heard twenty-two-year-old Mel Tormé sing at the Bocage, a Hollywood nightclub, and offered him a part in *Good News*. Although the part was small, Tormé accepted, not least because it brought him professionally level (or so he thought) with MGM contract player Ava Gardner, whom he was dating.

After the stage success of *Brigadoon* (1947), Alan Jay Lerner was invited to come out and just take a look around—maybe an idea for a movie would develop. Lerner's first good idea became *Royal Wedding*. For the songs, Freed adroitly paired Lerner with Burton Lane, the composer of 1947's other British Isles fantasy-fable *Finian's Rainbow* (lyrics by Yip Harburg). *Royal Wedding* gave us Astaire dancing on the ceiling to "You're All the World to Me" (actually an old melody of Lane's, lyrics by Harold Adamson, and entitled "I Want to Be a Minstrel Man") and the marvelous ballad "Too Late Now."

On the Culver City lot, Freed deferred to no one except Mayer. "How ya fixed, L. B.?" Lillian Ross quoted Freed as addressing Mayer. The two men were in touch by intercom several times a day. The studio line went: "If you want to shave Freed, you've got to lather L. B. Mayer's ass." Freed was aware that Mayer granted him an autonomy that few other men in motion pictures enjoyed; Mayer knew that Freed, given a free hand, would produce profitable films for the studio.

Neither songs nor the movies were Freed's passion; orchids were. As Freed aged, that passion grew and consumed more of his time. He was particularly proud of a pure white orchid he'd created. Freed came to the studio wearing beautiful suits and blackened fingernails from digging around his orchids. Oscar Levant liked to say, "Arthur is so rich that he doesn't get manicures like ordinary mortals. He eats his breakfast with one hand and sticks the other hand out the window."

But Freed, if not warm, was human. Apart from orchids, his blood was stirred by a young dancer from upstate New York named Lucille Bremer.

"I was trained in ballet," Bremer said, "and was dancing at the Versailles Restaurant in New York when producer Arthur Freed and some others from MGM came in one evening. Evidently they liked what they saw because they asked me to come to Hollywood." Bremer had also danced as a Rockette at Radio City and appeared in a minor role in *Lady in the Dark*. She arrived in Culver City on a Friday, was instructed to read the *Meet Me in St. Louis* script over the weekend, and report to work on Monday.

Freed, possessed of a keen ear and an unerring eye, was determined to make Bremer a star. Buoyed by Judy Garland and a sturdy ensemble, Bremer was adequate and pretty in *Meet Me in St. Louis*. But Freed wanted more for her—and, by most accounts, from her. So he purchased Ludwig Bemelmans's *Yolanda and the Thief* as a starring vehicle for her, and he commanded Irving Brecher to adapt it. Although Brecher found the Austrian artist-author (best known in the United States for his children's book *Madeleine*) extremely companionable—"He couldn't draw an egg that wasn't funny," Brecher said—he sensed there was no movie in it. Freed turned the recalcitrant Brecher over to Sam Katz, formerly a nationally feared theater owner (of Balaban and Katz) and now, as executive producer of the musical division, nominally Freed's boss. A roughneck who didn't mince words, Katz had once dismissed the entire score of *The Wizard of Oz* as being "above the heads of children," particularly disliking "Over the Rainbow."

"Kid, close the door," Katz said to Brecher. "You know, we made a lot of money with Arthur. We owe him something. This one is for Arthur." When Brecher still resisted the assignment, Katz tried another tack. "What's your salary?" Twelve-fifty a week, Brecher replied. Katz pretended not to hear him and kept asking the screenwriter to repeat the figure. "Did you say two thousand dollars?" said Katz. "Four firm years at two thousand, with twelve weeks off with pay?"

Brecher took the assignment. And Freed kept faith in his discovery. He collaborated with Harry Warren on songs for the movie—"Will You Marry Me?" and "Coffee Time" got some airplay—proving he could still do some lyric spadework if he were motivated. But the completed *Yolanda* confirmed Brecher's fears; it was one of the few times Fred Astaire would publicly deride a picture in which he appeared. Lucille Bremer failed to catch fire. Freed was saved from greater embarrassment when, in 1948, his protégée married Abelardo Rodriguez, son of a former president of Mexico, and retired from the movies.

If Freed was devastated, he didn't show it. His unit had rapidly become the single most powerful, innovative moviemaking force on the Metro lot. A great deal of its success was due to the Texas-born Edens, who had a hand in every component of a Freed production. "Roger was not, in essence, a modest fellow," Simone said of Edens. "He was a well-mannered person who would express his negative opinion about something in a high-class manner." For a while Edens seemed to *be* the Freed Unit. His expansiveness was a welcome contrast to the boss's dour, withdrawn moodiness. Where Freed's office was like a formal drawing room—books perfectly aligned, valuable paintings hung straight, untouchable antiques—Edens's office was defined by the grand piano in the middle of the room. Music and games supplied the tone. Edens and Kay Thompson shared a birthday, November 9 (Edens was six or seven years older), which became an annual celebration for the unit: Edens played, Thompson sang.

With *The Pirate* (1947), Kay Thompson began her long goodbye to MGM, her contribution far louder and more influential than her four-year tenure would suggest. There were other vocal coaches and arrangers on the lot, to be sure—notably Bobby Tucker, whose background was in choral music—but none as dynamic as Thompson. At age thirty-five or so, Thompson was determined to resume her performing career. She had worked on half a dozen Freed productions, most expertly on the propulsive vocals for the Harry Warren–Johnny Mercer songs in *The Harvey Girls* (1946). (Think of the rung-climbing structure of "On the Atcheson . . . on the Atcheson Topeka . . . on the Atcheson Topeka and the San-ta Fa-aay.") And she'd changed the way Edens—and, by extension, the entire Freed Unit—thought about vocal numbers in the movies. For the Cole Porter songs for *The Pirate* (Gene Kelly and Judy Garland, directed by Garland's husband, Vincente Minnelli), Thompson's vocal arrangements were, according to Simone, "so overpowering that the whole thing was like the Metropolitan Opera."

Thompson's last official work for Metro was on *Good News* (1947). Freed had long wanted to remake the 1927 DeSylva-Brown-Henderson show (which had been filmed by MGM in 1930). *Good News* captured the rah-rah, extracurricular spirit of the '20s, when as

Roger Edens, George Sidney, Judy Garland on set of *The Harvey Girls* (1946)
Courtesy Academy of Motion Picture Arts & Sciences and Turner Entertainment

Robert Hutchins of the University of Chicago had said, "colleges con-
fused themselves with country clubs." Before he got a script from
Comden and Green, Freed offered to turn the project over to Sam
Coslow, who was—as Freed had been—trying to make the transition
from songwriter to producer. Coslow thought the project antiquated.
"There's a world war on," Coslow explained to an astonished Sam Katz

Good News (1947)
Courtesy the author

about why he was declining, "and I feel anything we make should be vital and significant. Who the hell cares about a story concerning the outcome of a football game?"

Kay Thompson's vocals may not have been significant but, with their fraternal, hand-clapping energy, they were certainly vital. Thompson structured the vocals so that they bounced, ran away from each other, and came together—something like students in love.

Needing a higher voice for the "Be a Ladies' Man" number to complement Peter Lawford, Mel Tormé, Ray McDonald, Tom Dugan, and Lon Tindall, Thompson brought in her paramour, eighteen-year-old Andy Williams. Williams was already familiar with movie ghosting jobs: his was the singing voice that emanated from Lauren Bacall's mouth in *To Have and Have Not*.

With a minimum of fanfare Thompson bid farewell to Edens and Salinger, to infant goddaughter Liza Minnelli and her pal Garland, and went to Las Vegas where she obtained a divorce from radio director Bill Spier. She wrote herself a nightclub act. A penthouse office was maintained for her at MGM, but Thompson was almost never there. She moved back to New York and settled into the nightclub Le Directoire (formerly the Café Society Uptown). For the next four years Thompson, backed by the Williams Brothers—Andy, of course, plus Richard, Robert, and Donald—beckoned to Manhattan's cabaret night creatures, most of them unaware of Thompson's contribution to the movie musicals they'd enjoyed.

In January 1954, Thompson began a new act at the Plaza Hotel. It was here, apologizing in a little girl's voice for arriving late to a rehearsal, that six-year-old Eloise was born. Introduced at the Plaza to a twenty-eight-year-old man named Hilary Knight, Thompson knew she'd found the perfect illustrator for her recent creation. *Eloise* ("A Book for Precocious Grown Ups"), the story of a little girl living at the Plaza, was published in November 1955. It was considered a classic before the new year arrived.

Despite the literary triumph, Thompson didn't ignore her music *or* the movies. She composed "Promise Me Love," a minor hit for Andy Williams, and wrote and recorded (for Cadence) her own "Eloise" song, which quickly sold half a million units. She also took her first major movie role, the brassy, long-legged fashion editor Maggie Prescott, said to be modeled on *Harper's Bazaar* editor Carmel Snow, in *Funny Face*. The production was overseen by old friend Roger Edens, who with Freed's blessing had stepped over to Paramount to make it, escorted by Salinger and a squadron of MGM arrangers to attend to the Gershwin tunes. Although *Funny Face* is prized by lovers of musicals for its framework of Avedon-like fashion photographer Fred Astaire taking pictures of Audrey Hepburn, there is to my mind only one truly wonderful

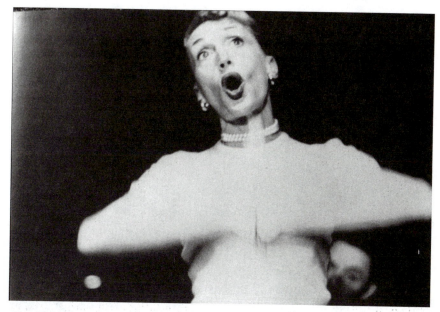

Kay Thompson
Photo by Milton Greene

sequence: Thompson and Astaire parodying the beatnik scene as they dance to "Fascinating Rhythm."

The box-office and critical success of *Good News* in 1947 cemented Arthur Freed's power. Yet the MGM executive staff, resenting the producer's close ties to Mayer and his increasing autonomy, tried to cut him down to size whenever it got the chance. One chance came after screenwriter Irving Brecher, whose relations with Freed had never been especially cordial, was assigned to work on the project *Summer Holiday*, a musical remake of Eugene O'Neill's comedic drama, *Ah, Wilderness!* As Brecher told it, director Rouben Mamoulian instructed him to show his latest draft to Freed. Freed read it and pronounced it "shit." He hollered at Brecher, "Get out of here, you sheenie bastard!" Shocked that one Jew could call another Jew such a name, Brecher reported the remark to Benny Thau.

"Would you mind telling this story to L. B. Mayer?" asked Thau. In Mayer's cream-colored office, flanked by Thau and other executives,

Brecher told the story to Mayer, who promptly called Freed on his intercom. "Yes, Chief!" said Freed, and rushed right over.

A humiliated Freed was made to apologize to Brecher. For the silently smirking executives, the slur at Brecher had been the perfectly curved scythe to cut down Freed.

But *Summer Holiday* (1948) was Brecher's last assignment for MGM. Less than three years later, Mayer was gone, too. And Freed's greatest musicals were still to come.

In those years of the late '40s, Freed, Edens, and Simone never seemed to stop. Lela Simone, everywhere at once, joined Jesse Kaye to put together the first complete soundtrack recording for MGM Records, *Till the Clouds Roll By.* Working with music librarian George Schneider, "an absolute genius, a wonderful old man," Simone compiled preview music tracks. She coached with pianist Harold Gelman, who arrived at the studio in 1945, consulted with cinematographer Peter Ballbusch, who was responsible for most of the montage shots in MGM musicals, and with Al Akst, Freed's brother-in-law, who edited most of the Freed Unit's movies until Adrienne Fazan arrived to take over the more sophisticated material.

For years Simone and her third husband, film editor Al Joseph, couldn't get away together—not with Freed insisting that everything had to be done yesterday. At the behest of producer Pandro Berman, Freed and Edens permitted her to play a Chopin prelude for *The Picture of Dorian Gray*; Simone had to diplomatically fend off ardent advances from the director, Albert Lewin. She could hold her own. For years she stood up to Metro music chief Nat Finston, who couldn't abide women in his department. Tensions eased when Izzy Friedman took over in 1945, and smoothed out completely when Richard Powers, a hands-off administrator, took over from Friedman in 1946. "Powers was more of an executive," Simone said. "He didn't pretend to know anything about music. He was very polite, very nice, and did exactly what we asked him to do."

The Freed Unit was fairly well insulated from the music department's old-fogeyism and ignorance. And it got a boost of adrenalin when, during preparations for *On the Town* in August 1949, Johnny Green was appointed head of music.

At once funny and self-important, consummately political and fiercely loyal, Johnny Green was born in 1908 in New York to a wealthy banking and construction family. (Greenhaven, Long Island, is named after his father.) A piano prodigy, young Johnny played for George Gershwin, entered Harvard at fifteen and graduated at nineteen. Although he had already published a hit song, made arrangements for Guy Lombardo, and palled around the Midwestern outposts of show business with a young publicist named Lew Wasserman, Green became a stockbroker—the career choice that pleased his father. He soon found himself in psychotherapy. He quit Wall Street and went to work as a rehearsal pianist at Paramount's Astoria studios. He resumed writing songs with his old buddy Edward Heyman, a sausage heir who had written shows at the University of Michigan. The team wrote a torch song for Gertrude Lawrence called "Body and Soul." The song was merely part of a package of four that Lawrence bought outright. When Libby Holman asked to sing the song in the revue *Three's a Crowd* (1930), Green and Heyman had to get the rights back from Lawrence. For years "Body and Soul" generated more income than any other American song.

Green knew he had a magic touch. With Heyman he wrote "Out of Nowhere" (Bing Crosby's first solo recording, 1931), and "I Cover the Waterfront" for the 1933 independent film of the same name, based on Max Miller's stories about San Diego. For several years Green was a fixture on New York's podia, leading a dance band on the roof of the St. Regis, conducting in the pit at various Broadway theaters, and fronting radio orchestras.

Jack Benny brought Green to Los Angeles in 1942 as a comic foil (Green was an incurable ham with a penchant for speaking in dialect, usually Yiddish) as well as music director for his radio program. Roger Edens knew Green from New York and brought him to Metro's music staff. Balding, elfin, and usually grinning, Green scored, orchestrated, or conducted at least two dozen MGM pictures, winning a best musical direction Oscar for Freed's *Easter Parade*, before becoming head of music. Green got his promotion from new production chief Dore Schary. Mayer, "the Chief," was on his way out, and Freed had little use for Schary. The feeling, alas, was mutual.

Within the Freed Unit it was felt that Lennie Hayton, who was then married to Lena Horne, coaxed more swing than Green from the musicians. But Green possessed a light touch, assembled wonderful musical talent, and did his damndest to administrate. He reveled in the sumptuousness of his office quarters, his bank of telephones, and his attention to detail, sometimes to the point of pettiness. According to Lela Simone, Green could get exercised about how much music paper was being wasted. Upon his promotion he instituted weekly Thursday morning meetings. His first departmental meeting, according to Miklos Rozsa,

> when he had to pass on to us a directive from the new head [Schary] was (at least for me) disturbing. The new chief wanted to hear the tunes in the musicals and not the orchestrations. (This was a thrust at the enormously gifted Conrad Salinger, the arranger responsible for most of the MGM musicals' distinction.) If in the dramatic pictures he had to choose between the "Steineresque" and the "Coplandesque," he preferred the former. I asked meekly whether I would be permitted to continue to be "Rozsaesque," but my sarcasm wasn't much appreciated.

When Broadway conductor Jay Blackton (*Oklahoma!, Annie Get Your Gun*), still young but already frail in his five-foot, polio-stricken frame, arrived at the studio in 1951 to conduct Pasternak's new *The Merry Widow,* he reported to his first weekly meeting. There he found himself face to face with men whose original or adapted scores he had long admired, among them Kaper, Rozsa, David Rose, David Raksin, Jeff Alexander, and Van ("A-Tisket, A-Tasket") Alexander. Green, with a fresh carnation in the buttonhole of his expensive suit, gestured grandly behind his huge desk and said, "Fellas, I want you to meet Jay Blackton. He's coming to work with us and show us how to make musicals." Blackton felt like shrinking to the bottom of his chair. This was especially puzzling because it was Green himself who had recruited Blackton after hearing him conduct *Call Me Madam* tryouts in Boston.

"You know, he overacted enormously," Simone said of Green, "then he tried to rearrange his department so that everything that [was] happening in the music department [was] of total importance. He wanted to establish himself as a king, [an] absolute monarch."

Jay Blackton and Marlon Brando preparing for film version of *Guys and Dolls* (1955)
Courtesy Louise Blackton

Although he still took his cues from Edens and Salinger when working with the Freed Unit, Green didn't hide his authority at Metro. Living with his third wife, former U.S. Olympics swimmer and MGM actress Bonnie Walters, and their daughters, Green settled into a comfortable professional life of composing, conducting, and acting important.

The first Freed production during Green's long tenure as head of music was *On the Town*. From Columbia Pictures, Green lured over Saul Chaplin (né Kaplan), the tall, rabbity-looking Brooklynite who had willed himself to keep working after a painful split from longtime collaborator Sammy Cahn. At penny-pinching Columbia, Chaplin was used to working on several scores at once for Morris Stoloff. At MGM, however, Green allowed him to concentrate on one project at a time. Chaplin was the kind of musician who could do just about anything—compose, accompany, arrange when Salinger was overworked—and he did it for *On the Town*.

Despite its place as a seminal musical in the MGM catalog and in Freed's own list of productions, *On the Town* is a lesson in how removed Hollywood product could be from its source. Gradually Roger Edens cut away most of Bernstein's music. The gorgeous songs "Some Other Time" and "Lucky to Be Me" were scrapped because they slowed the action. Sinatra, petulant about being required to show up for other players' numbers as though he were a "chorus boy," extracted from Freed a promise that he could sing the ballad "Lonely Town"—but that too was never filmed. Bernstein, already distressed by the chipping away of his score, grudgingly agreed to go to Culver City to write seven extra bars for one song. "And Bernstein came," Simone recalled, "ate lunch in the little restaurant, mostly with us, didn't speak a word and left again. It was fantastic." Simone wasn't even certain that Bernstein wrote the seven extra bars.

On the Town won Academy Awards for conductor Lennie Hayton and for Roger Edens, the two names submitted by music chief Johnny Green at Edens's own direction. Chaplin, who had orchestrated half the score—staff arranger Wally Heglin pitched in—felt cheated out of credit. But Edens maintained a tight grip on the music end of the Freed Unit, and only Freed himself had the authority to overrule him. Film historian Gerald Mast wrote, "Every Edens song for the film ('Prehistoric Man,' 'Main Street,' a vapid title tune, and 'You're Awful') is hackwork—the kind of musical garbage that proved the inferiority of Hollywood musicals to Broadway buffs." The picture is flat, yes, but it's not garbage; it's musically thin, but enough, *just* enough, of the music supplies the pulse of a postwar New York romp.

On the Town is a typical Freed production in that it boasts a lot of dancing by men, a loose-limbed, energetic script by Comden and Green, and not a thought in its head. Politics and current events are absent from Freed's musicals; they almost invariably move through a lush, highly stylized, Technicolor world, motorized by an extraordinary dancer, singer, or both. These pictures were helmed by a small cadre of Freed-approved directors, all of them dancers (Kelly, of course, Stanley Donen, Charles Walters, and Robert Alton) or sympathetic to dance (Minnelli, Richard Thorpe, and George Sidney). In a Freed musical, dance provided the engine, music the fuel, and the destination was good feeling. "You can't sell futility," Freed told Lillian Ross in 1951. He was referring to John Huston's movies, particularly *The Red Badge of Courage* and *The Treasure of the Sierra Madre*. "Fundamentally, a picture is not complete unless an audience is out there. Without an audience, you don't know where the laughs are. This is show business. You need laughs. You need cheerfulness. That's the whole reason for show business in the first place." Hiroshima, Nuremberg, McCarthyism—none of it was even hinted at in the Freed musical.

An American in Paris came out of Freed's conviction that the title alone supplied the basis for a story, set to Gershwin songs. Alan Lerner put together a script; Vincente Minnelli was brought in to direct. Saul Chaplin, with Ira Gershwin looking over his shoulder, combed the Gershwin catalog. For his leading lady, Gene Kelly lobbied for Leslie Caron whom he had seen dance in the Ballets des Champs Elysées. French musical comedy star Georges Guetary was signed (his rendition of "I'll Build a Stairway to Paradise" is a throwback to the lavish production numbers of the first movie musicals), along with the essential Oscar Levant—how could you mount a Gershwin project without that virtuoso of modern-day neuroses?

To some viewers, *An American in Paris* feels at once bloated and fey—a Technicolored balloon that floats nowhere—and too much of it sits heavily upon Caron's arguable charm. But the picture was a smash. It also won several Academy Awards, including best picture, and music awards for Johnny Green, who conducted, and the redeemed Saul Chaplin, who arranged. Gene Kelly was awarded an honorary Oscar for "brilliant achievement in the art of choreography on film." Freed, already the most successful musicals producer since the birth of the movies, received the Irving Thalberg Award. At fifty-seven, he was at the very top of the profession. It did not reduce his standing that he also happened to produce that year's Oscar show, held on March 20, 1952, at the Pantages Theater in Hollywood.

An American in Paris wasn't that year's only Freed production. After years of courting Oscar Hammerstein, Freed finally mounted another *Show Boat*. Louis B. Mayer attended the preview and wept. As later recorded by Lillian Ross, Mayer sat in his office:

> "I saw *Show Boat* and the tears were in my eyes. I'm not ashamed of tears. I cried. I'll see it thirteen times. Thirteen times! Tears! Emotion!"
>
> "It's great entertainment," Freed said. "It's show business."
>
> Mayer stared across the top of Freed's head. "There's a singer in the picture," he went on. "Black. He has one song. He"—Mayer jabbed a finger in Freed's direction—"got the man to come all the way from Australia to sing this one song. The way he sings it, it goes straight to the heart."

Lela Simone corroborated that William Warfield was located in Australia and summoned to California; and when he sang "Ol' Man River" on Metro Stage One, everybody, Freed included, gathered to listen in astonishment. Even with a lion like Paul Robeson in the path, Warfield made the song his own. (Salinger did the arrangement.)

When director George Sidney took sick, Roger Edens stepped in without fuss to complete his scenes. Ava Gardner, the most ravishing movie star of her generation played Julie—a casting coup that probably brought a few extra million viewers into theaters—but Edens and Simone were utterly horrified by her singing voice. At the last minute they dubbed Gardner's voice with Annette Warren's, though Gardner's voice was used for "promotional purposes" on the MGM recording.

◦   ◦   ◦

In 1951 the Freed Unit was at its most powerful. Knowing that the receipts Freed carried around in his pocket were accurate indicators of the profits he made for the studio, Schary largely left him alone. After more than a decade producing under his own name, Freed wanted a picture that meant something extra to him. *Singin' in the Rain,* like *Easter Parade* (Irving Berlin) and *An American in Paris* (Gershwin) before it, was built around a song catalog—but in this case the catalog belonged to the producer and to his former partner, Nacio Herb Brown.

Comden and Green were engaged to turn out a screen story. Attempting to match the period setting to the time when the Freed-Brown songs were first heard, Comden and Green seized on the era when silent films went to sound. Their first pass at a script focused on a silent cowboy actor who, blessed with a magnificent voice, becomes a star with the advent of the talkies. (Metro contract star Howard Keel was to play the lead.) But the essential woodenness of the concept gave way to a song-and-dance man: Gene Kelly. El Paso native Debbie Reynolds, discovered a couple of years earlier in Burbank, California, had already appeared in MGM's *Three Little Words* as boop-boop-de-boop vaudevillian Helen Kane (Kane herself ghosted Reynolds's singing). Reynolds was signed for *Singin' in the Rain* and, except on "Would You," where she was dubbed by Betty Noyes, she did her own singing. But in 1951 her speaking voice still sounded too Texan, so in the famous scenes in which Reynolds appears to be dubbing for Jean Hagen as the aluminum-voiced silent-screen actress Lily Lamont, it is actually Hagen, speaking normally, dubbing herself.

The score moved fluidly through the Freed-Brown catalog, with an addition by Edens, Comden & Adolph Green ("Moses Supposes"), and an old Freed lyric ("Fit as a Fiddle") to music by Russian-born Al Hoffman (best known for his music for Disney's *Cinderella*) and long-time collaborator Al Goodhart. One of the new songs by Freed and Brown, who had remained friendly in the thirteen years since their professional split, was "Make 'Em Laugh," in which Donald O'Connor sings and acts out to cheer up buddy Kelly. When Irving Berlin appeared on the set and heard "Make 'Em Laugh," he expressed concern that it sounded suspiciously like "Be a Clown," from Cole Porter's *The Pirate.* Nobody, least of all Freed, wanted to investigate this. Pirated songs or not, *Singin' in the Rain* was the most exuberant Freed musical yet. The songs—arranged by Salinger, Skip Martin, Wally Heglin, and Bob Franklyn—were given an extra squeeze by Lennie Hayton, conducting the MGM Orchestra.

After Freed and Brown got their shot at immortalizing part of their song catalog on film, it was Dietz and Schwartz's turn. Or, more accurately, it was Dietz's turn. Dietz, like Freed and Brown, had been an MGM employee in its earliest years—earlier, even, than Freed or Brown. In 1917, working for advertising man Philip Goodman, Dietz was assigned to design a trademark for Samuel Goldwyn's film company. Dietz came up with Leo the Lion—a laughing lion adorned *The Jester*, Columbia College's humor magazine—and the Latin motto *Ars Gratia Artis* ("Art for art's sake"), a stroke of advertising genius. Upon discharge from the Navy a few years later, "Freckles" Dietz found a permanent job in Goldwyn's publicity department. By 1924, when former employer Philip Goodman produced Dietz's first Broadway show *Dear Sir* (music by Jerome Kern), Dietz's day job fell under the auspices of Goldwyn's newly formed company, Metro-Goldwyn-Mayer.

In 1951 MGM bought the rights to the 1931 Dietz-Schwartz revue *The Band Wagon*. Comden and Green, on a roll after successes with *Good News, On the Town,* and *Singin' in the Rain,* went to work, basing their story on the physical difference between stars Astaire and the leggy Charisse (who was at least an inch taller than her male lead). Ingeniously, they flipped the boilerplate of the typical backstage musical so that it was the veteran rather than the newcomer who saves the troubled show. The role of the temperamental director was originally conceived for Clifton Webb, as a cross between Orson Welles and Jose Ferrer, but finally went to longtime song-and-dance man Jack Buchanan. In fact, Buchanan was an inspired choice. He had introduced "By Myself" in the 1937 Dietz-Schwartz show *Between the Devil,* which also included the "Triplets" number. Also gathered from various Dietz-Schwartz shows were "New Sun in the Sky," "I Love Louisa," "Dancing in the Dark," "Shine on Your Shoes," and "Louisiana Hayride."

The movie production needed something more—not just more music, but a high-voltage number that encapsulated what it means to entertain. So Dietz and Schwartz headed west. Each man had spent a fair amount of time in California. Schwartz lived for much of the '40s in Beverly Hills. He had produced the Columbia musical *Cover Girl* and Warners' *Night and Day,* and done some of his best composing during the war. With Frank Loesser he wrote "They're Either Too Young or Too Old," sung by Bette Davis in *Thank Your Lucky Stars,* and with Leo Robin wrote the songs for *The Time, the Place and the Girl,* which includes "A Gal in Calico" and the under-recorded "I Happened to Walk Down First Street." After he returned to New York in 1946 for the production of *Park Avenue* (lyrics by Ira Gershwin), Schwartz was determined to compose only for the theater.

Dietz was frequently in Culver City for his duties as director of advertising-publicity-exploitation for Loew's, Inc., but he officially resided in Greenwich Village and reported daily to the Loew's offices high atop Broadway and Forty-fifth Street, where he served dutifully as Nick Schenck's yes-man. "Anything that makes money we're *for,*" he told Lillian Ross. "You know, I'm not of the school that believes that popular entertainment need be art. And neither is Schenck. He's a showman. That's our business."

Dietz and Schwartz convened in Los Angeles. The Dietzes rented Celeste Holm's Brentwood house and had the MGM props department roll in a Steinway. Schwartz set music to Alan Lerner's voiceover spoof (spoken by Fred Astaire) of Mickey Spillane's "The Girl Hunt," which became Astaire and Charisse's climactic dance routine. Then Schwartz and Dietz wrote "That's Entertainment," the number that supplied the movie's musical frame. The song immediately took its place alongside "There's No Business Like Show Business" as one of the great show-business anthems. Adolph Deutsch conducted, and Salinger, Skip Martin, Bob Franklyn, and Sandy Courage worked on the charts. For dreamy urban romanticism, Salinger's arrangement of "Dancing in the Dark" is peerless.

Dietz continued his executive work for Loew's. As battlelines were drawn between Nick Schenck, who was still chairman, and powerful stockholder Joe Tomlinson, who lobbied to restore Mayer as studio head, Dietz sided with his New York–based boss. It was a smart alliance; Mayer lost his bid to return to MGM and remained with his new employer, the Cinerama Corporation. By 1954, at fifty-eight, Dietz was suffering from *paralysis agitans,* an early stage of Parkinson's. He resigned within the year to concentrate on writing.

Meanwhile, Schwartz had begun writing music for one of Mayer's planned Cinerama productions, *Paint Your Wagon,* with Lerner participating but without his usual partner, Frederick Loewe.

Arthur Schwartz
Courtesy ASCAP

(The movie wouldn't be made for another fifteen years, and Schwartz had nothing to do with it.) Natty, highly cultured, and speaking in a quasi-British accent that covered his Brooklyn roots, Schwartz caromed between the coasts in perpetual search of funds. For the Esther Williams *Dangerous When Wet* (1953), Schwartz and Johnny Mercer came up with an underrated, delightful score, of which "I Got Out of Bed on the Right Side" remains the most popular. Despite projects like these, much of Schwartz's best work was founded on autumnal harmonies. "I See Your Face Before Me" and "Something to Remember You By" are two examples.

A deeply melancholy man, Schwartz plunged into even darker waters when the first Mrs. Schwartz, Katherine Wright Carrington, died of a cerebral hemorrhage on April 2, 1953. With Dorothy Fields in 1954, Schwartz wrote a second Broadway musical, *By the Beautiful*

Sea, starring Shirley Booth. He accepted an assignment from Paramount producer Paul Jones to underscore the Dean Martin–Jerry Lewis comedy *You're Never Too Young* (1955). The idea to hire Schwartz may have come from Lewis, who loved "By Myself" and, after his split from Dean Martin, pointedly made it part of his nightclub routine. Schwartz spent his last quarter century seething at rock 'n' roll's hegemony over popular music. An insomniac, he would lie awake nights listening to the radio, as his son Jonathan wrote, waiting "for a melody of his own to jump out from the din of contemporary songs."

Arthur Schwartz's harmonies—what Nelson Riddle called his "low string writing" and a cello-like sensibility—were ideal for an orchestrator like Conrad Salinger, who had his own darkness to contend with. Completing an assignment, Salinger would exhaust himself, then drink to relax. Celebrating the end of recording *On the Town*'s music, Salinger was drinking with Edens and Saul Chaplin at Romanoff's when Oscar Levant came by to say hello. Salinger, deep in his cups, draped himself over Levant and slurred, "Oscar, whaddya say we get drunk?" "Connie, you're living in a flashback," Levant said. Yet Salinger was "a very civilized man," according to Lela Simone, who was his landlady for a while. "Connie did it all."

So did Adolph Deutsch. Born in London in 1897, Deutsch wrote for Paul Whiteman and for Broadway revues. Deutsch and Salinger had worked as music director-conductor and orchestrator, respectively, on the 1931 show *Here Goes the Bride,* with music by Johnny Green and lyrics by Edward Heyman (and a book by cartoonist Peter Arno), and both worked on the orchestrations for Rodgers and Hart's 1935 show *Jumbo.* Mervyn LeRoy lured Deutsch out to Warners. By 1949 he was at Metro as a utility man. Salinger and Edens had remembered him from Broadway as plodding and old-fashioned; but when Edens heard Deutsch conduct his own arrangement of "The Hat My Dear Old Father Wore" for *Take Me Out to the Ball Game* (1949), he said, "That man has got to come to work for us!"

Besides Deutsch, Metro music had orchestrator Bob Franklyn (whose brother Milt handled most of the cartoon orchestrations at Warners). Alexander "Sandy" Courage established himself early as a reliable orchestrator long before he became one of television's most respected composers; he contributed to *Star Trek* and *The Waltons*. Robert Van Eps could arrange the dance rhythms of "Varsity Drag," then move out of the unit to orchestrate the studio's more old-fashioned operetta product (*Rose Marie* and *The Student Prince*). Axel Stordahl followed Sinatra out of Tommy Dorsey's band and served as his personal orchestrator for his early film work, most memorably on Sinatra's Hollywood Bowl solo on the Cahn-Styne "I Fall in Love Too Easily" from Pasternak's *Anchors Aweigh*. French-born Leo Arnaud shuttled between orchestrating for Georgie Stoll and just about anything needed by the Freed Unit. Arnaud became confidant and in-house mentor to an impossibly young orchestrator named André Previn.

"From the very beginning," Lela Simone said, "André had, at the studio and outside, the reputation of being a special talent and a talent that is going to bloom into something big."

André Prewin (the original spelling) was born in Germany in 1929. His mother, Charlotte, was born in Alsace, but both sides of his family were of Russian-Jewish extraction. His father, Jack Prewin, was a lawyer whose prominence couldn't protect the family from the Nazis. In 1938, they fled to New York. Jack's cousin, Charles, by then the head of music at Universal, had already changed the surname so that he wouldn't be called "Prune."

The Previns also went west. Jascha Heifetz, the sternest of perfectionists, could hear that André had a gift, and suggested that the boy take lessons from Max Rabinowitz, whose hands, scurrying across the piano keys, were undoubtedly the most photographed in the movies. This gave Previn a taste of the bitter pride felt by émigré musicians who were sometimes employed by the studios. At thirteen, in 1942, Previn enrolled at Beverly Hills High School. He took a few lessons in theory from Ernst Toch, but it was a poor match—the brash little kid and the dignified old Austrian, though each had fled Hitler, had no rapport at the time. Then came painful but rewarding study with Joseph Achron, the Russian violinist also recently arrived in Los Angeles. When Previn turned in a fugue for a quartet, Achron pored over it, conceding that the adolescent's composition contained not a single mistake, until he suddenly slapped the page and said, "Aha! I knew it! Hidden parallel fifths!"

Before he was sixteen, Previn went to MGM to audition as an onscreen child pianist. He had no camera presence, but Johnny Green could tell how gifted he was. Joe Pasternak put him to work on *Holiday in Mexico*—Jane Powell falls for pianist Jose Iturbi—and Previn wrote variations on "Three Blind Mice" that impressed everyone at the studio. In fact, Iturbi was regarded on the lot as a virtuoso, but was incapable of Previn's level of invention.

Under the auspices of its production triumvirate—Freed, Cummings, Pasternak—the entire Metro music department was finally coming out of the nineteenth century. The old order was still represented by Stothart, who worked practically up to the day of his death in 1949. For *Undercurrent,* a *Gaslight* clone that might be charitably described as one of Katharine Hepburn's (and Vincente Minnelli's) mistakes, Stothart instructed Previn to embellish a cello theme from Brahms's Third Symphony. "Four minutes long I need. And make it big. I want it really *big!*"

Previn made it big, and then some. He worked as a pianist on *It Happened in Brooklyn,* played Johnny Green's adaptation of Copland's *El Salón México* in *Fiesta* (1947)—Ricardo Montalban's feature debut—and, like every other young composer-arranger on the lot, simplified arrangements for Georgie Stoll, who liked to conduct from a plain lead sheet, without a lot of fancy stuff that he couldn't understand. Leo Arnaud gave Previn a book on orchestration by Charles-Marie Widor. Previn began to hang around Miklos Rozsa's bungalow where the Hungarian composer received musicians visiting from all over the world. And, like so many of his older colleagues, Previn took up with Mario Castelnuovo-Tedesco, who became his most important teacher.

Previn's second assignment as music director was the Jack Cummings production of *Three Little Words,* the biopic of songwriting partners Bert Kalmar and Harry Ruby. (In a letter to Ruby, screenwriter George Seaton insisted the three little words weren't "I love you" but "I owe you.") Aided by Arnaud's orchestrations, Previn took old-fashioned Tin Pan Alley songs and made them glitter like diamonds. On "Thinking of You," Previn's underscore gets Fred Astaire and Vera-Ellen aloft, flies them to Latin America in a few chords, and executes a perfect three-point landing atop a mythic penthouse. Although *Three Little Words* wasn't Freed's, his fingerprints were all over it; as in the Freed Unit's productions, dance was snugly joined to a story. On a radio program within the movie, Phil Regan sang "You Are My Lucky Star," giving credit to Freed and Nacio Herb Brown.

Stothart died during the film's production, and his contribution to Kalmar and Ruby's early success (on *Good Boy* in general and "I Wanna Be Loved By You" in particular), though always questionable, was ignored in the movie. Supervising all this music, Previn was twenty and unworldly, but it didn't prevent him from instigating a romance with beautiful cast member Gloria DeHaven, who was playing her own mother, Mrs. Carter DeHaven. As the picture wrapped, Previn received his draft notice. Months later at Camp Cook, Previn got a wire informing him he'd been nominated for an Academy Award for *Three Little Words*. He didn't win, but the nomination, coming when he was barely old enough to vote, placed him in the exclusive club of highly sought-after music men.

Assigned to the Presidio, Previn soon met the man who would change the course of his career. Pierre Monteux was serving his last months as director of the San Francisco Symphony. Monteux assured Previn that he could handle the classical repertoire, taught him to conduct, then reined him in when Previn began to emulate Leonard Bernstein's overwrought style.

When his army stint was over, Previn returned to Metro. This was the period in which his new classical training and his jazz piano playing intersected with nonstop work. Married to singer Betty Bennett, Previn breathed music day and night. With Saul Chaplin he shared musical direction chores on *Kiss Me, Kate,* then provided the stark score for the action thriller *Bad Day at Black Rock,* which Schary personally produced. Previn was dismayed when Schary, one of the least musical of movie executives, wanted bugle calls in *Bad Day*'s underscore to point up a character's heroism.

After *Bad Day* came one of his more important assignments for Freed, *It's Always Fair Weather.* Initially conceived as a ten-year reunion of *On the Town*'s three sailors, the project went into a considerably more interesting direction when MGM declined to reuse either Sinatra, whose price was too high, or Jules Munshin. Kelly was set, of course, and Comden and Green were still at the top of their screenwriting game; but because Leonard Bernstein had no intention of working again for Hollywood (his *On the Waterfront* score was done in New York and entirely on his terms), the composer's job fell to Previn. With Bobby Tucker and Jeff Alexander aiding on vocal arrangements, Previn did it all—composing, orchestrating, conducting—and the results were dazzling. Songs like "Thanks a Lot But No Thanks" (sung by Dolores Gray) and "Situation-Wise" (Dan Dailey) weren't hummable so much as smart and cynical. "I Like Myself" was Kelly's rollerskating variation on "Singin' in the Rain."

But *It's Always Fair Weather* flopped, perhaps because, as Freed might have pointed out, audiences couldn't tell where the laughs were; cutting cynicism doesn't necessarily foment the "good cheer" that translates into box-office receipts. The picture's failure didn't hurt Previn, however. He worked simultaneously on parts of *Kismet, Invitation to the Dance,* and the earliest preproduction stages of *Silk Stockings*—all Freed productions that were less successful than had been hoped.

Of these, the most ambitious was *Invitation to the Dance,* a nod to Gene Kelly, who had become Metro's most important musical star since the departure of Judy Garland in 1950. Still heady from the *An American in Paris* accolades, Kelly envisioned a feature-length program of ballet, with himself as principal dancer. But the music had to be original, it was decided, and of course balletic. Lela Simone brought to Freed's office some recordings of compositions by Jacques Ibert, who already had had a long, distinguished career scoring films, including Orson Welles's 1948 *Macbeth.* Freed listened to the records and said, "That's it. That's the man." While Ibert was in London composing the commedia dell'arte section of the movie, his daughter either fell or flung herself down a flight of stairs at his house in Versailles; it was subsequently ruled a suicide. Simone, who was in England to supervise recording at MGM's Elstree Studio, went to sit with Ibert, "a very controlled man," until dawn, when he could get passage back to Paris. After handling funeral arrangements and his daughter's affairs, Ibert quietly went back to work.

The situation was more problematic, though hardly tragic, when conductor John Hollingsworth recorded music that Malcolm Arnold had composed for the "Ring Around the Rosy" segment; upon recording the first section, Hollingsworth turned to Simone and muttered, *"Gotterdammerung!"* for Arnold's thunderous Wagnerian music would have dwarfed Kelly's dancing. André Previn was quietly brought in to rescore the segment. A couple of years later, when *Invitation to the Dance* was finally released, Previn received a Screen Composers' Association award for his part of the score.

Previn's marriage to Betty Bennett had foundered, and a brief romance with the nectar-voiced Peggy King followed. King had worked at Metro, notably as the Garland-like party guest singing "Don't Blame Me" in *The Bad and the Beautiful.* Meanwhile, Previn was positioning himself to leave the movies. By 1953 William Wyler's invaluable former associate producer Lester Koenig, blacklisted and unrepentant, was back on his feet after founding Contemporary Records. Koenig didn't interfere with his jazz artists but was a stickler for the right sound, which he mixed himself in Contemporary's Los Angeles warehouse-studio. Previn made several recordings for Koenig, often as part of the small combo Shelly Manne and His Friends, alternately known as André Previn and His Pals. (Of these, the undisputed hit was the August 1957 recording of *My Fair Lady* selections, the kind of jazz album that even nonjazz fans picked up.) Then, some fifteen years after breaking off his teenage studies with Ernst Toch, Previn recorded Toch's Piano Quartet for Koenig's "Forgotten Music" series. Previn's classical phase shifted into high gear (he has not downshifted since) with recordings for Schuyler Chapin's Masterworks series at Columbia Records.

Around that time Previn visited George Szell, newly arrived in Los Angeles to conduct its Philharmonic. Previn proposed recording Richard Strauss's *Burleske in D Minor for Piano and Orchestra* with Szell. In his room at the Beverly Wilshire, Szell instructed Previn to "play" the score on a tabletop. When he complained that Previn was playing too slowly, Previn said, "Well, Maestro, the reason it sounds so slow is that I'm not used to this table. My dining room table at home has much better action." Unamused, Szell invited Previn to leave. There was no Szell-Previn recording made of *Burleske.*

•   •   •

Previn's Metro colleagues were just as busy, and not always for Freed. Up to 1955, Jack Cummings continued to produce high-quality work, including the glossy remake of *Roberta, Lovely to Look At,* and the rollicking (if overrated) *Seven Brides for Seven Brothers,* which was propelled more by Michael Kidd's bounding choreography than the songs by Johnny Mercer and Gene DePaul. (The music, however, received top-drawer treatment from orchestrators Salinger, Courage, and Arnaud, with Adolph Deutsch conducting.) Joe Pasternak made *The Student Prince* using only Mario Lanza's voice, because Lanza had ranted and gorged his way right off the soundstage. (Edmund Purdom walked through the role.) *Hit the Deck,* despite the great Vincent Youmans songs ("Hallelujah," "More Than You Know," "I Know That You Know"), came off as waterlogged.

The best Pasternak picture turned out to be *Love Me or Leave Me,*

Doris Day, James Cagney, and Harry Bellaver in *Love Me or Leave Me (1955)*
Courtesy Turner Entertainment

the biopic of Ruth Etting. With a tough script by Daniel Fuchs and Isobel Lennart and an especially crusty performance by James Cagney as Marty ("The Gimp") Snyder, *Love Me* featured Doris Day singing Tin Pan Alley standards by Roy Turk and Fred Ahlert ("Mean to Me"), Walter Donaldson alone ("At Sundown") and with Gus Kahn (the title tune), Joe McCarthy and Jimmy Monaco ("You Made Me Love You"), and Ted Koehler and Rube Bloom ("Stay on the Right Side, Sister"). Audiences responded warmly to these resurrected classic songs, which were stripped of glamor and all the more effective for it. For the movie, Nicholas Brodzsky and Sammy Cahn teamed up again for a new song, "I'll Never Stop Loving You," which Doris Day has since owned. (Ava Gardner, originally slated for the role, would have made a vastly different but perhaps equally interesting Etting.) The music director's credit went to Georgie Stoll, though Percy Faith conducted the best-selling Columbia album of Day's numbers. Although Joe Pasternak lasted into the mid-'60s at Metro—far later than any other important picture-maker of the era—he wouldn't make a better movie.

There were, to be sure, a few other Metro producers besides Freed, Cummings, and Pasternak who could handle musicals. The most important of these was probably Sol C. Siegel, who produced *High Society*. Siegel ran an independent company, and signed with Metro in 1955 for three pictures, of which *High Society* was the first. Formidable and, like Freed, impressed by talent but not celebrity, Siegel borrowed Saul Chaplin as music director. Chaplin's first assignment was to go to New York and check on Cole Porter, who was writing songs for the project. Hardly relishing the prospect of having to criticize one of his idols, Chaplin went to see Porter at his thirty-third-floor apartment at the Waldorf Towers. Aided by canes for his increasingly useless legs, Porter welcomed him, sat down at one of his two grand pianos, and played one of the new songs. Chaplin thought the melody lovely but all wrong for the scene it was to be heard in, and feigned enthusiasm. "I can tell from your reaction that you have certain reservations about the song," Porter said. He demanded honesty.

For three weeks Chaplin dined with Porter, who had his own table at each of three or four of the best East Side restaurants, accompanied him to the theater—intermissions were spent in Porter's limousine where Porter could rest his legs without people gawking at him—and gave his critiques of the new songs. Porter could no longer play piano with much clarity, yet oddly he still wrote music in the neatest hand. Chaplin found a manuscript of the unfinished "I Love You, Samantha" and urged Porter to complete it.

By the time Chaplin had to return to Hollywood, Porter had completed all but one song, the party duet for Bing Crosby and Frank Sinatra. Then, Chaplin, waiting in Sol Siegel's office, came across sheet music for "Well, Did You Evah?" which was originally heard twelve years earlier in *DuBarry Was a Lady*. To pick up some pointers as he worked on the Louis Armstrong–Bing Crosby duet "Now You Has Jazz," Porter had Fred Astaire, then wrapping *Silk Stockings* for Arthur Freed, take him to a Jazz at the Philharmonic concert. (The setting for *High Society* was transferred to Newport to tie in the Jazz Festival.) "True Love," the most treacly song in the score, became a hit. But the one great number is, of course, the reconstituted "Well, Did You Evah?" with Sinatra ("Don't dig that kinda croonin', chum") and Crosby ("Say, you must be one of the newer fellas") trading carefully staged ad libs.

Critics compared *High Society* unfavorably to its source *The Philadelphia Story*. (*Time* pronounced Porter's score "fair to maudlin.") But the music got expert treatment from Chaplin and co-music director Johnny Green, from orchestrator Nelson Riddle, whose association with Sinatra was then about three years old, and from Conrad Salinger, whose sensuous arrangements made even Grace Kelly seem warm-blooded.

A whole slate of successful musicals, however, wasn't going to put things right at MGM, which had to be dragged kicking and screaming into the television age. L. B. Mayer's comeback attempt in 1954 had been successfully blocked. But Dore Schary's tenure, supported by Nicholas Schenck as a way to keep Mayer out and infused with profits from the very musicals that Schary disdained, was in deep trouble. Unlike Warners or Universal, which began retooling for TV production early in the '50s, Metro sniffed at network television until it negotiated with CBS to begin broadcasting *The Wizard of Oz*, the first feature to be shown on prime-time network television, in November 1956—four telecasts at $225,000 per showing. More people watched a single telecast than in the movie's entire theatrical exhibition history. Freed's work as producer, though uncredited on *The Wizard of Oz*, was making money for the studio in a new way. Even with the *Wizard* deal, however, Metro just couldn't get the hang of it. By the close of 1956, longtime Loew's accountant and general manager Joseph Vogel had taken over as president (Schenck was tossed the title "Honorary Chairman") and settled $1 million on Dore Schary to go home.

But Arthur Freed and his unit remained. Freed's biggest musical, *Gigi,* was already in preparation. Colette's sixty-page novella *Gigi* (1945) had already been filmed as a straight French drama in 1948 starring Daniele Delorme. Anita Loos turned it into a play, its first production in 1954 starring Audrey Hepburn. It was at this stage, at least two years before MGM's wholehearted involvement, that Arthur Freed handed Lela Simone a French synopsis of Colette's story and said, "I can't understand a goddam word." Simone translated the synopsis, and rights to Loos's play were secured.

While Alan Lerner was with *My Fair Lady*'s tryout in Philadelphia, Freed flew in and approached him with the idea of doing *Gigi* as a musical. Lerner had other things to think about, of course, but he finally read the novella and saw the possibilities, especially if he could build up the part of Honoré for Maurice Chevalier. Freed and Vincente Minnelli, who had signed on to direct, concurred. There was a sturdy architecture to this, for Chevalier had charmed his way through the ground-breaking movie musicals of a quarter century earlier—*The Love Parade, One Hour with You,* and *Love Me Tonight*—and so much hinged on his participation in *Gigi,* the last great construction of the Freed Unit.

Initially Lerner intended to write only the screenplay and leave the score to another team. Gradually, however, he became more interested in having a hand in the songs. Lerner and Loewe had a standing agreement: each would get first refusal to participate whenever the other got an offer. So Lerner went to Loewe who, committed to the stage and to chemin-de-fer (but not necessarily in that order), declined. Told by Freed not to worry about a composer, and encouraged by the promised participation of Cecil Beaton, Lerner went home to New York to work on the screenplay. Only when he showed Loewe a late draft and suggested that the music had to be written in Paris—well, this was Fritz Loewe's cup of tea.

In France, in addition to writing songs with Loewe, Lerner took long-distance instruction from Freed: see Audrey Hepburn about the title role. Hepburn graciously said no. In London, Lerner went to see Dirk Bogarde, whom he wanted for Gaston (Bogarde said yes), then

Leslie Caron (yes, with reservations, due to her poorly reviewed appearance in the London production of Loos's play). But Bogarde fell out because J. Arthur Rank wouldn't release him from his contract. Louis Jourdan, a casting proposal of Freed's, took his place. Once the songs were completed, Freed assigned André Previn to go to France with the rest of the crew. Previn had already impressed Lerner and Loewe with his *My Fair Lady* jazz album. He seemed to be the natural choice as music director. In Lerner's top-floor suite at the Georges V in Paris, Freed, his crew, and Howard Dietz listened to most of the score. Later Dietz congratulated Freed, "Arthur, this will be the most charming flop you've ever made."

Shooting proceeded in Paris, with Previn supplying only piano accompaniment to the numbers; fully made orchestrations and arrangements were being prepared in California by Sandy Courage, Al Woodbury, and Connie Salinger. Salinger had begun to sign his own name to music scores for some minor MGM pictures like *The Last Time I Saw Paris,* an Elizabeth Taylor–Van Johnson romance that bore little relationship to the Kern-Hammerstein song, and *Gaby,* a remake of *Waterloo Bridge* starring Leslie Caron. But he continued to serve Freed as needed.

The actors eventually flew to California for looping, and Lerner and Loewe went along to complete "I'm Glad I'm Not Young Anymore" and "The Night They Invented Champagne." Chevalier, a pro down to his cuticles, was always ready for as many renditions as necessary. Caron, however, couldn't hear how unlovely her singing voice was, so Previn discreetly arranged for American singer Betty Wand to dub her the following day. (Lerner remembered Marni Nixon, not Wand, dubbing for Caron.) Freed, surprisingly circuitous for so powerful a producer, procrastinated in confronting Caron, who learned she was being dubbed only after she arrived at the studio. According to accounts by both Lerner and Simone, Caron made it hellish for the musicians involved.

The initial preview, in Santa Barbara, seemed too slow, and the exteriors shot in California looked like—well, like California, not Paris. The orchestrations were judged too lush and overpowering, not the more intimate Broadway pit sound that Lerner and Loewe wanted. When production chief Benny Thau refused to okay an additional $300,000—the money Freed figured was needed to repair the film—

Lerner and Loewe offered to buy the negative for $3 million that they didn't have. Their bluff paid off: Joe Vogel approved the $300,000; new scenes were shot, and new orchestrations made and recorded.

At this point Lela Simone, who waited on Freed in the office and on the soundstage, quit. She had worked too many years without a break, running interference between the Freed Unit and the Metro music department without encomium. Of her two closest colleagues, Edens was trying in vain to continue to produce on his own, and Salinger, who had done more to shape the music of the MGM musical than any other musician, was being held responsible for the negative reaction to *Gigi*'s songs. Simone flatly refused to re-record songs, as charted by Salinger's team, that sounded fine to her ears. She joined Franz Waxman in Rome, where he was composing music for Fred Zinnemann's *The Nun's Story,* and married him in August 1958. Later that year, *Gigi* was released to great acclaim. Despite its record-breaking number of Oscar nominations—nine, plus an honorary award for Chevalier—Lela Simone ignored the movie. During its first wide release, the studio musicians were out on strike (unsuccessfully, it turned out), and whatever ambivalence Simone may have felt about leaving MGM vanished.

Funny Face had put Roger Edens on the map as a producer. But Edens was steeped in a musical regimen that required elaborate blocking, rehearsal, and polish, and the studios wouldn't, or couldn't, supply those anymore. Screenwriter Helen Deutsch credited him with the better musical sections of *The Unsinkable Molly Brown* (1964). A year before he died in 1969, he served as consultant to old pal Gene Kelly on *Hello Dolly!* (1969), his one job at Twentieth Century-Fox. But both Lawrence Weingarten and Ernest Lehman, *Molly*'s and *Dolly*'s producers respectively, knew considerably less about musicals than Edens did, and it may be that Edens required Freed or someone like him—someone who had his knowledge but was even stronger—to function at his best. Or it may be, having coached Ethel Merman and Judy Garland into stardom, that he had done his job and was no longer needed. Garland's musical heiress, Barbra Streisand, arrived on the movie scene confident and fully formed, requiring absolutely nothing from Edens. Like Lela Simone, Johnny Green left Metro in 1958. He had run the shop for a good nine years and built the most versatile music department in the industry. Green briefly took a job in television at Desilu. Yet the movies continued to exert their pull, and he became a freelancer for the first time in nearly twenty years. In 1960 Robert Wise, slated to direct *West Side Story*, said to Saul Chaplin, "You're in charge of the music. Pick anyone you want [to conduct] except one guy—Johnny Green." When Chaplin asked why, Wise explained, "When I was at Metro and had appointments with him, he kept me waiting in his outer office for hours. He never stops yapping and telling dialect jokes and wasting a lot of time." Chaplin, however, considered Green irreplaceable—musically, Green was patient and always ready to fix a score, in this case one well-loved by American theatergoers and record buyers. Chaplin confronted Green, who was stunned and saddened that anyone thought of him as Wise did. Green agreed to Chaplin's lean terms, asking only for an office—a perk he'd become used to in his years at Metro. *West Side Story* subsequently won best score Oscars for supervisor Chaplin, orchestrators Sid Ramin and Irwin Kostal, and conductor Green. But Green's most impressive work came at the end of the '60s, in the film version of *Oliver!*, one of the few truly great post-Freed musicals.

Unlike his assistants, musicians, and stars, Freed remained at Metro, where he'd been employed since 1928. But of course it was a different studio: no official music department anymore, no more Freed Unit after the decamping of Edens and Simone, no more Chief ("How ya fixed, L. B.?") to praise or chide him by intercom. With Previn supervising the music, Freed produced *Bells Are Ringing* (1960), which "The Kids," Comden and Green, had written with Jule Styne for Broadway. It was watchable—barely. Minnelli directed, but his once lush interiors were now less inviting, and the dancing, already pared down for *Gigi*, was reduced to practically nothing.

That same year Freed also leaned on Previn for *The Subterraneans*, a timid adaptation of a Kerouac novel. In it Carmen McRae sang Freed's and Harry Warren's "Coffee Time." The irony was that the movie's jazz musicians—Gerry Mulligan, Shelly Manne, Art Pepper, and Jack Sheldon among them—were contacts of Previn's, whom Freed now needed more than Previn needed him.

Freed hung around as a movie elder, a nagging reminder that the golden era of the movie musical had passed. In a photograph taken in April 1963, Freed, seated between seventy-fifth birthday boy Irving

Berlin and a tired, puffy Vincente Minnelli, smokes a cigarette and appears delighted: with the company? with himself? As always, Freed is hard to read. He died in April 1973, two months after his younger brother Ralph ("How About You?"). *Say It with Music,* Freed's long-time pet project built around Irving Berlin's song catalog, remained unfilmed. It was the era of the independent writer-director, as well as the rock 'n' roll soundtrack, and the Arthur Freed brand of musical was widely regarded as quaint.

After *Gigi* was wrapped, Previn, remarried to MGM lyricist Dory Langdon, worked on the music for *Cat on a Hot Tin Roof* (1958) with Charles Wolcott and Jeff Alexander. (Because of the musicians' strike, the score was recorded in Europe. Officially the picture has no music credit.) Then Previn balked at working with Mario Lanza, whom he regarded as a boor. Previn joined his wife and Johnny Green on Columbia's expensive, troubled *Pepe,* the Cantinflas vehicle that helped depose Morris Stoloff as music head after nearly thirty years. By 1962 Previn was conducting in the concert hall. At Lerner and Loewe's insistence he was music director for the film version of *My Fair Lady* (released by Warners in 1964), and with Lerner wrote *Coco,* a musical comedy about Coco Chanel, in 1968. That same year he served as music director for the wan film version of *Paint Your Wagon.*

In the fall of 1961 the Previns were living on Bel-Air's fashionable Stone Canyon Road. The fire that swept through Bel-Air that autumn sidestepped the Previns' but burned to the ground the house recently acquired by Connie Salinger. Homeless, Salinger moved in with a young friend named David White. Since the *ritard* ending of the Freed Unit, Salinger had scored *Lonelyhearts,* a Dore Schary production based on Nathanael West's novella *Miss Lonelyhearts,* now remembered primarily for being one of Montgomery Clift's post-accident curiosities. Like so many colleagues, Salinger had had to accept television work, and he was no longer a member of any royal family, musical or otherwise. On June 17, 1962, unable to shake the depression that had set in with the destruction of his house and papers, Salinger took an overdose of sleeping pills. His few obituaries identified him primarily as the composer of the theme to the TV situation comedy *Bachelor Father.*

TEN

JUST MAKE UP YOUR MIND
THE SCREEN COMPOSERS'
ASSOCIATION AND HUAC

One evening in 1913, Victor Herbert and his good friend Giacomo Puccini walked into Shanley's Times Square restaurant, where a small orchestra was playing Herbert's score from *Sweethearts,* then playing on Broadway. Herbert accepted this as common practice, but Puccini was outraged; such piracy would not be permitted in Europe, where composers were paid a fee for the public performance of their works!

Herbert discussed the incident with some of his musical friends. A meeting was called at Luchow's restaurant in Manhattan in October 1913; in attendance were seven composers, including Herbert, plus Herbert's frequent lyricist Glen MacDonough and publisher Jay Witmark.

The American Society of Composers, Authors and Publishers was officially formed three months later at the Hotel Claridge, near Times Square, with one hundred and seventy composers and authors and twenty-two music publishers attending. The new organization, commonly known as ASCAP, gingerly filed suit against Shanley's.

It took a while for the case to be decided, but it was worth the wait. Chief Justice Oliver Wendell Holmes, Jr., read the unanimous 1917 Supreme Court decision in favor of Herbert over Shanley's: "If music did not pay it would be given up. If it pays it pays out of the public's pocket. Whether it pays or not, the purpose of employing it is to profit and that is enough." ASCAP had its first major victory, vindicating its very existence.

But motion-picture theater owners, claiming that music constituted no substantial part of what they offered the public, ignored the 1917 ruling. In addition, the theater owners thought of music publishers as ungrateful for all the songplugging they received from house orchestras that accompanied motion pictures. ASCAP, the theater owners argued, was a monopoly formed to restrain trade.

For several years ASCAP could neither fight nor collect. In 1921, however, a *Ziegfeld Follies* songwriter named Gene Buck took over as president, and the organization got down to business. Many more composers, authors, and publishers were signed up. Buck spearheaded a 1925 fight against Cincinnati radio station WLW for refusing to pay royalties for the ASCAP-represented songs they played. ASCAP won again, and this time the court ruling was enforced. Other radio stations soon fell into line. Due to ASCAP's royalty collections, some popular songwriters became extremely wealthy.

Despite these victories, ASCAP did not treat its Hollywood members as well as its original, primarily New York-based, membership. By the early '40s, film composers realized they were getting little in the way of ASCAP royalties, no matter how popular their compositions were. ASCAP's classification system placed film composers at the bottom rung of popular music makers. The justification wasn't that the music was unimportant or second-rate; it was that it was composed to order and had been already paid for by the composers' employers.

On November 3, 1942, forty film composers met at the Beverly Hills Hotel. "It was at the instigation of Max Steiner," said long-time Universal composer Hans Salter. "[He] found out that his publisher was collecting royalties and he didn't get any, so he started the ball rolling." Other film composers, though less prodigious than Steiner, shared his experience. The composers voted unanimously to send a telegram of protest to ASCAP about the classification system, signed by Max Steiner, Victor Young, Herbert Stothart, Arthur Lange, Roy Webb, Adolph Deutsch, and Leigh Harline.

Movie composers and songwriters had remained largely unorganized in the fifteen years since sound entered the medium, and it was the massive loss of royalties that now galvanized the composers into action. After the meeting at the Beverly Hills Hotel, six of the original forty composers—Deutsch, Harline, Lange, Steiner, Webb, and Young—plus the English composer Anthony Collins (1893–1963) and Disney music man Edward Plumb, continued to meet regularly as the Film Composers' Committee.

On March 5, 1943, the Film Composers sent a letter to ASCAP outlining this problem:

> ASCAP income from Motion Picture Theatres in 1942 totalled $1,100,000.00.
>
> The net balance after deducting 19% administration costs and 50% for the publishers' share is . . . $445,500.00.
>
> A film composer who is a charter member of the Society, and who has written at least twelve picture scores for a major studio every year for the past seven years, receives per quarter . . . $5.00.
>
> Another composer of seven picture scores annually for a major studio, admitted to ASCAP in 1941, receives per quarter . . . $30.00.

In other words, the film composers saw in ASCAP's distribution practices a gross inequity in which film composers were paid so much less than, say, Broadway composers or even songwriters who merely published their work without writing to order for the studios. Five dollars every three months? Copyists made that in an hour.

In *The Gold in Tin Pan Alley*, Hazel Meyer referred to ASCAP's method of payment as being "based on an intricate system of intangible values such as: How long had the publisher been a member of ASCAP? How valuable was his catalog? How recently did he have a substantial hit?" Members of the Film Composers felt caught in this web. Without sheet music sales or radio airplay to quantify its value, a film score was shrugged off as inconsequential by ASCAP, no matter how many people might have paid to see the film.

To be fair, ASCAP executives, most of them based in New York and steeped in the old Tin Pan Alley ways, had no way of knowing what a film composer actually did. In late 1943, Adolph Deutsch, unofficially proclaimed the group's leader, fired off a statement to ASCAP:

> There are numerous zones of misunderstanding and lack of comprehension in the higher places of ASCAP that must be corrected or dissipated before we can reach the level of intelligent discussion. The screen composer of today bears not the slightest resemblance to the "scorer" of the silent films. In the early 1920s a director of film music needed nothing more than a good musical memory and familiarity with the content, moods, etc., of the popular standard, semi-classical and classical works, mostly in the public domain. Today, in Hollywood, such a person could not qualify or receive an assignment as a film composer. Instead, you will find these old time "scorers" holding such jobs as music librarians, copyright clerks, selectors of sound track for newsreels and advertising trailers, and copyists. In spite of the fact that for more than a decade the musical scores of films have consisted of original composition, a few ASCAP representatives in the talks with us have revealed their apparent ignorance of this fact. . . .

For the next year or so, the Film Composers chipped away at ASCAP's granite-like misunderstanding of their function. These men were, after all, creating music that was already among the most popular in America. In 1938 alone, the Frank Churchill–Larry Morey songs from *Snow White* sold more than 1,500,000 disks. Two years later Steiner's *Gone with the Wind* theme was all over the radio, and Harline's *Pinocchio* songs were sold in music shops across the country. The paltry royalties these composers received gave no indication of the popularity of their compositions. The composers had more to gripe about than just the distribution of royalties: for those composers, no matter how accomplished, who had not actually their own music published, admission to ASCAP was denied.

Finally ASCAP was willing to talk seriously. Jerome Kern, not technically a film composer—he did not compose musical underscores—but perhaps the most revered songwriter in Hollywood (and one of ASCAP's biggest money earners), hosted the first informal discussion between representatives from the two factions at his Beverly

Hills house. At a later meeting in July 1945, New York attorney Leonard Zissu was present as the Film Composers' counsel.

Negotiations moved slowly. The Film Composers, now known officially as the Screen Composers' Association (SCA), suffered setbacks with the deaths of Kern in December 1945, and, in 1947, ASCAP's John Paine, who had been particularly sympathetic to the composers' aims.

Meanwhile, ASCAP was fighting a young rival organization. As far back as September 1939, the National Association of Broadcasters had convened in Chicago to create an organization to challenge ASCAP's monopoly on pop music publishing and licensing. One month later, Broadcast Music, Inc. (BMI) was formed. Guided by attorney Sidney Kaye, BMI blew the music business wide open, because it turned to musical areas traditionally shunned by ASCAP, although its attempts to sponsor hit-making contests proved dismal. Through the 1940s, while ASCAP continued to rely on Tin Pan Alley songwriting, with a heavy dependence on music written for Broadway. BMI's royalty structure gave prominence to country and western music, gospel, even the blues. BMI's control of copyrights for Cuban composer Ernesto Lecuona (1896–1963), who wrote such standards as "Malaguena" and "The Breeze and I" and worked on Twentieth Century-Fox musicals such as *Sweet Rosie O'Grady*, helped to saturate the airwaves with Latin music.

On every front, ASCAP had to compromise, or it would quickly become irrelevant. It didn't immediately rework its intricate classification system, but it began to renegotiate with film composers and songwriters on a case-by-case basis. By 1948, fifty-six-year-old songwriter Fred Ahlert ("Mean to Me" and "Walkin' My Baby Back Home") had taken over the ASCAP presidency, with Gustave Schirmer and Oscar Hammerstein serving as vice presidents, and songwriter Ray Henderson as treasurer. For the Film Composers Committee, Adolph Deutsch assumed the official title of President. Offices were set up at 8782 Sunset Boulevard.

The long process of reviewing applicants' written film scores began. After the Screen Composers' Association (SCA) review committee had looked at the scores, letters of acceptance or rejection were sent out. Decisions tended to be swift. Rejections were kind, pointing out that: (1) the music in question wasn't comprised of original work but rather an orchestration of existing work; and/or (2) the applicant could apply again at a later date.

Despite the notorious backbiting of film composers, the SCA promoted a fraternal feeling. It heartily backed RKO film noir specialist Roy Webb when Webb charged that studios were withholding foreign royalties for its motion-picture music. In June 1949 a greater scandal, one that allied SCA members with their employers, erupted when Daniele Amfitheatrof returned from a seven-week conducting tour of Europe to report that American features were being redubbed wholesale, including their music. Of forty-six movies that Amfitheatrof had seen, even *The Wizard of Oz* had been rescored. The SCA was able to stop European redubbing of American films, but not before millions of European moviegoers had seen these movies with new, hastily assembled scores.

In 1950, ASCAP and the SCA each received a tremendous blow when Judge Vincent L. Leibell ruled ASCAP in violation of antitrust laws for collecting *twice* on film music: once from producers for the right to employ its music; once from theater owners for the right to exhibit it. ASCAP was ordered instead to collect a single fee for each piece of film music. But the result was that ASCAP stopped paying film composers for exhibitions of the films that included their work.

By then, however, the Screen Composers' Association was serving its membership in more immediate ways. For years, for example, composers were forced to accept the long-time practice of a studio's music chief signing his name to a picture on which more than one composer worked. At Universal in the '30s, music chief Charles Previn was often credited as a film's composer, even though Previn's sole musical (i.e. non-administrative) contribution was conducting. It was a practice that supposedly simplified matters and kept composers working anonymously. It was bad enough to be cheated out of a music credit because your contribution wasn't deemed important enough—at MGM, a fine musical mind like Saul Chaplin often swallowed such humiliation—but it was even worse when the boss took the credit. Columbia's Morris Stoloff, though widely considered knowledgable and gentlemanly, often signed for scores that he had only conducted.

On June 12, 1952, from the SCA offices on Sunset Boulevard, Deutsch wrote to Universal's Joe Gershenson: "At the last meeting of the Board of Directors of the Screen Composers' Association, it was reported that Universal's production *Scarlet Angel* had carried the screen credit of 'Music by Joseph Gershenson.'" The actual composers of *Scarlet Angel*'s score were Milton Rosen (then assistant music chief), David Tamkin, Herman Stein, and the very young Henry Mancini. Deutsch's letter continued:

> In view of the strong sentiments expressed by those of our members who contributed to the music for this production, it was the Board's wish that I convey to you their suggestion that future screen credit and cue sheet listings be by use of the phrase "Musical Direction by Joseph Gerhsenson" as more accurately reflecting your contribution. . . .

Gershenson, well-liked by his staff, cut back on the practice of taking a 'Music By' credit. For a while, though, the practice was continued at other studios.

Later that year, Deutsch and his board rolled up their sleeves to fight the not uncommon practice of executives or producers pocketing their composers' royalties. They used as a test case a complaint by composer Dave Torbett, who accused former Monogram Head of Music Eddie Kay of keeping Torbett's incoming ASCAP checks—as though Kay owned the composer himself. Through member Nathan Scott, a western score specialist at Republic, the SCA also kept watch over the exploitation of pre-existing "track"—previously recorded music that was often cannibalized by picture makers in order to avoid new music fees.

Apart from its policing and bargaining, the SCA provided its members with a new fraternity—one that, with strong legal counsel and some money behind it, carried some muscle. Hans Salter said, "When I came to Hollywood the film composers were on the lowest rank of recognition. They were not organized, it was everybody for himself."

The association went to great pains to take care of its own. One example: By 1950 composer Werner Heymann was in deep emotional crisis. Born in Germany in 1896, Heymann had emigrated to the United States in 1933 after working for several years as musical director at UFA in Berlin, and for Max Reinhardt. His most notable Hollywood work had been for Lubitsch—*Ninotchka* (1939), *The Shop*

Luncheon honoring Colonel Bramwell Coles of the Salvation Army, hosted by Meredith Willson at Beverly Hills Friars Club, September 17, 1946. *seated left to right*: Franz Waxman; Dimitri Tiomkin; Meredith Willson; Colonel Bramwell Coles; Earl Lawrence; William Grant Still. *standing left to right*: Abe Meyer (MCA agent); Leith Stevens; William Broughton; Anthony Collins; Johnny Green; Miklos Rozsa; Victor Young; Werner Heymann; Leo Shuken; Arthur Bergh; Alexander Steinert; Robert Emmett Dolan; Frank Skinner; Wilbur Hatch; Carlos Morales; Louis R. Lipstone
Courtesy John Waxman

Around the Corner (1940), and *To Be or Not to Be* (1942). On this last picture, Heymann's music was considered inadequate, his score "Mickey-Mousing" (or musically mimicking) the action, forcing Lubitsch to call in Miklos Rozsa, who had originally rejected the assignment because of the script's satirical tone. Rozsa, like so many Europeans working in Hollywood, didn't believe there was anything funny about the Nazis. Grateful to Rozsa for bailing him out with an acceptable score, Heymann showered him with presents. Heymann appeared to have a bottomless humility, and the '40s weren't kind to him. His services were required less frequently—though he did earn an Oscar nomination for his musical adaptation of Kurt Weill's

Knickerbocker Holiday, with Charles Coburn croaking "September Song"—and by the end of the decade he was chronically despondent. During the first week of April 1950, Heymann deliberately took an overdose of morphine. Some sources have Heymann dying on April 8; in fact, Heymann, indigent, was fighting for his life at County General Hospital in Los Angeles. Adolph Deutsch appealed for funds from twenty SCA colleagues, with David Buttolph handling distribution. All twenty composers, plus Heymann's old UFA colleague Billy Wilder, contributed to Heymann's medical costs. Heymann recuperated and eventually returned to Germany, living comfortably for another decade.

There was one problem the SCA could not take care of, however—one that no other motion picture organization handled any better, either. The SCA could not indemnify its members from a twentieth-century witch-hunt.

۰ ۰ ۰

The blacklist hit only a few film composers hard. With some important exceptions, the House Un-American Activities Committee (HUAC) called as witnesses far fewer Hollywood musicians than, say, writers or actors. There were a couple of obvious reasons for this disparity. Communistic fervor is more difficult to read into a composer's theme than a bit of dialogue or screen action. The composer works in the shadows, not in the spotlight. It was a much greater coup for HUAC to hook a John Garfield, known to millions as a movie star, than a composer like Hanns Eisler, who was known to several hundred colleagues for his film scores (*None But the Lonely Heart,* among others) and for one of the first books exclusively about film music, *Composing for the Films.* Although Eisler's prose can be read as ideological—"shot through with the whole dialectic materialism," according to Hugo Friedhofer—it was stretching it to label it subversive.

As a European émigré composer, Eisler (born 1898) was typical of the legions of film composers who worked in Hollywood; as an avowed Communist, he was an anomaly. Most musicians who had fled Eastern Europe, and Russia in particular, had had firsthand experience with totalitarianism, whether of the Nazi or Stalinist brand, and tended to go cold when the Party made overtures. In fact some émigré musicians, like Russian-born Boris Morross, who served as Paramount's head of music from 1937 to 1939 and also found time to publish *My Ten Years as a Counterspy*, wore their anti-Soviet sentiments early and proudly. Eisler, on the other hand, made no secret of being influenced by Brecht, or of serving as Charles Chaplin's music advisor when Chaplin, in the last months of 1947, was defending himself from charges that he was a "Communist sympathizer." In addition, Eisler's brother Gerhart had been arrested as a Soviet spy and held by the U.S. Immigration Service, while the Eislers' sister, Ruth Fischer, testified against both of them.

HUAC had rolled right over Gerhart Eisler, who refused to cooperate, but had a trickier time with Hanns. When HUAC's investigator, Robert Stripling, characterized Hanns as "the Karl Marx of Communism in the musical field," Eisler replied that he was flattered. When Stripling baited the composer about a statement he'd made concerning music as an instrument of revolution, Eisler calmly stated, "I think in music I can enlighten and help people in distress in their fight for their rights. . . . The truth is, songs cannot destroy Fascism, but they are necessary. . . . If you don't like them, I am sorry; you can listen to 'Open the Door, Richard.'"

There was nothing the Screen Composers' Association could do to protect Eisler. He was deported as a Communist and resettled in East Germany, where he composed the young nation's national anthem.

In Hollywood, red-baiting had been practiced all through the '40s. Hugo Friedhofer recalled lecturing on music at the Peoples Education Center (on Vine Street), which Louella Parsons had dubbed "The Little Red School House" as far back as 1942. This made Friedhofer, like the Center's full-time faculty, suspect.

By and large, composers were less suspect than songwriters, whose tools included (potentially subversive) lyrics, and whose product was more widely disseminated over the airwaves. Jay Gorney and Yip Harburg had written "Brother, Can You Spare a Dime?," the classic Depression song that was construed by some witch-hunters as expressing Communist ideology. By 1953, Gorney and his wife, Sondra, had been named by several friendly witnesses to HUAC. Harburg (a family friend who tried to recruit my mother, then a teenager, to the Communist Party in 1948) was asked in 1950 by MGM to write a "clearance letter" that would explain his inclusion in *Red Channels,* the infamous list of "subversives" in the entertainment business. Taking the high road, the salty Harburg invoked his authorship of such lyrics as "God's Country" to prove his patriotism. After the SCA brought lyricists into its ranks, in 1955, it still couldn't aid Harburg in cracking his lingering blacklisted status. Harburg was reduced to obsequious correspondences and taking meals with men he couldn't stand but who might help clear his name.

Composers without an "Over the Rainbow" on their resume fared worse. In 1953 MGM music man George Bassman, who had composed "I'm Getting Sentimental Over You," and his wife, Kay, were named to HUAC. Bassman is credited with the fine underscore for *Ride the High Country*, the 1962 Sam Peckinpah western, but his career had suffered mightily in the preceding decade.

Jerry Fielding, the young big-band arranger who showed tremendous promise as a composer, was also blacklisted in 1953, before he'd even got started. For the balance of the '50s Fielding worked in Las Vegas. In 1961, to score the overbaked film adaptation of Allen Drury's *Advise and Consent*, Fielding was brought back to Hollywood by Otto Preminger, who was making a second career of putting blacklisted writers and musicians on his productions. After that came work for Peckinpah (*The Wild Bunch*), and television scoring (*Barnaby Jones* and many, many others) that made him financially secure but musically restless.

In that same ominous year, 1953, composer Sol Kaplan was identified by John Garfield as his "friend." A founding member of the Screen Composers' Association, Kaplan had received his first screen credit at Twentieth Century-Fox for *Tales of Manhattan* (1942), and he was now back at Twentieth after spending much of the '40s scoring B product at Eagle-Lion. The Fox executives, rattled by Kaplan's publicly voiced relationship to Garfield, decided it would be best to fire him. When Kaplan pointed out that *every man* at the studio was friendly with the beleaguered actor, he was reinstated. But when called to testify on April 8, 1953, Kaplan took a challenging stance against the HUAC. The executives panicked again. Returning to the studio, Kaplan was advised to smooth things over by meeting privately with a Committee member. But Kaplan didn't feel there was anything to smooth over; in his opinion, he hadn't done anything wrong. Two days later he was fired for a second and final time.

A newspaper account described Kaplan as "the tall, blond musical director at MGM." This was, in fact, Saul Chaplin, who was an ardently liberal Democrat but had had no traffic with HUAC. Chaplin felt shunned by many of his colleagues; he felt worse when he heard himself desperately explaining that the newspaper had him confused with Kaplan.

Kaplan took his family to New York and spent several lean years. In 1962 writer-director Carl Foreman, himself a victim of the blacklist, took Kaplan under his wing to compose music for his new movie, *The Victors*. It's hard to say if Kaplan was responsible for the inclusion in the film of Beethoven's Fifth or Sinatra's wrenching version of "Have Yourself a Merry Little Christmas" (played against the firing-squad execution of an American deserter during World War II); but Kaplan is certainly the composer of "My Special Dream," the jewel-like theme that runs through the war picture and plays like a poignant rebuke to the witch-hunt.

Other film composers were graylisted. Elmer Bernstein and Alex North had strong leftist connections and didn't apologize for them. In 1950 both men were just getting started in Hollywood; still viewed as Easterners, they had less to lose than established film composers like Bassman and Kaplan.

David Raksin handled it another way. Long after it was over, it remained the darkest episode in his life. While still fairly new to Los Angeles, Raksin had been a member of the pro-Loyalist Musicians' Committee to Aid Spanish Democracy. He joined the Communist Party in 1938, but renounced his membership after Germany and Russia divided Poland between them in September 1939. Raksin remained liberal and brash. But when called to give testimony on September 20, 1951, Raksin was jittery about embarrassing his employer, MGM. At the time Raksin's MGM contract was nearing its end, and his wife, frightened by the star-chamber tone of the HUAC hearings, was in no position to calm him. Before the committee, Raksin made a passionate defense for having joined the Communist Party thirteen years earlier—and then named eleven Communists, including John Howard Lawson, Waldo Salt, and Budd Schulberg.

Raksin has punished himself ever since.

● ● ●

Raksin was neither helped nor hindered by the Screen Composers' Association, of which he'd been an especially active member. The SCA could fight the blacklisting forces no better than more established, better-endowed Hollywood unions. It only offered its few victims a place to come back to.

In 1953 the SCA led to the formation of the Composers Guild of America, which in 1955 transformed itself into the Composers and Lyricists Guild—recognition among the musicians themselves that a lyric could make a song memorable, which in turn tended to help a movie and its music. This was the middle of the decade in which the title song became an essential component of a score, and the lyricist's contribution could no longer be downplayed.

In addition, other unions had made inroads into the musical ramparts of the studios. ASCAP, which maintained offices on Hollywood Boulevard, now fought for rather than against the film composers. The American Society of Arrangers, which included many of the Composers' Guild members, became a solid union unto itself. The American Guild of Musical Artists, which represented the leading stars and musicians in classical music and opera (its president in 1950 was Lawrence Tibbett), opened a Hollywood branch. And in 1952 Musicians Local 47, the "white" union, amalgamated with Local 767, the "colored" union. Musically and professionally, doors were swinging open.

The SCA occasionally glanced over at England, where the Composers' Guild of Great Britain operated with somewhat more decorum than its American counterpart. Based in London, the CGGB wasn't tied directly to the British film industry, but practically all of its officers were working, or had worked, extensively in film. In 1955 its president was Ralph Vaughan Williams, then seventy-six years old; its council included William Alwyn, Arthur Benjamin, Sir Arthur Bliss, and Sir William Walton, while John Addison and Malcolm Arnold served on the executive committee. The CGGB could afford to be decorous, of course, because its members didn't face the built-in enmity that existed between the Hollywood film composers and their bosses. In British culture, the composer was of the highest rank, not the lowest.

Miklos Rosza, the Hungarian who had come to America by way of British film scoring, took over the American Composers' Guild presidency from Deutsch in 1956. Fourteen years after the first informal meetings, the Guild had largely attained its goals: higher royalty payments from ASCAP, and greater recognition for film (and then television) underscoring. In the early '60s, with most major studio music departments dismantled and most film composers using agents to negotiate and serve as watchdogs, the Guild's influence over movie music business diminished.

But its roster of music men, at its peak, was an honor roll of Hollywood's greatest. It represented cowboy songwriters (Ozzie Caswell) as well as cartoon scorers (Carl Stalling, Scott Bradley). It watched over its members' work, and got tough with producers and music department heads when necessary. Yet there was a kindness about its management, due in no small part to Adolph Deutsch's delicate diplomacy.

Through the life of the Screen Composers' Association only one composer was admitted without review of his written scores: in 1949 Deutsch and the board of directors voted an honorary membership to Dr. Ernst Toch. Though largely having withdrawn from film work by then, Toch was held in the highest esteem by film composers, many of them current or former students who would always be more financially secure than he. Toch had a sixth sense about harmony, however idiosyncratically he might bend it for his own use, and great dignity. The highest salaries in Hollywood couldn't buy that.

ELEVEN

I ONLY KNOW I MUST
BE BRAVE

WESTERN MUSIC IN THE MOVIES

Western music and the movies grew up together. In 1908, when Saint-Saëns wrote the first known film score, Texas folklorist John A. Lomax published *Cowboy Ballads*, which introduced "Home on the Range" and "Git Along, Little Doggies" to American readers and musicians. The Lomax collection crystallized the image of the singing cowboy roaming the great Western panoramas.

There was just a grain of truth to the image. The great Texas historian J. Frank Dobie described "the picture-show version" as:

> Gay cowboys dressed in silk and silver rode over the fenceless grass and sang their way up the long cattle trail. Cattle kings ruled over ranges as big as European principalities and had feuds with sheep kings. Princesses waiting to be queens were coming out of the castles; villains were behind the bushes. . . .
>
> In reality, when the wholesale driving of Texas cattle north began, cattle kings did not exist. Ranch homes, mostly small frame houses, were on unfenced lands to which anybody's cattle came and from which the owner's strayed. The manner of controlling them was not in the least kingly. The cowboys were neighborhood friends,

and they had no more finery about them than a wagonload of cottonpickers.

Two silent Western epics, *The Covered Wagon* (1923) and *The Iron Horse*, (1924) attempted to correct the more romantic notions about the West. These went out to the biggest cinemas, accompanied by scores for live orchestra composed by Hugo Riesenfeld and Erno Rapee, respectively. But most of the silent Westerns were cheaply, formulaically made, and harnessed the glossier Western images for their stories. Little money was spent commissioning live music to accompany them. As film historian William K. Everson pointed out, "Exciting *agitato* themes were an absolute essential to the genre, often literally making the difference between a gripping Western and a dull one." Action was what the Western-going public wanted, and the music had to enhance that action.

Sound made trouble for the Western, as it did for most genres; in the first three or four years of talkies there was plenty of dialog but little or no music. In 1931 RKO's *Cimarron* was released with a patchy Max Steiner underscore. Steiner's previous handling of Western music was of the show-biz sort—he had conducted *Rio Rita* on Broadway—and *Cimarron* was typical of the era in that its underscore could be heard only occasionally. "In the early sound period," Everson writes, "musical scores were suspect and considered totally artificial in the new 'realistic' medium of talkies," and this was especially true of the Western, which had fewer opportunities to use source music—no radio, no phonograph, maybe a dance hall scene.

The symphonic Western score was still being developed. Ferde Grofé's *Grand Canyon Suite*, dazzling in its orchestral colors, debuted in 1931. Aaron Copland was just beginning to toy with motifs that sounded Western (*El Salón México* was first heard publicly in 1938). In Hollywood, Gerard Carbonara seemed to have a knack for underscores that at least sounded Western, a weird hybrid of old-fashioned chase music and wagon-wheel rhythms. According to the cue sheets for *Stagecoach*, Carbonara, a concert violinist born in 1886 and raised in New York City, contributed greatly to the 1938 score, though he remained uncredited. Paramount staff composers Richard Hageman, John Leipold, Leo Shuken, and W. Franke Harling combined to win the Academy Award for music; but it was Carbonara's motifs, coupled with the folk songs selected by Paramount music chief Boris Morross, that stood out. In 1939 the Western score still depended largely on musical Americana that was used to evoke "the big country." Stephen Foster's "Jeannie with the Light Brown Hair" and "Bury Me Not on the Lone Prairie" ran through *Stagecoach* and other large-scale Westerns because directors like John Ford identified with them, and because audiences knew them as well as any American music.

Before original Western underscores hit their stride, however, it was the singing cowboys, Gene Autry and Roy Rogers, who attracted attention. Occasionally their songs were written by staff musicians, but more often the singing cowboys arrived with their own material, or had established contacts with writers they felt comfortable with. Sound man Murray Spivack said, "At Republic, the cowboy singers, Autry and Rogers, always had songwriting friends, who were paid one time only for use of the song in the film and perpetual publication rights."

The older of these two cowboy stars was born Orvon Gene Autry in Texas in 1907, but raised in Oklahoma. After a stint in Tulsa, where he gained the nickname "The Yodeling Cowboy," Autry went to New York to record for Victor, accompanied by the Marvin Brothers— Frankie and Johnny—who also wrote and performed. A series of radio appearances launched Autry nationwide, and he became the most popular of country-blues singer Jimmie Rodgers's followers, able to sing and yodel with an enviable naturalness. It was this ease that made Autry so attractive for cowboy movies, beginning with *Tumbling Tumbleweeds* (1936). The picture was a hit. "Overnight every studio began to test its horse opera aspirants for vocal qualifications," wrote the editors of *Variety*. The Singing Cowboy instantly established himself as a sub-genre of the Western.

Bill C. Malone, in his book *Country Music U.S.A.*, points out that Autry's sound over the next few years was softened by his music director Carl Cotner. Cotner led the Cass Country Boys and also arranged Autry's music for his radio show "Gene Autry's Melody Ranch," which debuted in 1940.

If radio was central to Autry's endurance, it played a briefer but equally important role in the career of Roy Rogers. Born Leonard Slye in 1911 in southern Ohio, and raised there, Rogers was still performing under his birth name in 1934 when he formed the Pioneer Trio with Bob Nolan (born Robert Clarence Nobles, originally from New Brunswick, Canada), and Missourian Tim Spencer. Joined by the Texas-born Farr brothers, Hugh (vocals, fiddle) and Karl (guitar), the group renamed itself the Sons of the Pioneers. More stylistically if less geographically Western than other cowboy groups, the Sons went to Los Angeles and garnered a huge radio audience on KFWB.

The Sons of the Pioneers showed up in *Rhythm on the Range* (1936) with Bing Crosby and Martha Raye leading the cast. Crosby sang "Empty Saddles," with lyrics by the Boston-born Billy Hill, to music by J. Keirn Brennan. Johnny Mercer, expanding his already vast range, supplied "I'm an Old Cowhand," which became a standard even before the movie completed its first theatrical run. Bob Nolan, the Sons' chief composer, also contributed songs.

Leonard Slye left the Sons in 1937 and signed a contract with Republic as Dick Weston, a name he discarded before the year was out. The Sons of the Pioneers replaced him with tenor Lloyd Perryman and began to record for RCA. The newly named Roy Rogers got his movie break when Autry suddenly bowed out of *Under Western Stars*. Rogers sang "Dust," which Johnny Marvin, who had remained all these years with Autry, had written for his old pal. Rogers's popularity took off during the war, when Autry was in the service and absent from the screen.

There were plenty of Autry-Rogers imitators, some of them more accomplished musicians with more sophisticated, or more authentic ("hillbilly"), material; but they lacked that elusive star quality. Tex Ritter came closest to combining musicianship with screen presence. Originally from East Texas, Woodward Maurice Ritter (born 1905) was a glee-club singer at the University of Texas before briefly attending law school at Northwestern University. After some radio appearances, he made his way to New York and became an actor, attracting notice in Lynn Riggs's play *Green Grow the Lilacs* (the source for Rodgers and Hammerstein's *Oklahoma!*). His storytelling made him especially popular with urbanites who otherwise had little interest in the cowboy ethos.

Ritter made his first recordings in 1933. Movie producer Edward

Slim Andrews and Tex Ritter in *Rolling Home to Texas* (1941)
Courtesy the author

Finney "discovered" Ritter in 1936 and called him to Hollywood. Ritter made his feature debut in *Song of the Gringo,* and for the next few years made singing Westerns, with Finney producing, at Monogram, Columbia, Universal, and PRC (Producers Releasing Corporation). On *Take Me Back to Oklahoma* (1940), Johnny Bond became Ritter's band-leader, and the two would be nearly inseparable for the rest of Ritter's career.

The year that Ritter entered the movies, so did Ray Whitley, who had written Autry's hit "Back in the Saddle Again" with Fred Rose. Jimmy Wakely sang his way through several Monogram Westerns of the '40s. Wakely had a voice but came off on film as bland—an odd contrast to his recordings which, Bill Malone points out, included one of country's first "cheating" songs, "One Has My Name, the Other Has My Heart." After World War II, Rex Allen backed himself on guitar while singing in a bushel of Republic Westerns. On or off his horse, Koko, Allen was sympathetic and likable.

All of these singing cowboys were helped by a small circle of songwriters. Johnny Marvin, older than Autry by a decade, remained with him until his death in North Hollywood at forty-seven. Fred Rose (born 1897), who also wrote for Autry, began as writer-arranger for Paul Whiteman in the '20s, moved west to Chicago to work as a pianist, then farther west and into pictures, where he wrote "Take These Chains from My Heart" and "Blue Eyes Crying in the Rain." For *Ridin' on a Rainbow* (1941), Autry and Rose collaborated on "Be Honest with Me," kept on the air for months by Bing Crosby's recording under John Scott Trotter's baton. When the singing cowboy faded from the silver screen, Fred Rose moved to Nashville, working as a music publisher (successfully marketing Hank Williams's songs) until his death. In the late 1930s Cindy Walker arrived in Hollywood from south Texas with her mother, Oree, who transcribed and played her teenage daughter's songs, and also wrote for Autry. Crosby's recording of "Lone Star Trail" helped get Walker a contract with Decca.

The singing cowboys and their writers worked at various small studios, including Monogram, Eagle-Lion, and PRC, but the most productive Western studio was Republic. Westerns could be made more cheaply there. Sets, costumes, even scripts were continually recycled to lower costs and maximize profits.

Jule Styne, who had arrived in Los Angeles to work as a vocal coach at Twentieth Century-Fox, moved over to Republic after Darryl F. Zanuck cut his music staff by three quarters in 1940. In fact, Zanuck arranged for Styne's Republic job but first wanted the songwriter-pianist to accompany Fox star Constance Bennett on an eight-week tour, to promote her new line of beauty products. During the tour Styne played piano behind Bennett's parlando singing, and the pair became romantically involved. At each new hotel, Bennett discreetly referred to Styne as her fiancé. The romance, however, didn't survive the return to Los Angeles, partly because Styne was still married, mostly because he was now reporting to work at Republic, where he earned $145 per week—hardly a salary to keep a movie star in furs.

The Republic Studios were located in North Hollywood, at what was formerly the Mack Sennett Studio (and, of late, part of CBS). Founded in 1935 by tobacco dealer Herbert John Yates, Republic specialized in low-budget Westerns but made pictures in all genres. At the time of Styne's arrival, the studio's head of music was Cy Feuer, a former trumpeter who would go on to produce Frank Loesser's Broadway musicals. Feuer shared his Republic music position with Raoul Krashaar, who specialized in cobbling together cowboy music for pictures like *The El Paso Kid* and *Alias Billy the Kid.*

Before he was given music to write, Styne was assigned to check synchronization for Smiley Burnette, Republic's perennial cowboy sidekick. But Styne gradually got his chance. For a Roy Rogers picture, director Joe Kane wanted Styne to write a song called "I Love Watermelon." His sensibilities bruised, Styne couldn't get Feuer to countermand the request, so he sat down and made a tune, with lyrics supplied by studio writers Sol Meyer (later to write for Glenn Miller's air force unit) and George Brown. Styne, born on the London prairie and raised in the Chicago wilderness, became as adept as any composer at laying out the melody of a cowboy song. For Autry, Styne wrote "Purple Sage in the Twilight," which the star crooned with relish. "Jule, boy, I think I like that song," Autry said.

Feuer was drafted and went to war. Styne got his young racetrack crony Walter Scharf hired as music director. Then Styne began a songwriting collaboration with Sammy Cahn—his Western song days were soon over—and Scharf, bursting with energy, moved over to Universal. Republic went through whole platoons of cowboy songwriters under subsequent music chiefs Morton Scott (father of saxophonist Tom Scott), Jerry Roberts, the tireless and beloved Stanley Wilson, and Mort Glickman.

Because of its high-volume Western product, Republic had a reputation for cheapness. Musically, however, it was practically lavish. In 1945, Stage 12, known as the Music Auditorium, was completed and quickly established itself as one of the most desirable recording studios in town.

And Republic didn't stint when it came to its composers and lyricists. Foy Willing, a founding member of the Riders of the Purple Sage, poured out songs for the Westerns and occasionally appeared onscreen. Pianist Robert Armbruster came on board, eventually receiving critical acclaim for his *Western Ballet,* written outside of his studio responsibilities. The rotund Perry Botkin handled guitar and ukelele duties. Aaron Gonzales moonlighted as an aircraft engineer and as conductor of the house band at the Beverly Hills Hotel. The Dutch-born piano prodigy Richard Hageman maintained an international career as a serious concert musician while scoring a series of Westerns on the tracks of *Stagecoach.*

Paul Mertz (born 1904) arranged the music for virtually all of Autry's pictures; under the name Paul Madeira, he wrote the standard "I'm Glad There Is You" with Jimmy Dorsey. Oakley Haldeman liked to write weepy songs with Texas references. Practicing architect Walter Kent ("I'll Be Home for Christmas" and "The White Cliffs of Dover") arrived at the studio in 1943. Johnny Lange—no relation to Arthur, though also from Philadelphia—was an excellent cowboy lyricist, though he may be best remembered for "Clancy Lowered the Boom." (Lange was nominated for an Oscar in 1950 for "Mule Train," sung by Vaughn Monroe in *Singing Guns.*) Republic also attracted Tin Pan Alley writers who could use a quick buck, a film credit, and, as often as not, an easy way to dust off and modify a trunk tune. Even Stanley Adams, already an ASCAP director and later to become its president, got into the act with songs for *Saddle Pals* (1947).

Probably the most crucial individual to the Republic Western sound was R. Dale Butts. Butts was a respected pianist-arranger in Chicago when his wife—also named Dale, a big-band singer from Texas—was invited to Hollywood. Butts followed and scoured the studios for work. Jule Styne, an acquaintance from Chicago, introduced him to Walter Scharf, who hired him to work at Republic. Within weeks, Butts's marriage ended without acrimony. After an apprenticeship as an orchestrator, Butts began to compose his own scores—sometimes as many as six a year, some of them for his former wife and her co-star and new husband, Roy Rogers.

·   ·   ·

Studios less closely associated with Westerns than Republic had their share of cowboy songs, some of them lasting far longer than Jule Styne's "I Love Watermelon." After Johnny Mercer's 1936 "I'm an Old Cowhand," there was a slew of Western songs rolling off Hollywood's highest-priced keyboards. "Cow Cow Boogie," which was originally composed by Charles Davenport in 1928 as a ragtime piece, was given new commerical life when Gene DePaul, Don Raye, and Benny Carter remade it into a hit song for *Reveille with Beverly,* the 1943 Columbia all-star musical. The song was popularized by Ella Mae Morse's recording, and people thought of it as an old cowboy song. That same year the Gershwins' *Girl Crazy* was filmed again—to my mind the best Gershwin on film—with Judy Garland and a male chorus doing "Bidin' My Time," at once parodying and paying court to the loping cowpoke songs collected by John Lomax.

Hollywood Canteen (1944), which grew out of the John Garfield–Bette Davis creation of a servicemen's center, featured several songs by several writers, but when Roy Rogers and the Andrews Sisters sang Cole Porter's "Don't Fence Me In," an instant classic was made. Porter had originally written the song for Fox's 1934 *Adios, Argentina.* Producer Lou Brock had found a poem called "Don't Fence Me In," written by self-styled cowboy Bob Fletcher of the Missoula (Montana) Power Company. Porter bought the rights to the poem for $150, scrapped most of it, and wrote his own lyric around the title. The picture remained unproduced, and Porter forgot about his Western parody.

"Don't Fence Me In" was one of several songs plucked by *Canteen* producer Walter Gottlieb from Warners' shelves, where it had been set aside for a musical biopic of Will Rogers. Then, out of nowhere, Twentieth Century-Fox claimed to own it. When Jack Warner explained the situation to Darryl Zanuck—the number was already set in *Hollywood Canteen* and would have to be edited out if the rights weren't available—Zanuck gave it gratis to his former boss. By New Year's 1945 the Bing Crosby–Andrews Sisters version had topped the Hit Parade. Informed of the song's phenomenal success, Porter was reported to have dismissed it with "Oh, that old thing." A man named Ira Arnstein, who made a career of accusing established songwriters of plagiarism, sued Porter for $1 million for lifting the tunes of "Don't Fence Me In" and three other songs. America's "Tune Detective"

Sigmund Spaeth testified in court that yes, Mr. Arnstein owned the notes C, D, E, F, G, A, and B, and the others, too. The suit was later dismissed.

Frank Loesser, always a little jealous of the Porters and the Mercers who made it look so easy, weighed in with the lyrics to "I've Got Spurs That Jingle Jangle Jingle," with music by Paramount's long-time piano man Joseph J. Lilley. "Spurs" was written for the Fred MacMurray action movie *The Forest Rangers*—not a Western, exactly, but a firefighting outdoorsy romance. Loesser had already tried his hand at cowhide imitation with his work on *Destry Rides Again,* notably "See What the Boys in the Back Room Will Have"—music by Fred Hollander. "I think it was Lord Beaverbrook," film historian Richard Roud recalled, "who said that Marlene Dietrich standing on a bar in black net stockings, belting out 'See What the Boys in the Back Room Will Have,' was a greater work of art than the Venus de Milo."

The Western score was an artificial thing; just as cowboy songs were disseminated by radio, then widely imitated by writers who had never been within a thousand miles of a prairie, music for Westerns was composed out of a handful of folk songs, and then made into a "familiar" tapestry by the studios' symphony orchestras. As Dimitri Tiomkin told Tony Thomas,

> I would like to point out that much of the music that is accepted as typical of certain races, nationalities and locales is wholly arbitary. Audiences have been conditioned to associate certain musical styles with certain backgrounds and peoples, regardless of whether the music is authentic.

Given a few American-sounding tools, Viennese composers Max Steiner at Warners and Hans Salter at Universal created "authentic" Western music. French-born composer-arranger Lucien Calliet (born 1891) churned out Western scores primarily for RKO, as did the Polish-born, Berlin-trained violinist Paul Sawtell (born 1906). Karl Hajos (born 1889 in Hungary) music-directed dozens of Westerns for RKO and Paramount. Ozzie Caswell (born 1913 in Austria) worked primarily on Monogram's cowboy pictures, while moonlighting as an economics professor at Univeristy of Southern California. Fred Hollander was from Germany. These émigrés made up the Western sound as they went along. That European émigrés composed symphonic scores for Westerns points to how new and original the music really was. Aaron Copland said:

> There was a "market" for music evocative of the American scene— industrial backgrounds, landscapes of the Far West, and so forth. This kind of role of music, so new then, is now taken for granted by both entrepeneurs and composers. But in the late '30s and early '40s it was almost without precedent, and moreover, it developed at just the time when the economic pinch of the Depression had really reached us.

When Copland checked in with *The Red Pony* (1949), the score was lauded in Hollywood as achieving a stunning new plateau in movie music. Sections of his *Red Pony* Suite are laid out like childishly simple story episodes: "Morning on the Ranch" opens the suite, "Happy Ending" closes it. Dale Butts orchestrated most of the score; Steve Previn, André's older brother, was the music cutter. *The Red Pony* score was Western in the way that much of Copland's *Rodeo* and *Appalachian Spring* were—evoking a rural, wide-open America through the strains of folk tunes and cowboy songs.

Hugo Friedhofer, freely acknowledging his debt to Copland, wrote a terrific score for *Broken Arrow* (1950), and bales of chords were roped, at Alfred Newman's recommendation, into the 1955 *White Feather*. Newman himself scored *The Gunfighter*—strong work, though not as memorable as his exquisite music for the much earlier *My Friend Flicka* (1943), another contemporary Western.

If Copland, Friedhofer, and Newman were mining American folk music for their Westerns, surely Dimitri Tiomkin was mining Russian folk music. "A steppe is a steppe," whether in Siberia or Wyoming, seemed to be Tiomkin's angle. Tiomkin became so confident of his ability to handle a Western score, he almost swaggered. Among the scores he knocked off were *The Westerner* (1940) for Goldwyn; *Duel in the Sun*

(1947), with its seventy-five-piece orchestra and the Hall Johnson Choir singing beneath it, for Selznick; and *Red River* (1948) for Howard Hawks. But it was Tiomkin's Russian folk–derived theme for *High Noon* that blew Western movie music—in fact *all* movie music—wide open.

When Stanley Kramer, Boy Wonder of independent producers, screened *High Noon,* his latest, for Tiomkin, his assessment was "a real stinkeroo"—the entire picture consisted of Gary Cooper walking up and down the street. (Cooper's nemesis in the movie was played by country singer-comedian Sheb Wooley.) Tiomkin wrote the score and persuaded journeyman lyricist Ned Washington to provide words for a title song. That done, Tiomkin, in his theatrically fractured Russian-English, said, "Who can sing best Cowboy Song? Tax, dot's who!"

"Tax?" said a perplexed Washington.

"Tax Ritter! He sings cowboy songs like nobody. Get him on the telephone!"

Only a few days earlier, Tex Ritter had told his songwriting friend Johnny Bond, "I can't make a dime in Hollywood anymore. There's nothing for me here. It's all out there somewhere and I need something that will keep the price up, otherwise it's a losing proposition."

Then Tiomkin and Washington called.

Ritter and a few friends, including country guitarist Merle Travis, recorded the song, and it was added to the *High Noon* soundtrack. It didn't seem to help—the preview cards were still lousy. Capitol Records declined to have Ritter record the song, which had come to be known as "Do Not Forsake Me," because Ritter wasn't in the movie. So Tiomkin arranged a recording with Columbia's Mitch Miller, who quickly got Frankie Laine to sing it. This strategy had paid off handsomely in '49 with "Mule Train"—why not again? Hearing about the Laine session, which was already generating an industry buzz, Capitol ate crow, lassoed Ritter into the studio, and released the single on June 21, 1952, one week before Laine's. Ritter sang "Do Not Forsake Me" on the Academy Awards show, and the song won. Although Laine's version outsold Ritter's, both renditions helped put the picture over.

The success of "Do Not Forsake Me" also changed the rules of Hollywood songwriting. After *High Noon,* few major-studio features produced in the 1950s would be released without an exploitable theme song, with or without the title in the lyric.

Into the '50s the singing cowboy slowly vanished from the movies like locomotive smoke down the tracks. He was the victim of rising production costs, too many recycled storylines, changing public tastes, and just mundane aging: Autry, Ritter, and the more comical Dick Foran had all reached forty, while Rogers saw it coming 'round the bend. It was too costly and time-consuming to scout younger cowboy singers, who could make quicker money anyway by recording on the new long-playing record format.

Then there was television. The non-singing Bill Boyd had bought back his *Hopalong Cassidy* pictures, and financial returns on their telecasts prompted Autry to ride in his dust. Always a smart businessman, Autry took his music crew, his stallion, Champion, and sidekick Pat Buttram (in the old Smiley Burnette role) onto television in 1947 and never looked back. Roy Rogers and Dale Evans followed a couple of years later, occasionally visited by the Sons of the Pioneers. Most of the other TV Westerns didn't bother with singing; cowboy music was set aside for variety shows. What has come to be known as country-and-Western soon subsumed cowboy music, which could be "watched" on television in such early shows as *Eddy Arnold, Grand Ole Opry, Ozark Jubilee,* hosted by the ubiquitous Red Foley, and the Cleveland-based *Pee Wee King,* hosted by the bandleader-author of "Tennessee Waltz." Except for the occasional parody—Nat Cole and Stubby Kaye in *Cat Ballou,* for one—the singing cowboy disappeared from features.

With the singing cowboy gone, the Western score became grand and more sophisticated. Victor Young, in 1953 still Paramount's golden boy, wrote the score for *Shane*—"melodic and easy to remember," William K. Everson wrote, "but it is incurably romantic," and just too much of it. *Shane* strikes me as terribly overrated, a set of bloated Western archetypes, and Young's music seems to pour syrup over the whole concoction. More interesting was Young's earlier work on *Johnny Guitar.*

The better late-'50s Westerns were often the work of director Anthony Mann (*The Naked Spur, The Man from Laramie*), and, depending on the distributing studio, veteran composers such as Bronislau Kaper, George Duning, and Hans Salter. Daniele Amfitheatrof's music for *From Hell to Texas* (1958) captures the essential hard-riding sound of the '50s Western. Max Steiner created his last big Western score with

The Searchers (1956). The twenty-five-year-old André Previn wrote a stark, spare score for one of the best contemporary Westerns, *Bad Day at Black Rock* (1954).

The Big Country (1958), like most William Wyler projects, was driven partly by a great score, even if the mostly deaf Wyler himself couldn't quite hear it. Jerome Moross's music—whip-cracking, Coplandesque, and balletic—rode right into the national consciousness.

The same is true for Elmer Bernstein's music for the Mirisches' *The Magnificent Seven* (1960). Based on Akira Kurosawa's *The Seven Samurai* and directed by John Sturges (who made *Bad Day at Black Rock*), the movie is less interesting than its reputation suggests. But its score survives, due in part to the hit main theme recorded by guitarist Al Caiola, and to its later use by Philip Morris in its Marlboro commercials.

The big hit *How the West Was Won* (1962) was a Technicolor/Cinerama epic boasting a cast of thousands and *three* directors; it played a reserved-seat engagement in its first run. It was the Western's last stand on the silver screen. When an eye operation kept him sidelined, Dimitri Tiomkin had to bow out of his commission to write the score, and the job went to Alfred Newman. At sixty-one, Newman had slowed down a bit, no longer pouring out ten or twelve scores per year or handling his administrative responsibilities at Twentieth. His long-time vocal arranger Ken Darby remembered Newman expressing doubt about the MGM assignment: "'How the hell am I going to do anything original for *another* Indian chase?' and then [he went] home and [did] one. It was a series of brass punctuations in a complex scherzo, with the horses' hooves and Indian yells supplying the counterpoint."

Newman wove traditional works like "Battle Hymn of the Republic" and "When Johnny Comes Marching Home"—some of them with new lyrics by Sammy Cahn and Johnny Mercer—with original music by Darby, Robert Emmett Dolan, and himself. He got some help in the folk-song department from Dave Guard, a founding member of the Kingston Trio, who had left the trio in 1961 to form The Whiskeyhill Singers. As usual, Darby handled the vocals, and MGM sound editor Johnny Logan used some audio track recorded years earlier for *Raintree County*.

John Ford's *Cheyenne Autumn* (1964), scored by Alex North, was Warners' attempt to rescuscitate the dead genre. It didn't have a prayer. Why go to the movies when you could see the same thing at home—and done with more verve—on *Bonanza, The Big Valley,* or *Rawhide*? Most of these TV Westerns were scored by Hollywood veterans. The new medium was more watchable and eminently more listenable anyway. Television swallowed the genre as if it were the only grub left in the saddlebag.

*   *   *

The so-called spaghetti Westerns, produced in Italy in the mid-1960s, made Clint Eastwood a movie star and introduced Americans to the film music of Ennio Morricone. Morricone (born 1928 in Rome) came from a musical family—his father was a well-known trumpeter—and studied at the Conservatory of Santa Cecilia. Alfred Newman's score for *The Robe* (1953) turned his ears to the movies. Mario Nascimbene, the intuitive Italian who frequently scored American (*The Barefoot Contessa*) and British (*Room at the Top*) films, introduced Morricone to film composition when they worked together on *Barabbas* (1960), director Richard Fleischer's heavy-handed, guilt-and-redemption Roman epic. For Morricone, it was a start.

Sergio Leone grudgingly hired Morricone to score his *A Fistful of Dollars* (1964)—the director had been unimpressed with the composer's previous scores but was in a bind. Everything about the movie, including the music, stretched the spaghetti Western genre's archetype. Based on Kurosawa's *Yojimbo,* Eastwood played The Man with No Name, caught in the middle of two violent factions. Amusingly, both Leone and Morricone employed Americanized pseudonymns—Bob Robertson and Dan Savio, respectively—to sign their work.

What made Morricone's score distinctive for *A Fistful of Dollars*—and the scores for its descendants, *A Few Dollars More* (1965), *The Good, the Bad, and the Ugly* (1967), and *Once Upon a Time in the West* (1969)—was its variety of crisscrossing themes, which owed more to the hi-fi exotica recorded by the likes of Martin Denny and Les Baxter than to anyone's idea of Americana. Morricone liked to isolate a character with a single instrument—the trumpet, of course, was the one he used most, though he famously used the harmonica in *Once Upon a Time in the West* for Charles Bronson's character—obscuring the fact that his ensembles were usually as large as American studio orchestras. The Morricone sound became so influential that audiences mistakenly assumed he'd scored *Hang 'Em High* (1968), Clint Eastwood's and director Ted Post's Hollywood version of the spaghetti Western. The twangy score was by Dominic Frontiere.

When Westerns returned to the American screen, their makers usually tried something new with music. Arthur Penn's *Little Big Man* (1970) employed folk-blues guitarist John Hammond, Jr., in its unique scoring process. John Strauss, who composed the scurrying little theme for Nat Hiken's TV series *Car 54, Where Are You?*, worked on the picture in New York as music cutter under supervising editor Dede Allen. Strauss recalled, "I was brought out [to Hollywood]. . . and introduced to the music editor . . . and she said, 'Who is your orchestrator, and who is your this, and who is your that?' And I said, 'It's John Hammond, Jr., and he's going to improvise music while watching the film.' And it was like 'Whaaat?!'" Hammond, son of the great aristocratic jazz impresario John Hammond, played harmonica and acoustic guitar and used his voice to achieve some astounding effects.

"And it was such a right choice," Strauss concluded, ". . . and the whole structure worked beautifully."

A Man Called Horse (1970) was scored by Leonard Rosenman, and *The Return of a Man Called Horse* (1976) by Laurence Rosenthal, and both scores are worth repeat hearings. Rosenman (born 1924) came to films after his piano student, actor James Dean, recommended him to Elia Kazan to score *East of Eden* (1955). Rosenthal, two years younger than Rosenman, began his career by providing incidental music for Broadway plays. One of them, *The Miracle Worker*, was for director Arthur Penn, who subsequently hired him to score the movie. The *Man Called Horse* scores, though different, both have angular textures, mixing American Indian forms into a twentieth-century musical vocabulary.

Upon completion of filming of *McCabe and Mrs. Miller* (1971), perhaps the most idiosyncratic Western yet made, there was still no music. Director Robert Altman stalled his backers at Warners for time. He went to Europe to take a break, where he heard a record by Leonard Cohen. *This is it! he thought. This is the* McCabe *music!* With Cohen's own flat vocals and a wood-nymph background chorus, the songs aren't specifically Western, yet they contribute—along with the snowy land-scapes, the gaslight, the opiated haze, and the uncomplicated bawdi-ness—to weave what Pauline Kael called "a beautiful pipedream of a movie." The soundtrack had no cracking whip, no thundering string section, no quotations of folk or cowboy songs, no ride-into-the-sunset motifs. It had only a Canadian droning his poetry, owing nothing to silk and silver or the long cattle trail.

TWELVE

LEAVE YOUR WORRIES ON THE DOORSTEP
JAZZ ARRIVES BY STREETCAR

Jazz, deeply embedded in American culture by the time the movies had soundtracks, was a natural musical style for the medium. The music is sexy, suggestive, and energetic; its players are colorful, their performances dynamic, and far more interesting than the staid demeanor of the average classical musician. For these reasons, jazz was employed by the movies from the dawn of the sound era. King Vidor's *Hallelujah!* (1929) wove primitively recorded spirituals, blues, and a smattering of Irving Berlin through the story of a black cotton picker.

In the '30s the studios poured out musical pictures by the bushel, usually show-biz stories that featured some jazz because it was "hot" and evocative of the big city. Much of this was Latin-tinged percussion and big-band music, with Afro-Cuban rhythms to accompany dancing.

The arrival of short music films known as "Soundies" in 1940 brought truer jazz performances directly to movie audiences. Soundies weren't played in the auditoriums but in theater lobbies, projected inside complex little machines akin to jukeboxes. They were developed by a jukebox company, Mills Novelty, in Chicago, which called its player the Panoram. Its president, Ralph Mills, in partnership with James

Roosevelt, son of the U.S. president, hired songwriter Sam Coslow to provide the films themselves.

Coslow was well connected in jazz circles and had no trouble persuading dozens of jazz folk to make Soundies. Because their success was predicated largely on how many theaters rented these machines, Soundies could afford to showcase talents who weren't necessarily mainstream—gritty, unrepentant blues singers like Jimmy Rushing. By the late 1940s, television killed off Soundies—never more than a novelty anyway—and in fact later co-opted the films themselves. Jazz shorts continued to be produced but were projected in the main auditoriums again, accompanying the features.

The most important of the non-Soundies jazz shorts was probably Warners' 1944 ten-minute *Jammin' the Blues,* featuring filmed transcription of three songs: the title improvisation; "The Midnight Symphony"; and "On the Sunny Side of the Street." Photographed by Gjon Mili and supervised by jazz impresario Norman Granz, the players were Harry Edison (trumpet), Lester Young and Illinois Jacquet (tenor saxes), Marlowe Morris and Garland Finney (pianos), John Simmons and Red Callendar (basses), Sid Catlett and Jo Jones (drums), and Mary Bryant (vocal), with Archie Savage dancing in the background. Because Warners wanted the film to play in the South, where integrated bands were still taboo, the one white performer, guitarist Barney Kessel, played in the shadows to shade his white skin; his hands were stained with berry juice for close-ups.

Of course Hollywood's jazz films whitewashed the issue of race. Typical was the MGM-produced "Honeysuckle Rose" short. The song was originally written in 1928 by Fats Waller and Andy Razaf for a revue at Connie's Inn in Harlem. The film showed two white men writing the song—while they were in jail! Waller was indifferent, if not amused, but Razaf was incensed. He wrote an angry letter to L. B. Mayer. Instead of responding directly to Razaf, Mayer announced in *Variety* that the songwriters were "poor sports" who should have been grateful that their song was showcased. Razaf wanted to know how Mayer "would've placated Irving Berlin if they had presented a scene showing 'Alexander's Ragtime Band' written by a colored boy behind bars."

Duke Ellington appeared in both features and short subjects long before his ground-breaking recordings of the late '30s and early '40s. His first film appearance was in the nineteen-minute *Black and Tan Fantasy* (1929), centered, of course, around his own famous composition. "Black and Tan Fantasy," by most accounts, was inspired by his great growling trumpeter, Bubber Miley, who had already been replaced by Cootie Williams by the time the film was made. Ellington's second appearance was in the 1930 Amos 'n' Andy feature, *Check and Double Check.* Movies were easy for Ellington. He was strikingly handsome, and his band, possessed of an oceanic sound that transposed well to a soundtrack, swung forcefully. In 1934 Paramount put him to work, first in *Murder at the Vanities,* then in Mae West's *Belle of the Nineties.* That same year, in what must be one of the strangest ghost jobs in the history of the movies, Ellington dubbed Guy Lombardo's piano playing in *Many Happy Returns,* a Burns and Allen vehicle.

Ellington's most creative period as a composer came after he left Hollywood in the '30s. It was during this time that he composed, with various collaborators, "In a Sentimental Mood," "Caravan," "I Let a Song Go Out of My Heart," "Prelude to a Kiss," and "In a Mellow Tone." When Ellington returned to Los Angeles, by then enthroned as the dashing prince of American jazz, it was to appear in *Cabin in the Sky* (1942).

Cabin in the Sky's other royal musician, Louis Armstrong, was by contrast all over Hollywood. The sparkling presence, with a congeniality that would later cause some of a younger generation to brand him an Uncle Tom, the virtuosic renderings of Tin Pan Alley standards as well as the blues with both voice and trumpet—all these qualities attracted moviemakers to Armstrong. He seemed to glide effortlessly from picture to picture, always being Satchmo and sometimes single-handedly lifting the story material.

Armstrong couldn't do much with the ill-packaged *New Orleans* (1946), which purported to examine the origins of jazz and featured Billie Holiday in her only movie role (she played a maid). But he shook up his scenes with Danny Kaye (playing cornettist Red Nichols) like a crapshooter on a lucky streak in *The Five Pennies* (1959). And he was one of several jazz men—Benny Goodman, Lionel Hampton, Charlie Barnet, Tommy Dorsey, Louis Bellson, and Mel Powell were among the others—surrounding Danny Kaye in *A Song Is Born* (1948), a remake of *Ball of Fire*. (Those two hot-tempered bandleaders, Goodman and Dorsey, came to blows during the filming, inadvertently knocking down tiny music director Emil Newman in the process.)

Armstrong didn't score pictures; he didn't have to. The fine reception accorded his genius had turned him into a showman while still young, but he was at heart the first and greatest of improvisers. Armstrong had nothing to say as a film composer that he couldn't say more laconically by performing or recording. Like the music of Fats Waller, Armstrong's singing and blowing is essentially about joy, undiluted and undiminished by the vicissitudes of the characters—on the bandstand or on film—around him. Patronized by Bing Crosby in Cole Porter's 1955 *High Society*—"Say, Pops, you wanna grab a little of what's left here?" Crosby offers at the break of "Now You Has Jazz"— Armstrong sings easily against Crosby's unerring but rather stiff baritone. Even his appearance in *Paris Blues* (1961), playing the international celebrity that he was—with Ellington's lilting five-note figure playing in the soundtrack—seemed effortless compared with the hip poses of stars Paul Newman and Sidney Poitier. After a certain point in his film career, Armstrong no longer had to play, he just had to show up. Oddly, even in Bert Stern's gloriously photographed *Jazz on a Summer's Day*, a documentary about the Newport Jazz Festival of 1958, Armstrong's onstage demeanor was as significant as his musicianship. The movies, in fact, had long since served to make the two virtually indistinguishable.

Some jazz musicians had a screen presence almost as strong as Armstrong's. Fats Waller, though seen in only one important feature, *Stormy Weather* (1943), locked a movie camera in a love-grip and didn't let go. Few men of such girth have exuded such sexiness, a growling, mocking, eyebrow-bouncing sensuality that was ripe for the movies. Had Waller lived longer—he died just months after the release of *Stormy Weather*, at thirty-nine—he might have used the movies, or let the movies use him, in new musical ways. Also appearing in *Stormy Weather* was singer Dooley Wilson, always welcome on the screen but only marginally a jazz performer. In his most famous screen appearance, as Sam in *Casablanca* (1942), even his piano-playing was dubbed—either by Earl Roach or Elliot J. Carpenter—because Wilson simply didn't play piano.

Before principal photography began on *Casablanca,* producer Hal Wallis briefly considered making Sam female so he could use Hazel Scott, whom he'd heard in New York at the Café Society Uptown. Scott's piano could be heard in several movies, but after 1945, when she married controversial politician Adam Clayton Powell, she was graylisted by Hollywood. Hadda Brooks, often confused with Scott by audiences but more of a cabaret performer than a jazz one, was installed at the piano in the Hollywood nightclubs of *In a Lonely Place* and *The Bad and the Beautiful.*

In several forgettable pictures during the '30s to the 1943 *Stormy Weather,* Cab Calloway sprang up like a bandy-legged jack-in-the-box. *Stormy Weather'*s two romantic leads, Lena Horne and Bill Robinson, had far broader careers as all-around entertainers rather than as jazz performers, and it shows in *Stormy Weather.* (Despite a reputation as "bluesy," Horne never quite mastered the blues.) These were all fine musicians who rarely occupied the center of a Hollywood feature but always brought something to the party; as often as not, they *were* the party.

The same can be said for a white musician, pianist-composer Hoagy Carmichael. Carmichael's chord changes are the kind that jazz players love to use as a basis for improvisation. (Some sources say that "Stardust," which Carmichael wrote with Mitchell Parrish, is the most recorded American standard.) Carmichael was also comfortable darting impishly before the cameras. As early as *Topper* (1937), where he had a memorably sly moment singing his "Old Man Moon" with Cary Grant and Constance Bennett, his leprechaun's frame and flat Midwestern drawl grabbed viewers' attention. He graced a dozen other pictures, including *To Have and Have Not* (1944) and *The Best Years of Our Lives* (1946). By the time he appeared in Michael Curtiz's *Young Man with a Horn* (1949), Carmichael was, at fifty, the embodiment of insouciant, on-the-road jazz experience. With Carmichael onscreen you knew what you were getting: a rolling, laid-back melody played by spidery hands; a cigarette dangling at the edge of the mouth; a bottle of gin somewhere in the vicinity.

Hoagy Carmichael, Westwood Marching & Chowder Club, 1940
Photo by Bill Avery. Courtesy Terry Polesie

Gin played a large part in *Young Man with a Horn,* the fictionalized account of a Bix Beiderbecke–like cornettist, portrayed by Kirk Douglas. When released it was the most accomplished of the jazz features to come out of Hollywood. Kirk Douglas's hero, his performance dubbed by Harry James, was credibly self-destructive. What's missing from the movie—and, to a lesser extent, the soundtrack—is joy. Even James's solos are despondent and verging on self-pity. Oddly, given the grim storyline, Doris Day, as one of Douglas's love interests, sings ballads in her daisy-petal tone. The picture effectively, melodramatically depicts jazz as a toxic cocktail, one part gin and two parts fury. Oscar Levant attended a showing with Virgil Thomson: "When the lights went on after the cornball climax, Virgil's face was streaming with tears. 'What an awful picture,' he complained."

The movies made during World War II, like the war itself, cut a rug to the music of the big bands. Everybody danced, and everybody went to movies that featured dancing. Typically, in *You'll Never Get Rich* (1941), it wasn't enough that Fred Astaire was featured dancing with a favorite partner, Rita Hayworth; Martha Tilton (Benny Goodman's former "chick" singer), the Delta Rhythm Boys, and drummer Chico Hamilton were hired to enhance the onscreen party. Bandleaders like Artie Shaw and Tommy Dorsey appeared onscreen occasionally, Benny Goodman only somewhat more frequently.

Glenn Miller made only two pictures before his death. *Sun Valley Serenade* (1941) featured what may be the most famous dance-band tune of all time, "In the Mood," which tenor saxophonist Joe Garland originally wrote while playing in Edgar Hayes's Orchestra. (Garland's fellow musicians referred to "In the Mood" as his "Black Symphony.") *Orchestra Wives* (1942) included the great Harry Warren–Mack Gordon songs "At Last" and "I've Got a Gal in Kalamazoo." Miller's orchestra featured trumpeters Billy May and Ray Anthony, who would both become prominent musical directors in their own right. Of course actors were still plugged into the leads: in *Orchestra Wives,* Cesar Romero plays the pianist, George Montgomery the trumpeter, and Jackie Gleason the bassist; only Gleason could actually play—but not bass. Although its music wasn't jazz in the strictest sense—Whitney Balliett has called it "semi-jazz"—the Glenn Miller Orchestra's appearances were as close as American movie audiences would get to hearing complex big-band arrangements, most of them worked out by Bill Finegan, on a feature soundtrack. After Miller entered the army, his band took on even richer color, but he didn't live to make another picture.

All of these pictures used jazz in the foreground, to accompany established jazz performers. In the '40s, however, studios had begun to permit their composers to use minor jazz elements to accompany non-jazz scenes, notably on some noir soundtracks. *Crossfire* (1947) directed by Edward Dymytryk, was scored by RKO's versatile house composer Roy Webb, who had also composed the creepy scores for *Notorious* and *The Spiral Staircase.* (A native New Yorker, Webb's professional music career began as music director for Rodgers and Hart shows.) *Crossfire's* postwar military anti-Semitism theme may have suggested to Webb the piercing, dissonant chords that jangled beneath the violence onscreen.

Robert Siodmak's *Criss Cross*, a more typical example of the postwar film noir, was scored by Miklos Rozsa, with free and intimate writing for the woodwinds, particularly in the somber clarinet solos played in the *chalumeau* register.

But the studios, for the most part, were loath to introduce jazz into the background of a movie that didn't already contain jazz elements. Who could blame them? Schooled in the premise that the score of a picture should simultaneously support or emphasize the emotions generated by the screen story and be readily accessible to the moviegoing public, producers and studio executives shied away from jazz. Outside the movies the bebop revolution, generated by the likes of Charlie Parker, Dizzy Gillespie, and Thelonious Monk, made the music even more difficult to understand. How could moviemakers use jazz to complement a picture when they were themselves baffled by the music?

Even the studio composers and musicians resisted using jazz in a full score. Whatever interest they might have had in jazz and its complexities had been long since bred out of them by their scoring responsibilties. In 1973, Quincy Jones commented on the difficulty jazz composers had in getting a foothold in Hollywood to Fred Baker:

> The traditional school of Hollywood film composers shared a certain attitude as to what movie music was all about: they established the basic style and created the tradition. Some of those composers were very good and some were not so good, but collectively they formed a kind of ruling dynasty that locked up movie music for thirty years. No one—white *or* black—got into that scene. It was really tight. And then the word *jazz* had a funny effect on them. They would use jazz sometimes, but never for an entire score. They'd call in the cats from the jazz bag—Calvin Jackson or Phil Moore or Benny Carter—to do maybe one number for Lena Horne, but another guy would write the music for the rest of the picture.

The jazz-oriented composers and musicians called upon for such incidental chores rarely received credit; like screenwriters who did patch jobs, their lucrative checks were their rewards. Sometimes their movie-scoring peers didn't even know their names.

Race undoubtedly played a hand in creating this situation, because most of the jazz composers were black. Will Vodery (born 1885), composer of the "Darktown Poker Club," worked as an orchestrator at Twentieth shortly after sound was introduced. Bandleader and saxophonist Benny Carter, in Hollywood from the mid-1940s, can be heard on *An American in Paris* (1951) and heard *and* seen playing flute in *The Snows of Kilimanjaro*. (There's a wonderful horrible moment in *Kilimanjaro* when Ava Gardner, listening to Benny Carter's flute solo, purrs, "That African has no piety.") After working for the great bandleader Jimmie Lunceford, Sy Oliver served time as an arranger at both Twentieth and MGM. Philadelphia pianist Calvin Jackson also became a staff arranger at MGM. Phil Moore, who dropped his piano career after hearing Art Tatum's playing, worked notably on *A Song Is Born*. If the arrangements of these men weren't necessarily jazzy, their employment helped clear the musty hallowed air of film orchestration.

Of the white Hollywood music men, Ray Heindorf may have been the most jazz-inclined. Heindorf had been Warners' most versatile musicals man since the mid-'30s, enriching the Warren-Dubin songs for the Busby Berkeley musicals as well as later product like *Yankee Doodle Dandy*. He was also an enthusiastic fan of jazz pianist Art Tatum, whom he recorded at a soiree held in his home in 1956. It was appropriate that Warners assigned Heindorf to orchestrate *A Streetcar Named Desire* (1951), with a score by a composer then new to Hollywood, Alex North.

Alex North was brought onto the project by director Elia Kazan. In his 1989 autobiography, Kazan explains why he selected North:

> [He was] a good family friend (until I gave my testimony to the House Committee on Un-American Activities five years later, after which he became a less good family friend). Alex knew jazz, which was—New Orleans!—what I wanted. The score may have surprised Irene [Mayer Selznick, the producer], but I believe she was pleased with it.

In fact, Kazan had combined a jazz soundtrack with a New Orleans setting in his previous picture, the thriller *Panic in the Streets* (1950). Shot on location, the film portrayed Richard Widmark trying to track down a carrier of bubonic plague; its soundtrack uses Benny Carter's alto sax sparingly, with Helen Humes's voice riding in and out. With Alex North contracted for *Streetcar*, Kazan knew he'd get an even fuller, jazz sound.

It may have been *Streetcar*'s setting that inspired North to use jazz, as Kazan suggests. The train motif comes out of the very foundation of American blues and jazz. To express Blanche DuBois's emotional unraveling, North uses colliding, piteous chords—a standard score played by a string orchestra would have made her grotesque—and Stanley Kowalski's alternating brutality and childishness seem to demand a jazz background. Some of North's music, particularly a cue accompanying a shot of Kim Hunter descending the stairs, was deemed "too carnal" by the studio.

Pete Kelly's Blues (1955) must have seemed like a natural. As the band-leading trumpeter, producer-director Jack Webb displays as much verve as a corpse, and the movie itself is hardly more alive. But Webb, like Clint Eastwood, was a jazz-crazy, political conservative, and surrounded himself with the likes of Peggy Lee and Ella Fitzgerald. Ray Heindorf conducted the band that played songs by several different music-and-lyricist teams.

More interesting was the music for *The Wild One* (1954). The mordant, often terrifying score is credited to Leith Stevens, who had led a jazz band on the radio in the '30s and began his film career in 1941. In '42 he provided the score for *Syncopation*, which purported to trace the history of jazz, with Jackie Cooper (ghosted by Bunny Berrigan) playing a trumpeter on the rise. Stevens's jazz credentials were impeccable: bandleader for CBS radio's *Saturday Night Swing Session*, among other gigs. But an industry scandal exploded when trumpeter Shorty Rogers (born Milton Rajonsky in 1924), who had contributed identifiable arrangements to several pictures, audaciously sued for credit on *The Wild One*. Rogers lost his lawsuit—the compos-er's credit stayed with Stevens—but Hollywood was put on notice: credit to the house composer would no longer be taken for granted.

Shorty Rogers was on hand again to help Elmer Bernstein orchestrate his music for *The Man with the Golden Arm* (1955). Adapted from Nelson Algren's novel about a Chicago drummer and junkie named Frankie Machine, *The Man with the Golden Arm* required a soundtrack that didn't flinch at cold-turkey terror. Bernstein supplied it. Shelly Manne pounded the skins for the film's soundtrack and tutored Frank Sinatra to play like a real drummer. In some ways the music is as annoying as the picture itself: the brass screams relentlessly as if trying to compensate for the script's lack of energy.

Much better, partly because the movie is so much better, is Bernstein's pulsating, dark-soul-of-Broadway score for *Sweet Smell of Success* (1957). It's about the Walter Winchell-like smear campaign of a young jazz guitarist (played by Martin Milner). The scenes of the guitarist's group at work feature musicians such as Paul Horn on flute, Conte Candoli on trumpet, Chico Hamilton on drums, and, ghosting for Milner, John Pisano. But Bernstein's background score is equally brilliant, evoking a Manhattan that breathes scandal rather than romance, innuendo rather than fact, where a penthouse can be as forbidding as the state pen.

Sweet Smell's protagonist, just about as slippery and unheroic as the movies can tolerate, was played by Tony Curtis, who also played the jazz musician in *The Rat Race* (1960). Another Bernstein score about Manhattan, though a brighter, Technicolor one where love lurks at the top of the tenement stairwell, *The Rat Race* provided musician roles for pianist Joe Bushkin (who had appeared in Garson Kanin's stage version), saxophonists Gerry Mulligan and Paul Horn.

Within a couple of years, the urban romantic comedy became a safe vehicle for a semi-jazz score. Peter Nero composed the bright music for *Sunday in New York* (1963), with Mel Tormé handling the title song. Erroll Garner was hired by Paramount to add his rolling, gleaming-cuticle touch to *A New Kind of Love* (1963), though it was Leith Stevens who was credited with the score, primarily because he conducted the thirty-five-piece orchestra. Neal Hefti, who had played trumpet, written, and arranged for Count Basie, scored *Sex and the Single Girl* (1964), his first picture on a resume crowded with urban romantic comedies. (The *Sex and the Single Girl* soundtrack includes a cue called "City Style" that clearly anticipates Hefti's famous *Odd Couple* theme.) Pete Rugolo and Marty Paich, each from the Bay Area, worked on film scores between big band and recording assignments, while guitarist Mundell Lowe was just getting started as a film composer.

More than any other postwar jazzman, however, John Alfred Mandel seemed destined to compose for the movies. Johnny Mandel (born 1925) was educated at the Manhattan School of Music and at Juilliard; apprenticed with Van Alexander ("A-Tisket, A-Tasket"), who was subsequently part of Johnny Green's music department at MGM; and served as both trumpeter and trombonist in bands led by Joe Venuti, Boyd Raeburn, Jimmy Dorsey, Buddy Rich, and Count Basie. Mandel's big-band experience made him a master of the complex chart. At some point in the early '50s he made the leap into television, composing for *Your Show of Shows* and *G.E. Theater*. His first movie arrangements were for Arthur Schwartz's score for the Martin-Lewis comedy *You're Never Too Young*.

In 1958 Mandel shattered movie music with his score for *I Want to Live!* In the story of Barbara Graham (Susan Hayward), a West Coast hooker who goes to the gas chamber for a murder she probably didn't commit, Gerry Mulligan plays himself, the object of Graham's admiration—she digs his music, even when she hears it on a radio on death row. *I Want to Live!* is a rare example of jazz musicians actually playing much of Mandel's sultry, languid score, who are well integrated into the plot; it's easy to believe that Graham, in her hard-bitten insolence, enjoys the music of Mulligan and his sidemen, including Red Mitchell (bass), Pete Jolly (piano), Frank Rosolino (trombone), Bud Shank (alto sax and flute), Art Farmer (trumpet), and the ubiquitous Shelly Manne (drums).

Despite the complexity of, or because of, many of his arrangements, Mandel wrote an idiosyncratic shorthand to his musicians. Wanting a certain sound from his lead trumpet, for instance, he would write on the score "Miles" (for Miles Davis). Meanwhile, the chord changes in his movie themes made them attractive to jazz artists. "Emily," from Mandel's score for the 1964 *The Americanization of Emily,* has been beautifully covered by pianists Bill Evans and Dave McKenna. And his theme to the 1970 *M*A*S*H* became a jazz club staple when the television series was in its heyday a few years later.

Composers who worked far outside the studio system had, as always, a freer hand. Harmonica virtuoso Larry Adler, unable to work in Hollywood once he was blacklisted, went to Great Britain and came up with one of the most pleasing of all film scores for the 1953 comedy *Genevieve*. (Adler's success in England was mirrored in America by Eddy Manson, the former Harmonica Rascal whose *Little Fugitive* score was a small gem.) Miles Davis's 1958 score for *L'Ascenseur Pour l'Echafaud* (aka *Frantic*) was so intense that audiences of the time thought of it as foreground, rather than background, music. The score was given a sharper edge by French saxophonist Barney Wilen, who had absorbed bebop while living in the United States during World War II and later composed a series of soundtrack scores for director Edouard Molinaro. Trumpeter Dizzy Reece helped turn a familiar little British thriller, *Nowhere to Go* (1958), with a script partially credited to Kenneth Tynan, into a moody film noir. Although veteran film composer Phil Green got the music credit for the '59 Scotland Yard mystery *Sapphire* about the murder of a "passing" college student, it's widely agreed that John Dankworth gave the score its edge. The great pianist-composer Thelonious Monk played under almost all of Roger Vadim's *Les Liaisons Dangereuses* (1959); in addition, one party scene included drummer Kenny Clarke and the stunning trumpeter Lee Morgan.

Vadim's sometime producer Raoul Levy signed John Lewis—pianist and composer with the famous Modern Jazz Quartet—to write a score for a picture called *Sait-On Jamais*, literally, *One Never Knows* but released in the United States as *No Sun in Venice*. Even better was Lewis's work for *A Milanese Story* (1961), which he completed in a mere six days while holed up in a Milanese hotel. Lewis had previously scored Robert Wise's heist thriller *Odds Against Tomorrow* (1959), including the widely admired "Skating in Central Park," in New York.

Also in 1959, bassist-composer Charles Mingus and his aggregation worked on John Cassavetes's *Shadows* (1959). Mingus's saxophonist Shafi Hadi is credited with "Saxaphone [*sic*] Solos." The first scene takes place outside Birdland in midtown Manhattan, and in a subsequent scene costar Ben Carruthers tells a story about Bird (Charlie Parker [1920-1955]), whose canonization had found its way onto the screen. THIS FILM IS AN IMPROVISATION says the title card at the end, aligning itself with the soul of jazz.

These were relatively small jazz groups at work—"combos," as they were called at the time—and Hollywood was still comparatively slow to pick up the beat. Duke Ellington was called back into movie service to write the score for Otto Preminger's *Anatomy of a Murder* (1959), with its bluesy chiaroscuro main theme. As if to tie in the music organically, Jimmy Stewart played a lawyer who liked to toy with jazz lines on his piano; in one scene he even sits in with Ellington who plays a pianist called Pie-Eye. The score was so well received that Ellington gladly composed for *Paris Blues,* with its catchy title figure, and *Assault on a Queen* (1966), a Frank Sinatra caper picture which, despite its star and a Rod Serling script, has only its turbine-driven music to recommend it.

As the new decade rolled in, even the Beats had become acceptable—a condition that made them passé, as so frequently happens when something rebellious or naughty is co-opted for mass consumption. Arthur Freed, with his great movie musical work behind him, hired André Previn to write a jazz score for the film adaptation of Jack Kerouac's *The Subterraneans* (1960). David Amram had already earned the respect of classical and jazz musicians and had had some minor scoring experience working on photographer Robert Frank's independent classic, *Pull My Daisy* (1959), which featured Allen Ginsberg and Gregory Corso. Elia Kazan brought in Amram to work out some Dixieland and symphonic music for *Splendor in the Grass* (1961). The completed *Splendor* score is based on a simple ballad blown sweetly over the credits and a few times through the movie, but it would be stretching it to call it jazz.

Later that year, Amram was called to Los Angeles to score John Frankenheimer's *The Young Savages.* As soon as he stepped off the plane, he was confronted by a Hollywood moviemaking system mired in protocol and oblivious to the way more independent-minded jazz composers worked:

> I went to the screening of *The Young Savages* and was really impressed. Although parts of it were Hollywood at its worst, there were flashes of brilliance that John [Frankenheimer] had brought with him from his television days. I could see that the musical possibilities were enormous. I decided to use a jazz orchestra for the parts

that were concerned with life in Spanish Harlem and to use an ensemble of fifty-five men for the parts that could be more symphonic, even though the orchestra music had elements of jazz in it as well. I was sent to see the studio music director to get oriented.

"Okay, kid," he said. "I want you and your helpers—"

"Excuse me," I said, interrupting him. "I don't use any helpers. I write my own music."

"Look, kid," he said. "I've been in this business for twenty-six years. You don't have to bullshit me. Everyone out here has ghost writers and helpers."

"I'm sorry," I said. "I write my own music."

"Well, all right," he said. "A lot of kids do when they first come out. At least tell your orchestrators that—"

"I'm sorry," I said, interrupting again. "I don't use anyone to orchestrate my music either. I orchestrate, compose and conduct my own music."

"What?" he said, looking at me as though I were insane.

"What's so amazing about that?" I inquired. "It's not that hard."

"All right," he said. "I know plenty of wise guys who thought they knew it all. When you get to the studio you'll see. If you go overtime, you'll never be asked back here again. The best way to succeed in this business is to be like everybody else."

Although his recollections of Hollywood make him shudder, Amram came up with a score for *The Young Savages* that reeked of the streets far more authentically than the movie version of *West Side Story*, which got all the attention that year. Nine months later, Frankenheimer's *The Manchurian Candidate*, one of the few brilliant black comedies to come out of the studio system, was released with a fine Amram score. But for jazz to remain alive and throbbing in the movies, composers like Amram had to be hungrier than he was. Willing to work for less money and greater respect, Amram finally turned his back on the movies and never regretted it.

With few exceptions, it would be well into the new decade before producers would allow jazz to fill an underscore. Amram played French horn on Jerry Goldsmith's underrated, jazz-inflected score for *Seven Days in May* (1964). *The Cincinnati Kid* (1965) had Lalo Schifrin's patented percussive sound, bebop, and tango rolled into one. That same year, Quincy Jones's music for *The Pawnbroker* became the touchstone for jazz soundtracks to come. Freddie Hubbard's trumpet solos burn over the shots of Spanish Harlem, and Jones's orchestra takes his bluesy charts at breakneck speed.

In the 1970s, when the old Hollywood system briefly (and wisely) deferred to the more maverick, independent filmmakers, jazz players could sink their chops into glossy movie material without the terrible aftertaste of executive meddling. *The French Connection* (1971) made a fortune partly because of trumpeter Don Ellis's ophidian score, which came at the viewer like a speeding elevated train over a curvy avenue. The period culminated in a jazz-idiom score by Jerry Goldsmith—for *Chinatown* (1974)—featuring the trumpet playing of studio veteran Uan Rasey cutting through the Los Angeles night. Of course Goldsmith was already an established film composer. But without Alex North's work twenty-five years earlier, without Quincy Jones's work in the '60s, the *Chinatown* music might well have been just a compilation of foxtrot records.

◦   ◦   ◦

In 1937, the year that *Chinatown* was set, Henry Mancini was a thirteen-year-old flute student in Pennsylvania. At seventeen he had tried and failed at arranging for Benny Goodman. In the '50s as a member of the music staff at Universal, he worked as arranger and musical director on *The Glenn Miller Story* (1954) and *The Benny Goodman Story* (1955). After he wrote the creepy underscore for Orson Welles's *Touch of Evil* (1958), Henry Mancini began to stand out of the pack. His training in piano and in jazz forms, coupled with a natural musical glibness, would make him the ideal movie composer for the '60s. "Like Mancini," producers would request of their composers. Some of them got it—especially the ones who hired Mancini himself.

THIRTEEN

A PASSING BREEZE FILLED WITH MEMORIES
HENRY MANCINI, FROM UNIVERSAL TO INTERNATIONAL

Introduced by Vincent De Rosa's French horn before the chorus, "Days of Wine and Roses" marks the high point of the movie industry's practice, instituted in the late '40s and refined through the following decade, of commissioning songs to herald the film's title. It also marks the high point of Henry Mancini's art. The song comes from the 1962 Blake Edwards movie of the same name, and the lyrics were written by the most versatile of Hollywood lyricists, Johnny Mercer, then fifty-three.

Blake Edwards had been, and would remain, the director whom Mancini most liked to work with. Mancini and Johnny Mercer had just scored a smash hit with "Moon River," the centerpiece of Mancini's score for Edwards's *Breakfast at Tiffany's*. Although only fifteen years older than Mancini, Mercer represented a much older generation of Hollywood music men—Tin Pan Alley–trained writers who possessed a touch of the poet. After Mercer completed his lyric for "Days of Wine and Roses," he and Mancini played it for Edwards and the movie's costar, Jack Lemmon, at a huge Warners soundstage. "I went to the piano and started in middle C and went up to A," remembered

Mancini. Mercer sang the lyric in his shaggy tobacco drawl. "When we were through," Mancini wrote, "there was a long, long, heavy, terrible silence." Mancini and Mercer needn't have worried—the silence was the sound of the listeners trying to keep from crying.

Mancini worked again with Mercer ("Charade," "The Sweetheart Tree" from *The Great Race*) but "Days of Wine and Roses" was pretty hard to top. Mancini was then thirty-eight and already had had a decade of solid movie work behind him.

Even if his output hadn't been so prodigious, even if he had not won four Academy Awards and twenty Grammys, Henry Mancini would occupy a unique position among film composers. No Hollywood musician before him had become so famous as a performer of his own music; no other film composer came close to scoring so many popular hits. Although he liked to say that he "never trusted this thing called success," Mancini had undeniable ambition, lucky timing, and a melodic facility that made him the envy of his many colleagues.

Born in Cleveland in 1924, Henry Mancini grew up in and around Pittsburgh. At eleven he was taken to Loew's Penn Theater to see his first movie, Cecil B. DeMille's *The Crusades,* the famous director's 1935 entry on the long shelf of his glossy, artbook histories. Mancini was overwhelmed by the soundtrack, with Rudolph Kopp's score played by a full orchestra over DeMille's extravagant, evangelical scenes. At the time Mancini played flute and piccolo with the Sons of Italy Band, in Pennsylvania's Beaver Valley.

Mancini stayed with flute—he was first flautist in the Pennsylvania All-State High School Band—and soon became intrigued by jazz. A slightly older black trumpeter showed the fourteen-year-old a nine-six chord, which produced a modern, Ellingtonian sound. Mancini tried his hand at arranging by simultaneously reading a score while listening to a record. Benny Goodman's recording of "Flat Foot Floogie" especially perplexed him: how in the world did Goodman get that sound?

As he closed in on high-school graduation, Mancini studied with conductor-reedman Max Adkins. (Among Adkins's students was Jerry Feldman, two years older than Mancini, who later changed his name to Jerry Fielding.) When Goodman came to Pittsburgh, Adkins brought around the kid, who was permitted to try an arrangement; Goodman bought it.

With Goodman's encouragement, Mancini went to New York to be near the band's home base, and took a room at the Piccadilly Hotel. His first performed arrangement, "Idaho," proved disastrous for the band, and Goodman's support quickly evaporated. Remaining in town to audition at Juilliard (then located at Claremont Avenue and One-hundred-and-twenty-second Street), Mancini managed to fake his way through "Night and Day." It was enough to get him in.

Mancini became a proficient pianist at Juilliard, but the war prevented him from graduating: he was drafted. When he learned that Glenn Miller was in Atlantic City to form his new army band, Mancini hoped against hope that he could join it. Miller was pleasant and encouraging, but judged Mancini too inexperienced. Instead Mancini was assigned to the 28th Air Force Band. For the next few years, Mancini immersed himself in the big-band arrangements that would inform the rest of his career.

After Glenn Miller's plane was lost over the English channel on December 15, 1944, Jerry Gray, composer of the Miller standards "Pennsylvania 6-5000" and "String of Pearls," took over the Air Force wing of the Miller band. When the war ended, Gray turned the band's leadership over to singer-saxophonist Tex Beneke but stayed on as arranger. This was the band that Mancini, already familiar with the classic Miller arrangements, joined as pianist:

> I was not called on to write arrangements, but if I had an idea for an original instrumental, I'd go to Norman [Leyden] and Tex, and Tex would say, "Go ahead." I did some backgrounds for the singers, and I got my first experience writing for strings. I was most adept at ballads, although I did some up-tempo arrangements.

This was an educationally seminal time for Mancini. He was absorbing the newer, jazzier arrangements that came primarily from the pens of big-band horn players. The complex chords that had thrilled Mancini as a boy now became part of his bag of tricks.

Around this time, singer Ginny O'Connor arrived on the Beneke bandstand. She had previously sung with the Mel-Tones, Mel Tormé's vocal quintet. The Mello-Larks was the singing group within Beneke's band, and O'Connor's chirpy alto fit into it perfectly. O'Connor and

Mancini fell in love. Her Teamster father drove trucks for MGM, and O'Connor knew there was music work to be had there. She persuaded Mancini to come off the road and move to Los Angeles.

Jerry Gray was best man at the Mancinis' wedding, in Hollywood in 1947. Mancini began to study at the Westlake School of Music, and privately with Czech composer Ernst Krenek, Dr. Alfred Sendrey (whose son Albert arranged at MGM), and everyone's favorite teacher, Mario Castelnuovo-Tedesco. MGM, however, proved to be a closed shop; Mancini had to find another way in.

An assignment to score a radio adaptation of *A Tale of Two Cities* led to work for David Rose, whose songs "Holiday for Strings" and "Our Waltz" had already become standards. Still waiting for his own movie assignment, Mancini became an arranger for dance director Nick Castle. Castle had even less work in pictures, so to make ends meet he created nightclub acts for stars who were also getting less picture work. Mancini was invited to handle the music. This gave him, if nothing else, some experience dealing with movie-star temperaments. He collaborated with Castle on his first published song, written expressly so they could join ASCAP (1951). Mancini published the song himself; most of the five hundred printed copies never left his San Fernando Valley garage.

Despite his ASCAP membership and some work in and around Los Angeles, Mancini's progress seemed slow. Back in Pennsylvania, his father bemoaned the son's failure to get a degree that would have enabled him to teach. A dashed-off arrangement of "Skip to My Lou" for Jimmy Dorsey caught the ear of Milt Rosen, the Juilliard-educated assistant to Universal's music chief Joe Gershenson. "The studio had a few musicals coming up," Mancini wrote, "and needed somebody experienced in modern dance-band writing, as opposed to the European symphonic approach to scoring that predominated in movies at that time."

Mancini is only partly correct. Actually, Universal's musicals slate was a direct response to MGM's Freed Unit, which was steadily turning out one powerhouse musical picture after another. But Universal certainly had the talent. Under Joe Gershenson, the Russian-born (1904) conductor-arranger who had run Universal's music department since 1941, the contracted composers held their own.

At the time, Universal's main composers were Frank Skinner (born 1897) and Hans Salter (born 1896). Skinner began his career as a riverboat pianist, moved to New York to arrange for Tin Pan Alley, and then went to Hollywood in 1935 after Jack Robbins, who was already MGM's music publisher, took over Universal's publishing as well. His colleague Hans Salter, with whom he wrote horror movie scores (*The Wolf Man, House of Frankenstein*, etc.) in the '40s, described Skinner's capabilities: "He was very adaptable and very, very ingenious in developing a style of his own, so before I got there he did practically most everything including orchestrations and so on." If Skinner developed a trademark, it was an overwrought tension that spiced melodramas of the Ross Hunter variety: *Magnificent Obsession, Imitation of Life, Back Street* (the 1941 version as well as the 1961), and *Madame X* (scored when Skinner was sixty-eight). In 1950, Skinner published *Underscore*, one of the earliest book-length treatises on motion-picture scoring.

Consistently overworked, Skinner often needed a last-minute hand to complete a job. Salter said, "If you gave Frank Skinner two months to write a score he would be behind the eight ball at the end because he didn't start [until] two weeks before the recording date." Skinner would compose a sequence, and Salter would begin its orchestration while Skinner took a nap at the studio; then Skinner would compose another, and the process would continue.

Skinner stood up for Salter when the latter became a U.S. citizen. Salter was an Austrian émigré who scored films at UFA in Berlin until Hitler took power. He had initially studied medicine, but teachers such as Felix Weingarten and Alban Berg recognized his musical talents. By 1922 Salter was conducting for silents. He arrived in Hollywood, via Paris, in 1937, and his old pals Henry Koster, Felix Jackson, and Joe Pasternak got him into Universal. Deanna Durbin musicals and Johnny Mack Brown westerns followed. By the time Mancini arrived on the lot, Salter, at age fifty-five, was the dean of Universal composers.

Besides Skinner and Salter, the Universal composing staff included veteran Heinz Roemheld; William Lava, a Minnesota native whose theme to *Cheyenne* may be familiar to TV viewers; the jazz arranger

Shorty Rogers; and Herman Stein, the department's utility infielder, who composed without a keyboard. Orchestrating their work was David Tamkin, a fine composer in his own right. Tamkin came out of Frank Capra's war-film unit, arriving at Universal-International while still in uniform. Through the late '40s, Tamkin orchestrated his colleagues' compositions while tinkering with his own opera, *The Dybbuk*. Directed by actor-director Irving Pichel, *The Dybbuk* was well received when finally presented at New York's City Center in 1952. But Tamkin was so disenchanted that he vowed never to write another. He told *L.A. Daily News* columnist Mildred Norton: "You can't live by writing operas these days. I wrote *The Dybbuk* twenty years ago. It took me that long to peddle it."

This was a pretty solid staff for Mancini to join. Mancini and Herman Stein worked together on more than a hundred Universal features, including entries in the Ma and Pa Kettle and Abbott and Costello series. (A surprising number of memorable tunes come from Abbott and Costello pictures, including the great "I'll Remember April" from *Ride 'Em Cowboy*.) Mancini recalled: "Joe Gershenson would call in Herman Stein and me to look at a picture. Herman and I would decide where the music would go and discuss it with Joe—or with the producer, if he came around. Usually, though, the producer was off in another part of the factory making his next picture." Mancini and Stein would "spot" the picture, choosing the sequences that needed scoring, and then composing for each one, usually with a leitmotif or -motifs.

Mancini got on-the-job training at Universal—one of the last film composers to work in such a system—by composing with older, more experienced colleagues. He also learned a lesson that served him well over the next thirty years: Music for a comedy didn't have to be goofy; the comedy on the screen would take care of that.

Through the '50s, Decca Records and its president, Milton Rackmil, acquired increasing control over Universal-International. Oddly, this didn't translate into the production of more musical pictures; in fact, musical production was cut back. Rackmil, almost alone among studio owners, had a special interest in television.

Yet two subsequent musical pictures, both right up Mancini's alley, would gain the facile young composer the attention he deserved. *The Glenn Miller Story* (1953) used Mancini's charts and one lovely original, "So Little Time," a wistful trombone piece that anticipates Mancini's more celebrated ballads to come. It helped that Gershenson's studio orchestra could so closely replicate the emotional tone of Miller's band. *The Benny Goodman Story* (1956), though considerably less satisfying, proved to the music boys that Mancini knew what he was doing.

In 1957 Mancini was assigned to Orson Welles's one Universal picture, *Touch of Evil*, contributing a particularly creepy underscore. Meanwhile, he was composing cues (brief bits of music) for Blake Edwards's pictures that were usually attributed to Frank Skinner. Patches of the *Mister Cory* soundtrack (Skinner's music credit) sound like Mancini's snazzy later work on the TV series *Mr. Lucky*. Mancini also contributed songs to pictures that he didn't score. Actor Jeff Chandler, an aspiring lyricist, worked with Mancini on "One Desire" for the Ross Hunter weeper *All I Desire,* and on the title song for *Six Bridges to Cross,* which Sammy Davis, Jr., recorded immediately after the desert auto accident that cost him an eye. Sometimes the reverse procedure took hold: Mancini wrote a background score to Edwards's comedy for Bing Crosby, *High Times,* but the hit song from it, "The Second Time Around," was written by Hollywood's then premier team, Sammy Cahn & Jimmy Van Heusen. (Mancini, imitating Crosby, became a pipe smoker.)

Although he had an extensive resume at Universal, Mancini was given a pink slip along with most of the music staff after MCA bought the studio in February 1959. Almost every department was retooled for quick, high-volume television production. Fortunately, Mancini already had a toe in television.

Blake Edwards brought him on to write music for his TV series *Peter Gunn* (1958–59). The series had a great impact on film composers and the general public for its jazzy score. No less exacting a critic than Vernon Duke called *Peter Gunn*'s music "'progressive jazz' (and very good of its kind, too)." The weekly scoring sessions initially included the young pianist John Williams. When Williams departed he was replaced by the great jazz player Jimmy Rowles, who became a Mancini favorite.

The TV series *Mr. Lucky* followed; Edwards had acquired the rights to the title from RKO, which had released the Cary Grant–Laraine Day picture. Mancini's themes for both shows were hits on the pop charts.

Mancini was now Edwards's composer of choice. The timing was right. As the movie studios began to dismantle their music staffs, directors and composers sometimes formed alliances. The most prominent of these alliances was between Alfred Hitchcock and Bernard Herrmann. Edwards and Mancini—each man untethered to a studio— formed a similar unofficial partnership. When Edwards contracted with Paramount Pictures to direct *Breakfast at Tiffany's*, naturally he wanted Mancini to work with him again.

The transition wasn't smooth. Mancini was furious to learn that, acceptable as his score was, producers Marty Jurow and Richard Shepherd were hiring a Broadway composer, who would presumably be more familiar with the story's locale and tone, to write a song for the picture. Mancini's MCA agent Henry Alper advised him not to rock the boat. Mancini had already composed an appropriately light and glittery theme—it made you feel that, like the store at Fifty-seventh and Fifth, you were at the center of the universe—and its use of wordless voices became a Mancini trademark.

Mancini's anger—rare, by all accounts, but formidable when it surfaced—paid off, and he got the call to write the big song after all. Now he didn't quite know what to do. Watching *Funny Face* on television, he gauged Audrey Hepburn's limited range, barely more than an octave, as she sang the Gershwins' "How Long Has This Been Going On?" Mancini determined to keep his song in that range. He spent a month thinking about it, then one night went to his rented piano—and out came the melody in half an hour.

For the lyric, Mancini proposed Johnny Mercer. The two had first met when Mercer heard the "Joanna" theme from *Peter Gunn* on his car radio and phoned the station to find out what it was. Mercer agreed to write the *Breakfast at Tiffany's* lyric but, because rock 'n' roll was marching through the land, didn't have much hope for commercial success.

"Had Johnny been a military man," Mancini wrote, "he would have been another Patton. He used to attack a song three ways. He could hear a melody and see different angles from which to approach it and then write three different lyrics, each one valid, each one fully worked out, and each one different from the others."

Mercer originally called the completed lyric "Blue River," but a perusal of ASCAP titles showed that several songs, many by his friends, already had that title. "Red River" was considered, then rejected because of its possible confusion with "Red River Valley." "Moon River" was the answer.

After *Breakfast at Tiffany's* previewed in the Bay area, Mancini and several principals joined Paramount chief Martin Rackin to celebrate. Rackin began as a screenwriter in the '40s—he wrote Martin and Lewis's *The Stooge* (1951)—and subsequently turned to producing.

"We were all sitting around, nobody saying anything," Mancini wrote. "Marty Rackin had his arm on the mantelpiece of the fireplace. He was very New York and personable, a tall, trim, and lovely man in his 40s, with fine features.

"The first thing Marty said was, 'Well, the f**king song has to go.'"

The song stayed. Mancini thought that Hepburn's recording of "Moon River" was the best, the most genuine reading. On the soundtrack album, however, a mixed male-female chorus sings the song; Hepburn, not a recording artist, was seen as a liability on record, so her voice isn't heard. The *Breakfast* album was important to the industry even before Mancini and Mercer won the Academy Award for best song of 1961. (Mancini also won for best score.) The original RCA cover featured Hepburn plaintively facing the camera, wearing her sleeveless black cocktail dress, with a slightly less innocent air than she was permitted in the movie. (Readers of the Truman Capote novella may recall that Holly Golightly was a worldlier call girl than her movie counterpart.) The album was the first full soundtrack album, despite Hepburn's aural absence, that Mancini conducted, and it was the first of the composer's soundtrack albums for RCA—a string of recordings that stopped only after sixteen years and several dozen albums.

Mancini's instrumental single of "Moon River" went gold, then platinum; Jerry Butler's vocal recording was almost as successful. Andy Williams, who had the biggest hit of all, initially turned it down.

According to Susan Sackett's *Hollywood Sings!*, Williams was button-holed by Mancini and Mercer in a Beverly Hills restaurant. He took the song to his orchestra leader, Archie Bleyer—whose bands had been premiering songs since 1930—and Bleyer said, "I don't think the kids will buy a song that has the phrase 'huckleberry friend.'"

Much has been made of Mercer's "huckleberry friend," which is said to evoke Mark Twain and maybe the Mississippi River that flows down to Holly Golightly's (and Mercer's) Southern roots. In fact, the phrase's preciousness partly accounts for my own indifference to "Moon River." The song feels coy rather than profound, simplistic rather than simple. "Moon River, wider than a mile" sounds like a dummy lyric. The song feels false, just as the film's last scene, in which a forlorn, rain-drenched Holly calls for her lost cat ("Cat! Cat!"), seems false.

Yet "Moon River" is a favorite of many people who otherwise have little interest in movies or their music. And "Moon River" aside, there's a lot of terrific music on the soundtrack, which was orchestrated by Jack Hayes and Leo Shuken. The early track "Something for Cat" brings in a Latin big-city beat. Mancini's jazzy piano and pugnacious brass voicings evoke the Kennedy era's nightlife. The swirling flute from "The Big Blow Out" (heard over the bash that Holly throws for herself) was the sound of every midtown party that had pretensions to bohemia. "Holly," the theme that underscores the character's essential loneliness, is played by a plaintive trombone (shadings of Glenn Miller again) before the strings come in.

For the 1962 Academy Awards, Mancini was also nominated for his theme song for the Bob Hope comedy *Bachelor in Paradise*. That song is so much more pleasing than "Moon River," probably because it's clear and unpretentious. Mack David, composer Hal David's older brother, wrote the lyrics for it, giving the song a jaunty, know-it-all motor.

At the '62 Oscar ceremony held at the Santa Monica Civic Auditorium in March, Andy Williams sang "Moon River"—a shoo-in for best song. The revelation, however, was Ann-Margret's rendition of "Bachelor in Paradise," which showcased her milk-fed figure and suggested that big things would happen to her.

That same month, Mancini was working on Howard Hawks's *Hatari!* Having dismissed the first composer on the project, Hawks offered Mancini the use of instruments he'd brought back from Africa. Huge pea-pod–like winds, thumb pianos, and shell gourds gave Mancini indigenous sounds to work with. Seeing the rhythmic swaying of elephants in the film, Mancini thought they were walking eight-to-the-bar, reminding him of an old Will Bradley boogie-woogie, "Down the Road a Piece." The combination led Mancini to write "Baby Elephant Walk," employing an electric calliope to simulate the elephant's tipsy movement.

Days of Wine and Roses followed. Firmly in place was Mancini's recording arrangement at RCA, the recording company said by audiophiles to have the best stereophonic sound in the business—the "shaded dog" of the logo connoted excellent engineering. To his TV work, Mancini and his partner, Larry Shayne, a music publisher whom Mancini had met at Universal, had exclusive rights, though he had to share royalties on his movie work, including "Moon River" (Paramount) and "Days of Wine and Roses" (Warners). In addition, Mancini was helped by his battery of agents and advisors— MCA music guru Abe Meyer; agent Al Bart, who had been brought into the music business by army buddy Elmer Bernstein; and Bobby Helfer, who had for years managed studio orchestras before producing soundtrack recordings. Mancini, in his polite, elegant way, showed the industry that a film composer could write, conduct, record, and reap greater rewards from his work.

When Blake Edwards adapted William Goldman's novel *Soldier in the Rain* (but didn't direct), he brought Mancini aboard. The movie didn't seem to know what it was—comedy? melodrama? male-bonding tragedy?—but Mancini's main theme, introduced by Mannie Klein's trumpet, dripped like amber. Edwards wrote and directed *Experiment in Terror*, which featured Mancini's genuinely chilling theme, made by the plucking of two autoharps, tuned to slightly different pitches—one played by Bob Bain, the other by veteran studio guitarist-leader Jack Marshall; the resulting sound is close to that of a zither.

MCA concert broker Jerry Perenchio persuaded Mancini to tour, making him the first film composer to perform his own film music on the road. Jet travel was now commonplace, making it fast and cheap for Mancini and his musicians to cover the globe. It helped that Mancini had no fear of flying. At the same time, Hollywood studios had cut way back on production at home and were relying increasingly—through prefinancing, distribution, or both—on foreign-made product. As television skimmed audiences, inveterate moviegoers demanded things they couldn't see on TV: naked or semi-naked flesh; more realistic locales instead of the old studio sets; and wide-screen projection. The boom in international (read: European) production was a boon to a fast, dependable, inventive composer like Mancini.

In 1963, Mancini was called to London by director Stanley Donen, who was making *Charade* there. Mancini rented a piano and installed it in his suite at the Mayfair Hotel. Johnny Mercer added lyrics, and lightning struck a third time for their hit title tune. *Arabesque,* another London-based picture for Donen, and a Universal melodrama called *Moment to Moment,* arrived within a year or so. Awful as it is, *Moment to Moment* boasts a dark, lovely title tune. (It also boasted Honor Blackman, just as *Arabesque* had Sophia Loren. Such statuesque international stars kept the cameras rolling, which in turn kept Mancini working.)

Blake Edwards returned to comedy with his Inspector Clouseau series. The "Pink Panther Theme" drew on the justifiably famous David DePatie–Friz Freleng animated titles; it remains a signature tune for the series of films. Summoned to Rome during filming, Mancini had to come up with a song for Fran Jeffries to sing in Italian. Mancini wrote the melody on the plane, then hired Franco Miglacci, who had written the Italian lyric to the hit "Volare," to write lyrics. "Maglio Stasera" became, in Johnny Mercer's American version, "It Had Better Be Tonight."

A Shot in the Dark and *The Great Race* followed. Mercer wrote lyrics to *The Great Race*'s "The Sweetheart Tree." Natalie Wood "sang" it (she was dubbed by Jackie Ward), and a bouncing ball was shown onscreen to invite a singalong. Mercer wasn't available to work with Mancini on Warner Bros.' *The Out of Towners,* which was about conventioneers Glenn Ford and Geraldine Page meeting and falling in love in Manhattan. So Mancini called in Jay Livingston and Ray Evans. After reading the script, Livingston and Evans came up with the title "Dear Heart," and Mancini worked his melody, with its wagon-wheel rhythm, around the phrase. Jack Warner heard the song and changed the title of the picture—leaving the former title for the sour Neil Simon comedy made at Paramount in 1970. Mancini and Larry Shayne asked Warner to release *Dear Heart* in time to qualify for the Oscars. Warner agreed, provided Mancini and Shayne put up the local (i.e., Los Angeles) ad money, $10,000. It was worth it. The song "Dear Heart" got its Oscar nomination, and royalties poured in, the tap gushing with sales from recordings by Andy Williams and Jack Jones.

Two for the Road's score, which was probably Mancini's favorite, is memorable partly for Stephane Grappelli's mercurial violin (which, for contractual reasons, is sadly absent from the soundtrack album). *Wait Until Dark*'s music is carefully thought out: Mancini composed for two pianos—one tuned to 440 hertz (cycles per second), the other a quarter-tone flatter—played by Pearl Kaufman and Jimmy Rowles.

Rowles played Mancini's cocktail piano musings on the soundtrack of Edwards's *The Party*, with Plas Johnson, who tooted "The Pink Panther Theme" on his tenor saxophone, contributing some surprisingly soulful work. (The male-female vocal chorus on the soundtrack is playfully named The Party Poops.)

Between assignments for Edwards, Mancini worked on other pictures, not all of them happily. His score sounds all wrong for *The Molly Maguires*; it's too studied, too self-consciously reaching for poignancy. He was dismissed from *Frenzy*; Hitchcock replaced him with English film composer Ron Goodwin. His conducting work on *That's Entertainment!* (1974) was lucrative, all right, but seems to waste his considerable talent in the service of rescuscitating movie musical numbers that already had been made with more punch.

Of Mancini's post–*Pink Panther* work for Edwards, the most celebrated is probably the music for *10*, and for *Victor/Victoria*. The Oscar-nominated song from *10*, "It's Easy to Say," strikes me as an anachronism; it makes Dudley Moore's songwriter character seem much further out of touch than his Malibu residence suggests. The songs for *Victor/Victoria*, written with Leslie Bricusse, lack the musical vulgarity necessary to put them across. (The show's commercially successful transfer to Broadway has more to do with Julie Andrews's star power than with Mancini's music.)

Mancini's financial success was so great that it made him an easy target. Pauline Kael, savvy as she is about all kinds of music, sounded as though she were blasting Mancini's entire career when she wrote, "When a movie costs over eleven million dollars, a composer who skimps [on the music for *Molly Maguires*] must value his creativity very highly indeed." In a 1982 radio interview with WNEW-AM personality Jonathan Schwartz, Mancini's colleague Nelson Riddle blamed him for including the "obvious" crescendo of Ravel's *Bolero* in *10*. But the use of *Bolero* wasn't Mancini's decision—it had been written into Blake Edwards's script—and a listener can sense Riddle's barely contained jealousy as he spoke. Whenever his work was referred to as "elevator music," Mancini's stock response was "Everybody's in the elevator. It's a very crowded place."

When Henry Mancini began his career in Hollywood he brought with him something new: a dance-band rhythmic bent greatly aided by a facility for the quick phrase; the quick phrase, in turn, brought out the best in his already renowned lyricists. Mancini was lucky enough to arrive on the scene just as the old studio system, for better or worse, was beginning to unravel. At his death in 1994 he was godfather to a generation of film composers who were unafraid to try sweeping themes as well as hummable melodies.

Mancini started out in a field that traditionally required its practitioners to remain anonymous, or at least totally focused on movie work. Applying his considerable business acumen, he evolved into a one-man music industry—a household presence, if not a household name. With a legacy that includes more than eighty record albums, he escorted his listeners from Hollywood B product to some of the snazziest television music ever composed, and finally to a wider, international audio world that took in Latin, African, and Mediterranean musics. Always facile, he sometimes managed to be profound.

FOURTEEN

MAKES NO DIFFERENCE WHO YOU ARE
THE ANIMATION COMPOSERS

Working out of a Harlem studio, Austrian-born Max Fleischer made some of the most original and vital black-and-white cartoons with his brilliant team of animators. Some of these were part of the "Bouncing Ball" singalong series created by Fleischer and his team in 1924. The bouncing ball itself wasn't animated; it was a luminescent ball, held at the top of a long stick by one man, while another man rolled a cylinder that contained written song lyrics. One of the first bouncing ball shorts was *Oh, Mabel* (1924), based on a song written by Gus Kahn and bandleader Ted Fiorito. Animator Richard Huemer recalled:

> It was all so successful that when they ran *Oh, Mabel* at the Circle Theater, in Columbus Circle, New York, it brought down the house, it stopped the show. They applauded and stamped and whistled into the following picture, which they finally stopped and ran *Oh, Mabel* again, to the delight of the audience. I always say that was an indication of what sound would someday do for the animated cartoon, because basically it was a "sound" idea.

While Fleischer was producing more bouncing ball shorts, his friend Hugo Riesenfeld introduced him to sound wizard Lee DeForest.

Working out of his Phonofilm lab in Manhattan, DeForest added sound to *Oh, Mabel* and other shorts in the series.

DeForest went to Hollywood in 1927 to lend his expertise to the first sound musicals. At the same time Fleischer, then in his late thirties and the most prominent animator in New York, aligned himself with Paramount Pictures. This gave him an infusion of cash; equally important, it enabled him to use the huge song catalogue that the studio controlled. In the next few years, Fleischer cartoons featured such Paramount-connected recording artists as Rudy Vallee, the Mills Brothers, and Cab Calloway.

The sound shorts with Calloway were especially inventive. *Minnie the Moocher*, featuring Calloway's rolling eyes and elaborate, bandy-legged presentation, was an instant classic. His 1933 *Snow White*, four years before Disney's, included several tunes from Paramount's *The Big Broadcast*; Calloway's voice emerged from an animated ghost on stilts.

The Fleischer cartoon music was usually jazzy and never less than sophisticated. Two young men, hired in the early '30s, were largely responsible for it. Sammy Lerner (born 1903) was a Romanian who had moved to the United States as a child and had earned a living as a songwriter for, among others, Sophie Tucker. Four months younger than Lerner, the New York native Sammy Timberg came from a theatrical family and studied music with the legendary Rubin Goldmark.

Lerner and Timberg had a lot to work with. In 1930, Fleischer animator Grim Natwick conceived of Betty Boop, based on actress Helen Kane and voiced by Mae Questel. Wearing a hula skirt, Betty Boop introduced another notable Fleischer character in a 1933 short called *Popeye the Sailor*, boasting the first appearance of the prematurely wizened, muscle-bound seaman. Initially, Popeye was only a minor character in Elzie Segar's comic strip *Thimble Theater*, which also introduced Olive Oyl; by the time Fleischer put them onscreen, Popeye was already the more popular of the two. Timberg was away on his honeymoon, so Lerner got the call to compose a Popeye theme, which put the character across to audiences who had never seen the comic strip.

During the '30s, working on his own, Lerner wrote lyrics for Gerald Marks's "Is It True What They Say About Dixie?" and provided English words to Fred Hollander's "Falling in Love Again." Timberg handled the bulk of the Fleischer music chores. From a small combination of instruments, he extracted a warm sound that wasn't unlike the music Leroy (Roy) Shield wrote for Hal Roach's early Laurel and Hardy and Our Gang two-reelers.

The astounding success of Disney's feature-length *Snow White* (1937) led Paramount to push Fleischer into preparing a feature. This, coupled with a strike at Fleischer's New York studio, encouraged him to build a bigger studio—in Miami, far from New York *and* Hollywood. Within six months, the Fleischer brothers chose *Gulliver's Travels*. While the Fleischer team worked on the project in Miami, Paramount assigned its ace songwriting team, Rainger & Robin, to write the songs. As it turned out, the movie's one important song, "It's a Hap-Hap-Happy Day," was written by Timberg, Al Nieberg, and Winston Sharples, and was subsequently used in dozens of Paramount cartoons. Sharples (born 1909) soon took over as Paramount's music director for cartoons, while Timberg handled the music for the studio's animated *Superman* series.

Gulliver's Travels was a box-office failure. Paramount let the Fleischers go; the Miami operation was dismantled. For a while the brothers continued cartoon production, but it didn't pay. Max Fleischer went to Detroit to make industrial and educational films for the Jam Handy Organization. Dave Fleischer moved to Hollywood, working first at Columbia, then at Universal.

Universal was where Walter Lantz (born 1900), the creator of Woody Woodpecker, got his start. Lantz devised and drew the opening animation sequence for *The King of Jazz* (1930), depicting Paul Whiteman as a big-game hunter, with Bing Crosby's singing voice coming from Whiteman's mouth.

Lantz and his wife, actress Grace Stafford, were honeymooning at June Lake, near Yosemite, when they were continually distracted by a woodpecker boring a hole in their cabin roof. Out of that experience, Woody Woodpecker was born and drawn in 1940. The original Woody was a scary creature, with a saber-like beak, bad teeth, and fat feet. The bird's image was gradually softened. Although animation stalwart Mel Blanc supplied Woody's speaking voice, it was Grace Stafford's voice making the woodpecker's trademark cry "Ha-ha-ha-*HA*-ha!"

In 1948 the Woody Woodpecker feature *Wet Blanket Policy* introduced "The Woody Woodpecker Song," sung by Grace Stafford.

Nominated for an Oscar, the song was written by lyricist Ramez (Ramey) Idriss and his composer-arranger partner, George Tibbles. (The team had previously written musical material for The Ritz Brothers and Jimmy Durante.) By the summer of 1948, "The Woody Woodpecker Song" was playing everywhere, due partly to the enthusiasm of children who'd seen the movie, but also to Kay Kyser's hit version. Danny Kaye, singing with the Andrews Sisters and backed by the Harmonica Gentlemen, also had a hit with it. Mel Blanc wanted his share. He sued for royalties, lost, so he made his own recording of the song, which probably netted him more money than any court would have awarded him.

During Woody Woodpecker's heyday in the 1940s, Lantz liked to use nineteenth-century classical music fragments to accompany his films, because he didn't have to pay for them. His Swing Symphony series was another matter. Its music director was Darrell Calker (born 1905), an affable man who graduated from the Curtis Institute and then composed ballet scores for the Ballets Russes de Monte Carlo and Sadlers Wells Royal Ballet. In Los Angeles, Calker maintained a wide network of jazz musician friends, including Nat Cole, who lived in town, and Meade Lux Lewis and Jack Teagarden, who passed through now and then.

"Darrell would say, 'I can get King Cole,'" cartoon director Shamus Culhane remembered. "So we'd get some song [that Cole] would normally play in a nightclub and do that. That would be a pre-synched thing and we'd animate to that, but the rest would be ad-lib music that Darrell would write."

In the 1950s, long-time orchestrator Clarence Wheeler replaced Calker as Lantz's music director; Calker subsequently handled westerns for Eagle-Lion. Wheeler toned down the Lantz music, moving it closer to the styles of other cartoon outfits. Eugene Poddany, who had been a music copyist at Warners, followed Wheeler's tenure. Calker returned in the early '60s, then Walter Greene, another veteran of western programmers, served as Lantz's last official music head. (The similar resumes of Calker and Greene, and other composers as well, might suggest a musical affiliation between cartoon and western scores. In fact, the frequent crossover had more to do with budget constraints frequently imposed on and by both kinds of films.) Long before Walter Greene's days with

Lantz, television had bled the Woody Woodpecker cartoons—indeed, the entire Lantz product—of its insolent, irresistible jazz.

Like Woody Woodpecker, Mighty Mouse began as a cartoon character for the movies and only later landed on television. Mighty Mouse was a product of Terrytoons, the company run by early animator Paul Terry and based in New Rochelle, New York. Using music only after 1942, Terrytoons relied on composer Philip Scheib for most of its product; Tom Morrison provided the lyrics and the mouse's speaking voice. (The original stentorian voice that declared "Here I come to save the day!" belonged to Roy Halee, who would later produce Simon & Garfunkel.)

In 1952 CBS began televising the *Mighty Mouse* series. Three years later the sixty-eight-year-old Paul Terry sold his company outright to CBS. The new Terrytoons artistic staff soon included former jazz musician Ernest Pintoff and the young Jules Feiffer. In the '60s a young animator named Ralph Bakshi was making television's *Deputy Dawg* for Terrytoons. When Bakshi entered feature-length animation with *Fritz the Cat* (1971), its slamming, orgiastic rock 'n' roll—utterly appropriate to the cartoon—would have had Paul Terry gnashing his teeth.

o   o   o

With his prowling, priapic swagger, Fritz the Cat was the Anti-Christ to Walt Disney's forest of cuddly cartoon characters. The Disney music also tended to be soft and sylvan. That doesn't take away from its frequent flashes of genius.

The light began with Walt Disney (born 1901) himself, in Kansas City, Missouri, where Disney became a commercial artist after serving as an ambulance driver in France in World War I. Disney was in his early twenties when he and Ub Iwerks, a friend from his adolescence, began making animated commercials to be shown in cinemas. At one of the cinemas, Kansas City's Isis Theater, an older musician named Carl Stalling (born 1888) was the organist.

With a $250 loan from Stalling, Disney went to Los Angeles. A cartoon sale took him to New York, and on the cross-country trip back he conceived Mickey Mouse. The first two Mickey Mouse cartoons, *Gallopin' Gaucho* and *Plane Crazy*, were silent releases that went begging. Fortunately, Disney's failure to place them coincided with Warners' release of *The Jazz Singer*. Disney realized that sound was a must; for animation, that also meant music.

The third Mickey Mouse movie was *Steamboat Willie*. Disney brought in Wilfred Jackson, an animator who could play the harmonica, and, using a metronome, tried to time Jackson's playing of "Steamboat Bill" and "Turkey in the Straw" to the film. It was a crude way to synchronize sound to action, but it was enough to encourage Disney to try to fit *Steamboat Willie* with a soundtrack. Disney returned to New York to record it. Carl Edouarde, the longtime Strand Theater music director, was engaged to conduct his orchestra. The first recording was disastrous: Edouarde didn't know what to make of Disney's cue marks and finally ignored them, timing his conducting to the action on the screen as he did when conducting for the silents; meanwhile, radio tubes blew left and right, and the orchestra's bass overpowered everything else. A second session went more smoothly. Disney, knowing that his only hope of selling the first two Mickey Mouse cartoons was to provide them with sound, dropped them off in Kansas City to see what Stalling could do with them.

With the new soundtracks—and Disney himself supplying Mickey's famous falsetto—Mickey Mouse became a star; Stalling soon moved to Los Angeles; and Disney began to build his empire, founded on music almost as much as animation. Stalling suggested the "Silly Symphony" series, which quickly became the industry's most successful use of music in cartoons. The first Silly Symphony was *Skeleton Dance* (1929); Stalling based his score on Grieg's "March of the Dwarfs," from the *Lyric Suite*. Disney had Stalling's services until 1930, when their common friend Ub Iwerks, under contract to MGM, hired him away.

With Stalling gone—he would return, off and on, until 1936—Disney had to assemble a new music department. The new hires revolved around Frank Churchill (born 1901), a Maine native whose family moved to California's Central Coast when he was a boy. At fifteen, Churchill was playing piano professionally in Ventura, fifty miles north of Los Angeles. After a brief stay at UCLA and a dance-band tour of the Southwest and Mexico, he joined Disney in 1931 as a pianist-arranger. Churchill had a facility for creating melodies that clung to your brain. For eighteen months he worked first on several

Frank Churchill
Courtesy ASCAP

Silly Symphonies, then on *Three Little Pigs* (1933). Churchill wrote "Who's Afraid of the Big Bad Wolf?" in a matter of minutes. (The cartoonists' impression of the wolf was said to be based partly on Broadway producer Jed Harris; twenty years later, Laurence Olivier claimed that his conception of Richard the Third was inspired by both.) Contract screenwriter Ted Sears provided a dummy lyric to Churchill's tune, including the famous phrase that became its title. Ann Ronell, a protégée of George Gershwin, soon supplied an entire lyric, beginning her long Hollywood career.

"Who's Afraid of the Big Bad Wolf?" emerges in bits and pieces in *Three Little Pigs*; the song isn't folded into the narrative in the way Disney would later attempt, but bubbles up every now and then, played by the three pigs. (Carl Stalling was the pianist for the piano-playing pig.) Still, the song became immensely popular, due partly to Disney's new publishing agreement with Sol Bourne, general manager of Irving Berlin Music.

If Churchill was a quick tunesmith, his opposite number initially seemed to be Leigh Harline, who had joined Disney in 1932 at the age of twenty-five. Harline, fair-haired and calm where Churchill was dark and nervous, had a symphonic sensibility that made him a valued arranger for the Silly Symphonies. Harline gained company attention for his score for *The Old Mill* (1937), the first cartoon to use the multiplane camera that could glide into and across a drawing, giving a three-dimensional effect.

Snow White was the culmination of all of Disney's animation and musical experiments of the Silly Symphonies. The first animated feature (82 minutes) was three years in the making. Ted Sears was one of eight writers adapting the Brothers Grimm tale; Larry Morey, who provided the song lyrics, was one of six directors. For the figure of Snow White, a local teenage actress named Marjorie Belcher, later known as dancer-choreographer Marge Champion, served as the animator's model.

Churchill had a reputation for ignoring Disney's musical instructions, waiting instead until the cartoon's other components were locked in place before he began work on the songs. Once he got started, however, he and Morey wrote more than twenty songs for *Snow White*, of which eight were used, with orchestrations by Harline and Paul J. Smith, a UCLA graduate who would become essential to Disney's live-action product twenty years later. "Some Day My Prince Will Come" had been planned early and, as predicted, became a huge hit, along with the Seven Dwarfs' numbers "Heigh-Ho" and "Whistle While You Work."

Snow White's voice was supplied by Adriana Caselotti, who had an operetta-like warble then very much in vogue. Sound effects specialist James MacDonald, who took over as the voice of Mickey Mouse in the '40s when Disney became wrapped up in his other responsibilities, yodeled for the dwarfs, whistled for the calliope, and sneezed as Sneezy. The *Snow White* songs made up the first album of original movie music ever released. (The 1939 *Wizard of Oz* album was the second.) The score was ignored by the Motion Picture Academy, which didn't know what to do with music that came from a cartoon, but six of the songs landed on the Hit Parade in 1938.

With *Snow White*'s success, Disney began to prepare *Pinocchio*. Leigh Harline was assigned to score and write several songs, with Ned Washington writing lyrics and Paul Smith supplementing Harline's work. "When You Wish Upon a Star," "Give a Little Whistle," "Hi Diddle Dee Dee (An Actor's Life for Me)," and "I've Got No Strings" were all part of the Harline-Washington score. Cliff Edwards, known professionally as Ukelele Ike and performing in movies since 1929, was the voice of Jiminy Cricket, which was a creation of the Disney studio, not from the Carlo Lorenzini source material. The *Pinocchio* record album, the first to exploit the word *soundtrack*, sold almost as well as the *Snow White* album.

But the movie was not a commercial success at first. And Walt Disney wasn't happy with *Pinocchio*'s music—until Harline and Washington won the 1940 best-song Academy Award for "When You Wish Upon a Star," and Harline won for best score. Suddenly *Pinocchio*

Leigh Harline
Courtesy ASCAP

contained Disney's favorite music. Harline was so annoyed by Disney's blithe about-face that he never worked for Disney again. Freelance, he went on to provide background scores for *The Pride of the Yankees* (1942), *You Were Never Lovelier* (1942), and *The Sky's the Limit* (1943). Disney eventually made "When You Wish Upon a Star" the theme of his long-running TV series.

While the studio was making *Pinocchio*, it was putting the finishing touches to its *Fantasia* (1940). The project's genesis may have occurred in an accidental meeting at a Los Angeles restaurant between Disney and Leopold Stokowski. Disney wanted to animate Paul Dukas's orchestral piece *The Sorcerer's Apprentice* (based on a poem by Goethe) as a short, with Stokowski conducting; Disney hoped to record the score using then new stereophonic technology. The English-born leader of the Philadelphia Orchestra not only had recent Hollywood experience but had also made some early stereophonic recordings for Bell Labs and knew his way around a multichannel console.

The short grew into a two-hour feature that included seven other animated works: Bach's *Toccata and Fugue in D Minor*; Tchaikovsky's *Nutcracker Suite*; Stravinsky's *Rite of Spring*; Beethoven's *Pastoral (Sixth) Symphony*; Ponchielli's *Dance of the Hours*; Schubert's *Ave Maria*; and Mussorgsky's *Night on Bald Mountain*. Stokowski recorded *The Sorcerer's Apprentice* in Hollywood using studio musicians, then went back to Philadelphia to record the remaining seven pieces, some of which were selected by music authority Deems Taylor. At Stokowksi's side was Disney music supervisor Edward Plumb, a Dartmouth man who had arranged for Vincent Lopez and Johnny Green. (Among the composers at the Disney studio it was said that Plumb's arrangements were the most complex.) Also on hand were music editors Steve Csillag and George Adams.

When he saw and heard the results, Disney conceived a kind of perennial series of *Fantasia*, much like Paramount's *Big Broadcast* and Warners' *Gold Diggers*, with new musical selections introduced every few years. That idea proved financially prohibitive, as did the retention of the soundtrack's stereophonic sound, which was dropped during World War II in favor of cheaper, standard monophonic sound.

Dumbo (1941) harked back to a less pretentious Disney. The underscore was by Oliver Wallace (born 1887), and Frank Churchill and Ned Washington wrote the songs, including "When I See an Elephant Fly." For *Bambi* (1942), Churchill was re-teamed with Larry Morey—their "Love Is a Song" threads through the entire score. The orchestrations were by Disney staffers Frederick Stark and Sid Fine, and by Charles Wolcott, the gentle pianist-arranger from Michigan who had previously arranged for Paul Whiteman and André Kostelanetz.

As early as 1938, Churchill had begun working on the *Bambi* underscore, but gradually his work was discarded. This only added to Churchill's nervous depression and dependence on drink. In February 1942, Churchill and Oliver Wallace accepted Academy Awards for *Dumbo*'s score. Wallace was then at work on a title song for *Der Fuehrer's Face,* featuring Disney's second most popular character, Donald Duck. A month after accepting his Oscar, Frank Churchill, drinking hard on his ranch in Newhall, California, took out a shotgun and killed himself.

Walt Disney, though politically conservative, was professionally adventurous. He branched out with a series of Latin American–flavored cartoons that were meant, like their live-action counterparts produced at other studios, to garner an audience that wasn't directly affected by the war in Europe. Under the auspices of Nelson Rockefeller and Jock Whitney's Motion Picture Unit of the newly established Office of Inter-American Affairs, a Disney crew was dispatched south to plan new pictures. On these films—*Saludos Amigos* and *The Three Caballeros* were the best known—Charles Wolcott emerged as the most important music man, though his only prior exposure to Latin music was through bandleader Xavier Cugat.

The other music man at Disney who emerged during this period was lyricist Ray Gilbert. A Hartford native, Gilbert had come out of vaudeville. Disney's South American trip inspired Gilbert's lyrics for the rest of his career. He contributed most of the lyrics to Disney's *Make Mine Music* (1946), working with former Warners composer Allie Wrubel and Disney staffer Eliot Daniel. With Wrubel, Gilbert won an Oscar for "Zip-a-dee-doo-dah" from Disney's mostly live-action *Song of the South* (1947). Based closely on Joel Chandler Harris's Uncle Remus tales, the picture was blasted by the NAACP and other groups for promoting white master–black slave stereotypes, which Gilbert's lyrics cheerfully perpetuated. Through the 1950s Gilbert published many Latin-flavored lyrics. In the following decade his career enjoyed a rejuvenation when he provided English lyrics to such marvelous Antonio Carlos Jobim tunes as "She's a Carioca" and "Dindi."

Disney's live-action animated follow-up to *Song of the South* was *So Dear to My Heart* (1949). Burl Ives performed "Lavender Blue (Dilly, Dilly)," Eliot Daniel's and Larry Morey's adaptation of a bawdy seventeenth-century English folksong. "Lavender Blue" was nominated for a best-song Oscar and was widely recorded. *So Dear to My Heart* had other musical pleasures, including the spaciously happy "County Fair," written by that old Burbank team, Mel Tormé and Bob Wells.

Cinderella (1950) was a return to the animated feature, kicking off what many cartoon lovers regard as the studio's greatest era. Disney himself hired Al Hoffman, Mack David, and Jerry Livingston to write songs for the film because he was impressed by their Perry Como hit, "Chi-Baba Chi-Baba." For *Alice in Wonderland* (1952), Disney turned to the ever-fertile Sammy Fain and lyricist Bob Hilliard. (The team had already written Bing Crosby's hit "Dear Hearts and Gentle People," and Hilliard and Richard Miles had written "The Coffee Song," which Sinatra subsequently popularized.) The *Cinderella* songwriting trio pitched in, as did the always underrated team of Don Raye and Gene DePaul.

Peggy Lee was signed by Disney to provide voices for *Lady and the Tramp* (1955), but her enthusiasm for the project suggested to Disney that she should actually write the songs. She was paired with Sonny Burke, the long-time arranger and Decca A&R man who had also turned out some lovely melodies ("Black Coffee," "Midnight Sun"). Lee was then under contract to Decca; to hear her tell it, Burke called *her* to collaborate on *Lady and the Tramp*. During post-production and recording of the Burke-Lee songs, relations between Lee and Disney were warm; one of the dogs voiced by Miss Lee was even named Peg in her honor. When *Lady and the Tramp* was re-released in 1986, however, Lee was insulted when the Disney organization offered her a mere $500 to promote the movie.

Sleeping Beauty (1959) was the last of the '50s animated features for Disney. The scoring responsibilities went to George Bruns, a crew-cut, defensive tackle-sized trombonist who had joined the studio in 1953. Bruns's whimsical musical sensibility can be heard in a lot of his work, especially his Disney TV theme, "The Ballad of Davy Crockett." For *Sleeping Beauty,* Bruns adapted Tchaikovsky. Later, he did the same with Victor Herbert for *Babes in Toyland,* Disney's first live-action musical. Meanwhile, Disney continued to use a platoon of lyricists— Mel Leven, Tom Blackburn, Hazel George (who used the nom de plume Gill George), and former radio singer Bobby Worth—who had been already employed by the studio in various capacities.

The hiring of the Sherman brothers was a new development for Disney. Like Livingston & Evans, the Shermans wrote music *and* lyrics, their responsibilities often overlapping. Their employment turned out to be the studio's best musical bargain.

Robert (born 1925) and Richard (born 1928) Sherman were the sons of composer Al Sherman ("For Sentimental Reasons," "You Gotta Be a Football Hero"). Al Sherman had worked as a pianist for New York–based film studios during World War I, and tried to dissuade his sons from going into the same business. The brothers' late '50s, self-produced song called "Tall Paul" was heard by someone in the Disney organization and appropriated for Annette Funicello. For several years the Shermans—their slightly cherubic, big-eyed, Mediterranean faces unmistakably marked them as brothers—wrote songs for Annette. One of those was for a TV film called *The Horsemasters* (1961), which brought the brothers to the attention of Walt Disney himself.

Disney assigned the boys, then in their early thirties, to write songs for a Hayley Mills picture tentatively titled *We Belong Together.* One of the songs, "The Parent Trap," was so promising that it became the new title of the film. Another, "Let's Get Together," had the kind of bubblegum catchiness that stuck to your brain.

By 1962 the Shermans were Disney's house songwriters. Most of their work was for the studio's live-action product, which was increasing in volume, partly because it could be turned out so much more rapidly than animation, partly because the studio's contract players—Fred MacMurray, Hayley Mills, Tommy Kirk—proved capable of drawing preadolescent audiences away from television.

In 1963, the Shermans scored their first Disney animated feature, *The Sword in the Stone.* For the Pepsi-sponsored UNICEF exhibit at the 1964 World's Fair, in Flushing Meadows, New York, Disney asked the Shermans for music—not the cacophony of styles that would naturally arise from an international children's exhibit, but a simple song unifying those styles. The result was "It's a Small World," surely the most famous song to come from any exposition anywhere in history.

The Shermans had a hand in choosing which P. L. Travers stories about the magical nanny would be adapted for *Mary Poppins* (1964). Working with screenwriter Don DaGradi, the Shermans moved the setting from the 1920s back to Edwardian London, which enabled them to draw from old Cockney and music hall styles. "Super-cal-i-fragil-istic-ex-piali-docious" was an expansion of a made-up word the Shermans recalled from summer camp days in the Adirondacks. "Chim Chim Cheree" emerged from Robert Sherman's waltzlike line for Dick Van Dyke's chimney-sweeping character, Bert: "One chimney, two chimney, three chimney sweep." "Feed the Birds," with its poignant, Brahmsian texture, became Walt Disney's favorite song. At the end of the work week, on a Friday evening, Disney would invite the Shermans into his office, pour them each a scotch, then nod to Richard Sherman to go to the piano. "Play the song," Disney would urge.

Under Irwin Kostal's music direction, *Mary Poppins* was the last great live-action Disney feature to use a lot of animation. (The 1977 *Pete's Dragon*, with songs by Al Kasha and Joel Hirschhorn, animated only the dragon.) Kostal went on to co-music direct Julie Andrews's next musical movie, *The Sound of Music.* The Shermans, meanwhile, stayed with Disney for several more years. The animated *The Jungle Book* (1967) gave new life to the career of Phil Harris, who supplied the voice of Baloo the bear. (The film's hit song, "The Bare Necessities," was actually written by Terry Gilkyson.) Other animated films followed for the Shermans, notably *The Aristocats* (1970), which included their title song performed by Maurice Chevalier—something of a coup for the brothers because Chevalier had recorded Al

Sherman's "Living in the Sunlight" three decades earlier. But Disney had died at the end of 1966, and without his personal stewardship the studio's films seemed to go flat.

*   *   *

Disney's first great music man had been Carl Stalling. But it wasn't for Disney that Stalling proved so valuable.

In 1936 Stalling left Universal and Ub Iwerks to work at Warners. There were at least three distinct advantages to his shift: Warners would pay more for pop songs and already owned a massive catalog; they boasted a much bigger orchestra than Disney or Iwerks could or were willing to pay; and Stalling's old Kansas City friend Leo Forbstein was head of music there.

There was another important Kansas City connection: newspaper-cartoonist-turned-producer Leon Schlesinger, who had the heady title of Warners' general manager of the by-products division, had recommended Stalling for a position in the music department. Through Schlesinger, Warners had agreed to distribute the cartoon product of former Kansas City animators Hugh Harman and Rudolph Ising. Harman and Ising took the name Looney Tunes for their series as a response to Disney's Silly Symphonies—this was still six years before Stalling arrived at Warners—and put on their first Looney Tune, *Sinkin' in the Bathtub*, in 1930. The title was taken from "Singin' in the Bathtub," written by Ned Washington, Herb Magidson, and Michael Cleary for Warners' 1929 *Show of Shows*. For its theme song, Looney Tunes used the Cliff Friend–Dave Franklin "The Merry-Go-Round-Broke-Down." Later, Schlesinger, Harman, and Ising conceived the Merrie Melodies series (which used "Merrily We Roll Along" as its theme) specifically to exploit the vast Warners catalog.

Stalling's talents were well known by the time he arrived at Warners. At forty-eight, he was a pretty good pianist with a working knowledge of orchestration. What made him so valuable for cartoon music, however, was his steel-trap musical mind; he seemed to have schools of songs and bits of classical melodies swimming around his brain. Animator Chuck Jones said, "[Stalling] developed a memory which related to the titles, so if you had a woman with a red dress on, he always played 'The Lady in Red.' If it was anything to do with food, he played 'A Cup of Coffee, a Sandwich, and You,' because his computer would deliver that song."

Not a jazz fan himself, Stalling was greatly aided by his orchestrator Milt Franklyn, a native New Yorker who had worked at Paramount Publix and Loews theaters as conductor–master-of-ceremonies before landing at Warners in 1935. Franklyn coaxed goofy sounds out of unlikely instruments. The music got an added layer of jokiness from Tregoweth (Treg) Brown, the startlingly inventive sound-effects man who had formerly been a guitarist-vocalist with Red Nichols and his Five Pennies.

Listening to Stalling's compositions and piano work, Franklyn's orchestrations, and Treg Brown's sound effects, you begin to feel like a Freudian analysand whose couch is suddenly folding up on you. The music tickles and gurgles, hammers and caresses. And all the while it's quoting the Warners catalog. "You Oughta Be in Pictures" or "You Go to My Head" stumbles through a Stalling composition; around the bend comes a burlesqued version of Jolson singing "September in the Rain." Musically, everything was a gag to Stalling, a bony man with a little mustache. It made for some very relaxed music-making. Animator Bob Clampett remembered the Stalling recording sessions:

> Many's the time that Carl, Treg and I waited while the fifty-piece Warner Brothers orchestra would finish recording the score for a Bogart or Bette Davis feature, and then bat out one of my Bugs Bunny or Porky shorts. When Leo Forbstein told them to put our cartoon scores on the stands, a wave of relief would spread through the entire orchestra. Suddenly, two violinists would pop up and begin dueling with their bows, or some such horseplay. Others would call out things in jest, and by the time Carl stepped to the podium, raised his baton and they broke into the unnaturally rapid tempo of our Merrie Melodies theme song . . . they would be in a completely different mood for Bugs than for Bogey.

Humor permeated the recording studio before the first musical note was sounded. "Production number thirteen ninety-two, 'The High and the Flighty,'" the recording engineer announces to the orchestra (as recorded on *The Carl Stalling Project*) and you can hear the musicians breaking up at the pun on Warners' recent Tiomkin-scored airliner drama.

By the time Looney Tunes and Merrie Melodies amalgamated in 1943, Stalling's sensibility had been so whittled by animation scoring that live action just didn't inspire him. He worked on one reel only of the Jack Benny comedy *The Horn Blows at Midnight* (1945) before being replaced by the more appropriate Franz Waxman. It was the cartoons that got Stalling's blood racing, and their titles identified his blood type as !#$!!!*?!-positive: "Rubber Dog," "Marching Pink Elephants," "Orchestra Gag," "Ghost Wanted," "Variations on Chinatown, My Chinatown," "Porky in Wackyland"—you get the idea. Steve Schneider, author of *That's All, Folks!*, estimated that Stalling scored in the neighborhood of six hundred cartoons over twenty-two years—an astonishingly prolific output. For about a quarter of all that music, Stalling exploited material by other writers. Warren and Dubin were studio favorites, of course, as were M. K. Jerome and his frequent lyricist Jack Scholl. Robert McKimson contributed melodies like "Hillbilly Hare."

But the undisputed champ of all outside writers was Raymond Scott. A Scott composition like "Dinner Music for a Pack of Hungry Cannibals" was the kind of musical tidbit that made Stalling lick his chops.

Carl Stalling and Raymond Scott never met. In fact, Scott didn't watch cartoons until 1988 when he suffered a stroke that left him largely speechless. There's no evidence that Scott liked what Stalling did with his tunes, which, once they were sold to Warners, were out of his hands.

Scott was born Harry Warnow in Brooklyn, in 1908 or 1909. His older brother, Mark, earned a living as a professional musician, but Harry had more of a scientific bent and intended to become an engineer. Mark urged him to attend the Institute of Musical Art (which became the Juilliard School), paying his tuition and buying him a Steinway grand. Upon his graduation in 1931, Harry went to work at CBS as a pianist. Bored with radio's standard big-band fare, he began to compose his own pieces. Whether the pieces qualify as jazz, as their fans claim, is debatable: they left no room for improvisation, though they were singularly eccentric.

In 1936, Harry Warnow plucked a name from the Manhattan phone book: *Raymond Scott* had a good sound to it. As pianist-composer-leader, Scott soon formed his "Quintette" (*sic*)—although the group employed six musicians, he liked the sound of the word. Later there were seven members.

Eccentric? That wasn't the half of it. Scott gathered some terrific musicians, then had them make "silent music" by miming the playing of their instruments. An early radio piece was called "War Dance for Wooden Indians," based on "an old Indian legend"—written by Raymond Scott, of course.

The most durable Quintette was comprised of Scott; drummer Johnny Williams, father of film composer John Williams; Louis Schoobe (bass), Dave Wade (trumpet), Dave Harris (saxophone); and Peter Pumiglio (clarinet). Record producer Al Brackman brought the Quintette to the (Irving) Mills studio at 1776 Broadway to lay down a dozen sides. Scott insisted on recording at night, when no one else was around, and put a microphone in the men's room to add echo and get a bigger sound.

With "In an Eighteenth Century Drawing Room," Scott's updating of Mozart's C Major Piano Sonata (K. 545), the Quintette caught the attention of David O. Selznick, and they were summoned west. For Selznick's *Nothing Sacred,* (1937), scored mostly by Oscar Levant, the Raymond Scott Quintette provided a background version of "Columbia, the Gem of the Ocean." But Scott the mad innovator and Selznick the control freak didn't get along, so Scott took the boys and his music over to Twentieth. Louis Silvers plugged the Quintette into *Happy Landing* (1938). "The Toy Trumpet," originally composed for Mark Warnow's Christmas 1936 edition of *Your Hit Parade,* supplied a rousing finale to the Shirley Temple movie *Rebecca of Sunnybrook Farm* (1938).

Scott didn't care for Hollywood, and Hollywood didn't know what to do with Scott, whose "kittenish" jazz was unclassifiable and adamantly refused to swing. Scott returned to New York, composing and tinkering in his Long Island workshop. He became a music director for CBS radio, organizing one of the first integrated radio bands.

The Raymond Scott Quintette (sextet) in *Happy Landing* (1938)
Courtesy Raymond Scott Archives

He also began work on his one Broadway musical, *Lute Song*, adapted by Sidney Howard and Will Irwin from the Chinese classic *Pi-Pa-Ki*. Bernie Hanighen, whom Scott knew from CBS, wrote the lyrics, and Mary Martin starred when the show opened on Broadway in 1945.

Warners had bought much of the Scott catalog two years earlier. It was already soundtrack fodder. "Scott's idiosyncratic compositions," his archivist Irwin Chusid wrote, "toodled along at Keystone Kop tempos interrupted by hairpin-turn rhythmic shifts and over-the-cliff dynamic spirals." Carl Stalling first appropriated the Scott tune "Dinner Music for a Pack of Hungry Cannibals" for the 1943 *Greetings Bait*. Later that year Scott's "Powerhouse" showed up in *Porky's Pig Feet*, along with his compositions "The Penguin" and "Twilight in Turkey." Ten other Scott titles were used by Stalling in a whopping one-hundred-and-seventeen Warners cartoons, with Bugs Bunny chewing and sauntering through endless renditions of "Powerhouse."

In the early '40s Scott took on another responsibility: the education of a Chicago teenager named Dorothy Collins. With her mother, Collins moved to New York and became Scott's musical protégée. "Raymond made me practice eight hours a day," Collins told the *New York Times* in April 1971, when she was about to appear in Stephen Sondheim's *Follies*:

> He'd have me sing something like "The Man I Love" and at the same time he'd sit at the piano and play all sorts of dissonant things. I learned to keep on pitch that way, no matter what. Today, when Hal Prince and Stephen Sondheim praise the way I sing, they're really praising Raymond. But at the time, I felt I was ready for the booby hatch.

Scott's tutelage was anything but lecherous; according to Collins, she had a crush on Scott, who took nearly a decade to regard her as anything other than a pupil. Scott was divorced from Pearl Stevens in 1950, and married Dorothy Collins in 1952. By then Collins was a regular on *Your Hit Parade,* where her pretty and prim appearance helped the show make the transition from radio to television. Scott had taken over the *Hit Parade* orchestra in 1949 upon the death of his brother, Mark. "Be Happy, Go Lucky" went the jingle that Scott composed for sponsor Lucky Strike. One of Scott's workshop creations, amusingly named the Karloff (after the horror-film star), produced electronic sounds—such as a sizzling steak, bubbling liquid—that Scott could use for composing, particularly for commercials.

By 1957 Scott had finished work on his Clavivox, a keyboard that imitated the human voice in its ability to slide over notes. This was also the year that Scott and Collins were axed from *Your Hit Parade.* Their common employment over, their marriage lasted another eight years. In the early '70s, with his third wife, Mitzi, Scott moved tons of equipment to the San Fernando Valley. Before his death in 1995, he heard his music played constantly on television's *Ren and Stimpy Show,* a smirky descendant of Bugs Bunny and Daffy Duck.

If Scott virtually ignored the way Warners used his music—he just cashed the checks—cartoon music was practically Carl Stalling's whole

Raymond Scott composing at home on Long Island, 1940s
Courtesy Irwin Chusid and the Raymond Scott Archives

life. In the '50s most of his music was composed for Chuck Jones's cartoons. For Jones's *What's Opera, Doc?* (1957), Stalling boiled Wagner's *Ring* cycle down to a six-minute operatic chase between Bugs Bunny (sung by Mel Blanc) and Elmer Fudd (Arthur Q. Bryan).

In 1958 the musicians' strike brought silence to Warners. Stalling, then seventy, saw it as a good time to retire. During the strike John Seely compiled stock music track from the Warners library. The following year Arthur Q. Bryan died, and Mel Blanc's attempts to replace him as Elmer Fudd's voice were usually off by a half whine. After the strike ended, orchestrator Milt Franklyn took over as cartoon composer. Franklyn died in 1962, and William Lava, formerly on staff at Universal, came in. But Lava's musical mind was too sober to handle animation.

Chuck Jones, working with his wife, Dorothy, made the feature-length *Gay Purr-ee* (1962), an animated musical with Disney-size ambitions. Mort Lindsay handled the musical chores, primarily because his long-time boss, Judy Garland, supplied the voice for the kitten Mewsette. Nearly a quarter century after *The Wizard of Oz*, Harold Arlen and Yip Harburg provided the score.

Although released by Warners, *Gay Purr-ee* was produced by UPA (United Productions of America). One of the more innovative animation companies, UPA was seen in the postwar years as the Anti-Disney, its spare style and quiet satire in counterpoint to its monolithic Burbank neighbor.

UPA got a boost when Columbia, dissatisfied with the product of its own subsidiary Screen Gems, contracted to distribute its cartoons. The company was then guided artistically by animator John Hubley. Between Hubley and UPA president Stephen Bosustow, some of the best voice and music people in the business were hired. *Gerald McBoing Boing* (1951), from a Dr. Seuss story about a boy who speaks in sounds rather than words, was scored by the New York–based composer Gail Kubik; the second Gerald McBoing Boing cartoon was scored by Ernest Gold. Preparing the first "Mister Magoo" shorts, Hubley brought comedian Jim Backus into the studio and had him improvise.

Madeleine (1952), from the beloved Bemelmans book, and Thurber's *A Unicorn in the Garden* were scored by David Raksin. These, along with UPA's *Giddyap*, are more recognizable as Raksin than as "cartoon music" and solve problems quite different from those he set for himself at MGM.

The MGM cartoon music man was Scott Bradley. Like Carl Stalling, Bradley was born in and formed by the nineteenth century; he was cigarette-thin and wore glasses and a little mustache. Like Stalling, Bradley worked for Harman-Ising (in 1934) and drew on a wide musical background for his cartoon work. His "Tom and Jerry" scores were constructions of controlled madness, and they tended to shoulder more weight than Stalling's, if only because the series had considerably less dialog than, say, the garrulous Bugs Bunny cartoons.

Unlike Stalling, Bradley could score live action as well as animation. (*Courage of Lassie* [1946] and the 1950 Red Skelton vehicle *Yellow Cab Man* are two examples.) And he was known to write difficult, virtuosic parts. "He is going to break my fingers," sighed MGM concertmaster Lou Raderman about Bradley's compositions. Perhaps the most famous of these was for *The Cat Concerto*, the Tom and Jerry short in which Tom is the pompous pianist playing Liszt's Hungarian Rhapsody while Jerry sleeps inside the piano. (The running gag is that Tom, agitated as he becomes, never loses the beat.) The actual playing was done by John Crown, the Los Angeles–based pianist whose fingers seemed to be everywhere at once.

Bradley wasn't unaware of his contribution to MGM's cartoon music. Asked to lecture on the subject to Miklos Rozsa's university class, Bradley brought a Tom and Jerry cartoon, which he projected with his accompanying music track. The classroom rocked with laughter. To emphasize how important his own contribution was, Bradley then showed the cartoon with the sound turned off.

The students roared anyway.

FIFTEEN

MAKE IT MINE, MAKE IT MINE, MAKE IT MINE!
THE RISE OF THE MOVIE SONG

Tex Ritter's hit recording of "Do Not Forsake Me" was so successful in selling *High Noon* that it became clear to picture-makers that if they could publicize their product through a song—disseminated on record, in jukeboxes, and on radio—they could profit from both the increased popularity of the film and the income from the recording. Moviemakers quickly learned how to exploit the music in their product—especially the music from non-musicals, in which a single song could be readily identified with that product. With some of the best songwriters in the country under contract, why not have them write to order, then use the result to sell their movies to the public? This was also a way to use radio to promote films against the upstart medium television, which was eroding the audience for movies.

Radio—which had once been a diverse medium of drama, comedy, and variety, as well as music—began to feature mostly music and talk in the late 1940s. Live radio programs were less novel than live TV. Disk jockeys proliferated. The term *disk jockey,* in fact, originated as a pejorative term in the pages of *Variety* in the 1930s; these radio announcers "rode" records ("disks") to fill air time when the station had run out of live programming. This period saw the rise of shows like Al

Jarvis's "Make-Believe Ballroom" on KFWB in Los Angeles, featuring nothing but new recordings. Martin Block co-opted the show's title for his WNEW show in New York, attracting a sizable audience beginning in 1934 while other stations were preoccupied with the Bruno Hauptmann trial and subsequent execution.

With recorded rather than live music starting to dominate the airwaves, the power to promote a record shifted from music publishers, who could give or take at will permission to use material, to radio shows presided over by disk jockeys. The DJ, as he was now called, was simultaneously a broadcast personality, a tastemaker, and even at times a journalist who could give his listeners an "intimate" profile of the recording artist whose records were being spun. The need for record companies to ingratiate themselves with DJs planted the seeds for payola, the scandals involving illegal payments to radio personalities to get airtime for recordings.

As television began to dominate live performance broadcasting, record-spinning personalities held ever more hegemony over popular music. To demonstrate the DJs' increasing power, Tin Pan Alley historian Hazel Meyer tells the story of disk-jockey Al "Jazzbo" Collins, based in 1948 at a Salt Lake City radio station. Bandleader Art Mooney prevailed upon Jazzbo to play his new recording of "I'm Looking Over a Four-Leaf Clover" on his jazz program. After sampling it for the first time along with his audience, Jazzbo was irked that the recording turned out to be a conventional, banjo-heavy rendition. Expressing his displeasure—first at being duped by Mooney, then by his listeners' surprisingly positive response—Jazzbo flipped the "repeat" switch on his turntable so that the record played over and over. The radio station was deluged with calls—so many that the station manager himself, dismayed to hear "I'm Looking Over a Four-Leaf Clover" on his car radio, couldn't get through. When the manager arrived at the station, he found his star DJ reading a book. With the Art Mooney record twanging in the background for perhaps the thirtieth time, Al Collins looked up from his book and said, "Hey, Daddy-O." Collins's stunt inadvertently boosted the record's sales.

Al Collins probably never played Doris Day's recording of "It's Magic" on the air. But when it comes to the exploitation of movie songs, "It's

Magic"—recorded in 1948, three years earlier than the theme song from *High Noon*—was one of the first.

Doris Kappelhoff (born 1922) changed her name to Doris Day while still living in her hometown of Cincinnati. She apprenticed with the bands of Bob Crosby, Fred Waring, and, most important, Les Brown, turning Brown's composition "Sentimental Journey" into a 1944 hit. Warners signed her but didn't quite know what to do with her. Sammy Cahn arranged for Day to test for director Michael Curtiz, for the singing lead in *Romance on the High Seas* (1948). Betty Hutton had been slated for the role, but pregnancy forced her to bow out. Day's chances to replace her didn't look good: she was up against Marion Hutton, Betty's sister, and Janis Paige.

Cahn rehearsed Day singing the Latinish "On a Rainy Night in Rio" from Warners' *The Time, the Place and the Girl* by Leo Robin and Arthur Schwartz. Day sang it for Curtiz standing absolutely still. "You move a little, dolling," Curtiz said. Day tried. It didn't look great in the studio; but when the test was screened in the projection room, the place exploded. Day won the part; Janis Paige was given a role with higher billing but less to do. Day sang several songs, but it was Cahn and Jule Styne's "It's Magic" that made the greatest impression. The film's title was changed to *It's Magic* when it was exported to Great Britain, reflecting the song's success. Day's recording went platinum— it was released at all three phonographic speeds—and several other popular versions followed, notably by Dick Haymes and by Sarah Vaughan.

Not everyone was bowled over by the strapping, freckled blonde. In the *New York Times*, Bosley Crowther wrote, "Maybe the Warners figured they had a new Betty Hutton in her but, even with other assets, she still lacks Miss Hutton's vital style." Crowther said that Day's voice was "nothing to herald." Jack Warner found Day "sexless."

But Day would become the most important female conduit for the movie songs of the '50s. A year after "It's Magic," Day recorded another batch of Cahn-Styne songs for *It's a Great Feeling* (1949), including the popular title tune. But these were negligible compared to the Sammy Fain–Paul Francis Webster songs for *Calamity Jane* (1953). "Secret Love" became the number-nine single for 1954. In 1956, Livingston and Evans's "Whatever Will Be, Will Be" from *The Man Who Knew Too Much* ended the year in the number-five slot.

Songwriters Cahn and Styne, meanwhile, had come to a cross-roads during the making of *Romance on the High Seas*. Up to that point, they had had a pretty good run together in Hollywood. Their movie songs included "I'll Walk Alone," introduced by Dinah Shore in *Follow the Boys* (1944), Cahn's lyric an answer to Frank Loesser's "I Don't Want to Walk Without You, Baby." (Both tunes were written by Styne.) The Christmas perennial "Let It Snow," "I Fall in Love Too Easily," and the near-perfect "Time after Time" all came out of their film work.

Since the filming of *It Happened in Brooklyn* (1947), when Styne got wind of Cahn's intention to work with Harry Warren, things between them had never been the same. With the success of their *High Button Shoes* (opening October 9, 1947), Styne found himself pulled to Broadway. In his mid-forties, Styne at last got the respect that had eluded him in Hollywood. Cahn, by contrast, was oversensitive to New Yorkers' criticism of his lyrics, and anyway was more entrenched in the sun-and-fun bachelor life that southern California offered.

Cahn returned to Hollywood and began to write regularly with Nicholas Brodszky, a cousin of producer Joe Pasternak. Brodszky, said Cahn, "had patent-leather hair and [a] kind of shape that, if you pushed him over, he'd roll back up." Because Brodszky's name is less well known than Cahn's other collaborators, this new partnership appears to have been a demotion; in fact the Cahn-Brodszky team came up with highly exploitable movie songs. At the top of the list is "Be My Love," which Mario Lanza sang in *The Toast of New Orleans* (1950). The song became Lanza's personal theme song, and his RCA recording was still outselling his other releases three years later. Cahn and Brodszky wrote several songs for Jane Powell and Vic Damone in *Rich, Young and Pretty* (1951), then turned out "Because You're Mine," the title tune for the 1952 Lanza picture. During production, Lanza exhibited the arrogant, abusive behavior as well as the gargantuan eating and drinking appetites that would eventually kill first his career, then him. Cahn next part-nered with Vernon Duke, "the single most talented composer I ever worked with." (This remark, found in Cahn's memoir *I Should Care*, may have prompted Jimmy Van Heusen to say in 1979 that Johnny Burke was probably his best lyricist, "with Yipper Harburg a pretty close second.")

By early 1954, Jule Styne had become a prominent theatrical producer and composer. The formidable Richard Rodgers demonstrated his respect by permitting him to produce the revival of *Pal Joey*. Styne's *Gentlemen Prefer Blondes*, with lyrics by Leo Robin, introduced Carol Channing to Broadway.

Styne remained on tolerable terms with Sammy Cahn, largely through their common friendship with Frank Sinatra, whose career was on the upswing since his appearance in *From Here to Eternity*. From Twentieth Century-Fox, producer Sol Siegel called Cahn and Styne together to take a look at *We Believe in Love*, a Jean Negulesco picture about three American women looking for love in Rome. Cahn and Styne's creative chemistry was instantly reignited, and they completed the song "Three Coins in the Fountain" in a few hours. A campaign was begun to change the title of the movie to the song's title, an old industry practice when producers thought they had a winner. Darryl Zanuck said yes, but his boss, Spyros Skouras, who had to market the picture, said no. Styne booked a flight on Sinatra's plane home from Europe, where he was spending weekends with current flame Ava Gardner, to talk him into recording the song; the recording was made the next day. It was all the ammunition Zanuck needed to change the title. *Three Coins in the Fountain* (1954) is a terrible movie, but it got a tremendous boost from Sinatra's title track. The Four Aces had 1954's sixth biggest hit with it.

"Three Coins" was Cahn and Styne's swan song. Styne returned to New York and became the clown prince of Broadway composers, working in an instantly identifiable pit-band idiom that would delight theater audiences for another twenty years. Cahn began to write with Jimmy Van Heusen, the Hollywood musicians' favorite bachelor. A high percentage of their output was written for Frank Sinatra.

◦   ◦   ◦

It's easy to take the position that Sinatra is the greatest popular music recording artist of our time. People who hate Sinatra really hate Sinatra, often for extramusical reasons. In top form, however, Sinatra stepped inside a lyric with his whole being—something that can't be said consistently of any other singer. Mel Tormé could do more with changes, inverting and bending them any way he wished; Tony Bennett is invariably more likable; and Vic Damone's blessed with purer voice and diction. But Sinatra, especially from his late thirties to his early fifties, sang not only as a singer's singer but as a songwriter's singer, finding swing even in a swamp.

Yet as movie singers go, Sinatra is important more for his contributions offscreen than on. Astaire and Crosby, each blessed with unerring rhythm, moved through their pictures with a grace and sincerity that Sinatra couldn't deliver. Sinatra never lacked sex appeal—few actors have looked so persuasively at their female costars—but he lacked conviction. Too often he shrugged through his movie roles; at times his baby blue eyes became more annoying than attractive. Too often he seemed to portray nothing so much as the star who was deigning to appear.

Consequently, I would rate Danny Kaye a more convincing onscreen singer—certainly a more entertaining one. And Sinatra's Rat Pack crony Dean Martin performed a whole folio of songs, particularly in his pictures with Jerry Lewis, that he delivered with more credibility. Of course, Sinatra had his onscreen musical moments, most notably the "Well, Did You Evah?" duet with Crosby in *High Society*. Too often, though, the camera lens couldn't capture the way Sinatra got inside a lyric.

All that said, Sinatra was indispensable as a movie songplugger. Once he'd regained his position atop the show-business heap, he could sell a nursery rhyme. He gave a beautiful reading of the title tune by Karger and Wells from *From Here to Eternity* (1953) that promoted the picture for years. In *Young at Heart* (1954), the Warners remake of *Four Daughters*, Sinatra sang the title tune by long-time jazz arranger Johnny Richards and lyricist Carolyn Leigh.

Once Sinatra began to sing songs by Sammy Cahn and Jimmy Van Heusen—the first was "Love and Marriage," written for the TV version of *Our Town* (1955)—he virtually owned the songwriters as well as the songs. *The Tender Trap* (1955) is precisely the kind of Sinatra picture that makes you want to strangle the arrogant, unctuous star, but the Cahn–Van Heusen title tune swings effortlessly. "All the Way" was the Oscar-winning song from *The Joker Is Wild*, the 1957 biopic of the craggy, hard-drinking and -gambling comedian Joe E. Lewis, and it became a signature Sinatra song. (Its screen rendition is fuller, more romantic, than Sinatra's Capitol recording, although both were arranged by Nelson Riddle.)

Cahn and Van Heusen wrote several non-movie songs for Sinatra, the best of which show up in his '50s Capitol albums arranged by Nelson Riddle or Billy May. *Come Dance with Me* and *Come Fly with Me* helped define a whole swinging-bachelor ethos, promoted by Sinatra but created in large part by Cahn and Van Heusen. The rakishly tilted hat, the loosened necktie, the on-his-heels posture—the images that went into Sinatra's recording persona were powerfully seductive to women and men alike. And pulsing through that persona was Cahn and Van Heusen's jaunty, come-on rhythm.

"High Hopes," from *A Hole in the Head* (1959), was a case in point. Stumped for a lyric to Van Heusen's bouncy melody, Cahn drew inspiration from Van Heusen's former collaborator, Johnny Burke, playing off of Burke's lyric to "Swinging on a Star," with its tongue-in-cheek animal references. A chorus of children who sang with Sinatra (and whom, the recording session tapes demonstrate, he put at ease) helped to give the song a core of innocence. The song was co-opted for John F. Kennedy's presidential campaign; the social reciprocity between the Rat Pack and the Kennedy clan, if you recall, soaked up more ink than all the Republicans combined.

Sinatra didn't appear in *High Time* (1960), in which Crosby sang "The Second Time Around," but it was Sinatra's recording of the song that made the charts and inspired another picture, which took the song's title. "Come Fly with Me" was lifted from the Billy May–arranged Capitol album and given to Frankie Avalon to introduce in the 1962 movie of the same name, a kind of *Three Coins in the Fountain* about stewardesses (in the parlance of the era). Nelson Riddle handled the arrangement again for *Come Blow Your Horn*'s '62 title tune: "Make like a Mr. Milquetoast, you'll get shut out" counsels the lyric. There was nothing meek about Sinatra, Cahn, or Van Heusen.

A while before *Come Blow Your Horn* was produced at Paramount, the studio hired Cahn and Van Heusen to write songs for Fred Astaire's new film, *Papa's Delicate Condition*. Adapted from a memoir by silent-film star Corinne Griffith, the picture was to be produced by composer Robert Emmett Dolan. Astaire himself had wanted Johnny Mercer, who had come up with the music *and* lyrics for "Something's Gotta

Give" for him in *Daddy Long Legs* (1955). (Sinatra's Capitol recording of the song was another smash hit.) But Mercer wasn't available this time. Neither was Sammy Cahn, who was working with Brodszky on another Mario Lanza picture. Too enthusiastic, or maybe just too sane, to turn down a commission to write songs for Astaire, Cahn negotiated to write separately with both Brodszky and Van Heusen. For Astaire, Cahn and Van Heusen wrote "Call Me Irresponsible," which Astaire loved. Then came a tune called "Walking Happy," an ideal number for the screen's greatest dancer, especially since he had lost some speed but none of his grace.

Then, suddenly, Astaire moved on to another commitment. When the *Papa's Delicate Condition* project was resuscitated in 1962, its two new producers, Jack Rose and Marty Rackin, wanted no songs. "Call Me Irresponsible" remained in the film only because Jackie Gleason, who was now starring, liked it so much. "Walking Happy" was cut from the release print but became the heart of Cahn and Van Heusen's second Broadway show together. Sinatra took vocal ownership of "Call Me Irresponsible," its lyrical murmurs of apology and adoration placing it deep inside the Sinatra persona.

"Pocketful of Miracles" was written for director Frank Capra's film of the same name (released in 1961), and boasted another jaunty, very Van Heusen melody. Sinatra wasn't in the picture—Glenn Ford starred opposite Bette Davis in a creaky adaptation of a Damon Runyon story that Capra had already filmed once—but he took the tune onto the charts. As in "High Hopes," the recording featured a chorus of children and a lot of la-la-laing. Cahn's word-stretching lyric was so eccentric that other singers left the song alone.

In 1958, Van Heusen had composed a lovely title melody for Stanley Donen's *Indiscreet.* Four years later, Cahn added a lyric—too late to publicize the picture, but in plenty of time for Sinatra to pick it up and record it.

Cahn, with or without Van Heusen, turned out title-tune lyrics at an alarmingly fast pace, including songs for *The Long Hot Summer* (1959, music by Alex North), *The Best of Everything* (1959, music by Alfred Newman), and *Where Love Has Gone* (1964, with Van Heusen). Cahn's record-holding twenty-six Academy Award nominations, unlikely to be broken in this or the next century, attest to his dominance in the field. Even if you don't care for his lyrics, you'd be hard-pressed to think of a songwriter who so tirelessly plugged his own work. Brash, ambitious, and unapologetic, Cahn could write in an elegiac style that wasn't embarrassing. "September of My Years," to Van Heusen's melody, was written for Sinatra's 1964 Reprise album of the same name.

In and out of the recording studio, involved with or apart from the movies, the three men—Sinatra, Cahn, and Van Heusen—moved together with an astonishing creative rapport. This may have been a function of their closeness in age: there was less than three years' difference between the oldest, Van Heusen, and youngest, Sinatra. Whatever accounted for that rapport, it reached its zenith with "My Kind of Town," from *Robin and the Seven Hoods* (1964). There were other Cahn–Van Heusen songs in the picture, but "My Kind of Town" immediately elbowed aside Fred Fisher's barrelhouse "Chicago" as *the* Chicago song in Sinatra's catalog: he sang it twice on the 1967 album *Sinatra at the Sands.*

"My Kind of Town" was the last great Cahn–Van Heusen movie song for Sinatra. The Chairman of the Board (as disk-jockey William B. Williams dubbed him) continued to record the team's songs, but they weren't movie songs. "Everybody Has the Right to Be Wrong" and "I'll Only Miss Her When I Think of Her" were from the Broadway musical *Skyscraper* (1965).

Movie soundtracks were changing rapidly, and the recording industry was changing with it. The old Hollywood royalty was running scared, occasionally even paying court to the usurpers. Crosby, who had introduced more Jimmy Van Heusen tunes than Sinatra had, put out an album called *Hey Jude, Hey Bing.* Sinatra twisted to cover hits like "Mrs. Robinson." The rock explosion shattered the old musical alliances. Cahn and Van Heusen wrote a very singable title tune for *Thoroughly Modern Millie* (1967), but this was an old-fashioned assignment and unlikely to be reprised. Another Julie Andrews title tune, for *Star!*, died a quiet death, as the movie did.

Sinatra kept retiring, then returning. Van Heusen actually did retire. In the early '70s, he married Bobbie Perlberg, widow of producer William Perlberg, and kept to his Yucca Valley ranch house. Cahn, incapable of retirement, became an unattached lyricist-for-hire. In the

'70s this made for some amusing alliances. It was exactly like Cahn to hook up with George Barrie, CEO of Fabergé, who composed the theme song for the 1973 *A Touch of Class*. Barrie relaxed in his New York office by playing an electronic keyboard. Cahn, once upon a time a ferrety little fiddler from Brooklyn, wanted to touch class in the worst way. Perhaps no one told him that his lyric-writing was all the class he needed.

Apart from Cahn and Van Heusen, Sinatra was still king of the movie song. Even when he was not the recording artist on the soundtrack, he turned certain songs into diamonds. On his Reprise album *Softly, As I Leave You*, he makes the Johnny Mandel–Johnny Mercer song "Emily" his personal lullaby, and adds dignity to the Cy Coleman–Peggy Lee nursery-school march "Pass Me By" from *Father Goose* (1964). In 1966 Sinatra recorded "Strangers in the Night," from that year's comedy-thriller *A Man Could Get Killed*. The picture wasn't much—James Garner is mistaken for a spy in Lisbon—but the international cast plays gamely, and Bert Kaempfert's song sold the picture to audiences. ("Strangers in the Night" is probably the German bandleader's best-known song. The jewelbox tune "Wonderland by Night" is often mistakenly attributed to him.)

On the screen, Sinatra played a series of cops, both bad and good, which may have been closer to his bone, but his performances were just as unpersuasive as in earlier roles. He was still available to sing movie songs, if they felt right, but he was losing his writers. Johnny Mercer's death in June 1976 hit Sinatra particularly hard. His spirit was revived somewhat with the following year's success of the theme to *New York, New York*. John Kander and Fred Ebb were no strangers to the movies—they wrote "How Lucky Can You Get?" for Streisand in *Funny Girl* (1975)—but most of their music was for Broadway, specifically for Liza Minnelli, including the shows *Flora, the Red Menace* and *Cabaret* and the TV special *Liza with a Z*. In director Martin Scorsese's retromusical, Minnelli plays a songwriter and the title song is supposedly her latest composition. Many moviegoers embraced Minnelli's rendition, but it was Sinatra's recording that captured the most hearts.

·   ·   ·

In *New York, New York,* Minnelli also sang "A New Kind of Love to Me"; in 1963, Sinatra's version of the song became the title tune of a Paul Newman–Joanne Woodward comedy for Paramount. The tune had been composed more than thirty years earlier by Sammy Fain. In each subsequent decade Fain had composed some marvelous movie songs—"That Old Feeling" was from 1937, "I'll Be Seeing You" from 1944—but a great deal of his output was for Broadway, much of it written with long-time partner Irving Kahal. After Kahal's death in 1942, Fain spent an increasing amount of time in Hollywood. At some point, shortly after movie songs were being driven hard onto the airwaves, he hooked up with lyricist Paul Francis Webster.

Webster had arrived in Hollywood in 1935 to write lyrics for Shirley Temple. Second only to Ned Washington as the industry's most successful free-roaming lyricist, Webster's best lyrics had been written for Betty Hutton's unique, raucous style. (A good example is "Doctor,

Sammy Fain
Courtesy ASCAP

Lawyer, Indian Chief," to Hoagy Carmichael's tune, featured in 1945's *The Stork Club*.)

By the time Webster partnered with Fain, his style had mellowed. "Secret Love," from *Calamity Jane*, was an early Fain-Webster hit. It paved the way for their best-loved number, "Love Is a Many-Splendored Thing." The line is taken from the 1913 poem "The Kingdom of God" by the inspirational English poet Francis Thompson. ("The angels keep their ancient places;/Turn but a stone, and start a wing!/'Tis ye, 'tis your estranged faces,/That miss the many-splendored thing.") Fain and Webster wrote a perfectly acceptable song to the film's original title, *A Many-Splendored Thing*, but when Twentieth Century-Fox changed the title, presumably for marketing purposes, the team wrote new music as well as lyrics. The Four Aces, who'd had such a hit with "Three Coins in the Fountain," scored again with the Fain-Webster song.

Fain and Webster weren't joined at the hip. After lyricist Ned Washington became increasingly involved with ASCAP responsibilities, Dimitri Tiomkin, now coveted for his ability to turn out a marketable title tune, needed a lyricist for the theme for *Friendly Persuasion*. Webster happily signed on to write the Quaker-style, second-person lyrics. The problem was that Jessamyn West, who had written the stories about post–Civil War Quaker life on which the movie was based, wanted to write the lyrics herself. Tiomkin prevailed upon director William Wyler to run interference with West. After Tiomkin and Webster completed "Thee I Love," the main theme that is otherwise known simply as "Friendly Persuasion," they persuaded West to listen to the song. At last West gave her approval and backed away from lyric-writing. The tune may be Tiomkin's dreamiest melody. (His melody for 1954's *The High and the Mighty* anticipates "Friendly Persuasion"'s long, bending lines.) The song hit the airwaves courtesy of the young Pat Boone.

Like it or not, Pat Boone played a crucial role in the rise of the movie song. Boone was a freshly scrubbed Southern boy, born in Florida and raised in Texas. While he was a Columbia University undergraduate, New York provided him with music-business contacts. The contacts led him to try to conquer Nashville at twenty-one. For Dot Records, Boone recorded the over arranged, laughably stiff cover versions of rock 'n' roll hits like "Tutti Frutti" and "Long Tall Sally" that have been cited as examples of white exploitation of black-created music. In any case, his commercial success enabled Boone to step back into a more comfortable singing personality; "Thee I Love" from *Friendly Persuasion* was his first great hit in this new style. "Love Letters in the Sand," the 1931 song by J. Fred Coots, kept Boone's recording career on the fly.

For a while, Boone covered a geographic triangle, with Hollywood, Nashville, and New York as its three points. Twentieth Century-Fox cast him in *Bernardine* (1957), a high-school comedy. But it was *April Love* later that year that went through the roof. The movie's source material was a 1944 Fox picture starring Jeanne Crain, *Home in Indiana*, which anticipated the Rodgers and Hammerstein remake of *State Fair* (1945). "April Love" can be heard as a hosed-down version of "It Might as Well Be Spring." During Christmas week of 1957, Boone's recording, arranged by Billy Vaughn, reached number one on the charts. A few months later, Boone graduated from Columbia. By then he had four children with wife, Sherle (daughter of country-and-western star Red Foley), and two million-dollar contracts: one for television, one for the movies.

Standing beside Boone as a movie song stylist of the '50s was Johnny Mathis. One year younger than Boone, Mathis was signed in 1956 as a jazz singer by Columbia Records, but the great A&R man Mitch Miller pointed him toward ballads. "Chances Are" was written for him by Perry Como's former pianist Robert Allen and by veteran lyricist Al Stillman. For the 1957 movie *Lizzie* (Eleanor Parker, like Joanne Woodward's Eve, had the three faces of a schizophrenic), the team wrote "It's Not for Me to Say." "Wild Is the Wind" was the turgid, humorless title tune for the 1957 Paramount melodrama; Tiomkin and Ned Washington were the responsible parties. Mathis made up for it with the Fain-Webster title tune for *A Certain Smile* (1958), another in the series of lush CinemaScope romances released by Fox in the late '50s.

Fain and Webster continued to work together, writing "A Very Precious Love" for *Marjorie Morningstar* (1959), and a title tune for *Tender Is the Night* (1962), a surprisingly agile melody married to what must have been a challenging lyric. Even at seventy-five, in 1977, Fain was contributing songs to Disney's *The Rescuers*. Webster, five years younger than Fain, really came into his own in the '60s. "The Green

Leaves of Summer" was part of Tiomkin's score for the John Wayne *The Alamo* (1960). Its music and lyrics made it sound like a nineteenth-century folk tune. The misconception was fostered by the Brothers Four recording, made after the picture's release.

Because producers find it easy to pigeonhole songwriters, much as they pigeonhole actors, Webster was given lyric-writing work on some of the bigger epic themes of the decade. When Rozsa composed the music for *El Cid*, Webster supplied the "Love Theme," otherwise known as "The Falcon and the Dove." For the love song to *Mutiny on the Bounty*, Webster wrote a lyric, "Follow Me," to Broni Kaper's gorgeous music. Webster wrote "So Little Time" with Tiomkin for the Samuel Bronston production *55 Days at Peking.*

After Johnny Mercer had first crack at providing a lyric for Johnny Mandel's theme to the Burton-Taylor Big Sur romance *The Sandpiper* (1965), Webster was brought in, and came up with "The Shadow of Your Smile." The lyric sounded to the jilted Mercer "as if it were about a lady with a slight mustache." Mandel possessed a very interesting harmonic style—lean and pastel-colored; if it was like anyone else's, it was perhaps his slightly younger French colleague Michel Legrand. I can't be the only listener who has mistaken one for the other. "A Time for Love," for instance (from the painfully wrongheaded 1966 adaptation of Norman Mailer's *An American Dream*), could have been written by Legrand with Alan and Marilyn Bergman instead of Mandel and Webster. After the collaboration with Mandel ended, Webster still took assignments, usually working with the tireless Fain. However, by 1968 work began to dry up for them.

Nearly seventy, Dimitri Tiomkin was hired to score *A Town Without Pity* (1961). No matter how high a fee he commanded, Tiomkin was a bargain. His frequent lyricist Ned Washington, a former vaudeville agent and sketch writer, was barely less expensive because he had more film song hits to his credit than anyone in town, including Sammy Cahn. To Tiomkin's hard-driving "Town Without Pity" tune, Washington wrote what could have been mistaken for a rock lyric. In fact, many listeners assumed that the song was written by its Connecticut-born recording artist Gene Pitney, because Pitney was

Dimitri Tiomkin and Franz Waxman at SACEM dinner hosted by Georges Auric, early 1960s
Courtesy Olivia Tiomkin Douglas

also a successful songwriter (e.g., Ricky Nelson's hit, "Hello, Mary Lou").

Some of the famous movie themes of the '50s sound Tiomkin-like in their deceptive simplicity, even though Tiomkin had nothing to do with them. Certainly Alex North's "Unchained Melody" has the quasi–folk tune feeling of Tiomkin's songs. The lyrics were by Hy Zaret, a longtime lawyer who had begun to write seriously while serving in Special Services during World War II. The song was sung in the film by Al Hibbler—it remains its single best reading—but the huge hit, virtually owning the pop airwaves in the summer of 1955, was by Les Baxter. Baxter's version incorporated what he called his "velvety low unison" vocal arranging. (The Capitol album credits a group called The

Notables with the singing.) Several versions followed, none of them anywhere near as popular, until the Righteous Brothers (baritone Bill Medley, tenor Bobby Hatfield) covered it in 1965; their version was used in the 1990 tearjerker, *Ghost.*

Although he denied any calculation in the way he made his records, Les Baxter knew what he was doing, whether he was making Cuban-flavored albums, cocktail music, or movie themes. His recording of "Ruby," the theme to *Ruby Gentry* (1952), was a marvelous number, with Danny Welton's harmonica providing the steam. (An actor as well as musician, Welton appeared in *The Wild One;* in a 1995 radio interview on KPCC-FM in Los Angeles, Welton suggested that Baxter grabbed a lot of musical credit that didn't belong to him.)

"Ruby" was composed by Heinz Roemheld, with lyrics subsequently added by the great Tin Pan Alley freelancer Mitchell Parish. Even if Jennifer Jones (as Ruby Gentry) slinking around the bayou makes you giggle, the song is sublime. David O. Selznick, offering free advice as usual, particularly where it concerned his wife Jones, told producer-director King Vidor to obtain the services of Victor Young to underscore the picture and, as he'd done on so many films, come up with a hit title tune like "My Foolish Heart." Young wasn't available; Roemheld was.

◦   ◦   ◦

Selznick took pride in his musical taste, and this resulted in the first major title tune in the '50s, "The Third Man Theme." *The Third Man* (1949) was one of the few pictures David O. Selznick distributed without having much say in the production—director Carol Reed, working independently in England where the film was first released, closely followed Graham Greene's screenplay. But Selznick had unbridled enthusiasm for Anton Karas's zither music, which outsold every other 1949 recording in England and wound up as the third best-selling record in America in 1950. The story goes that Carol Reed wandered into a Grinzing tavern one evening while filming *The Third Man.* Karas (born 1906), a former locksmith and now the house musician, so impressed the director with his zither-playing that Reed insisted he accompany him back to England to write the music for the picture. Reluctantly

Karas scored the picture, which yielded the famous title theme, and became wealthy enough to buy his own tavern in Grinzing.

In the year "The Third Man Theme" hit the *Billboard* charts, a considerably darker movie theme by Bronislau Kaper accompanied George Cukor's MGM weeper *A Life of Her Own* (1950). The Lana Turner picture slid in and out of theaters without much notice. (Turner was about a decade too old to credibly play a fashion model.) Because the picture was barely noticed, Kaper reused the theme for *Invitation* (1951), a suspenser that's not better so much as louder. "Invitation" has been a favorite among jazz musicians thanks to its interesting chord changes; the peripatetic Paul Francis Webster added lyrics, but they're negligible—it's the tune that's recorded over and over. (Kaper was a master at recycling his better melodies. His "Green Dolphin Street," from the 1947 MGM movie of the same name, has an attractive half-tone progression that you can hear in "While My Lady Sleeps" from the 1941 *Chocolate Soldier.*)

In the 1950s, Bronislau Kaper was MGM's answer to Dimitri Tiomkin—a composer who could write an effective underscore and also produce an exploitable title tune. *Lili* (1953) was based on a screenplay by MGM contract screenwriter Helen Deutsch. Two years earlier, Deutsch had written the script along the lines of *The Red Shoes*, in which ballet was an integral part of the narrative, "so that if you took the ballet out you couldn't know what it was about, instead of interpolated musical numbers." According to Deutsch, the studio insisted she accept source material, a Paul Gallico short story titled "The Man Who Hated People," first published in the October 28, 1950, edition of the *Saturday Evening Post*, about an emotionally withdrawn puppeteer.

In the early '40s, Deutsch had published her own short story, "Song of Love," that included a lyric derived from medieval choruses. "It was like 'Hey, nonny, nonny,' and the 'Hey, lilly, lilly' was a very common thing that the twelfth-century singers used. I took that lyric, which I didn't expect them to use; I thought they'd get a real songwriter. Instead, Broni Kaper wrote this beautiful melody—that's what made the success of the song, that divine melody." "Lilly" became "Lili" to match the spelling of the name in the script. According to Deutsch, Pier Angeli had already been cast to star, but Leslie Caron won the title role after the producers took another look at *An American in Paris.*

Caron sang "Hi Lili, Hi Lo," explaining to costar Mel Ferrer, "It's just an old song I used to sing with my father." A waltz, the song was orchestrated by Bob Franklyn to have the texture of a carnival tune. Producer Edwin Knopf assured Deutsch that "Hi Lili, Hi Lo" was a shoo-in for the 1953 Academy Award for best song. Deutsch claimed to hate her own lyrics, but confessed she was looking forward to the recognition, to say nothing of the salary boost, that an Oscar would bring.

Deutsch was in New York when she got a call from Johnny Green. "I've got bad news," Green began. "'Hi Lili, Hi Lo' is not eligible for an Academy Award. Broni Kaper can get it for the score. But you can't get it for the song because you told them, you idiot, that the lyric came from a short story you wrote." Deutsch blamed Sammy Cahn for lobbying against the song, though she knew him only as a rabid self-promoter who hadn't yet won an Oscar himself. (He would win the following year for "Three Coins in the Fountain.") The best-song winner of 1953 was the Fain-Webster "Secret Love," while Kaper did take home the best-score statuette for *Lili*.

No matter. *Lili* was such a resounding success that MGM reconvened most of its team—producer Knopf, director Charles Walters, choreographer Roland Petit, and Caron—to film Deutsch's Cinderella story *The Glass Slipper*. Deutsch and Kaper again collaborated on a song, "Take My Love." Deutsch didn't like this lyric, either. A line from the song goes "Turn to me and take my love." "What the hell do you think that *means?*" Deutsch shouted at me when I asked her about the line several years ago. Considerably more florid than "Hi Lili, Hi Lo," the song evokes candelabra and fluttering draperies. In *The Glass Slipper*, Michael Wilding (Elizabeth Taylor's second husband) sits at a piano and sings "Take My Love," but it was Eddie Fisher (Taylor's fourth husband) whose recording turned it into a minor hit.

The two Kaper-Deutsch collaborations had a Gallic quality. So, in a more overt way, did the theme to Chaplin's *Limelight* (1952), whose music credits were a mess. Chaplin seized his usual composer's credit, but an arbitration later determined that he had plenty of help from Raymond Rasch and Larry Russell. Rasch was a former dance-band pianist from Ohio. Russell, married to songwriter Inez James (*"Vaya Con Dios"*), had a greater Hollywood presence, arranging for Victor

Young, Gordon Jenkins, and then Dinah Shore. Because *Limelight* wasn't exhibited in Los Angeles in 1952, due to political harassment of its director, it failed to be considered for an Academy Award. Over the next two decades the theme was recorded by dozens of conductors, notably Mantovani. Then, in 1972, a brief Los Angeles run made the theme eligible in the Best Score category. By that time Raymond Rasch had been dead for twelve years, Larry Russell for eighteen; Chaplin survived for another five.

Moulin Rouge was also released in 1952. The highly fictionalized biopic was beautifully scored by French film veteran Georges Auric; its most famous song, "The Song from Moulin Rouge" is frequently known as "Where Is Your Heart?" A French lyric, *"Le Long de la Seine,"* was written by Jacques Larue, who had written many songs for Chevalier; William Engvick, a favorite lyricist of Alec Wilder's, provided the English version. In *Moulin Rouge,* Muriel Smith ghosted the singing for Zsa Zsa Gabor. A few weeks after the picture's release, Percy Faith's orchestral version, with a brief vocal chorus by Felicia Sanders, hit the airwaves and ended up the number-one song of 1953.

Percy Faith (born 1908), the Canadian composer-arranger, played piano for the silents, but fire damaged his hands badly enough to make him turn to arranging in his early twenties. Experience with the CBC and NBC radio orchestras helped mold a rich orchestral style. By 1950, Faith's conducting and arranging career dovetailed with the still-infant, increasingly popular long-playing record. Like other popular conductors with greater tools at their disposal—Les Baxter, André Kostelanetz, Hugo Winterhalter, Enoch Light, Si Zentner, to name a handful—Faith turned out album after album of "easy listening" music. He became the Los Angeles–based music director for Columbia Records but kept one baton waving across the movie studios.

The hand-in-glove relationship between the record companies and the studios was cemented in the 1950s. A company like Capitol—founded in 1942 by Glenn Wallichs, Buddy DeSylva, and Johnny Mercer— became increasingly adept at exploiting the product that came from the movies. Particularly because of DeSylva and Mercer, Capitol had a kissin'-cousin relationship with Paramount Pictures.

Capitol wanted Dean Martin to record "That's Amore," from Martin and Lewis's Paramount comedy *The Caddy* (1953). Martin was slated to sing the Neapolitan "Come Back to Sorrento" for a scene, but Harry Warren, who knew an overused love song when he heard one, prevailed upon producer Paul Jones to let him try composing a new number. Warren's lyricist was English-born Jack Brooks, who also played a decent piano, used a cigarette holder and ran with Martin and Lewis. Martin hated "That's Amore" and balked at re-recording it for Capitol. As a compromise, Paramount gave Capitol the rights to release the soundtrack version. The record sold two million copies. The song galvanized Martin's singing career, became his theme song (until it was displaced by Ken Lane's "Everybody Loves Somebody Sometime"), and has since been a musical staple in movies about urban Italian-Americans.

Warren and Brooks were on the case again for Martin and Lewis's *Artists and Models* (1955), perhaps the boys' most sustained piece of mayhem. The delightful title tune is sung by Dean Martin, but it's the ersatz Italian song "Inamorata," sung by Dino and reprised by Lewis and Shirley MacLaine, that has stayed in the standard repertoire. As in most of Martin and Lewis's movies, the music was punched up by music director Walter Scharf, with an assist on vocals this time by Norman Luboff.

After Martin and Lewis split up, Warren continued composing songs for Lewis's pictures. But Warren's most famous title tune from this period was for Cary Grant in "An Affair to Remember," the 1957 Fox film of the same name. The lyrics were by Harold Adamson; there was something so right about two songwriting veterans, each in Hollywood for twenty-five years, writing together for the first (and last) time. Director Leo McCarey, a native Angeleno who liked to sit in his car and write, also took a credit on the song. Harry Warren had worked with the best lyricists in town, most productively with those two portly gentlemen, Al Dubin and Mack Gordon, and he had worked hard, always decrying his anonymity in a business that still glorified Broadway composers. His melody for "An Affair to Remember," according to Stanley Green, was his twenty-sixth attempt at a workable tune, yet it sounded typically effortless—a grand slice of Puccini. Vic Damone's reading of it over the opening credits is flawless. Deborah Kerr sings it later, in French, dubbed again by Marni Nixon. The song has a Tiffany elegance. But I confess I miss in it the younger Harry Warren, the endlessly inventive piano man whose music barrelled toward you like a locomotive that occasionally jumped the tracks.

For Warren, "An Affair to Remember" was his final hit. Through the 1960s and 1970s, Warren was still available for work. With the young Michael Feinstein serving as his arranger-amanuensis, he went to the piano each day to construct his songs. In his eighties, Warren worked toward the realization of a beloved project, *Manhattan Melody,* for Paramount. The project never got much past the wishing stage. When Harry Warren died in 1981, *Fame* had just swept the Academy's music awards. *Fame* moved the old backstage musical out to the midtown streets and had the kids dancing on taxicabs, but the streets had no grit, the taxis had no rattle.

 ⚬   ⚬   ⚬

At the end of the 1950s, the frenzy for movie themes still hadn't abated. The advent of the stereo disk in 1958 was making the LP more attractive than ever to consumers, and individual tracks were being carried on FM radio which, unlike AM, could broadcast in stereo. Sometimes this enhanced sound was even better with movie themes that hadn't yet been given lyrics. Before Mack Discant supplied a lyric to Max Steiner's "A Summer Place," Percy Faith's orchestral version (based on Ray Heindorf's arrangement) of the theme filled airwaves in the summer of 1959.

Black Orpheus, an exotic, foreign film featuring an equally exotic score, also arrived in 1959, beginning a new wave of international music rolling toward American shores. This was partly due to changes in Hollywood itself. Throughout the '50s, as they struggled to compete with television, the studios gradually slowed production and began to concentrate on distribution. Foreign product was often cheaper, making American distribution feasible, and exotic enough to draw some audiences away from their television sets. The rise of the great postwar directors—Rossellini, Bergman, Fellini, Kurosawa, Antonioni—took place on foreign shores, not inside the dying Hollywood system. Unable to ignore these inroads, the industry gave its first foreign-language film award in 1957 (to the beautiful Fellini film *Nights of Cabiria*).

Franz Waxman and Ray Heindorf at Laurel Awards Ceremony, 1958
Courtesy John Waxman

Black Orpheus was the 1959 winner, and its music may have been the primary attraction. The lovely ballad "Manha de Carnival" and the rollicking "Samba de Orfeu" were contributed to the film by the Rio de Janiero guitarist Luiz Bonfa (born 1922). "A Felicidade" was composed by Antonio Carlos Jobim (born 1927), whose catalog rolled in with the waves when the bossa nova craze arrived here three years later.

In 1960 the most popular lyricless theme was probably the theme to Billy Wilder's *The Apartment*. A year earlier, Adolph Deutsch had worked with Wilder's long-time pal Matty Malneck to compile the 1920s music for *Some Like It Hot*. Deutsch was then signed to score *The Apartment*. But the best-remembered theme from the movie was lifted from the 1949 British movie *That Dangerous Age* composed by Charles Williams, and known as "Jealous Lover." (The United Artists soundtrack album of *The Apartment* lists Deutsch as the composer and makes no mention of Williams.) Ferrante & Teicher made its hit recording.

After the failure of the 1958 musicians' strike, the studios depended increasingly on outside artists like Ferrante and Teicher and Percy Faith to exploit their music. With the proliferation of European-made pictures, music naturally came from European musicians as well. In 1960 the great international hit was Manos Hadjidakis's theme song for *Never on Sunday*. Hadjidakis had been composing for the movies since the mid-'40s. The *Never on Sunday* theme sounded so fresh because Hadjidakis employed the bouzoukia, a traditional Greek folk instrument, with apparent abandon—*swing*, if you like. A Greek lyric, "Children of Piraeus" in English, was transposed by Billy Towne into "Never on Sunday." (Sunday is the day that Melina Mercouri's Illya studies Greek drama.) Don Costa released the title song as a single, and the song was nominated for an Oscar best song of 1960.

Beside the Cahn–Van Heusen "Second Time Around" and the Tiomkin-Webster "Green Leaves of Summer," the other nominees that year were Johnny Mercer's title song for *The Facts of Life*, a Panama and Frank comedy in which Bob Hope and Lucille Ball contemplate an extramarital affair, and the Previn-Langdon "Faraway Part of Town" from *Pepe*. The studio publicity machines went into overdrive; so did the nominees themselves. Cahn in particular took pot shots at Tiomkin for being ungracious when "Three Coins in the Fountain" won the '54 award over "The High and the Mighty." "Tiomkin has stimulated a virus that has infected every branch of the music industry," Cahn kvetched to *Los Angeles Times* columnist Joe Hyams. Tiomkin defended himself by saying, "I suffer for recognition here and the Academy Awards show to me is recognition." In March 1961, days before the Awards show, Sammy Cahn sent out this lyric, "Five Songs for the Oscar" (to the tune of "Three Coins in the Fountain"), to Academy members:

> Five songs for the Oscar, each one claiming it's a click
> Just one song will be chosen, which one will the voters
>   pick?
> Five songs for the Oscar, each one covered by an ad

Equal time cries Tiomkin, and we mustn't make him mad
Ernest Gold implores the lads, dig the music not the ads
Five songs for the Oscar, each one praying for a sign
Langdon, Cahn, Webster, Mercer, or the Greek* would
   like it fine
Make it mine! Make it mine! Make it mine!
*(Who can pronounce the name?)

The Greek won. Absent from the Awards show, Hadjidakis didn't receive his statuette until Jayne Meadows, who had accepted it for him, took it home to New York and mailed it from there.

For a movie songwriter, an Oscar was the ultimate. But you didn't need one if your song sold a lot of records. So even old themes were dressed up with lyrics for the LP buyer. The specialist in this field was Mack David. Embellished by Mack David's ink, Steiner's "Tara's Theme" became "My Own True Love." Rozsa's *Spellbound* theme got the David treatment, and David provided the English lyrics to *"La Vie En Rose."* Never one to shrink from a challenge, David even managed a passable lyric to Ernest Gold's marathon theme for *It's a Mad Mad Mad Mad World* (1963).

Mack David's kid brother, Hal, was no longer a kid by 1963. Forty-two years old at the time, Hal David had met Burt Bacharach in New York's Brill Building a few years earlier. Bacharach was a handsome, soft-spoken pianist, the Kansas City–born (1928) son of writer-editor Bert Bacharach, and he'd been accompanying Vic Damone and Steve Lawrence, among others, in addition to trying to establish himself as a composer. Perry Como had turned Bacharach's "Catch a Falling Star" into a hit, and Marty Robbins had made the Bacharach-David "Story of My Life" into a signature song. They scored with several pop hits, including "Blue on Blue," "Don't Make Me Over," and "Johnny Get Angry."

In 1963, when everyone in Los Angeles had turned down the assignment to write an exploitation song for the Paramount comedy *Wives and Lovers,* Bacharach and David accepted from New York. The song wasn't heard in the movie, but the subsequent Steve Lawrence recording did the job. With politically correct feminist hindsight, "Wives and Lovers" has been jeered at—I have heard it described as foul—but it's certainly livelier than most of the Bacharach-David songs to come: minor key emotions presented in major keys, the pangs of romance salved by impressionistic tonal colors and eccentric time signatures.

The team moved to Los Angeles and were on everybody's short list of movie songwriters. Bacharach occasionally composed an entire score, but it was his ability to turn out quick, highly marketable melodies that endeared him to the studios. That Bacharach and David didn't *need* film work made them all the more attractive, particularly after forging a deal with Scepter Records and Dionne Warwick. "A House Is Not a Home" was written for the 1964 film about New York madam Polly Adler. "What's New Pussycat?" was written in London, while the swinging 1965 comedy was being filmed, and rocketed Tom Jones to the top of the charts. "Alfie" did a smashing job of publicizing the 1966 film, which was quickly covered by a dozen singers but was sung during the closing credits by, of all people, Cher. The movie *Casino Royale* (1967) was a parody of the James Bond films—their gorgeous, unavailable women, exclusive hotel and casino settings and high-tech accoutrements—that didn't quite come off. (As Ian Fleming cautioned, you can't spoof a spoof.) But the *Casino Royale* soundtrack album, highly prized among collectors for its recording technique, contains some Bacharach gems. The "Casino Royale Theme," played by Herb Alpert and the Tijuana Brass, could serve as the cocktail theme of the '60s, evoking the bizarre junction of tuxedoes and psychedelia. "The Look of Love," a much heavier tune (lyric by David), was sung by the underrated Dusty Springfield. The Sergio Mendes & Brasil '66 recording became a major hit.

Sergio Mendes's records were distributed by A&M, which was owned by Herb Alpert and Jerry Moss—and housed, by the way, in the old Chaplin studios on La Brea Avenue in Los Angeles. The Bacharach-David alliance with Alpert made them all wealthier than Hollywood musicians had ever been before.

In a way, Bacharach and David were the perfect songwriting team for an increasingly schizophrenic Hollywood, where the old studio system had crashed but decisions were still being made by executives educated in that system. Bacharach and David rode high in a Hollywood that during Oscar-nominating time had ignored *all* the songs from the Beatles's *A Hard Day's Night* and *Help!* and Dave Clark Five's *Catch Us If You Can* and Gerry and the Pacemakers' *Ferry Cross the Mersey*, and John Sebastian's "Darlin', Be Home Soon" from *You're a Big Boy Now*. Establishment Hollywood wanted to belong to, if not reflect, what was going on outside of Beverly Hills, but no one quite knew how to negotiate it. At a late '60s party hosted by Adolph Green and Phyllis Newman, lyricist Dory Previn felt old and obsolete while the other guests, including her conjugal successor Mia Farrow, danced to lyricless rock 'n' roll.

For that era, Bacharach and David served quite nicely. Perhaps as a reward for producing so much commercial music, Bacharach and David's biggest hit, "Raindrops Keep Falling on My Head," was squashed into *Butch Cassidy and the Sundance Kid* (1969). Utterly incongruous to the action, the song was the equivalent of an early music video. The recording by B. J. Thomas, who got the assignment primarily because he shared a manager with Dionne Warwick, remained at number one for a month.

It was a strange year, 1969. At the Academy Awards show, conductor Lionel Newman, collecting his Oscar for best scoring of a musical (*Hello, Dolly!*), stood at the podium and said, "Lennie Hayton couldn't make it tonight, but I'm sure he's just as gassed as I am."

Despite Newman's hip vernacular, the nominated songs were of an older order. "Jean" was written by Rod McKuen for *The Prime of Miss Jean Brodie*. Oakland native McKuen had enjoyed a dual career as composer and poet—his volumes of poetry, particularly *Stanyan Street and Other Sorrows* and *Listen to the Warm*, seemed to be sold in every greeting-card and gift shop in the late '60s—and "Jean" was the biggest hit of his still young career. (The hit recording belonged to the British singer, Oliver.)

"Come Saturday Morning" from *The Sterile Cuckoo* was another best-song nominee in 1969, and its creation seemed to come at a crossroads for its writers: composer Fred Karlin was just beginning his movie career, lyricist Dory Previn (née Langdon) was nearing the end of hers.

Karlin (born 1936) had come up through the Eastman School and dance band apprenticeships, including important study with Stan Kenton arranger Bill Russo. Before *The Sterile Cuckoo,* Karlin had scored *Up the Down Staircase* (1967) and the Western *The Stalking Moon* (1968), and would go on to compose the seldom-heard electronic score for *The Baby Maker* (1970). "For All We Know" from *Lovers and Other Strangers* (1970) confirmed Karlin's viability as a songwriter.

Dory Previn had not had an easy time breaking into the male citadel of lyric-writing, even after she'd married André Previn. "Vernon Duke smiled indulgently when André said I was first-rate. 'There's no such thing,' said Duke, 'as a first-rate woman lyricist.'" When Previn mentioned Dorothy Fields, Duke pronounced Fields the exception to the rule.

But Dory Previn stayed in the game. The dark lyric to David Raksin's theme to *The Bad and the Beautiful* was hers, though written some years after the picture's release. During her marriage and professional alliance with André Previn, Previn wrote some extremely effective movie lyrics, notably "You're Gonna Hear from Me" from *Inside Daisy Clover* (1965) and "Gotta Get Off" from *Valley of the Dolls* (1967), which sounds like a Bacharach-David song. After the Previns' marriage broke up, Dory Previn made record albums and wrote books in a confessional mode. She had a lot to get off her chest. She added lyrics to Gato Barbieri's *Last Tango in Paris* theme, then largely withdrew from movie music. "Come Saturday Morning," turned into a hit by the soft-rock group The Sandpipers, was her last great movie song. Patronized by the likes of Vernon Duke, she paved the way for female lyricists Carole Bayer Sager, Carol Connors, and Marilyn Bergman.

Marilyn and Alan Bergman dominated Hollywood lyric-writing from the late '60s to the late '70s. Born in Brooklyn (Alan in 1925, Marilyn in 1929), the husband-and-wife team led a bicoastal professional existence long before they got movie work. They wrote special material for Fred Astaire, Jo Stafford, and Marge and Gower Champion before making their mark with Sinatra's recording of "Nice 'n' Easy." (The tune was by Alan Bergman's New York University classmate Lew Spence.)

The Bergmans' movie work took off with "The Windmills of

Your Mind" from *The Thomas Crown Affair* (1968). Noel Harrison sang it over the blinking-light credits. Even with all the circular imagery that the Bergmans toss into the lyric—"wheels within wheels," "snowball down a mountain," etc.—does any of it mean anything? Michel Legrand's music is typically weightless—that's part of his charm—and the Bergmans do little to ground it. "Why did summer go so quickly, was it something that I said?" is the most concrete line in the song, and it leads into their Legrand collaboration, "The Summer Knows" from *Summer of '42* (1971). Too often the Bergmans got by on emotions that had nothing to do with people.

Between "Windmills" and "Summer" came that fine song, "What Are You Doing the Rest of Your Life?" from the melodrama *The Happy Ending* (1969). In the movie the exquisite Jean Simmons weighs her options after boredom, alcoholism, and infidelity have splintered her long marriage to John Forsythe. The Bergmans do better here because the lyric is at once precise and in motion. A 1970 title tune with Legrand for *Pieces of Dreams* was a close cousin to "What Are You Doing the Rest of Your Life?" (Robert Forster portrayed a priest in love with social worker Lauren Hutton.)

The Bergmans moved on. They wrote lyrics for Henry Mancini, Maurice Jarre, and David Shire—all for movies caught in a no-man's-land of the 1970s, when the most interesting pictures were coming from a handful of mavericks. The Bergmans' most celebrated collaboration from this period was surely with Marvin Hamlisch, particularly on "The Way We Were." The song works on you, much as the 1973 movie itself does, though each ought to be highly resistible. The Bergmans are sometimes up to their old tricks ("Memories, like the colors of my mind"—huh?); but most of the lyric gets down to the business of evoking lost romance in innocent times. It's a good song, at least in Streisand's soundtrack version, although anyone with half a brain feels a little guilty liking it. Part of its charm is in Marty Paich's excellent arrangement, which touches the listener without spreading too much treacle.

The Bergmans and their various collaborators—especially Michel Legrand and Marvin Hamlisch—were the last important movie songwriters up to the mid-1970s. The literacy they brought to their projects is gone from the movies now; the romance is still there, but in an edgier, more external form. For all their poetic pretensions, the Bergmans are missed.

THREW A PARTY IN THE COUNTY JAIL

THE ROCK 'N' ROLL SOUNDTRACK

Blackboard Jungle (1955), based on an Evan Hunter novel, was a Richard Brooks film that purported to be a hard-hitting exposé of teenage hoodlum behavior in American high schools. Glenn Ford starred as Richard Dadier, called "Daddy-O" by some of his students. Despite its reputation for rock 'n' roll danger, *Blackboard Jungle* is a mainstream film with the tone of the button-down hipster, the guy who prefers a dry martini with his rebelliousness. The bold use of music disguises the movie's fundamental conservatism. (Of the baby they're expecting, Glenn Ford says to pregnant wife, Anne Francis, "It will have your looks and my brain.")

"Rock Around the Clock" by Bill Haley and His Comets made the movie famous—and vice versa. The song had been a minor hit for Decca, but its inclusion in the movie sent sales soaring—an additional half a million units were sold by the end of 1955. Because of the Bill Haley number, we often recall *Blackboard Jungle*'s soundtrack as being driven by rock 'n' roll. In fact at the time there wasn't much rock 'n' roll to speak of, either in or out of the movie. The other music on the soundtrack is Stan Kenton's "Invention for Guitar and Trumpet" and Bix Beiderbecke's "Jazz Me Blues." These latter two are melded into the famous sequence in which meek math teacher Richard Kiley's prized records are smashed. The musical director, igniting all this turbo-driven music and composing a separate theme, was the soft-spoken Charles Wolcott, long of the Disney organization. *Blackboard Jungle* was Hollywood through and through.

It was good old-fashioned censorship that gave the picture its notoriety. *Blackboard Jungle* was the American entry to the 1955 Venice Film Festival but Clare Boothe Luce, U.S. ambassador to Italy, had it removed. Asked for an explanation, Luce lay low but the U.S. delegation said officially that the film gave "an unflattering and unrealistic view of American school life." Glenn Ford's previous movie, *Interrupted Melody* (about opera star Marjorie Lawrence's fight against polio) was shown in place of *Blackboard Jungle.*

The Luce Affair, as it came to be called, was fraught with cultural symbolism. An American ambassador and a playwright of some accomplishment (e.g., *The Women,* filmed in 1939 by MGM), Clare Boothe Luce was also married to publisher Henry Luce, whose magazines *Time, Life,* and *Fortune* were guardians as well as makers of popular taste. By attempting to censor *Blackboard Jungle,* with its "frank" depiction of juvenile delinquency and its assaultive soundtrack, Luce inadvertently promoted it. Watching over the cultural ramparts, she must have been shocked to hear rhythm-and-blues–derived music drawn primarily from black sources shake up a movie audience.

Producer Sam Katzman, then enjoying a housekeeping deal at Columbia Pictures, quickly parlayed the notoriety of "Rock Around the Clock" into a movie of the same title featuring Bill Haley and His Comets (performing onscreen this time), The Platters, and Alan Freed, the country's most audible rock 'n' roll disk jockey. *Rock Around the Clock* was the first of many rock musicals that showcased black and white recording artists. Such onscreen racial integration, in which the black artists were shown not in a subservient role but on more of an equal footing with their white counterparts, added to the danger and excitement of the music itself. This translated into big box-office.

The rock phenomenon amused the Hollywood old guard, who viewed the music as a novelty and the public reaction to it as nothing more than teenage hysteria. Garson Kanin spoofed it all in a story called *Do Re Mi,* about a racketeer who gets involved with jukeboxes.

In 1956 at Twentieth Century-Fox, the project was taken over by the endlessly inventive, former cartoonist Frank Tashlin. Tashlin had begun his film career working as an errand boy for Max Fleischer in New York, and subsequently worked for Ub Iwerks and Warners before directing live action. By the mid-'50s, when *Do Re Mi* came along, Tashlin had been directing the better Martin-Lewis pictures.

Tashlin's version of *Do Re Mi* became *The Girl Can't Help It.* Tashlin exploited the excessive endowments of Jayne Mansfield as the blonde who doesn't want the stardom that racketeer Edmund O'Brien has mapped out for her; she wants a husband, a home, and children. Because Mansfield had no discernible musical talent—that was the point—she was given the opportunity to use her squeaky voice like a police siren to punctuate the rock-song parody "Rock Around the Rock Pile." Actually written by Bobby Troup and played by a band led by rock-movie regular Ray Anthony, the song was supposed to have been written by the racketeer while in prison for income-tax invasion.

The Girl Can't Help It was packed with an impressive array of musical stars, even while it parodied Sam Katzman's brand of rock 'n' roll quickie. The list of recording stars included Fats Domino singing "Blue Monday," The Platters singing "Great Pretender," Little Richard, Gene Vincent, The Treniers, Eddie Fontaine, The Chuckles, Johnny Olenn, Nino Tempo, Eddie Cochrane, and the exquisite Abbey Lincoln, then beginning more than a decade of occasional screen appearances.

Little Richard's version of "She's Got It" was an eye-opener—probably the first onscreen performance in a studio movie in which a black recording artist was shown with full-bodied, unapologetic sexuality. More placid but equally interesting was the way Tashlin presented Julie London singing Arthur Hamilton's "Cry Me a River." London plays the singer who makes haunting, diaphanous appearances in various settings—an effect that predates the MTV music-video style by thirty years.

The Girl Can't Help It benefitted mightily from being presented in Twentieth's CinemaScope format. Lionel Newman was the music director assigned to the project; Ken Darby was credited with vocal supervision, though it's tough to imagine Darby coaching, say, Little Richard. Although the picture managed to get in the last word on what was still an infant genre, the rock 'n' roll musical, not every review was favorable. *Newsweek* said, "The underlying theory behind the enterprise seems to be that if Elvis could do it, so could anybody."

Not exactly. While *The Girl Can't Help It* was playing its first run, Twentieth Century-Fox had already prepared Elvis Presley's film debut, *Love Me Tender*, with Lionel Newman supervising the music again. (The studio thought enough of the picture's box-office prospects to assign Edward Powell to the orchestrations.) Elvis's character didn't survive in his first picture—he was competing with brother Richard Egan for Debra Paget's affections—but it didn't matter: he sang four songs, including the title tune, which is based on the nineteenth-century American sentimental song "Aura Lee."

Elvis was clearly feeling his way in this old-fashioned Western; the studios, too, were searching for a vehicle that would capture the star's considerable stage magnetism. There had been nothing like the Elvis phenomenon since Sinatra in 1943–1944, and there'd be nothing like it again until the Beatles in 1963–1964. Although Sinatra's and the Beatles' earliest movies were better, Elvis's matinee-idol aura was beyond compare.

One of the songs that helped make Elvis famous was "Hound Dog," originally recorded by Big Mama Thornton in 1953. The "Hound Dog" writers, Jerry Leiber (born 1933) and Mike Stoller (born 1933), were transplanted Easterners. Leiber, the son of Polish-Jewish immigrants, absorbed black music and dialect while working at his widowed mother's Baltimore grocery store. Stoller grew up on Long Island idolizing the Harlem stride pianists, with his mother's love of show tunes thrown into the mix. Leiber and Stoller met in Los Angeles in 1949. Leiber was selling records; Stoller was taking composition lessons from Arthur Lange, whose 1945 scoring assignment *Along Came Jones* (with Gary Cooper) subsequently inspired Leiber and Stoller's hit for the Coasters.

As a result of the success of "Hound Dog," Leiber and Stoller were invited to write for the next three Presley movies. *Loving You* (1956) is widely regarded as a slightly altered Elvis biopic, with Lizabeth Scott playing a female version of Col. Tom Parker. *Jailhouse*

Mike Stoller & Jerry Leiber, New York City, 1959
Photo by Halley Erskine. Courtesy Mike Leiber and Jerry Stoller

Rock (1957) boasts that terrific title tune, with the essence of rock 'n' roll—"Once threw a party in the county jail"—imprisoned inside its lyric. *King Creole* (1958) is interesting primarily for being adapted from Harold Robbins's novel *A Stone for Danny Fisher* (published before Robbins became a one-man potboiling industry). *Loving You* and *King Creole* were made at Paramount, with the perenially game Walter Scharf handling the musical direction; *Jailhouse Rock* was filmed at Metro, where Jeff Alexander had the honor. Neither the songwriters nor the music directors had trouble with Elvis, whose behavior, it was said, was polite and professional.

Then Elvis was drafted. It was 1958, the year of the long studio musicians' strike. His army induction made his fans and handlers alike weep. In his absence, the most arresting rock 'n' roll on the screen could be heard in the edgy, cheap MGM B pictures, *High School Confidential* (1958) and *Girls' Town* (1959), with Mamie Van Doren doing her bad girl–good woman routine. Elvis, discharged in 1960, resumed his movie career with *G.I. Blues*, a box-office success but a tremendous comedown from the previous pictures.

The comedown would last for the next decade, until he stopped making movies altogether. During the '60s there were some small pleasures. *Viva Las Vegas* (1964) owes as much to George Sidney's expert direction and Ann-Margret's shimmying as it does to Elvis's performance. *Girl Happy* (1965), his eighteenth picture, is oddly watchable, perhaps because the old musicals master Joe Pasternak was at the helm. Elvis's pictures almost always made a profit, but musically the times were passing them—if not him—by. Joseph Lilley, the longtime Paramount music director, handled the music on several of these; as late as 1965, the conductor on Elvis's *Girl Happy* was Georgie Stoll, the quintessential company man at Metro's music department. In the '70s Elvis appeared strictly in concert movies. It was a relief—no more screenplays shoehorning him into unwieldy stories. Even during his bloated, jump-suited Las Vegas days, Elvis never forgot that rock 'n' roll ought to be hot enough to scorch.

The early '60s teen films set on the beaches of Florida or southern California were cool rather than scorching. Display bikini-clad girls and muscular lads, throw in a rock song or two and a romantic plot, and usually you made your money back.

Columbia's *Gidget* (1959) was one of the first, putting Sandra Dee on the beach, but it was more sentimental than the pictures to come, and the old-fashioned Hollywood music was by veteran George Duning. MGM's *Where the Boys Are* co-opted the old Fox formula of portraying several young women looking for boyfriends (if not husbands). This was another Joe Pasternak production, with Georgie Stoll conducting. Connie Francis, one of the three "good" co-eds of the four who arrive in Fort Lauderdale for Easter week, sang the title song. The music and the movie were only minimally rock 'n' roll, but they added the sun-and-fun ingredient that would be exploited over the next few years, particularly in the *Beach* series distributed by American International Pictures (A.I.P.).

A.I.P.'s *Beach Party* (1963) had Bob Cummings "studying" the mating rituals of young surfer types, with Dick Dale and the Del-tones playing their twangy surf music. What *Beach Party* was really about, however, was female bodies—Dorothy Malone's and Annette Funicello's, as well as those of the "beach bunnies." Beach Boys' guiding light Brian Wilson can be glimpsed as an extra in the film. The series probably hit its peak with *Beach Blanket Bingo* (1965), then rode downhill.

Ride the Wild Surf (1964) was produced at Columbia, but of the same ilk as the budget A.I.P. beach product. Les Baxter, who handled the background scores for many of the A.I.P. films, scored this one as well. The surf songs—including a roaring title tune that became an archetype of surf songs—were performed mostly by Jan and Dean, whose first hit, "Jenny Lee," went back to 1958, released on the Arwin label owned by Doris Day's husband Marty Melcher. A slightly older, budget version of the Beach Boys, Jan and Dean were very good at what they did until an auto accident left Jan in a coma for twenty-one days in 1966; he never fully recovered as a performer.

During the half decade of the beach movies' heyday, the focus shifted from the teen idols who'd been part of the so-called "Philadelphia sound" to a group of increasingly blonde, all-American non-musical actors. "The teen idols were white," Michael Shore and Dick Clark reminded readers of *The History of American Bandstand,* "but they were also heavily *ethnic,* specifically Italian. Thus, while ostensibly 'safe,' they also had a particularly exotic appeal to Middle America." Annette Funicello was from upstate New York; Frankie Avalon (Avallone) and Bobby Rydell (Ridarelli) were from Philadelphia; Connie Francis (Conchetta Franconero) was from New Jersey. In the *Beach* series, these stars sang songs by a battery of writers, notably Gary Usher and L.A. disk jockey Roger Christian. Eventually, they were edged out by non-musical actors—among them, Linda Evans, Noreen Corcoran, Tommy Kirk, Joel McCrea's son Jody, and Deborah Walley—who were less exotic but considered more photogenic. But the music itself began to run behind the times. Before the genre faded, its harmonizing godfathers, the Beach Boys, made only one on-camera appearance in *The Girls on the Beach* (1965). Ironically, that picture was about the title characters' failure to arrange for a local concert by the Beatles.

o   o   o

"People are talking about . . . The Beatle movie, *A Hard Day's Night*," whispered *Vogue* in 1964, "which, in spite of jiggly camera work and no plot, silverplates the boys' total appeal." Although *Vogue*'s single sentence got it half wrong—the camera work wasn't "jiggly," though much of it was hand-held, and there *was* a plot of sorts—the magazine was correct about the movie confirming The Beatles' appeal. There had been nothing like *A Hard Day's Night*.

Much of the credit ought to go to producer Walter Shenson (born 1921), an unusually kindly former publicist for Hal Roach who turned to scriptwriting and producing in the late '40s. Shenson hired playwright-television writer Alun Owen to prepare a script.

The Beatles emulated various American musical performers—McCartney was a fan of Fats Waller and Peggy Lee. Lennon went in for Little Richard and Chuck Berry. George Harrison listened to Carl Perkins. Collectively, however, they leaned heavily on the expert musical mind of George Martin.

Martin had begun producing comedy recordings for EMI's budget Parlophone label—in the 1950s, Spike Milligan and Peter Sellers of *The Goon Show*, then in the mid-'60s, the *Beyond the Fringe* team of Peter Cook, Dudley Moore, Jonathan Miller, and Alan Bennett. After a trip to Los Angeles, where he sat in on the recording sessions of Sinatra's *Come Fly with Me* (Billy May arranged and conducted), Martin returned to London determined to extract a better sound from his studio microphones. In 1962 Beatles manager Brian Epstein brought Martin a record that the Liverpool group had cut. Martin recalled: "I must admit, I didn't do a handstand and say, 'This is the next coming.' I said it was OK, interesting, and that I'd like to meet the guys, spend an afternoon in the studio with them, and we'll see what we can do." When Martin's colleagues at EMI learned he was producing a new group called the Beatles, with their idiosyncratic spelling, and heard the first recording, "Love Me Do," they said to him, "It's another one of your funny ones, George, isn't it?"

The money the boys earned was downright hilarious. Financially, in the beginning, they proved to be a greater phenomenon than even

Elvis Presley. *A Hard Day's Night* showed they were adorable screen actors as well. In addition to their previous hits "I Wanna Hold Your Hand," "She Loves You," "I Should Have Known Better," and "Anytime at All," the boys performed at least six other songs, including the puppyish "This Boy" and the title tune. All of these were credited to Lennon & McCartney; it was only years later that most understood the peculiar authorial arrangements: for the most part, John and Paul wrote separately, helping each other with a line or two but always taking co-credit. The title line came from Ringo, a fount of naive aphorisms.

"He would say to us, 'God, it's been a hard day's night,'" McCartney remembered. "We'd say, 'Say that again.' 'Tomorrow Never Knows' is also one of his. Ringo talked in titles. We had to follow him around with a notebook and a pencil. You never knew what he would say next."

Richard Lester, a Philadelphian who began his show-business career as a director and musician at local CBS stations, had been based in England since the late '50s. Lester also composed music which, like Frank Tashlin's experience as an animator, gave him a certain feeling for rhythm. Before *A Hard Day's Night*, Lester directed *It's Trad Dad* (1962, aka *Ring a Ding Rhythm*), a British variation on the old Sam Katzman formula. (Helen Shapiro and Craig Douglas were the adolescents championing rockers Chubby Checker, Gene Vincent, and Del Shannon, among others.) The movie itself is more "trad" than *A Hard Day's Night,* but you can pick up hints of what would become Lester's patented style: the easygoing action; the quick cuts; the gentle mockery. Add to it a Godard-like probing, unpretentious camera, and *A Hard Day's Night* visual style is in place.

Help! (1965) proved that, despite the same filmmaking unit on hand (except for writer Alun Owen), it was the Beatles being the Beatles that charmed; the songs, particularly "Ticket to Ride" and the title song, were marvelous, but the boys just weren't around enough. The Lester style, splashed with color, now seemed a little self-conscious as it chased a plot that had something to do with cults and Victor Spinetti acting officious.

But *A Hard Day's Night* imitations were already pouring into theaters, most of which lacked the original's spirit. *Having a Wild Weekend* (1965) supposedly portrayed a typical weekend in swinging London starring the pop group Dave Clark Five. Sadly, Clark lacked onscreen charisma, although costar Barbara Ferris is fascinating as a Mod model. It was director John Boorman's first film. *Ferry Cross the Mersey* (1965) was a vehicle for Gerry (Marsden) and the Pacemakers, another Liverpool group represented by Brian Epstein. The group competes in a band contest and sings "Don't Let the Sun Catch You Crying" and the title tune.

These were relatively innocent romps that came to seem quaint as grittier, raunchier bands ascended, and new film techniques—some of them, in fact, popularized by Richard Lester—invited experimentation. French art-director Jean-Luc Godard's *One Plus One* (1970, widely released as *Sympathy for the Devil*) interspersed sequences of the Rolling Stones in rehearsal and a recording session to make some inevitable, if not always comprehensible, statements about revolution. (Jagger working out the lyric to "Sympathy for the Devil" may be the best scene in the movie.) *One Plus One* was influential to filmmakers out of all proportion to its box-office take, which was nearly nil. It seemed to influence Lindsay Anderson's *O Lucky Man!* (1973), in which Alan Price, formerly of the Animals, sang and played a rock 'n' roll keyboard commentary on the narrative, a bleak contemporary *Candide*, with Malcolm McDowell as a coffee salesman on the rise.

Between *One Plus One* and *O Lucky Man!* came *Performance* (1970), with Jagger as a kind of townhouse satan giving refuge to on-the-lam gangster James Fox. The picture, by Nicholas Roeg and Douglas Cammell, tapped into Jagger's startling, androgynous charisma: when he lewdly sings "Memo from Turner" wearing a pin-striped suit, lipstick, and eye shadow, you know that some old rock 'n' roll mores are being shattered. Most of the music was handled by the Americans Jack Nitzsche and Randy Newman, each of whom would record frequently—Nitzsche primarily as producer, Newman as singer-songwriter—over the next decade.

Back in America, the singer-songwriters had taken over the rock scene. The first studio movie to clearly reflect this was *The Graduate* (1967). Director Mike Nichols was a Simon and Garfunkel fan, and invited Paul Simon to write several songs for the film. All of them were scrapped except "Mrs. Robinson," and Nichols added four previously recorded Simon and Garfunkel songs, including "The Sound of Silence" and "Scarborough Fair." Dave Grusin, then thirty-two, had just scored the Norman Lear production *Divorce American Style*; *The Graduate* was to be released by Embassy Pictures, of which Lear was the prime force, so Grusin was brought in to provide an underscore.

This was the musical set-up as *The Graduate* was being cut in the early spring of 1967. Simon and Garfunkel were piecing together *Bookends*, the "concept" album that remains their best, and put "Mrs. Robinson" on it. But Columbia Records, awarded soundtrack rights by Embassy, wanted a soundtrack album, too. Columbia A&R man Ed Kleban (who subsequently wrote the lyrics for *A Chorus Line*) pointed out that the label couldn't just re-release the four Simon and Garfunkel songs lifted from its own 1965 album *The Sound of Silence*. So Columbia included Grusin's underscore and released *The Graduate* soundtrack just weeks before *Bookends* in spring 1968. Sales for one boosted the other. The soundtrack album was the first to exploit its underscore—the connective musical tissue of the movie—along with its pop-rock songs.

Hollywood tried hard to replicate *The Graduate*'s critical and commercial success by pushing youthful alienation. But the few really interesting movies aimed at the youth market were awkward and cheaply made, away from the big studios. A.I.P.'s *Wild in the Streets* (1968), in which Christopher Jones plays a pop star turned U.S. president who institutes compulsory retirement at age thirty, featured a score by Les Baxter and songs by Brill Building stalwarts Barry Mann and Cynthia Weil. *Easy Rider* (1969) was released by Columbia but populated by A.I.P. veterans and filled out with songs by various bands, notably The Band's "The Weight" (by Robbie Robertson) and Steppenwolf's "The Pusher" (by Hoyt Axton). Best and gawkiest of all was Arthur Penn's *Alice's Restaurant* (1969), in which Arlo Guthrie's comic narrative slithered through the movie, with Pete Seeger brightening things in Woody Guthrie's hospital room, and Joni Mitchell's "Songs to Aging Children" eulogizing at the snowy, heartbreaking funeral in the Berkshires.

In this late-'60s period, rock 'n' roll documentaries most fluidly captured the ethos of the era and its music. The primitive mama of them all was *The T.A.M.I. Show* (1964), a Santa Monica Civic Auditorium concert—featuring James Brown, Smokey and the

Miracles, the Rolling Stones, and many others—recorded by television cameras and later transferred to film by Steve Binder. (The title stands for Teenage Awards Music International.) *Monterey Pop* (1967) was the marvelous filmed record of the Summer of Love festival in Monterey, California, highlighted by Janis Joplin's apoplectic "Ball and Chain," Jimi Hendrix's coital immolation of his guitar, and Ravi Shankar's raga. *Gimme Shelter* and *Let It Be,* both released in 1970 and, respectively, about the Rolling Stones and the Beatles, were not as much fun but revealed a lot—some of it inadvertently—about the two bands. *Woodstock* (1970) added widescreen and interviews to the genre; if everything seemed a little self-conscious, including the music, it was the price paid for being embraced by the mainstream. Like the pre-Vietnam rock 'n' roll musicals of the late 1950s, these rock documentaries gave movie audiences an earful they might not have been otherwise exposed to.

The same was true for *Shaft* (1971) and *Superfly* (1972). These were black urban crime thrillers—melodramas, really—that got tremendous mileage out of their scores. No one who saw its telecast can forget Isaac Hayes's Academy Awards show performance of his own theme from *Shaft,* seated at a mobile, illuminated electric keyboard and wearing a costume made of metal chains. This was audacious, unapologetically black, and terribly show biz. And the entire *Shaft* soundtrack was a smash hit.

Curtis Mayfield wrote and sang the theme to *Superfly* and its hit single, "Freddie's Dead." Mayfield, like Isaac Hayes, was born in 1942 and writing hits early—"For Your Precious Love" hit the charts when he was sixteen—with a style that soon evolved into an immediately identifiable sound, shooting off lightning bolts with his near-falsetto voice. Over the next few years Mayfield scored several movies in Hollywood.

But the wave of black films rolled back as quickly as it came in. Too many of the films aimed at black audiences were unnecessarily violent, pandering, and toted soundtracks that had the same quasi-Stax sound, with its gymnasium echoes and Steve Cropper–like guitar riffs. Far more influential during these years was Perry Henzell's *The Harder They Come* (1972), a cheaply made film that exploited reggae and an outlaw ethos. The movie sent audiences into stores to buy the soundtrack featuring Jimmy Cliff, and spawned another dozen reggae pictures. Meanwhile, Curtis Mayfield contributed to the small, often delightful *Sparkle* (1976), about a Supremes–like group with the statuesque Lonette McKee's great performance. And the comedy *Car Wash* (1976) neatly closed out the black-pop line with a terrific set of songs by Rose Royce. (A decade later Madonna had a hit record with one of them, "Love Don't Live Here Anymore.")

In 1977 the Bee Gees' songs for *Saturday Night Fever* swarmed all over the charts. Their songs, and a few by other artists, were expertly strung together by David Shire, one of the more versatile musicians in the business, for the film. The credit sequence, in which the title tune plays over a high-heeled John Travolta strutting along a Bay Ridge avenue, brought rock 'n' roll back to where it began in the movies: to the city streets and clubs, where danger lurks indifferently alongside the promise of one wild night.

Travolta was back the following year in *Grease* (1978), the spirited neo-'50s rock 'n' roll musical that proved to be Hollywood's last successful musical film. The songs, by Jim Jacobs and Warren Casey, had the appropriate Brill Building texture. In its first theatrical run, *Grease*'s phenomenal box-office receipts suggested not so much a wave of nostalgia as a weariness with the then-current rock scene, which was changing over from disco to punk.

The Sex Pistols, the Clash, the Ramones, the New York Dolls—these punk rock groups and others like them unquestionably brought something to the party. But their appeal lay primarily in their snarling, nihilistic attitude rather than their music, which was often devoid of harmonic structure and inaccessible to the casual listener. The willful lack of joy in punk rock—the lack, in fact, of any positive feeling—made it all wrong for Hollywood exploitation. (This was exactly the way most punk rockers wanted it.) While it dissipated, the punk scene became the subject of Penelope Spheeris's fine documentary *The Decline of Western Civilization* (1981). Focusing on the L.A.–based groups, including Black Flag and X, that performed blocks away from the movie studios, the documentary was as close as the movies dared get to punk. (*Decline* was financed outside the studio system.)

The Who, whose onstage antics anticipated the punks', had filmed their rock opera *Tommy* in 1975 (directed by Ken Russell), and now inspired Franc Roddam's 1979 feature *Quadrophenia*, which introduced the Police's bassist Sting to the screen. But the Who, like most of the bands at the forefront of '60s and '70s rock, splintered: flamboyant drummer Keith Moon died in 1978, and guitarist Pete Townshend would soon become an editor at the London publishing house Faber & Faber.

In American movies, the end of the decade of the rock singer-songwriter resulted in *One-Trick Pony* (1980), Paul Simon's wan examination of an aging musician. Within the next couple of years, rockers began to recede from the movie screen. By 1981 Hollywood had found gold in the linear electronic music of Tangerine Dream (*Thief* and *Risky Business*), the rock band from Germany, and Vangelis (*Chariots of Fire* and *Blade Runner*), the composer from Greece. Their music exploited the pulse of rock music but remained antiseptic. One missed the raucousness of Bill Haley and His Comets, the bawdiness of Little Richard, the ingratiating mischievousness of the Beatles.

WHERE HAVE YOU GONE, JOE DIMAGGIO?

Five months before *Saturday Night Fever* opened, John Williams's music for *Star Wars* poured out of cinema sound systems. Overnight, the symphonic score was made respectable again. After a decade of rock 'n' roll compilations, of quirky use of regional musical material with limited instrumentation, movie music was ready to return to the use of big orchestras. If *Star Wars* hadn't been a blockbuster, it wouldn't have happened.

Twenty years later, despite the increased versatility of electronic instruments, the avenue reopened by Williams remains open. "The orchestra has a limited sound palette, synthesizers a vast one," composer Trevor Jones (*Last of the Mohicans*) admitted to *Time* in September 1995. "But a synthesizer score sounds old very rapidly. Orchestral scoring is what you use for a longer shelf life." There are probably more proficient, symphonically versed film composers working now than ever before. Of those composers appoximately a generation younger than Williams, a few worth mentioning include Michael Convertino (*Guarding Tess*), Mark Isham (*The Moderns*), Hans Zimmer (*Beyond Rangoon*), Elliot Goldenthal (*Heat*), James Horner (*Glory*), Michael Kamen (*Brazil*), James Newton Howard (*The Fugitive*), and Danny Elfman (*Batman*).

Like the composers and orchestrators working in the first two decades of sound, these composers come primarily from the United States or from Europe, from working bands as well as from conservatories. Almost all of them are white and male. This suggests to some observers that movie music has barely progressed a note, that the closed-shop employment practices Quincy Jones decried almost thirty years ago still dominate. Bad as the movies have become, however—and I think that, by and large, the Hollywood product is dumber than ever—the music of these younger men has invigorated movie music. Despite the inevitable, occasional ripoff, their scores are surprisingly fresh.

Meanwhile, the one indisputably great American art form—popular song—is nowhere in evidence in the movies. That is to say it's everywhere, usually in the wrong place. Instead of commissioning original new songs that might enhance a film story, or at least showcase the talent of one of its stars, most movie studios are using generic or nostalgic rock music to promote the recordings of their subsidiaries (or, in the case of Columbia Pictures and Sony Music, their music-parents). The recording arms of these companies have become the contemporary version of the old-time music fitters. "The operative word is cross-promotion," Neil Strauss wrote in a recent *New York Times* article. "For a studio that just spent $70 million on a film and wants to gain an edge in an increasingly competitive marketplace, a successful soundtrack with big-name artists released in advance of the movie can be extremely helpful." This isn't far from what Sam Coslow had in mind when, seventy years ago, he extolled the talkies' ability to plug a song. But it's a long way down from Coslow's "Cocktails for Two" to Gravity Kills' "Guilty" (from the 1996 *Seven*).

The current state of affairs was a long time in the making. The conglomerization of the Hollywood studios began in the 1950s, when MCA took over Universal, and accelerated in the 1960s. The cocoon-like atmosphere of the studio music departments—administrative protection provided by former or working musicians who ran interference with the front office—collapsed during this period, following the 1958 musicians' strike. Younger composers and orchestrators went freelance. Younger songwriters, trying not to depend on movie work, aligned themselves with recording artists or went into television.

There's no turning the clock back, of course. Just as the movies can't recapture the late '30s heyday of screwball comedy, so movie music can't return to the days of sweeping, nineteenth-century–influenced themes or the marvelous movie standards written between the '30s and '50s. The movies move at their own speed: twenty-four frames per second and usually several months behind the culture as a whole. Fortunately, the musicians are better trained than ever, independent and remarkably adventurous. Among film professionals who work in and out of Hollywood, they may represent the best hope for making the movies new again.

ENDNOTES

Introduction: Where You're Terrific If You're Even Good

page 1. "Go to the movies": Duke, *Listen Here!*, p. 3.

page 2. "The night the film": Fordin, *Getting to Know Him*, p. 149.

page 2. "I walked over": Rodgers, *Musical Stages*, p. 165.

page 2. "After I had completed": Amram, *Vibrations*, p. 383.

page 4. "With the development": Robert Russell Bennett, "Orchestration of Theater and Dance Music," Taylor, ed., *Music Lovers' Encyclopedia*, p. 781.

Chapter 1: Smile Through Your Fear and Sorrow

page 8. "364,000 pianos": Douglas, *Terrible Honesty*, p. 365.

page 8. "impresario Mitchell Mark": Beynon, *Musical Presentation of Motion Pictures,* p. 6.

page 9. Saint-Saëns's score for *L'Assassinat du Duc de Guise* can be heard played by The Ensemble Musique Oblique, Harmonia Mundi label, recorded 1993.

page 10.   "A Bulgarian": American Film Institute Oral History with Hugo Friedhofer, conducted by Irene Kahn Atkins, p. 43.

page 10.   "Meanwhile Adolph Zukor": Blum, *A Pictorial History of the Silents,* p. 26.

page 14.   "Robert Hood Bowers": Bowers is listed many times in Gillian Anderson's *Music for Silent Films 1894–1929.*

page 14.   "'the best' movie music": Beynon, *Musical Presentation of Motion Pictures,* p. 48.

page 15.   "The two men began": The account of the Herbert-Dixon correspondence comes from Wayne D. Shirley, "A Bugle Call to Arms for National Defense! Victor Herbert and His Score for *Fall of a Nation,*" included in Newsom, ed., *Wonderful Inventions.*

page 16.   "The musical program": Shirley, "A Bugle Call to Arms," p. 183.

page 16.   "Schertzinger's score for *Civilization*": Schertzinger's score for *Civilization* was orchestrated for piano, two saxophones, strings and drums—a common instrumentation for live accompaniment to silent pictures.

page 16.   "Hope-Crosby *Road* pictures": Crosby, *Call Me Lucky,* p. 157. Bing Crosby said of Schertzinger, "He was a quiet fellow, used to directing his pictures in leisurely fashion. His awakening was rude. For a couple of days when Hope and I tore free-wheeling into a scene, ad-libbing and violating all the accepted rules of movie-making, Schertzinger stole bewildered looks at the script, then leafed rapidly through it, searching for the lines we were saying."

page 17.   "The efficacy of the original score": Beynon, *Musical Presentation of Motion Pictures,* p. 48.

page 17.   "The trap drummer": Friedhofer AFI interview, pp. 20–21.

page 18.   "[The orchestra] would play the first ten minutes": Oral History with Murray Spivack, Academy of Motion Picture Arts & Sciences, conducted by Charles Degelman, p. 18.

page 19.   "Bold, bumptious, and self-confident": Thomson, *Virgil Thomson,* p. 75.

page 19.   "He moved into the flat": Fitch, *Sylvia Beach and the Lost Generation,* pp. 191–192. As a pianist Antheil was as animated as anything on the screen in the 1920s. Adrienne Monnier, Sylvia Beach's lover, gave this account of his performing style: "When

[Antheil] plays his music he is terrible, he boxes with the piano; he riddles it with blows and perseveres furiously until the instrument, the public, and he himself are knocked out. When he is finished he is red, he sponges his forehead; he comes down from the ring with his forehead lowered, his shoulders rocking, his brows knitted, his fists still clenched tight. After a quarter of an hour he is in his right mind again; he laughs, he has forgotten everything."

page 19. "The motherly Beach described him": Fitch, *Sylvia Beach and the Lost Generation*, p. 150.

page 19. "Paris *Tribune* announced": Ibid., p. 191.

page 19. "claiming that the propellers": Ewen, *The New Book of Modern Composers*, p. 11.

page 20. "Until recently, Hans": The story of Erdmann's resurrected score comes from a "Morning Edition" interview with Gillian Anderson, conducted by Pat Dowell on National Public Radio and aired on Friday, August 5, 1994.

page 22. "For DeMille's *The Ten Commandments*": Larson, *Musique Fantastique*, p. 6.

page 23. "SPECIAL SCORE FOR 'Thief of Bagdad'": news clippings found in Mortimer Wilson Collection at the UCLA Archive of Popular American Music.

page 23. "More or less in the quasi-oriental idiom": Friedhofer AFI interview, p. 22.

page 25. "(Photographer Diane Arbus": Bosworth, *Diane Arbus*, p. 9.

page 28. "Alan Crosland didn't have the strength": Astor, *A Life on Film*, p. 48.

page 28. "But *The Jazz Singer*": Our identification with Jolson as the lead in *The Jazz Singer*, defying his cantor father on the Lower East Side, is so strong that it can be jolting to recall that Jolson, after spending his earliest years in Russia, actually grew up in the San Francisco Bay Area. His father was an Oakland tailor.

page 29. "The thing that threw me": Kobal, *Gotta Sing, Gotta Dance*, p. 31.

page 31. "Suddenly something goes wrong": Knight, *The Liveliest Art*, p. 155.

page 33. "Raksin was thrilled.": From David Raksin's excellent account in "Life with Charlie," in *Wonderful Inventions*.

Chapter 2: Every Note . . . Is Like a Lover's Kiss

page 37.   "We've had our eye": Coslow, *Cocktails for Two*, p. 95.

page 37.   "The system of planting": Meyer, *The Gold in Tin Pan Alley*, p. 222.

page 39.   "Winnie Sheehan attended a production": Midge Polesie's "Cafe Society" column, *What's Cookin' in New York*, July 3, 1954.

page 39.   "According to Butler": From the Directors Guild of America Oral History with David Butler, conducted by Irene Kahn Atkins.

page 40.   "Across town at Paramount": Early Paramount music personnel comes partly from Mark Evans, *Soundtrack: The Music of the Movies*, pp. 7, 15. The Paramount Circuit had long relied on husband-and-wife organists Jesse and Helen Crawford, so they too became part of the studio's original music department.

page 41.   "In late 1928 his publisher Max Dreyfus": Wilk, *They're Playing Our Song*, p. 101.

page 43.   "The voice, never weighty": F. Paul Driscoll, "I Dream of Jeanette," *Opera News*, August 1995, p. 50.

page 44.   "(Uncle Carl Laemmle": *Halliwell's Filmgoer's Companion*, p. 659.

page 45.   "Picture technicians weren't developed": Crosby, *Call Me Lucky*, p. 99.

page 46.   "Who is that guy?": Gilbert, *Lost Chords*, pp. 329–330.

page 49.   "By the end of 1929": Friedhofer AFI interview, p. 25.

page 49.   "Once a person's relation": McWilliams, *Southern California Country*, p. 336.

page 50.   "The best brains in town": *Reno Nevada Journal*, November 4, 1931.

page 51.   The account of the early years at Fox is drawn from the Friedhofer interview, and from Arthur Lange's unpublished memoir, found at the New York Library of Performing Arts.

page 54.   Material on Al Dubin comes primarily from McGuire, *Lullaby of Broadway*.

page 56.   "I couldn't stand it here then": Wilk, *They're Playing Our Song*, p. 119.

page 56.   "They're singing the wrong lyrics!": Harry Warren AFI Oral History, conducted by Irene Kahn Atkins, p. 33.

page 56.   "Give me thirty-two bars of schmalz": Ibid., p. 119.

page 57. "Forbstein's secretary told Al Dubin": Ibid., p. 46.

page 58. "One of the workmen complained": McGuire, *Lullaby of Broadway*, p. 128.

page 60. "universal church": Tyler, *Three Faces of the Film*.

page 60. "Jewish music": Douglas, *Terrible Honesty*, p. 358.

page 61. "Paired with Coslow": Caslow, *Cocktails for Two*, p. 99. Much of this material on the Hollywood days of Rodgers & Hart is drawn from Marx and Clayton, *Rodgers & Hart: Bewitched, Bothered and Bewildered*.

page 66. "opened the *Herald-Examiner*": Gary Marmorstein, "Lorenz Hart at 100," *Performing Arts*, May 1995, p. 19.

Chapter 3: Open Your Golden Gate

page 68. "Maximilian Raoul Steiner": Biographical material on Steiner is drawn from Gammond, *The Oxford Companion to Popular Music*, and Thomas, *Music for the Movies*.

page 70. "Music until then": Thomas, *Music for the Movies*, p. 113.

page 71. "In the scoring of his pictures": Behlmer, *Memo from Selznick*, p. 119.

page 72. "It is a hell of a feeling": Steiner quoted by Rudy Behlmer in booklet accompanying vinyl collection *Fifty Years of Film Music, 1923–1973*, Warner Bros. 1298, unpaged.

page 72. "Murray Spivack was unable to intercept": Spivack Oral History, AMPAS, p. 65.

page 73. "the second most powerful man": Wallis and Higham, *Starmaker*, p. 36.

page 73. "My first choice": Behlmer, *Memo from Selznick*, p. 193.

page 74. "the great Southern pieces": Ibid., p. 217.

page 74. "Steiner turned in his piano sketches": Friedhofer quoted in *Fifty Years of Film Music*.

page 74. "Sensing disaster": Behlmer, *Memo from Selznick*, pp. 228–229.

page 74. "In case you don't know it": Ibid., p. 231.

page 75. "Max had a way": Friedhofer AFI interview, p. 149.

page 75. "And of course": Ibid., p. 154.

page 75. *Casablanca* material drawn from Wallis and Higham, *Starmaker*, p. 90, and from Behlmer, *Fifty Years of Film Music*.

page 76. "Reviewing the Overture": Quoted by Slonimsky in *Music Since 1900*, p. 121.

page 77. "the motif of the cheerful heart": Ibid., p. 143.

page 77. "The boy has so much talent": Karlin, *Listening to Movies*, p. 284.

page 77. "Writing for the films": Ewen, *American Composers Today*.

page 78. "His copyist and amanuensis": Friedhofer AFI interview, p. 57.

page 79. "After arriving in": The account of Korngold's decision to stay in Hollywood is drawn from the *Fifty Years of Film Music* booklet, and from the PBS television documentary, *Music for the Movies: The Hollywood Sound*, telecast November 1995.

page 79. "*Robin Hood* is no picture for me": Behlmer, *Behind the Scenes*, pp. 84–85.

page 80. "freelancer Milan Roder": Friedhofer AFI interview, p. 125.

page 80. "I shall certainly be ready": Behlmer, *Inside Warner Bros.*, p. 142.

page 80. "Erich Korngold's music is good": Ferguson, *The Film Criticism of Otis Ferguson*, p. 416.

page 81. "As you know we have been receiving": Behlmer, *Inside Warner Bros.*, pp. 270–271.

page 82. "William Conrad, the square-jawed and -bodied actor": Thomas, *Music for the Movies*, p. 122. Conrad is unnamed by Tony Thomas.

page 83. "For more than thirty": Taylor, *Strangers in Paradise*, p. 49.

page 84. "composer Miklos Rozsa": Rozsa, *A Double Life*, p. 109.

page 84. "The Schoenberg story": this story has been told in various ways. See Taylor, *Strangers in Paradise*, p. 81, and Friedrich, *City of Nets*, p. 34.

page 84. "In 1909, when he was twenty-one": material on Toch drawn primarily from Lawrence Weschler's introduction to Toch's *The Shaping Forces of Music*.

page 86. "a master orchestrator": Chaplin, *The Golden Age of Movie Musicals and Me*, p. 70.

page 87. "Long ago, Dr. Rosenbaum's settings": Jarrell, *Pictures from an Institution*, p. 135.

page 87. "Warners released": Slonimsky, *Music Since 1900*, pp. 442–443.

page 88.   "While still in Paris": Baxter, *The Hollywood Exiles,* pp. 220–221.

page 89.   "Many congregated regularly": Ibid., p. 125.

page 89.   "Here many European emigrants": Dunaway, *Huxley in Hollywood,* p. 88.

page 89.   "Through the fund's influence": Taylor, *Strangers in Paradise,* pp. 139–140.

page 89.   "a musical academic": Baxter, *The Hollywood Exiles,* p. 202.

page 89.   "When a producer told": Rozsa, *A Double Life,* p. 114.

page 90.   "Determined to get Krenek": The Goldwyn story involving Ernst Krenek comes from Taylor, *Strangers in Paradise,* p. 84.

page 90.   "Hans Salter arrived": Most of the material on Hans Salter's early years is drawn from the Academy of Motion Picture Arts & Sciences Oral History. Salter was interviewed by Warren Sherk.

page 92.   "Like Salter, both men": a good account of the Deanna Durbin years at Universal is in Schatz, *The Genius of the System,* p. 238.

page 93.   "Before joining UFA": Thomas, *Music for the Movies,* p. 35.

page 94.   "In Paris": Zolotow, *Billy Wilder,* p. 51.

page 94.   "Within days of their arrival": Material on Jurmann and Kaper drawn partly from author's interview with Yvonne Jurmann, November 1995.

page 95.   "All God's Chillun Got Rhythm" can be heard on *Duke Ellington Presents Ivie Anderson.* Columbia KG 32064.

page 95.   "Two guys in San Francisco": Server, *Screenwriter,* p. 143.

page 96.   "Watery imitation Rachmaninoff": Smith, *Musical Comedy in America,* p. 332.

page 97.   "Alec Wilder's idea": Wilder, *American Popular Song,* p. 495.

page 97.   "In 1940 I had": Taylor, *Strangers in Paradise,* p. 230.

page 98.   "'insolent' rhythm": Tiomkin and Buranelli, *Please Don't Hate Me,* p. 51.

page 98.   "this is what an artist": Ibid., pp. 111–112.

page 99.   "Rasch's promotional material": Amberg, *Ballet in America,* p. 167.

page 100.   "To handle Tiomkin's music": Behlmer, *Behind the Scenes,* p. 32.

page 100. "Who does he think": Tiomkin, *Please Don't Hate Me*, pp. 185–186.

page 100. "A few weeks later": Material on Mischa and Constantin Bakaleinikoff is drawn primarily from the Bakaleinikoff Collection at the USC Cinema-Television Dept.

page 100. "Capra gave Tiomkin": Tiomkin, *Please Don't Hate Me*, p. 192.

page 101. "Later, at Chasen's": Ibid., p. 226.

page 101. "In 1945, David O. Selznick": Friedrich, *City of Nets*, p. 40.

page 101. "Tiomkin was a lousy composer": Arthur Morton interviewed by author, October 1996.

page 102. "Then there is the spectacular": Duke, *Listen Here!*, p. 309.

page 102. "Like Gershwin": Material on Duke's early years comes from Ewen's *American Composers Today* and *Panorama of American Popular Music*, p. 274.

page 103. "a movie caricature": Moross interviewed by Craig Reardon, April 16, 1979.

page 103. "We went to a preview once": Salter Oral History, AMPAS, p. 123.

page 104. "On September 13, 1944": The letter is quoted by Robert Evett in his essay on Schoenberg in *Atlantic Brief Lives: A Biographical Companion to the Arts*, pp. 683–84.

page 104. "The sextet wanted": The story of the Hollywood String Quartet's visit to Schoenberg's house is told by Tully Potter in his notes to the compact disk *Testament*, SBT-1031.

Chapter 4: Lonely Rivers Flow to the Sea

page 106. "In the early 1930s": Material on Lorentz is drawn primarily from Robert Snyder, *Pare Lorentz and the Documentary Film*.

page 106. "Fanfares, heavy orchestrations": Ferguson, *The Film Criticism of Otis Ferguson*, p. 456.

page 107. "Lorentz then consulted": Houseman, *Run-through*, p. 171.

page 107. "How much money": Thomson, *Virgil Thomson*, p. 259.

page 108. "Brant was such a natural": Ibid., pp. 260–261.

page 108. "This time Thomson": Ibid., p. 274.

page 109. "Lorentz, meanwhile": Copland and Perlis, *Copland: 1900–1942*, p. 290.

page 109. "Although no commission": Ibid., pp. 270–271.

page 110. "Like many New Yorkers": Ibid., p. 271.

page 110. "Left largely to his own devices": Ibid., p. 298.

page 111. "Just before the picture was released": Irwin Bazelon, *Film Music Notes, Vol. 2* (1949), quoted in Prendergast, *Film Music,* p. 95.

page 112. "(If you can't recall": "Plaisir d'Amour"'s transformation into the Presley hit "Can't Help Falling in Love" has a murky genesis. A credible version is that George David Weiss was asked to supply a lyric for the tune coming out of a music box in a Presley movie, and that his frequent partners, the famed A&R team Luigi Creatore and Hugo Peretti, made a new arrangement.

page 112. "Screenwriter Helen Deutsch": author's interview with Helen Deutsch, April 1983.

page 113. *The Big Country* score was recorded on vinyl on United Artists UAS 5004. A more complete, compact-disk version, with forty-two cues, can be heard on Screen Classics SC-1R-JM.

page 113. "Born in Brooklyn": Extensive material on the Young Composers' Group can be found in Copland and Perlis, *Copland,* pp. 190–207.

page 114. "vistas stunned him": Moross letter to Christopher Palmer, March 22, 1973.

page 116. Scores for *The Proud Rebel, Wagon Train, The War Lord, Rachel, Rachel* and several others are available on Silva SSD 1049.

page 116. *The Cardinal* was released on vinyl on Entr'acte ERS 6518. Notes by Royal S. Brown.

page 117. "Dishwater Tchaikovsky!": Moross interview with Craig Reardon, April 16, 1979.

page 117. "It stinks!": Copland and Perlis, *Copland,* p. 192.

page 117. "One of the Columbia": The account of Herrmann's early working relations with Welles comes from Houseman's *Run-through,* pp. 365–366.

page 118. "soundman James G. Stewart": Prendergast, *Film Music,* p. 54.

page 118. "Herrmann accompanies each scene": Christopher Palmer's notes were written for *The Classic Film Scores of Bernard Herrmann.* Charles Gerhardt conducting the National Philharmonia. Produced by George Korngold. RCA Victor 0707-2-RG.

page 119. "(In *Raising Kane*": Kael, *The Citizen Kane Book,* p. 67.

page 119. "text for Herrmann's *Salammbo*": Houseman, *Run-through,* p. 461.

page 122. "its high-pitched sounds": Leff, *Hitchcock & Selznick,* p. 165.

page 122. "Herrmann subsequently": "Portrait of Hitch" published by Sevenoaks, 1969.

page 123. "Of all Hitchcock's": An excellent version of the *Vertigo* score was recorded on compact disk by Sinfonia of London, conducted by Muir Mathieson. Mercury 422-106-2.

page 123. "Perhaps it's because": Alexander Walker interview with Hitchcock in *The Evening Standard,* March 24, 1965, quoted by David Thomson in *Movie Man,* p. 150.

page 123. "Hitchcock very rarely deals": Herrmann talks about film music on compact disk Milan DMG 731383643-2.

page 123. "Other TV work": Material on some of Herrmann's projects between the televised *A Christmas Carol* and *Taxi Driver* comes from David Benesty, interviewed by author, November 1995.

page 123. "In the year of *Vertigo*": Herrmann's scores for Charles Schneer were recorded on CD on *Bernard Herrmann: Classic Fantasy Scores.* ACN 7014.

page 124. "back to Los Angeles": Segaloff, *Hurricane Billy,* pp. 142–143.

page 124. "score was assembled": Friedhofer AFI interview, p. 127.

page 125. "Who's interested in your idea": Jerome Moross interview with Craig Reardon, April 16, 1979.

page 125. "For all of his facade": author's interview with David Benesty.

page 126. "The score was nominated": *Virgil Thompson,* p. 394.

page 126. "'Hollywood,' said Thomson": Ibid., p. 282.

page 126. "Another Martha Graham composer": Material on North is drawn from the Alex North Collection at the Academy of Motion Picture Arts & Sciences.

page 128. "I used to say": Karlin, *Listening to Movies,* p. 198.

page 129. *Spartacus* soundtrack (vinyl), MCA 1534.

page 129. "Mankiewicz, probably unsuited": Crist, *The Private Eye, the Cowboy, and the Very Naked Girl,* p. 13.

page 131. "On April 2, 1940": Material on Gold comes from the Ernest Gold Scrapbooks at the Academy of Motion Picture Arts & Sciences.

page 135.   "score unremittingly fills": *Halliwell's Film Guide*, p. 1005.

page 136.   "Elmer Bernstein appears": Some material on Bernstein is drawn from Zan Stewart, "Cinema Pianodiso," from the *Los Angeles Times* Calendar section, February 10, 1991.

page 137.   "It is repugnant": Thomas, *King Cohn*, p. 301.

page 137.   Parts of Bernstein's scores for *Sudden Fear, Sweet Smell of Success, The Man with the Golden Arm,* and *Walk on the Wild Side* can be heard on Choreo Records A-11.

page 138.   "padding and prowling": Christopher Palmer's notes accompany compact disk *Elmer Bernstein by Elmer Bernstein.* Composer conducts the Royal Philharmonic Pops Orchestra. Denon CO-75288.

page 138.   "I decided to focus": Ibid.

page 138.   Jack Jones's version of "Love with the Proper Stranger" can be heard on *Bewitched,* Kapp KS-3365. Only a few sequences of Bernstein's score for *Thoroughly Modern Millie* are included on the soundtrack, Decca DL 1500. By contrast, the *Hawaii* soundtrack—United Artists UAS 5143—is relatively rich and full.

page 140.   "When you do get to produce": Fintan O'Toole, "Elmer Bernstein Finds Himself in Tune with Movies," Arts & Leisure section, *New York Times,* October 28, 1990, p. 18.

page 140.   "Myself": Thomson, *Virgil Thomson*, p. 420.

Chapter 5: Work Like a Soul Inspired

page 142.   "In 1932": Material on Astaire's early years is drawn partly from Thomas, *Astaire: The Man, The Dancer.*

page 143.   "Absorbing these and the Castles' performances": Rosenberg, *Fascinating Rhythm*, p. 80.

page 143.   "These were the years": Kendall, *Where She Danced*, p. 182.

page 144.   "We would tell George": Rosenberg, *Fascinating Rhythm*, p. 26.

page 144.   "Gershwin sat down at the piano": Ibid., pp. 96–97.

page 145.   "Astaire's solo act": Douglas, *Terrible Honesty*, p. 360.

page 145.   "Of all the younger men": Farrar quoted on dust-jacket of Dwight Taylor, *Joy Ride.*

page 146.   "Mrs. Astor exclaimed": Green, *The Encyclopedia of the Musical Film*, p. 74.

page 148. "Hearing Borne work out": Croce, *The Fred Astaire & Ginger Rogers Book*, p. 91.

page 149. "Kern just never stopped": Server, *Screenwriter*, p. 194.

page 150. "Berlin owed his career": Douglas, *Terrible Honesty*, p. 374.

page 150. "Irving was so fecund": Server, *Screenwriter*, p. 190.

page 150. "Pandro Berman countered": Green, *Encyclopedia of Musical Film*, p. 285.

page 151. "Astaire went into the recording": Astaire's Brunswick recordings are collected on vinyl on Columbia PSG 32472.

page 152. "For 'Let's Call the Whole Thing Off'": Rosenberg, *Fascinating Rhythm*, p. 339.

page 154. "Arlene Croce reminds us": Croce, *The Fred Astaire & Ginger Rogers Book*, p. 154.

page 154. "Allan Scott was signed": Server, *Screenwriter*, p. 197.

page 157. "Kern, who suffered a fatal cerebral hemorrhage": Gary Marmorstein, "Music in the Air," *Stagebill, Show Boat* commemorative edition, 1996. The most poetic account of Kern's death is *Jerome Kern: His Life and Music* by Gerald Bordman.

page 158. "Crosby's original costar": Thomas, *Astaire: The Man, The Dancer*, p. 191.

Chapter 6: Or Would You Rather Be a Mule?

page 162. "When Leisen heard": Chierichetti, *Hollywood Director*, p. 120; Wilk, *They're Playing Our Song*, p. 106.

page 164. "In the movie the song was travestied": Sackett, *Hollywood Sings!*, p. 13.

page 164. "We'd get in the plane": David Butler Oral History, p. 183.

page 165. "I well remember a thin": Wilder, *American Popular Song*, p. 442.

page 165. "There was a little feeling": Butler Oral History, p. 187.

page 166. "contract stars Fred MacMurray and Jack Oakie": Green, *Encyclopedia of the Musical Film*, p. 239.

page 166. "for political good will": Crosby, *Call Me Lucky*, p. 168.

page 166. "He was the fastest": Butler Oral History, p. 186.

page 166. "When Burke wasn't available": Robert Tracy AFI Oral History, conducted by Irene Kahn Atkins, p. 365.

page 166. "The seed of the song": Sackett, *Hollywood Sings!*, p. 67.

page 166. "After eight years": quoted in accompanying booklet to Selections from *Going My Way* recorded on Decca A-405.

page 167. "When the sun goes down": Cahn, *I Should Care*, p. 167.

page 167. "Bessie with the Laughing Face": Chaplin, *The Golden Age of Movie Musicals and Me*, p. 69.

page 173. "Mel Tormé and Bob Wells": Tormé, *It Wasn't All Velvet*, p. 102.

page 175. "It has great weight": Wilder, *American Popular Song*, p. 448.

page 175. "One afternoon Burke": Cahn, *I Should Care*, p. 151.

page 178. "Someone at Paramount persuaded Cole": Sackett, *Hollywood Sings!*, p. 108.

page 178. "The reviews were so hostile": Shulman and Youman, *How Sweet It Was*, p. 166.

page 179. "Whatever the title": Sackett, *Hollywood Sings!*, pp. 137–138.

page 179. "Who's that little character": *The Frank Loesser Songbook*, p. 10.

page 179. "At first the kid": Ibid.

page 180. "Republic contract songwriter": Taylor, *Jule*, p. 83.

page 180. "Don't you ever": Ibid.

page 180. "the most popular songs": Fussell, *Wartime*, pp. 185–188.

page 181. "maybe about a hero": *The Frank Loesser Songbook*, p. 46.

page 182. "That's by the late Victor Young": *Sinatra at the Sands*, Reprise 1019.

page 183. "[Paramount's] chief composer": Rozsa, *A Double Life*, p. 131.

page 184. "[DeMille] had certain things": June Edgerton AFI Oral History, conducted by Irene Kahn Atkins, p. 536.

page 184. Sinatra's version of "Around the World in Eighty Days" was included on *Come Fly with Me*, Capitol SM-920.

page 185. "Writing a movie": *Chicago Sun-Times*, March 11, 1955.

page 185. "When Victor talked": Lee, *Miss Peggy Lee*, p. 188.

page 185. *The Jungle Book* album, RCA Victor DM 905. Miklos Rozsa conducted the NBC Orchestra. Sabu narrated.

page 186. "My contract with the picture": Rozsa, *A Double Life*, p. 131.

page 186. "In my naivete": Ibid., p. 132.

page 186. "Rozsa came in for more criticism": Ibid., p. 142.

page 187. "In order to capture": Ibid., p. 146.

page 188.   "Be sure to sell Ingrid's love": Rozsa, *A Double Life,* p. 147.

page 188.   "jazzy, xylophone Gershwinesque": Ibid., p. 148.

page 188.   Rozsa's epic scores were recorded on vinyl on *Miklos Rozsa Conducts His Great Film Music,* Angel S-36063.

Chapter 7: I Recall Picnic Time with You

page 190.   "Before he was twenty": Thomas, *King Cohn,* p. 11.

page 191.   "the operatic world": For a delightful analysis of opera stars in film, see David L. Parker's "Golden Voices, Silver Screen—Opera Singers As Movie Stars," *Wonderful Inventions.*

page 191.   "One way or another": Ibid., p. 85.

page 192.   "a dark-haired and very tall soprano": Thomson, *Virgil Thomson,* p. 139.

page 192.   "Moore went to see Harry Cohn": Thomas, *King Cohn,* p. 95.

page 193.   "At Cohn's instruction": Ibid., p. 97.

page 193.   "raising the standard": Ibid., p. 98.

page 193.   "(Cartoonist Al Capp": Parker, "Golden Voices, Silver Screen," p. 193.

page 195.   "Working in the Columbia Music Department": Chaplin, *The Golden Age of Movie Musicals and Me,* p. 46.

page 195.   "Hiya, Ruby!": Thomas, *King Cohn,* pp. 180–181.

page 196.   "Shrewdly, Stoloff": Rozsa, *A Double Life,* pp. 143–144.

page 196.   "Cornel Wilde is to be": Cahn, *I Should Care,* p. 85.

page 196.   "The Iturbi 78-rpm recordings": Prendergast, *Film Music,* p. 70.

page 196.   "I saw recently": Agate, *The Later Ego,* p. 354.

page 197.   "The lyric had been scrapped": Chaplin, *The Golden Age of Movie Musicals and Me,* pp. 51–53.

page 198.   "fiercely protective": Sackett, *Hollywood Sings!,* p. 13.

page 198.   "You worked a lot": Friedhofer AFI interview, p. 233.

page 200.   "a tall, amiable, rather gruff man": Chaplin, *The Golden Age of Movie Musicals and Me,* p. 14.

page 201.   "(The high point of the evening": Taylor, *Jule,* p. 93.

page 201.   "Jonie Taps is best described": Cahn, *I Should Care,* pp. 81–82.

page 202.   "Born in Richmond": Much of the biographical material on George Duning is drawn from the George Duning Scrapbooks at the USC Cinema-Television Library.

page 202. "There Duning met Arthur Morton": author's interview with Arthur Morton, October 1996.

page 204. "Are you nuts?!": Ibid.

page 205. "It was down to length": Kazan, *Elia Kazan: A Life*, p. 527.

page 205. "intrusive and inept-sounding": Prendergast, *Film Music*, p. 130.

page 206. "André Previn wrote"; "Hugo Friedhofer wrote": Previn's and Friedhofer's letters to Duning can be found in the Duning Scrapbooks, USC Cinema-Television Library.

page 207. "Record producer Bob Thiele": Phyllis McGuire quoted by Joe Smith in *Off the Record*, p. 60.

page 208. Duning's score for *Any Wednesday* was recorded on Warners W 1669.

Chapter 8: She Gave Your Very First Kiss to You

page 209. "Don' pinch mit the climaxes": Murray Spivack Oral History, AMPAS, p. 98.

page 209. "Newman, born in": Early biographical material on Newman comes partly from Thomas, *Music for the Movies*, pp. 54–55.

page 212. "The Great Engineer": Arthur Morton interview, October 1996.

page 212. "Joe Schenck was in Miami Beach": Taylor, *Jule*, p. 66.

page 212. "Styne was given an office": Ibid., p. 71.

page 213. "Between 1938 and 1943": Green, *Encyclopedia of the Musical Film*, p. 87.

page 213. "When the idea of a Berlin biopic": Behlmer, *Memo from Darryl F. Zanuck*, pp. 12–14.

page 214. "Jule Styne got the call": Taylor, *Jule*, p. 71.

page 214. "On days when they were expected": Ibid., p. 72.

page 214. "In 1929 he met Harry Revel": Gammond, *The Oxford Companion to Popular Music*, p. 485.

page 216. "cut the music department in half": Taylor, *Jule*, p. 73.

page 216. "Shirley Temple ended her stay": Behlmer, *Memo from Darryl F. Zanuck*, p. 37.

page 216. "After surgery": McGuire, *Lullaby of Broadway*, p. 145.

page 217. "the work of Mack Gordon": Kasha and Hirschhorn, *Notes on Broadway,* p. 78.

page 217. "which Alice Faye had to bow out of": Behlmer, *Memo from Darryl F. Zanuck,* p. 39.

page 217. Songs from the two Glenn Miller soundtracks were stunningly recorded on vinyl on *Glenn Miller's Original Film Soundtracks.* Twentieth Century-Fox-100-2.

page 218. "That sonofabitch could sell": Cahn, *I Should Care,* pp. 225–226.

page 218. "While Gordon and Warren were writing": Ibid., pp. 149–150.

page 218. "When I told him I was lonely": *Los Angeles Times,* June 3, 1949.

page 218. "In 1941 he asked Warners": McGuire, *Lullaby of Broadway,* pp. 153–154.

page 220. "On one of those trips": Ibid., p. 165.

page 221. "'Newman system' of scoring": Tracy AFI Oral History, p. 321.

page 221. "[Newman] was, of course, talented": Ibid., p. 336.

page 221. "He had a certain bravado": Spivack Oral History, AMPAS, p. 79.

page 222. "Darryl's idea in the very beginning": Friedhofer AFI interview, p. 151.

page 222. "Dear Al": Behlmer, *Memo from Darryl F. Zanuck,* p. 160.

page 223. "I remember the day": Tracy AFI Oral History, p. 325.

page 223. Much of the accounts of the scoring of *Laura, Forever Amber,* and *The Bad and the Beautiful* comes from Raksin's notes to his album *David Raksin Conducts His Great Film Scores,* RCA ARL1-1490. Raksin conducted The New Philharmonia Orchestra. *The Bad and the Beautiful* soundtrack has been reissued by Rhino Records, under the auspices of Turner Classic Movies, the composer conducting the MGM Orchestra.

page 224. "Alfred Newman came by": Prendergast, *Film Music,* p. 64.

page 224. "Raksin received one letter from an American soldier": Raksin wrote a booklet of essays, "David Raksin Remembers His Colleagues: Hollywood Composers," for the Stanford Theater Foundation, p. 25.

page 225. "De tune ends": author's conversation with David Raksin, October 1996.

page 225. "Raskin was invited by": In his discussion of *Force of Evil,* Raksin doesn't name Polonsky.

page 227. "While Raskin was composing": The Twentieth Century-Fox arrangers were described by Arthur Morton, interviewed by author, October 1996.

page 228. *The Robe* was recorded by Newman, conducting the Hollywood Symphony Orchestra, on Decca DL 9012.

page 229. "a man who knew everything": Ephron, *We Thought We Could Do Anything,* p. 153.

page 229. "[My father] worked": Thomas Newman interviewed by Pat Dowell, "Morning Edition" on National Public Radio, March 23, 1995.

page 229. "a matter of pride and muscle": Rodgers, *Musical Stages,* p. 237.

page 229. "*State Fair* is the most popular": Behlmer, *Memo from Darryl F. Zanuck,* p. 92.

page 230. "Too bad, Jay": author's interview with Jay Blackton, November 1990.

page 230. "syncophants laughed uproariously": Ephron, *We Thought We Could Do Anything,* p. 148.

page 231. "Few scores have more": Jack Smith, "The Sound Track," *Films in Review,* September/October 1995, p. 64.

page 231. "'difficult' composers": Fred Steiner's introduction to Robert R. Faulkner, *Music on Demand,* pp. 4–5.

Chapter 9: Waltzing in the Wonder of Why We're Here

page 233. "embarrassment of bad taste": Kobal, *Gotta Sing, Gotta Dance,* p. 133.

page 233. "I found myself": LeRoy, *Take One,* p. 137.

page 235. "a young German pianist": sequences on Lela Simone are drawn primarily from the Simone Oral History, conducted by Rudy Behlmer for the Academy of Motion Picture Arts & Sciences, and from biographical material provided by her son, Tomas Firle.

page 237. "ever curious": Thomson, *Virgil Thomson,* p. 157.

page 239. *Judy Garland Sings Selections from the Metro-Goldwyn-Mayer Pictures: Meet Me in St. Louis,* AE1 3101. Orchestra directed by Georgie Stoll.

page 240. "deemed ghoulishly pessimistic": Green, *Encyclopedia of the Musical Film,* p. 123.

page 240. "'The Trolley Song' was written": Hay, *MGM: When the Lion Roars,* p. 242.

page 240. "Songwriters Martin and Blane": *Martin & Blane Sing Martin & Blane.* Harlequin Records HQ-701. Notes by Bob Bach.

page 241. "When he was disgusted": Simone Oral History, AMPAS, p. 18.

page 241. "He wore armor, armor": Server, *Screenwriter,* p. 59.

page 241. "Asked to evaluate": Chaplin, *The Golden Age of Movie Musicals and Me,* p. 121.

page 241. "Although he knew perfectly well": Lerner, *The Street Where I Live,* p. 144.

page 242. Betty Comden and Adolph Green, *A Party with Betty Comden and Adolph Green,* Capitol Records WAO 1197. Notes are by the two songwriters about each other.

page 243. "Freed heard twenty-two-year-old": Tormé, *It Wasn't All Velvet,* p. 127.

page 243. "After the stage success": Lerner, *The Street Where I Live,* p. 139.

page 243. "How ya fixed": Ross, *Picture,* p. 168.

page 243. "If you want to shave": Server, *Screenwriter,* p. 63.

page 243. "Arthur is so rich": Chaplin, *The Golden Age of Movie Musicals and Me,* p. 121.

page 243. "I was trained in ballet": Bremer quoted in McLelland, *Forties Film Talk,* p. 19.

page 244. "He couldn't draw": Server, *Screenwriter,* p. 61.

page 245. "Roger was not": Simone Oral History, AMPAS, p. 116.

page 245. "so overpowering": Ibid., p. 55.

page 245. *The Pirate Ballet,* MGM E-540 (10", vinyl). Edens and Salinger stitched together several Porter tunes to create the ballet, conducted by Herbert Stothart.

page 245. *Good News,* MGM E-3771ST, conducted by Lennie Hayton.

page 246. "colleges confused": Smith, *Musical Comedy in America,* p. 265.

page 246.   "There's a world war": Coslow, *Cocktails for Two*, p. 235.

page 248.   "Thompson brought in her paramour": Simone Oral History, AMPAS, p. 30. Tormé, *It Wasn't All Velvet*, p. 129.

page 248.   "Williams was already familiar": Re Andy Williams's dubbing of Bacall: in *Bogart* (1997), Eric Lax recorded Bacall's claim that she did her own singing in *To Have and Have Not*.

page 249.   "Get out of here": Server, *Screenwriter*, p. 63.

page 250.   "an absolute genius": Simone Oral History, AMPAS, p. 298.

page 250.   "Powers was more": Ibid., p. 277.

page 251.   "Johnny Green was born": Charles Champlin, "Composer-Conductor John Green Dies at Age 80," *Los Angeles Times*, May 17, 1989. Gammond, *The Oxford Companion to Popular Music*, p. 242.

page 252.   "Green could get exercised": Simone Oral History, AMPAS, p. 85.

page 252.   "His first departmental meeting": Rozsa, *A Double Life*, p. 171.

page 252.   "When Broadway conductor Jay Blackton": Blackton interview with author, September 1989.

page 252.   "You know, he overacted": Simone Oral History, AMPAS, p. 85.

page 254.   "chorus boy": Chaplin, *The Golden Age of Movie Musicals and Me*, p. 117.

page 254.   "And Bernstein came": Simone Oral History, AMPAS, p. 60.

page 254.   "Every Edens song": Mast, *Can't Help Singin'*, p. 239.

page 255.   "You can't sell futility": Ross, *Picture*, p. 167.

page 256.   "I saw *Show Boat*": Ibid., 168–169.

page 256.   "Simone corroborated": Simone Oral History, AMPAS, p. 115.

page 256.   "At the last minute": Ibid.

page 257.   "Reynolds was signed": Green, *Encyclopedia of the Musical Film*, p. 260.

page 257.   "When Irving Berlin appeared": Simone Oral History, AMPAS, p. 315.

page 258.   "In 1917": Dietz, *Dancing in the Dark*, pp. 38–40.

page 259.   "Dietz was frequently": *Production Encyclopedia 1951*, p. 714.

page 259.   "Anything that makes money": Ross, *Picture*, pp. 212–213.

page 261.   *Jerry Lewis . . . Just Sings*, Decca DL 8410. Orchestra directed by Buddy Bregman.

page 261.   "for a melody": Jonathan Schwartz, "The Man Who Knew Fred Astaire," *GQ*, June 1990, p. 98.

page 261.   "low string writing": Ibid.

page 261.   "Oscar, whaddya say": Chaplin, *The Golden Age of Movie Musicals and Me*, p. 135.

page 261.   "a very civilized": Simone Oral History, AMPAS, pp. 115–116.

page 261.   "That man has got to": Fordin, *The World of Entertainment*, pp. 115–116.

page 262.   "From the very beginning": Simone Oral History, AMPAS, p. 65.

page 262.   "When Previn turned in a fugue": Bookspan and Yockey, *André Previn: A Biography*, p. 36.

page 263.   "Four minutes long": Ibid., p. 47.

page 263.   "I owe you": Seaton in letter to Harry Ruby, Harry Ruby Collection, USC Cinema-Television Library.

page 264.   "Previn was dismayed": Hugo Friedhofer AFI interview, p. 55.

page 265.   "Freed listened": Simone Oral History, AMPAS, pp. 133, 247–249.

page 265.   "The situation was more problematic": Ibid., pp. 139–140.

page 266.   "Previn made several": Gioia, *West Coast Jazz*, p. 278.

page 266.   "Around that time": Bookspan and Yockey, *André Previn*, p. 177. In his book *Piano Lessons*, Noah Adams recounts the identical story about Szell, but in his version it's pianist Leon Fleisher playing the tabletop.

page 267.   *Love Me or Leave Me*, Columbia CL 710. Orchestra conducted by Percy Faith. As of July 3, 1954, Ava Gardner was slated to play Ruth Etting in the movie, but everyone at MGM knew that Gardner couldn't sing well enough to preclude dubbing.

page 268.   "Siegel ran an independent": Chaplin, *The Golden Age of Movie Musicals and Me*, p. 153.

page 269.   "Porter had Fred Astaire": Eells, *The Life That Late He Led*, p. 300.

page 269.   "(*Time* pronounced": Ibid., p. 303.

page 269.   *High Society*, Capitol SW 750. Johnny Green conducting the MGM Studio Orchestra.

page 269.   "L.B. Mayer's comeback": Schatz, *The Genius of the System*, pp. 457–460.

page 270.   "By the close of 1956": Hay, *MGM: When the Lion Roars*, p. 299.

page 270. "I can't understand": Simone Oral History, AMPAS, p. 144.

page 270. "Freed flew in": Lerner, *The Street Where I Live*, p. 141.

page 270. "In France": Ibid., pp. 152–153.

page 271. "Arthur, this will be": Hay, *MGM: When the Lion Roars*, p. 315.

page 272. *Gigi*, MGM SE-3641. Music supervised and conducted by André Previn.

page 272. "She joined Franz Waxman": Simone Oral History, AMPAS, p. 165.

page 272. Main title music from *The Nun's Story*, from *Fifty Years of Film Music*, Warner Bros. 1298.

page 272. "Helen Deutsch credited": Deutsch interview with author, April 1983.

page 273. "You're in charge": Chaplin, *The Golden Age of Movie Musicals and Me*, pp. 182–183.

page 273   *The Subterraneans*, MGM SE3812ST.

page 273. "In a photograph": *That's Entertainment* booklet, Rhino Records R2 72182, p. 73.

Chapter 10: Just Make Up Your Mind

page 275. "One evening in 1913,": The account of ASCAP's formation is drawn primarily from Hazel Meyer's *The Gold in Tin Pan Alley*, pp. 80–82.

page 276. "It was at the instigation of Max Steiner": Hans Salter Oral History, AMPAS, p. 115.

page 276. "For several years ASCAP": Much of this material can be found in the Screen Composers' Association Collection at the Margaret Herrick Library, Academy of Motion Picture Arts & Sciences. Music archivist Warren Sherk has written an overview to the Collection.

page 276. "The composers voted unanimously to send": The letter was signed and sent on November 6, 1942.

page 277. "method of payment": Meyer, *The Gold in Tin Pan Alley*, p. 98.

page 278. "In 1938 alone": the figure comes from Abel Green & Joe Laurie, Jr., *Show Biz.*, p. 409.

page 279. "As far back as September 1939": Ibid., p. 91.

page 280. "In 1950, ASCAP and the SCA": Prendergast, *Film Music*, p. 57.

page 281. "At the last meeting": letter found in the Screen Composers' Association Collection.

page 281. "When I came to Hollywood": Salter Oral History, AMPAS, p. 61.

page 283. "Aldolph Deutsch appealed": Deutsch's solicitation of funds to pay Heymann's medical costs is in the Screen Composers' Association Collection.

page 283. "shot through with the whole dialectic materialism": Friedhofer AFI interview, p. 171.

page 284. Boris Morross's *My Ten Years as a Counterspy* was filmed by Columbia in 1966 as *Man on a String*.

page 284. "When HUAC's investigator": Friedrich, *City of Nets*, pp. 302–303.

page 284. "asked in 1950 by MGM": Navasky, *Naming Names*, p. 94.

page 285. "In 1953 MGM music man George Bassman": Vaughn, *Only Victims*, Appendix 1.

page 285. "identified by John Garfield": Cogley, *Report on Blacklisting*, pp. 110–111.

page 286. "A newspaper account described Kaplan": Chaplin, *The Golden Age of Movie Musicals and Me*, p. 148.

page 286. "Raksin had been a member": Navasky, *Naming Names*, pp. 249, 281.

page 287. "In 1955 its president was": Executive members of the 1955 Composers' Guild of Great Britain are listed in correspondence with the American guild, found in the Screen Composers' Association Collection.

Chapter 11: I Only Know I Must Be Brave

page 289. "The Lomax collection": Carlin, *The Big Book of Country Music*, p. 105.

page 289. "Gay cowboys dressed in silk": Dobie, *Up the Trail from Texas*, pp. 3–4.

page 290. "Exciting *agitato* themes": Everson, *A Pictorial History of the Western Film*, p. 124.

page 290. "In the early sound period": Ibid.

page 290. "According to the cue sheets": Gerard Carbonara's application to the Screen Composers' Association contains evidence of his contribution to the *Stagecoach* score.

page 291.   "At Republic": Spivack Oral History, AMPAS, pp. 74–75.

page 291.   "Overnight every studio": Green & Laurie, *Show Biz,* p. 408.

page 291.   "Autry's sound over the next few years": Malone, *Country Music U.S.A.,* p. 143.

page 292.   "The newly named Roy Rogers": Sackett, *Hollywood Sings!,* p. 23.

page 293.   "Wakely had a voice": Malone, *Country Music U.S.A.,* p. 144.

page 294.   "Cindy Walker arrived in Hollywood": Carlin, *The Big Book of Country Music,* p. 476. Malone, *Country Music U.S.A.,* p. 212.

page 294.   "In fact, Zanuck": Taylor, *Jule,* p. 73.

page 295.   "Jule, boy": Ibid., p. 86.

page 295.   "In 1945, Stage 12": *Production Encyclopedia,* p. 777.

page 296.   Material on R. Dale Butts is drawn primarily from an unpublished autobiographical essay donated by his family to the Margaret Herrick Library, Academy of Motion Picture Arts & Sciences.

page 297.   "Porter had originally written": Eells, *The Life That Late He Led,* pp. 217–219.

page 298.   "I think it was Lord Beaverbrook": *Halliwell's Film Guide,* p. 294.

page 298.   "I would like to point out": Thomas, *Film Score,* p. 128.

page 299.   "There was a 'market'": Copland quoted by David Hamilton in notes for *Aaron Copland Works for Piano 1926–1948,* New World Records 277.

page 299.   "When Copland checked in": Two fine versions, each played by the St. Louis Symphony Orchestra, of *The Red Pony* score: *Copland—Music for Films,* Leonard Slatkin conducting (RCA 09026-61699-2); and *Aaron Copland: The Red Pony,* André Previn conducting (Columbia ML 5983).

page 300.   "Who can sing best": Bond, *The Tex Ritter Story,* pp. 146–147.

page 301.   "melodic and easy": Everson, *A Pictorial History of the Western Film,* p. 208.

page 302.   "How the hell": Thomas, *Film Score,* p. 61.

page 302.   *How the West Was Won* was recorded by Alfred Newman conducting the MGM Orchestra, with the Ken Darby Singers, re-released by Sony AK 47024.

page 302. "Johnny Logan used some audio": AFI Oral History of sound editor Milo Lory, pp. 112–113.

page 303. Morricone's "spaghetti Western" scores can be heard on compact disk on *Ennio Morricone: The Legendary Italian Westerns,* RCA 9974-2-R. Notes by Didier C. Deutsch.

page 304. "I was brought out [to Hollywood] . . . and introduced": music editor-composer John Strauss, interviewed by author, November 1995.

page 305. "A beautiful pipedream": Kael, *Deeper into Movies,* p. 277.

Chapter 12: Leave Your Worries on the Doorstep

page 307. "The film showed two white men": Crow, *Jazz Anecdotes,* p. 146.

page 310. "Before principal photography": Behlmer, *Inside Warner Bros.,* p. 199.

page 311. "What an awful picture": Levant, *Memoirs of an Amnesiac,* p. 223.

page 312. "(Garland's fellow musicians": Bernhardt, *I Remember,* p. x; Coleman, *Trumpet Story,* p. 73.

page 312. For a fascinating musical take on *Spiral Staircase* and other postwar film noirs, hear Ran Blake, *Film Noir,* Arista 3019. Some of the selections were composed by pianist Blake, some by the films' composers.

page 313. "The traditional school": Quincy Jones quoted by Fred Baker, *Movie People: At Work in the Business of Film,* p. 187.

page 314. "a good family friend": Kazan, *Elia Kazan: A Life,* p. 339.

page 314. A brief excerpt from *Streetcar*'s score is included on Warners' *Fifty Years of Film Music,* Warner Bros. 1298.

page 316. *The Man with the Golden Arm,* Decca 8257 (vinyl).

page 316. Bernstein's title themes for *The Rat Race* and *Sweet Smell of Success* are recorded on *Movie and TV Themes Composed and Conducted by Elmer Bernstein,* Choreo A-11.

page 316. *Sunday in New York*'s bouncy title theme is included on *Mel Tormé Sings "Sunday in New York" and Other Songs about New York,* Atlantic 8091.

page 316. *A New Kind of Love,* Mercury MG20859.

page 316. *Sex and the Single Girl,* Warner Bros. 1572.

page 317. *I Want to Live!*, United Artists UAL-4005.

page 318. John Lewis's scores on vinyl include *No Sun in Venice*, Atlantic 1284, and *A Milanese Story*, Atlantic 1388.

page 319. *Anatomy of a Murder*, Columbia 1360.

page 319. The title theme to *Splendor in the Grass* can be heard on the vinyl recording *David Amram and Friends/ At Home and Around the World*, Flying Fish 094. Jerry Dodgion is the saxophone soloist.

page 319. "I went to the screening": Amram, *Vibrations*, pp. 367–368.

Chapter 13: A Passing Breeze Filled with Memories

page 322. This version of "Days of Wine and Roses" can be heard on Mancini's album *Our Man in Hollywood*, RCA-LPM-2604.

page 322. "I went to the piano": Mancini, *Did They Mention the Music?*, p. 111.

page 323. "modern, Ellingtonian sound": Ibid., p. 17.

page 324. "first performed arrangement": Ibid., p. 28.

page 324. "I was not called on": Ibid., p. 44.

page 324. "He was absorbing the newer": Re arrangers: Is it the passing notes routinely encountered by trombonists and trumpeters that often make them such great jazz arrangers? Or could it be simply that they often sit in the middle of the orchestra, where they can hear everything? Think of Billy May, Johnny Mandel, and Neal Hefti, to name three out of many.

page 325. "An assignment to score": On his WQEW-AM (New York) program, radio personality Jonathan Schwartz told the story of his father, Arthur Schwartz, seeing David Rose, whom he had never met, across the room at the MGM commissary. Schwartz went over and, in homage, hummed "Holiday for Strings" all the way through. Only when he was finished did he realize that his listener wasn't David Rose.

page 325. "The studio had a few": Mancini, *Did They Mention the Music?*, p. 59.

page 326. "He was very adaptable": Hans Salter Oral History, AMPAS, p. 70.

page 326. "If you gave Frank": Ibid., p. 60.

page 327. "Joe Gershenson": Mancini, *Did They Mention the Music?*, p. 70.

page 328. "'progressive jazz'": Duke, *Listen Here!*, p. 307.

page 329. "MCA agent Henry Alper": Mancini, *Did They Mention the Music?* p. 98.

page 330. "Had Johnny been a military": Ibid., p. 99.

page 330. "We were all sitting around": Ibid., p. 102.

page 330. *Breakfast at Tiffany's*, RCA Victor LPM-2362.

page 331. "Williams was buttonholed": Sackett, *Hollywood Sings!*, p. 163.

page 334. *The Party*, RCA LSP-3997. Plas Johnson has a particularly longing, soulful tenor sax solo on "Brunette in Yellow."

page 335. "When a movie costs": Kael, *Deeper into Movies*, p. 104.

page 335. "In a 1982 radio interview": Riddle was interviewed by Schwartz on September 12, 1982. The taped interview was broadcast on June 2, 1996, on WQEW-AM (New York).

page 335. "elevator music": Roth, ed., *Hollywood Wits*, p. 228.

Chapter 14: Makes No Difference Who You Are

page 336. "It was all so successful": Jon Newsom, "A Sound Idea," *Wonderful Inventions*, p. 62.

page 336. "While Fleischer was producing": Maltin, *Of Mice and Magic*, p. 93.

page 337. "Grim Natwick conceived": Maltin, *Of Mice and Magic*, p. 100.

page 337. "Wearing a hula skirt": Ibid., p. 107.

page 337. "Hal Roach's early Laurel and Hardy": Trained as a classical pianist, Leroy Shield composed hundreds of music cues for Roach's films in Hollywood, before returning to Chicago to resume work in radio. On August 30, 1994, Dutch bandleader Gert Jan Blom and audio engineer Piet Schroeders were interviewed on National Public Radio's "All Things Considered" to discuss their compact disk, *The Beau Hunks Play the Original Little Rascals Music*.

page 338. "Universal was where": Maltin, *Of Mice and Magic*, p. 162.

page 338. "were honeymooning at June Lake": Sackett, *Hollywood Sings!*, p. 101.

page 339. "By the summer": Ibid., p. 102. Danny Kaye's version is on the vinyl collection, *The Best of Danny Kaye*, MCA 1704.

page 339. "Darrell would say": Maltin, *Of Mice and Magic*, p. 172.

page 340. "belonged to Roy Halee": Ibid., p. 144.

page 340. "The first two Mickey Mouse": Tietyen, *The Musical World of Walt Disney*, p. 13.

page 342. "The cartoonists' impression": Holden, *Laurence Olivier*, p. 78.

page 343. "agreement with Sol Bourne": Tietyen, *The Musical World of Walt Disney*, p. 30.

page 344. Almost as popular as the original *Snow White* album of 78s was Lyn Murray's version on Decca A-368. Evelyn Knight sang Snow White's role.

page 345. "The project's genesis": Newsom, "A Sound Idea," p. 65.

page 346. "threads through the entire score": Ross B. Care, "Threads of Melody: The Evolution of a Major Film Score—Walt Disney's *Bambi*," *Wonderful Inventions*, p. 85.

page 346. "only prior exposure": Tietyen, *The Musical World of Walt Disney*, pp. 72–73.

page 347. "Disney himself hired": Ibid., p. 91.

page 347. "Peggy Lee was signed": Lee, *Miss Peggy Lee*, p. 147.

page 348. "late '50s, self-produced": Tietyen, *The Musical World of Walt Disney*, p. 124.

page 349. "expansion of a made-up word": Ibid., pp. 134–135.

page 349. "Chevalier had recorded": Ibid., p. 127.

page 350. "[Stalling] developed a memory": Maltin, *Of Mice and Magic*, p. 235.

page 351. "Stalling's compositions and piano": Much of Stalling's output for Warners was included on *The Carl Stalling Project* on Warners 9 26027-2, produced by Hal Willner and Greg Ford.

page 351. "Many's the time": Mike Barrier, Milton Gray, and Bill Spicer, "An Interview with Carl Stalling," from *Funnyworld*, No. 13, Spring 1971, p. 26.

page 352. "Scott was born": Much of the material on Scott was provided by Irwin David Chusid, director of the Raymond Scott Archives.

page 353. "An early radio piece": Ewen, *Men of Popular Music*, p. 183.

page 353. "Record producer Al Brackman": *The Swing Era: Vintage Years of Humor*, Time-Life Records, 1971, p. 49.

page 354. "Scott's idiosyncratic": Irwin Chusid, "Raymond Scott Remembered," *Animation*, Volume 6, Issue 4, Summer 1993, p. 43.

page 354.   Scott's more frequently used compositions can be heard on the Columbia CD, *The Music of Raymond Scott: Reckless Nights and Turkish Twilights*.

page 355.   "Raymond made me": "Three Show Biz Girls," *New York Times*, Arts & Leisure, April 4, 1971.

page 356.   "Stalling boiled Wagner's": Maltin, *Of Mice and Magic*, p. 268.

page 356.   "Elmer Fudd's voice": Ibid., p. 274.

page 357.   *Gay Purr-ee* was recorded on vinyl on Warners B 1479.

page 357.   Raksin's *Madeleine, A Unicorn in the Garden,* and *Giddyap* scores are included on the record accompanying *Wonderful Inventions*.

page 358.   "He is going": Maltin, *Of Mice and Magic*, p. 290.

page 358.   "Asked to lecture": Rozsa, *A Double Life*, p. 157.

Chapter 15: Make It Mine, Make It Mine, Make It Mine!

page 359.   "originated as a pejorative term": Meyer, *The Gold in Tin Pan Alley*, p. 124.

page 360.   "To demonstrate the DJs'": Ibid., pp. 132–133.

page 361.   "Betty Hutton had been slated": Sackett, *Hollywood Sings!*, p. 100.

page 361.   "Cahn rehearsed Day": Cahn, *I Should Care*, pp. 100–101.

page 361.   "Maybe the Warners": Sackett, *Hollywood Sings!*, p. 100.

page 362.   "when Styne got wind": Taylor, *Jule*, p. 113.

page 362.   "had patent-leather hair": Cahn, *I Should Care*, p. 224.

page 362.   "the single most talented": Ibid., p. 193.

page 362.   "with Yipper Harburg": *Los Angeles Times* Calendar, March 11, 1979.

page 366.   "which Astaire loved": Cahn, *I Should Care*, pp. 238–242.

page 370.   "problem was that Jessamyn West": Tiomkin, *Please Don't Hate Me*, pp. 242–243.

page 371.   "During Christmas week": Sackett, *Hollywood Sings!*, p. 144.

page 372.   "The misconception was fostered": Ibid., p. 161.

page 372.   "lady with a slight mustache": Wilk, *They're Playing Our Song*, p. 136.

page 373.   "velvety low unison": Smith, *Off the Record*, p. 68. Baxter's "Unchained Melody" was included on *Midnight on the Cliffs*, Capitol T 843.

page 374. "obtain the services of Victor Young": Behlmer, *Memo from Selznick*, pp. 393–394.

page 374. "Reed wandered into a Grinzing tavern": Gammond, *The Oxford Companion to Popular Music*, p. 310.

page 375. "*Lili* (1953) was based on a screenplay": Material comes largely from author's interviews with Helen Deutsch, March–April 1983.

page 378. "Martin was slated": Green, *Encyclopedia of the Musical Film*, p. 279.

page 378. "Warren's lyricist": Harry Warren AFI Oral History, p. 323.

page 378. "Martin hated": Sackett, *Hollywood Sings!*, p. 127.

page 378. "his twenty-sixth attempt": Green, *Encyclopedia of the Musical Film*, p. 5.

page 380. *The Apartment*, United Artists UAL 3105.

page 381. *Never on Sunday*, United Artists UAL 4070.

page 381. "A Greek lyric": Sackett, *Hollywood Sings!*, p. 118.

page 381. "I suffer for recognition": Wiley and Bona, *Inside Oscar*, p. 322.

page 381. "Five songs for the Oscar": Cahn's satirical rewrite of his own lyric is from the daily *Variety* column, "What's the Score?" by John G. Houser, March 29, 1961. The clipping is included in the Ernest Gold Scrapbooks, Academy of Motion Picture Arts & Sciences.

page 382. "Hadjidakis didn't receive": Wiley and Bona, *Inside Oscar*, p. 328.

page 382. "accompanying Vic Damone": Kasha and Hirschhorn, *Notes on Broadway*, p. 91.

page 383. Sergio Mendes & Brasil '66, *Look Around*, A&M SP 4137.

page 384. "At a late '60s party": Previn, *Bog-Trotter*, p. 53.

page 384. "remained at number one": Sackett, *Hollywood Sings!*, p. 198.

page 384. "Lennie Hayton couldn't": Wiley and Bona, *Inside Oscar*, p. 438.

page 385. "Vernon Duke smiled": Previn, *Bog-Trotter*, p. 35.

Chapter 16: Threw a Party in the County Jail

page 387. "The song had been a minor hit": Ehrenstein and Reed, *Rock on Film*, p. 15.

page 388.   "Garson Kanin spoofed it all": Garson Kanin's story, similar in texture to his *Born Yesterday,* was used as the book for the 1961
musical comedy *Do Re Mi,* with music by Jule Styne and lyrics by
Comden & Green. The original cast recording was made on RCA
Victor LSOD-2002. Phil Silvers played the would-be jukebox king.

page 390.   "The underlying theory": *Newsweek,* December 31, 1956.

page 390.   "The 'Hound Dog' writers": Material on Leiber & Stoller
drawn from author's "You Wuz High Class," *Performing Arts,*
November 1994.

page 393.   "Brian Wilson can be glimpsed": Ehrenstein and Reed,
Rock on Film, p. 113.

page 393.   "teen idols were white": Shore, *The History of American
Bandstand,* p. 26.

page 393.   "notably Gary Usher": Ehrenstein and Reed, *Rock on Film,*
p. 53.

page 394.   "People are talking": Drake, ed., *The Sixties,* p. 66.

page 394.   "I must admit": Smith, *Off the Record,* p. 203.

page 395.   "He would say to us": Ibid., p. 200.

page 395.   The *Hard Day's Night* and *Help!* soundtracks were really
compilations of The Beatles' songs. It wasn't until the animated
Yellow Submarine (Capitol SW 153) that a Beatles film included the
underscore, composed and orchestrated by George Martin.

page 396.   *O Lucky Man!,* Warner Bros. BS 2710.

page 397.   "Columbia A&R man Ed Kleban": Davis, *Clive,* p. 250.

page 397.   *Wild in the Streets,* Tower SKAO-5099.

Epilogue: Where Have You Gone, Joe DiMaggio?

page 401.   "The orchestra has a limited": *Time,* September 11, 1995.

page 402.   "The operative word": *New York Times,* September 2, 1996.

BIBLIOGRAPHY

Agate, James. *The Later Ego*. New York: Crown Publishers, 1951.

Amberg, George. *Ballet in America*. New York: New American Library, 1949.

Amram, David. *Vibrations*. New York: Macmillan, 1968.

Anderson, Gillian. *Music for Silent Films 1894–1929*. Washington, DC: Library of Congress, 1988.

ASCAP Biographical Dictionary. Edited by Daniel I. McNamara. New York: Thomas Y. Crowell, 1948.

ASCAP Biographical Dictionary. 3rd Edition. New York: ASCAP (and Lynn Farnol Group, Inc.), 1966.

Astor, Mary. *A Life on Film*. New York: Dell, 1972.

Atkins, Irene Kahn. *David Butler: Directors Guild of America Oral History*. Metuchen, NJ: Scarecrow Press, 1993.

Baker, Fred, with Ross Firestone. *Movie People: At Work in the Business of Film*. New York: Lancer Books, 1973.

Balliett, Whitney. *The Sound of Surprise*. New York: Dutton, 1961.

Barnes, Ken. *The Crosby Years*. New York: St. Martin's, 1980.

Baxter, John. *The Hollywood Exiles.* New York: Taplinger Publications, 1976.

———. *Hollywood in the Sixties.* London: Tantivy Press, 1972.

Behlmer, Rudy. *Behind the Scenes.* Hollywood, CA: Samuel French, 1989.

———. *Inside Warner Bros. 1935–1951.* New York: Simon & Schuster, 1987.

———, ed. *Memo from Darryl F. Zanuck.* New York: Grove Press, 1993.

———, ed. *Memo from David O. Selznick.* New York: Viking, 1972.

Bernhardt, Clyde. *I Remember.* Philadelphia: University of Pennsylvania Press, 1986.

Beynon, G. W. *Musical Presentation of Motion Pictures.* New York: G. Schirmer, 1921.

Blum, Daniel. *A Pictorial History of the Silents.* New York: Grosset & Dunlap, 1953.

Bond, Johnny. *The Tex Ritter Story.* New York: Chappell Music Co., 1976.

Bookspan, Martin, and Ross Yockey. *André Previn: A Biography.* Garden City, NY: Doubleday, 1981.

Bordman, Gerald. *Jerome Kern: His Life and Music.* New York: Oxford University Press, 1980.

Bosworth, Patricia. *Diane Arbus.* New York: Alfred A. Knopf, 1984.

Buxton, Frank, and Bill Owen. *The Big Broadcast 1920–1950.* New York: Flare/Avon Books, 1973.

Cahn, Sammy. *I Should Care.* New York: Arbor House, 1974.

Carlin, Richard. *The Big Book of Country Music: A Biographical Encyclopedia.* New York: Penguin, 1995.

Catalog of Victor Records. Camden, NJ: RCA Manufacturing, 1936.

Chaplin, Charles. *My Autobiography.* New York: Simon & Schuster, 1964.

Chaplin, Saul. *The Golden Age of Movie Musicals and Me.* Norman, OK: University of Oklahoma Press, 1993.

Chierichetti, David. *Hollywood Director: The Career of Mitchell Leisen.* New York: Curtis Books, 1973.

Cogley, John. *Report on Blacklisting 1: Movies.* Fund for the Republic, 1956.

Coleman, Bill. *Trumpet Story*. Boston: Northeastern University Press, 1991.

Copland, Aaron, and Vivian Perlis. *Copland: 1900–1942*. New York: St. Martin's/Marek, 1984.

Coslow, Sam. *Cocktails for Two*. New Brunswick, NJ: Arlington House, 1977.

Craig, Warren. *Sweet and Lowdown: America's Popular Song Writers*. Metuchen, NJ: Scarecrow Press, 1978.

Crist, Judith. *The Private Eye, the Cowboy, and the Very Naked Girl*. New York: Holt, Rinehart, Winston, 1968.

Croce, Arlene. *The Fred Astaire & Ginger Rogers Book.*. New York: Galahad Books, 1972.

Crosby, Bing. *Call Me Lucky*. New York: Simon & Schuster, 1953.

Crow, Bill. *Jazz Anecdotes*. New York: Oxford University Press, 1990.

Davis, Clive, with James Willwerth. *Clive: Inside the Record Business*. New York: William Morrow and Co., 1975.

Dietz, Howard. *Dancing in the Dark*. New York: Quadrangle, 1974.

Dobie, J. Frank. *Up the Trail from Texas*. New York: Random House, 1955.

Douglas, Ann. *Terrible Honesty: Mongrel Manhattan in the 1920s*. New York: Noonday Press, 1995.

Drake, Nicholas, ed. *The Sixties: A Decade in Vogue*. New York: Prentice-Hall, 1988.

Duke, Vernon. *Listen Here!* New York: Obolensky, 1963.

Dunaway, David King. *Huxley in Hollywood*. New York: Harper & Row, 1989.

Eells, George. *The Life That Late He Led*. New York: G.P. Putnam's Sons, 1967.

Ehrenstein, David, and Bill Reed. *Rock on Film*. New York: Delilah Books, 1982.

Ephron, Henry. *We Thought We Could Do Anything*. New York: W. W. Norton, 1977.

Evans, Mark. *Soundtrack: The Music of the Movies*. New York: Da Capo Press, 1979.

Everson, William K. *A Pictorial History of the Western Film*. New York: Citadel Press, 1969.

Ewen, David. *American Composers Today.* New York: H. W. Wilson Co., 1949.

———. *The New Book of Modern Composers.* New York: Alfred A. Knopf, 1961.

———. *Panorama of American Popular Music.* Englewood Cliffs, NJ: Prentice-Hall, 1957.

Eyman, Scott. *Ernst Lubitsch: Laughter in Paradise.* New York: Simon & Schuster, 1993.

Faulkner, Robert R. *Music on Demand: Composers and Careers in the Hollywood Film Industry.* New Brunswick, NJ: Transaction Books, 1983.

Feather, Leonard. *The New Encyclopedia of Jazz.* New York: Bonanza Books, 1960.

Ferguson, Otis. *The Film Criticism of Otis Ferguson.* Edited by Robert Wilson. Philadelphia: Temple University Press, 1971.

Fitch, Noel Riley. *Sylvia Beach and the Lost Generation.* New York: W. W. Norton, 1985.

Fordin, Hugh. *Getting to Know Him.* New York: Ungar, 1977.

———. *The World of Entertainment: Hollywood's Greatest Musicals.* Garden City, NY: Doubleday, 1975.

Friedrich, Otto. *City of Nets.* New York: Harper Perennial Library, 1987.

Furia, Philip. *The Poets of Tin Pan Alley: A History of America's Great Lyricists.* New York: Oxford University Press, 1990.

Fussell, Paul. *Wartime: Understanding and Behavior in the Second World War.* New York: Oxford University Press, 1989.

Gammond, Peter. *The Oxford Companion to Popular Music.* New York: Oxford University Press, 1991.

Gilbert, Douglas. *Lost Chords.* Garden City, NY: Doubleday, 1942.

Gioa, Ted. *West Coast Jazz: 1945–1960.* New York: Oxford University Press, 1992.

Green, Stanley. *The Encyclopedia of the Musical Film.* New York: Oxford University Press, 1981.

Halliwell, Leslie. *Halliwell's Film Guide.* 4th Edition. New York: Scribner's, 1983.

———. *Halliwell's Filmgoer's Companion.* 6th Edition. New York: Avon, 1978.

Haver, Ron. *David O. Selznick's Hollywood.* New York: Alfred A. Knopf, 1980.

Hay, Peter. *MGM: When the Lion Roars.* Atlanta: Turner Publishing, 1991.

Hentoff, Nat, and Albert J. McCarthy, eds. *Jazz.* New York: Rinehart, 1959.

Holden, Anthony. *Laurence Olivier.* New York: Atheneum, 1988.

Houseman, John. *Run-through.* New York: Simon & Schuster, 1972.

Jarrell, Randall. *Pictures from an Institution.* Farrar, Straus & Giroux, 1968.

Jezic, Diane Peacock. *The Musical Migration of Ernst Toch.* Ames, IA: Iowa State University Press, 1989.

Kael, Pauline. *The Citizen Kane Book: Raising Kane.* Boston: Little, Brown, 1971.

————. *Deeper into Movies.* Boston: Atlantic-Little, Brown, 1973.

Karlin, Fred. *Listening to Movies.* New York: Schirmer Books, 1994.

Kasha, Al, and Joel Hirschhorn. *Notes on Broadway.* Chicago: Contemporary Books, 1985.

Kazan, Elia. *Elia Kazan: A Life.* New York: Anchor Books, 1989.

Kendall, Elizabeth. *Where She Danced.* New York: Alfred A. Knopf, 1979.

Knight, Arthur. *The Liveliest Art.* New York: New American Library, 1957.

Kobal, John. *Gotta Sing, Gotta Dance.* London: Hamlyn, 1970.

Kronenberger, Louis, ed. *Atlantic Brief Lives: A Biographical Companion to the Arts.* Boston: Atlantic-Little, Brown, 1971.

Larson, Randall D. *Musique Fantastique: A Survey of Film Music in the Fantastic Cinema.* Metuchen, NJ: Scarecrow Press, 1985.

Lax, Eric, and A. M. Sperber. *Bogart.* New York: William Morrow & Company, 1997.x

Lee, Peggy. *Miss Peggy Lee: An Autobiography.* New York: Donald I. Fine, Inc., 1989.

Leff, Leonard J. *Hitchcock & Selznick.* New York: Weidenfeld & Nicholson, 1987.

Lerner, Alan Jay. *The Street Where I Live.* New York: W. W. Norton, 1980.

LeRoy, Mervyn. *Mervyn LeRoy: Take One.* New York: Hawthorn Books, 1974.

Levant, Oscar. *Memoirs of an Amnesiac.* New York: G.P. Putnam's Sons, 1965.

[Loesser, Frank.] *The Frank Loesser Songbook.* Text by Cynthia Lindsay. New York: Simon & Schuster, 1971.

McGuire, Patricia Dubin. *Lullaby of Broadway: Life and Times of Al Dubin.* Secaucus, NJ: Citadel Press, 1983.

McLelland, Doug. *Forties Film Talk: Oral Histories of Hollywood.* Jefferson, NC: McFarland & Co., 1992.

McWilliams, Carey. *Southern California Country.* New York: Duell, Sloan & Pierce, 1946.

Malone, Bill C. *Country Music U.S.A.* Austin, TX: University of Texas Press, 1991.

Maltin, Leonard. *Of Mice and Magic: A History of American Animated Cartoons.* Revised Edition. Plume/Penguin Books, 1987.

Mancini, Henry, with Gene Lees. *Did They Mention the Music?* Chicago: Contemporary Books, 1989.

Manville, Roger, ed. *International Encyclopedia of Film.* New York: Crown, 1972.

Marx, Sam, and Jan Clayton. *Rodgers & Hart: Bewitched, Bothered & Bewildered.* New York: Putnam, 1976.

Mast, Gerald. *Can't Help Singin': The American Musical on Stage and Screen.* Woodstock, NY: Overlook Press, 1987.

Meeker, David. *Jazz in the Movies.* New Rochelle: Arlington House, 1977.

Meyer, Hazel. *The Gold in Tin Pan Alley.* Philadelphia: Lippincott, 1958.

Navasky, Victor. *Naming Names.* New York: Penguin, 1981.

Newquist, Roy. *Showcase.* New York: Morrow, 1966.

Newsom, Iris, ed. *Wonderful Inventions: Motion Pictures, Broadcasting, and Recorded Sound of the Library of Congress.* Washington, DC: Library of Congress, 1985.

Palmer, Christopher. *The Composer in Hollywood.* London: Marion Boyars (Rizzoli), 1990.

Prendergast, Roy M. *Film Music: A Neglected Art.* New York: Norton, 1977.

Previn, Dory. *Bog-Trotter.* New York: Doubleday, 1980.

Production Encyclopedia 1951. Hollywood, CA: The Hollywood Reporter Press, 1951.

Rapee, Erno. *Motion Picture Moods for Pianists and Organists.* New York: G. Schirmer, 1924.

Rodgers, Richard. *Musical Stages.* New York: Random House, 1975.

Rosenberg, Deena. *Fascinating Rhythm.* New York: Dutton, 1991.

Ross, Lillian. *Picture.* New York: Avon Books, 1969.

Roth, K. Madsen, ed. *Hollywood Wits.* New York: Avon Books, 1995.

Rozsa, Miklos. *A Double Life.* New York: Wynwood Press, 1989.

Sackett, Susan. *Hollywood Sings!: An Inside Look at Sixty Years of Academy Award–Nominated Songs.* New York: Billboard Books, 1995.

Schary, Dore. *Heyday.* Boston: Little, Brown, 1979.

Schatz, Thomas. *The Genius of the System: Hollywood Filmmaking in the Studio Era.* New York: Pantheon, 1988.

Schneider, Steve. *That's All Folks!: The Art of Warner Bros. Animation.* New York: Henry Holt, 1988.

Segaloff, Nat. *Hurricane Billy.* New York: Morrow, 1990.

Server, Lee. *Screenwriter: Words Become Pictures.* Pittstown, NJ: The Main Street Press, 1987.

Shulman, Arthur, and Roger Youman. *How Sweet It Was.* New York: Bonanza Books, 1966.

Slonimsky, Nicolas. *Music Since 1900.* New York: Coleman-Ross, 1949.

Smith, Cecil. *Musical Comedy in America.* New York: Theatre Arts Books, 1950.

Smith, Joe. *Off the Record: An Oral History of Popular Music.* Edited by Mitchell Fink. New York: Warner Books, 1988.

Snyder, Robert. *Pare Lorentz and the Documentary Film.* Norman, OK: University of Oklahoma Press, 1968.

Taylor, Deems, ed. *Music Lovers' Encyclopedia.* Garden City, NY: Garden City Publishing, 1947.

Taylor, Dwight. *Joy Ride.* New York: G.P. Putnam's Sons, 1959.

Taylor, John Russell. *Strangers in Paradise: The Hollywood Emigrés (1933–1950).* New York: Holt Rinehart & Winston, 1983.

Taylor, Theodore. *Jule.* New York: Random House, 1979.

Thomas, Bob. *Astaire: The Man, The Dancer.* New York: St. Martin's Press, 1984.

———. *King Cohn.* New York: Putnam, 1967.

Thomas, Tony. *Film Score: The Art and Craft of Movie Music.* Burbank: Riverwood Press, 1991.

———. *Music for the Movies.* Cranbury, NJ: A.S. Barnes & Co., 1973.

Thompson, Kay. *Eloise.* Illustrated by Hilary Knight. New York: Simon & Schuster, 1955.

Thomson, David. *Movie Man*. New York: Stein & Day, 1967.

Thomson, Virgil. *Virgil Thomson*. New York: Alfred A. Knopf, 1966.

Tietyen, David. *The Musical World of Walt Disney*. Milwaukee: Hal Leonard Publishing, 1990.

Tiomkin, Dimitri, and Prosper Buranelli. *Please Don't Hate Me*. New York: Doubleday, 1959.

Toch, Ernst. *The Shaping Forces of Music: An Inquiry into the Nature of Harmony—Melody—Counterpoint—Form*. Introduction by Lawrence Weschler. New York: Dover Publications, 1977.

Tormé, Mel. *It Wasn't All Velvet*. New York: Zebra Books, 1990.

Tyler, Parker. *Three Faces of the Film*. New York: Thomas Yoseloff, 1960.

Vaughn, Robert. *Only Victims*. New York: Putnam's Sons, 1972.

Wallis, Hal, and Charles Higham. *Starmaker: The Autobiography of Hal Wallis*. New York: Macmillan, 1980.

Wilder, Alec. *American Popular Song*. New York: Oxford University Press, 1972.

Wiley, Mason, and Damien Bona. *Inside Oscar: The Unofficial History of the Academy Awards*. Edited by Gail MacColl. Updated Edition. New York: Ballantine Books, 1993.

Wilk, Max. *They're Playing Our Song*. Revised Edition. New York: New York Zoetrope, 1986.

Zolotow, Maurice. *Billy Wilder in Hollywood*. New York: G.P. Putnam's Sons, 1977.

INDEX

Italicized page numbers indicate photographs.